WHO KILLED KAREN SILKWOOD?

by
Howard Kohn

SUMMIT BOOKS   NEW YORK

Copyright © 1981 by Howard Kohn
All rights reserved
including the right of reproduction
in whole or in part in any form
Published by SUMMIT BOOKS
A Simon & Schuster Division of Gulf & Western Corporation
Simon & Schuster Building
1230 Avenue of the Americas
New York, New York 10020

SUMMIT BOOKS and colophon are trademarks of
Simon & Schuster
Designed by Eve Kirch
Manufactured in the United States of America

10 9 8 7 6 5 4 3 2 1

Library of Congress Cataloging in Publication Data
Kohn, Howard.
    Who killed Karen Silkwood?
    1. Silkwood, Karen, 1946–1974.   2. Kerr-McGee Nuclear
Corporation.   3. Uranium industry—United States—
safety regulations.   4. Murder—Oklahoma.   I. Title.
HV6529.S52K63   364.1'523'0924   81-16544
                                        AACR2
ISBN 0-671-43721-6
     0-671-43654-6 (Pbk.)

To my daughter, Elizabeth

It must be said that, except for the actual writing, Diana Romanchuk Kohn was an equal partner in the making of this book—more than equal in recording and documenting many of the details. Diana also kept us sane and happy during times that were quite the opposite, and for that alone she deserves a special tribute.

Foreword

The headline above the short AP dispatch was the sort you can't help remembering: WOMAN KILLED ON WAY TO SECRET MEETING. I clipped out the article and put it in my suitcase. It was 1974, the week before Thanksgiving, and my wife, Diana, and I happened to be in rural California on our honeymoon. When we got back to San Francisco I took the clipping to my editor at *Rolling Stone*. I said, "I'd like to take a few days to go to Oklahoma—" He wouldn't let me finish. "Forget it," he said. "I've got something else for you." Ignoring my clipping, he pulled out one of his own. It was the same AP dispatch, except from a San Francisco newspaper. A coincidence of little note, surely, but it meant I got the assignment. My editor said, "This woman had a bunch of documents from a nuclear factory, and she was on her way to deliver them when her car cracked up. It's some kind of weird. Why don't you go to Oklahoma and check it out. Take a couple of weeks."

I took six and a half years, off and on. Every time I was ready to call it quits, something new or somebody new showed up. Crazy tipsters, false leads, hostile footsteps on my trail, phone calls in the middle of the night—this case had them all. It was hard to let go, and not only because there was a mystery to be solved. Many of the people in this book are heroes; at least, what they did was heroic, and I use the term knowing it has gone virtually out of fashion. The dead woman's name was Karen Silkwood, and most of her life was distinguished by how ordinary it was, as ordinary as her death was extraordinary. The people who took up her cause were a lot like her. That is, they did not have much power or money, far less certainly than the forces they took on, and a great deal of what inspired this book was their amazing disregard for the impossible. As much as this case is about Karen Silkwood, it is even more about the people who came afterward: Kitty Tucker, Sara Nelson, Danny Sheehan, Peter Stockton, Bob Alvarez, Bill Taylor, Father Bill Davis. Without them, Karen's death would not have amounted to much more than that AP story, stuck in newspapers under curious question-mark headlines.

Kitty, Sara, Stockton, the others, however, I did not meet until later. None of them lived in Oklahoma, and Oklahoma was where I started. Oklahoma was home for the mystery; also home for the Kerr-McGee Corporation, which owned the nuclear factory where Karen had begun as a technician and ended as a spy; and home for Drew Stephens, who had been her boyfriend. Along with her parents, he suffered the most, but on my first trip to Oklahoma he was practically the only person to put aside grief and paranoia and talk openly. The men at the top in Kerr-McGee headquarters had a straightforward policy not to discuss the case with reporters, and they were meticulous about it. Karen's co-workers, the men and women in the nuclear factory, were closemouthed too—someone was dead and they didn't know whom to trust—but a few workers had taken Ilene Younghein into their confidence, and she took me into hers. Mrs. Younghein is a housewife and a hellraiser and one wonderful lady. In helping me, she stood up to considerable hostility from people who had long been part of her world. Much the same could be said about Steve Wodka and Tony Mazzocchi. They are health experts for the Oil, Chemical and Atomic Workers Union, and they were the first to call attention to the peculiar circumstances of Karen's death. By demanding an investigation, they did not make themselves popular; among their own union compatriots there was carping about how they were putting the nuclear industry and jobs therein at jeopardy.

Wodka and Mazzocchi were working out of Washington, D.C., and after Oklahoma, I went there: to interview them and to search through records that the Atomic Energy Commission was required to maintain. In a manner of speaking, that is how I met Kitty Tucker; she also was plodding through the records. Through Kitty, I met Bob Alvarez, her husband, and Sara Nelson, one of Kitty's best friends. Kitty and Bob and Sara are political activists, but, like Karen, they had grown up thinking nuclear power was safe and clean, that it was the good that had been salvaged from the bomb labs of World War II. From their involvement in this case, they found out different; they found out just how mean a little puff of radiation can be, and they became leaders in the movement to shut down nuclear reactors. It has been suggested that Karen died as a martyr to this movement. The truth is, the anti-nuclear movement was hardly in existence before 1975. But because of Karen's death, Kitty and Bob and Sara helped create it (along with thousands of others, of course, who had other impulses). They also created the Supporters of Silkwood, and lobbied a lethargic Congress for a full-blown investigation.

Chief of the congressional investigators was Peter Stockton. I had met him earlier, when he was reporting on the case for the National Public Radio. Stockton's investigation paralleled my own, but his was unarguably superior. Along with Win Turner, he was responsible for revealing the gross negligence in the official reports of the Oklahoma Highway Patrol, the FBI, the Justice Department. Stockton is a sort of throwback gumshoe and he is not at all self-promoting; long before I decided to write a book, he was sharing the results of his investigation, as an older brother might with a baseball mitt. Danny Sheehan picked up on the case where Stockton left off. He was at once lawyer, sleuth, rebel, missionary, orator, strategist, and his many sides, all of them forceful, made it seem as if a small army was gathered wherever he went. That was not far from reality. If Danny was not in the company of one of his three legal associates—Jim Ikard, Art Angel, Gerry Spence—he was hashing out strategy with his two sidekick detectives: Father Bill Davis, a Jesuit priest, and Bill Taylor, a former Marine cop. Each of them probably spent more time and talked to more people than I did, which is not an insignificant statement.

By rough count, I spent twenty-two months on the road, mostly in Oklahoma and Washington. The miles by car, plane, train, were in the vicinity of 75,000. Part of the time and distance also went into trips to Texas, Tennessee, New Mexico, Florida, Colorado, Michigan, South Carolina, Kentucky, Wyoming, and Georgia, where other pertinent events took place. Of these localities, the most important was Karen's hometown: Nederland, Texas. Her parents and her two sisters still live there. The Silkwoods were unfailingly forthright, and their courage ran deep, beyond what might be expected even from the depth of a family's love. Their cooperation was special, as was that of Jim Smith and Jack Tice, two of the factory workers who eventually did talk for the record. By that action they likely forfeited any chance of working ever again in the nuclear industry. Jean Jung, a crucial eyewitness who was among the last to see Karen alive, paid a price as high: she ended up leaving her job and going into hiding in another state. Allowing me to interview her there, she had to overcome a fear that was quite real.

The risks were not all the same, nor the emotion, nor the dimensions of cooperation, but all of these people invited me in some way into their lives. We ate and drank together, traded jokes, confessions; I stayed in some of their homes; there were parties, long nights of reminiscences, hugs, tears, shouts at the moon; I cross-examined them and pushed them sometimes to the point of heartbreak. In the beginning I was a stranger to every one of them. Now many are friends. The advantages of writing about friends are obvious. More obvious, perhaps, than the disadvantages: you tend to be tough on them, you tend to concentrate on their flaws; you do not want to cheat in their favor. They might have received kinder treatment from a writer who knew them less well.

Notwithstanding all their help, this book would not have been complete without the descriptions, the facts, the personal accounts provided by a number of other people. They cannot all be listed here, but I would like to thank Father Wally Kasubowski, Barbara Newman, Robyn Petty, Pat Austin, Alison Freeman, Rob Hager, John Seigenthaler, David Burnham, Joe Royer, Sherri Ellis, Dr. John Gofman, Congressman John Dingell, Imaging Spence, Dr. Thomas Mancuso, Jerry Stoll, Marion Edey, Frosty Troy, Michael Kennedy, Thomas Bamberger, Dr. Alice Stewart, Dr. George Kneale, Dr. Karl Morgan, Karen Miller, Bonnie Raitt, Jackson Browne, Anne Zill, Buzz Hirsch, Larry Cano, Michael Ward, Father Paul Gallatin, Dr. Dean Abrahamson, Dr. Donald Geesaman, Ted Sebring, Jack Taylor, Dwayne Cox, Alan Bromley, Joe Pennington, George Martin, Father Robert Taylor, Chris Beaver, Judy Irving, Sue and Michael Bowman, Vicki Monks, Lisa Honig, Justin Zinn, Ada Sanchez, Patty Neimond, Lesley Haas, Richard Rashke, Brett Bursey, Susan Urquia, Graham Nash, Susan Kellam, Becky Hardee, Peter Golden, Jim Garrison, Richard Pollock, Harold Smith, Dr. Helen Caldicott, Dr. Edward Martell, Ciji Ware, Mike Bates, Andrew Jaffe, Harvey Wasserman, Lieutenant Kenneth Van Hoy, Roberto Suro, Paul Wenske, Gene Triplett, Lynn Miller, Charles Thomas, Jeff Stein, and Howard Rosenberg. (One friend of Karen's, who is mentioned briefly, appears under a pseudonym—the other names are all real.)

Still others of importance consented to interviews albeit with limits. Lawrence Olson, the FBI's chief agent on the case, granted me an hour. Jackie Srouji, "the mystery lady," let me into her home, showed me some of her files, told me her version of certain events—though it must be said her version was not always consistent. John Keeney, a deputy attorney general for the Justice Department, answered some of my questions, as did Bill Paul, Bill Zimmerman, and Bill Teague, speaking on behalf of Kerr-McGee. (Most of the Kerr-McGee executives and their associates, though, declined interviews, in keeping with their self-imposed gag.) Judge Frank Theis permitted me to listen in on certain discussions in his chambers.

Out of such access and weeks of interviews—and tens of thousands of pages of investigative memos, congressional hearings, depositions, courtroom goings-on, affidavits, corporate records, government records, plus a variety of other written materials—was this book written. An afterword of footnotes was to be included, until it threatened to become as long as the text and had to be dropped. But the book throughout was made as accurate as possible by means of a system of cross-referencing and double-checking that we set up. I say "we," meaning Diana and myself. Both of us were involved in the case, as a team, from the beginning. Our own behind-the-scenes story, however, has been left out of the narrative. After some debate we decided not to insert ourselves as characters; along with dozens of others, we properly belong to the unspecified background. Nonetheless, we were present during much of what went on. Perhaps half of the book is drawn from direct observations. In my rendering, the dialogue and conversational tics should not be taken as absolutely literal, but everything is either a very close facsimile of what we saw and heard or, at least, is based on the best memory of other participants involved in the long struggle to vindicate Karen. Any rewriting I did was to benefit the transition from spoken to printed word, not to tamper with the meaning: that I tried to hold inviolate.

For Karen's feeling and words and actions I had to rely entirely on the people who had known her. The very fact that she was not around to say aye or nay undoubtedly affected what people said about her. Some people were overly protective, some overly cruel. Be that as it may, I'd like to believe that the picture of Karen's life, as presented, is honest and balanced and that no substantial part of it is missing. Indeed, my intentions were that for the book as a whole.

To the extent that I succeeded, I must again share the credit. Foremost of my editors were Jonathan Segal, Jim Silberman, Elizabeth Kaplan, and Kate Edgar at Summit; also, over the years at *Rolling Stone,* Christine Doudna, Sarah Lazin, Marianne Partridge,

Paul Scanlon, David Felton, Barbara Downey, Harriet Fier, Bob Wallace, Catharine Norton, Vicki Sufian, Maryanne Vollers, Linda Ross, David Young, and Tim White. A special acknowledgment must go to Jann Wenner, the *Rolling Stone* editor and publisher, who stood by this endeavor from start to finish, in a manner no one else in his position would or did. A number of good friends offered suggestions throughout. They included David Weir, Clark Norton, Daniel O'Leary, Tammy Jacobs, Tom Weir, David Fenton, Victor Kovner, Janet Sluizer, Susan Brenneman, Frank Browning, Frank and Mary Viviano, Kay Regar, Diane Reverend, Lynn Nesbit, Amanda Urban, and several already mentioned, two of whom bear repeating, Christine Doudna and Sarah Lazin. My thanks to everyone.

—Howard Kohn
May 1981

PART ONE

One

The sweetheart eyes, the devil in her, the sassy mouth—these were now taken for granted at the union meetings. As Karen herself was. But tonight everything about her was somehow more serious, less rah-rah. The talk she gave was in a register low and hoarse. Sitting down, she fell absolutely quiet. Skinny lady that she was, and rigid as she sat, she might have been a shadow. In this small crowd, here in the back room at the Hub Cafe, she was conspicuous only by how solitary she looked. She was like a kid pretending not to be scared. The men from the factory could see in her face some of her loneliness and fright and all the other things going on inside that God only knew. They would sneak a quick glance and, yes, they did feel a little sorry for her. But it was only in passing. Why waste themselves on someone so pretty? That was part of Karen's problem, of course. She was an awfully fine looker—too fine.

Karen had black hair and features of the sort that men remembered. The black of her hair made her skin all the more sheer and, tonight, all the more wan. She wore a black turtleneck, slacks in white-and-black plaid, white socks, black half-boots. The turtleneck and slacks were favorites. And they were warm. Though with the cold night outside, come down from the north, they could have been a lot warmer. Since sundown, winter had stolen across the brown hummocky fields to take autumn's place in the little Oklahoma town of Crescent. The cold hurt. It was the kind of cold that sucks heat from the furriest of animals, an unexpected, pounding cold, and Karen's coat was a thin leather one she had found in a flea market. So when she left the cafe, she ran hard, with the coat wrapped tight and her hair streaming behind. It took less than a minute to get to her car. She got in. But the cold was inside the car, too, and all the heater did was circulate it. The heater fan made a slow sound, a whine.

Karen's car was a Honda Civic hatchback, a foreign import uncommon for the early seventies. The exterior was a flashy white and the upholstery black. (White and black: the poet in her would have said they had become the colors of her world.) She had bought the Honda because it held like a wonder around corners, and she added the special-grip tires and wide-angle mirrors. On summer weekends Karen and Drew raced on the autocross circuit, she in the Honda, he in his red Austin-Healey Sprite convertible. Twist, brake, twist again, never blink—you had to navigate the pylons in a matter of seconds. Drew was fast: a water-skeeter on a pond was what she called him. She would never be able to match his clockings, especially the unbelievable fifty-point-seven. But she was almost as good. Up against other ladies she was better than good. Didn't she have a trophy to prove it?

Tonight her route was a two-lane track from Crescent to Oklahoma City, twenty miles of Highway 74, paved with tranquil faith. She knew it well. For two years she had driven it every day to and from work.

The wind was blowing out of the north, about fifteen miles an hour, hastening her tiny car toward a faded line where the sky touched the land. Six miles down the road, less than ten minutes from the cafe, there was a gravel driveway, faintly luminous. The driveway led to a fence and through a gate. The fence was a line of steel braids with an apron of barbed wire. Beyond was an asphalt parking lot, and on a low knoll beyond that, under floodlights, was a building. The building was set strangely close to the road for such an open, immense landscape. It had a flat roof, flat as the sky. The whole structure had been made innocent by milky brown paint. It could have been a warehouse, or a modern barn. There were hoofprints where cattle had grazed in the last wet days of autumn, but the hoofprints were outside the fence.

A white billboard out front explained in red and blue letters that this was Kerr-McGee property. In Oklahoma that was explanation enough—there were jobs inside. Other letters on the sign, smaller but in the same patriotic design, spelled out "NUCLEAR DIVISION." It was hard for Karen to remember that day two years ago, her first inside the nuclear factory. What had the Kerr-McGee man said? "This is the biggest breakthrough since the forties." He had shown her rooms where the air was filtered pure and people in white coveralls stood next to odd boxes of metal and Plexiglas. Now it seemed vague, that bright day when the poem had come to her like an augury.

> *The spirit of Will Rogers is alive and well*
> *outside in the green-gold land*
> *But inside the world belongs to Buck Rogers*
> *where our future is at hand.*

Karen could remember the poem, and the sterile rooms and the boxes. It was the jaunty pride she had lost.

Now every day inside the factory there were harsh accusing remarks. Bitch! Troublemaker! Hippie! What would happen if they discovered that she was also a spy? A spy? Yes, of course, that's what they would call her, if they knew about her pretending to put photomicrographs in a file drawer when she was actually taking them out, or if they knew about the extra copies from the Xerox copier that she had been slipping into her purse. Everything had gone into a manila folder, which was beside her on the front seat. The gauntness in her face showed how the life of espionage had affected her; so did her manacled grip on the steering wheel.

At fifty miles an hour her car sped past the parking lot and past the flat-roofed factory. The end of Highway 74, where it became an Oklahoma City street, marked the end of her journey. Drew was already there, waiting for her at the Holiday Inn Northwest. Also waiting was a reporter from *The New York Times*. And a man from the union. They had flown into town an hour ago for the occasion. The manila folder was for them. After tonight everyone who read the *Times* would know about Kerr-McGee's factory, and if Karen was successful, everyone would be stirred up, a little frightened. Like her.

It was about a quarter past seven. There was an aftertaste of iced tea on her tongue. She might well have wished for something a bit stronger, a bit more warming, but it had been weeks since her last time in the bars where she once had been a regular amidst the loud voices and the good-hearted sensual teasing and the bottles glowing in amber light. Perhaps later tonight she and Drew could go hoist a few.

Usually Karen had one foot heavy on the gas, the other held over the brake. She drove in much the same way that she composed her poems, with an anxious optimism about what lay ahead. In half an hour she would be at the motel and her mission would be done.

OKLAHOMA CITY. NOVEMBER 13, 1974. A tent of yellow cardboard on the dresser said "Welcome to the Holiday Inn." Drew Stephens shifted his eyes from the sign to a round synthetic-walnut table, to a beige phone, to an expressionless door. Any minute now, he thought, they would be hearing Karen's brassy knock.

Drew was slouched against black vinyl, one blue-jeaned leg slung over an armrest. He had middle-length tawny hair, a nicely trimmed beard, and a failed mustache. Direct, unboastful eyes suggested a lack of guile. For some time, off and on, he and Karen had lived together. When they first met, her dark lustrous curls had been short, her smile fleeting and bashful. Back then she looked somehow old-fashioned, but sexy in her girl-woman way. Lately he couldn't tell which she wanted to be, fun girl or uppity woman. Being her boyfriend could be very aggravating. *Very.* Right now she was more than two hours overdue, causing unrest in the motel room.

"Is she usually like this?" the older man asked. He was David Burnham, clean-shaven, pale, studious, a man about to enter his middle years. He was sitting on the edge of a bed. A yellow pencil and a thin brown notebook identified him as the *Times* reporter. Burnham had never met Karen, so he was trying to get an idea of what she was like.

"She's got her faults," Drew said quietly, "but being late isn't one."

The other man, in a business suit and matching tie, was Steve Wodka. From his straight, uncompromising mouth you would not have guessed he was a young man, only twenty-five. He had the look of someone who takes his work wherever he goes and the manner of someone who commands: men twice his age listened to him. Wodka had arranged this rendezvous, although, like Burnham, he was a stranger, from Washington, D.C. He worked there for the OCAW (the Oil, Chemical and Atomic Workers International) and had come to know Karen because she belonged to 5–283 Nuclear, an OCAW local here in Oklahoma. They were friends, but mostly over the long-distance wires; they had seen each other only three times.

Moving in quick steps, Wodka crossed the small room and halted again at the bed-side table. He picked up the beige phone. For most of the evening the phone had been dead, unaccountably, but now it buzzed an orderly buzz. He dialed and a voice came on the line. Drew listened unwillingly to Wodka's side of the conversation. It was a series of hoarse exclamations that went on for an astonishing, absurd length of time. "What?! What the hell—?!"

"Thanks," Wodka said, hanging up. The word sounded loud and severe in the hushed room. Drew felt anxiety like ice in his lungs. He could see that the note of gratitude was not right for the news. Wodka's face had sagged, shoulders too.

Wodka walked a few feet and shook his head. "Karen's car ran off the road," he said. "She's dead."

A truck driver, perched high in his cab and rolling along Highway 74, had spotted it about a mile past the Kerr-McGee factory. The white Honda was in the creek bed, lying on its side, almost hidden from view. Climbing out next to the culvert, the truck driver looked down. The scene was lit uncertainly by his lights, but on the ground he could see a manila folder that had spilled its contents. The wind snatched one of the papers away. Curling into a gust, it went skipping across mud and water. Along the shoulder of the highway the bluestem listed sideways, unable to snap back to attention.

A delicate arm, poking out a window, appeared to be waving for help. Getting closer, the truck driver saw a shoulder and a neck and a face. He shouted, but the woman made no response, and it was then he realized her arm was moving with the wind. Her other arm was flung up and over her face. Her head had fallen weakly to one side. She lay broken and unimportant across the black seat. The blood on her face was already crusted—she had died quickly.

Drew tried to say something, but the words were not distinct; they kept running down his throat. He jerked up and went to the sink. Wodka pulled his arms to his chest and collapsed into the abandoned chair. He said, apparently to no one, "It can't be true—how the hell can it?"

Burnham began putting on his coat. He was a newspaperman, and newspapermen do not have ordinary reactions. Every instinct demanded he rush to the scene. But it took him a few minutes before he got the two younger men to clamber into his rented car.

The three of them might have been plainclothes cops, gray-faced and drooping after a long stakeout. The power of the moment bound them together—they were caught up in the quest to find out how Karen had died, and why. Drew hunched in the back seat and called out occasional directions. Again and again hurt mounted in his eyes, stretching his cheeks, draining their color. His sculpted beard dropped to his chest. In the front seat Wodka tugged anxiously at a curly black mustache and kept a silent lookout. Burnham strained forward behind the wheel and shivered in his lightweight trenchcoat. The accelerator was hard to the floor despite the obvious futility in their speed.

It was dark—the only illumination came from their headlights, a furious arc that turned fence posts and telephone poles into predatory totems. In the blanching shadow they were like angels of death.

The prairie began at the road's edge, acres of grass bowed and burnt by the eternal wind. The prairie, most of it, was as remote as it had been fifty years ago, a hundred years ago, as remote and stubborn and blunt as it had always been.

Burnham drove past the culvert twice before Wodka could make out its outline. Karen's body had already been shuttled to a funeral home and her car towed away. But on the highway shoulder, in the mud and ruined grass, they could see the telltale signs of a recent disturbance. Drew stayed in the car while the other two, stepping gingerly, cast about. The red mud stained their shoes—red was the color of the earth here. Below them was the creek, a rivulet with a snaking line of muddy red rainwater, its path choked with brush and bluestem and goldenrod. They were looking for clues, but they didn't know the criteria, and all they found were a few morbid souvenirs: lengths of chrome peeled from their moorings; a moon-shaped racing mirror amputated with savage force; glistening slivers of glass; and daubs of orange, larger than the rest, from a roadside reflector that had been trampled under the bouncing car.

The instruments of death were the culvert's two concrete wing-walls, somber and gray, seven feet long, five and a half feet high. From the highway you could barely distinguish them. Most of the height was buried below ground level, enclosing the creek and forming its banks as it ran under Highway 74. Less than a foot of concrete protruded above ground, and even that disappeared as it sloped away from the road. A brittle fringe of bluestem, having escaped the tractor-mowers of summer, was tufted against the north wall. It added further camouflage. "Karen probably didn't see the damn thing until she was right on top of it," Wodka decided aloud. The accident had begun when her car swerved from Highway 74. It hit the north wall and jumped over, lurching forward, and caromed off the south wall. If she had turned in either direction, the outcome might have been different. Instead the first wall had acted like a daredevil's launch pad. When the Honda hit, its momentum carried it through the air and over the mud-water and against the other wall, then down into the creek.

That sequence was easily pieced together. But Wodka and Burnham were baffled by what preceded it. The car had crossed the center line, moving left to the wrong side of the road, and had gone off onto the left shoulder, a grassy embankment that dropped away sharply from the pavement. Yet the car had skittered a good length along the shoulder, almost a hundred yards, parallel to the road. "Why the hell didn't she get back on?" Wodka wondered. It was almost as if another car had driven alongside and forced Karen to stay on the shoulder. But there was no one to say for sure, so they retreated to their car. They continued along Highway 74, retracing her path. In ten minutes they were in Crescent.

Crescent is a hamlet with two stoplights, a post office, and not much else. Proceeding down the main street they passed the Hub Cafe. At the other end of town, across from a shrunken little train station, there was a Ford dealership with a garage and showroom in an adobelike structure. They pulled in. Ted Sebring, the owner, was president of the local chamber of commerce. About eight o'clock, as Sebring was having drinks with a few friends, a call had come over his CB scanner box. The police wanted his tow-truck. Dressed in immaculate hundred-dollar shoes, Sebring had brought along two of his men to do the muddy work in the creek. They had hauled the Honda here to his garage and locked it inside.

Yielding to the hour, approaching midnight, the three men from the Holiday Inn did not bother Sebring for a key. Instead they conducted an inspection through a large window crisscrossed with iron bars. In the spectral light they saw patches of spilled motor oil and discarded auto parts and other junk, pieces of metal. The tow truck sat in deep shadow. Pressing close to the glass, they could make out the winch handle and a hook from which the Honda hung on a taut cable like a toy. The exterior was dirty and crumpled, the interior a tangle of spewed-out wires and knobs. The motor and its parts had exploded the dashboard. Damage was concentrated on the driver's side. The left front fender was pushed back almost to the door, with the hood bent upright in a V shape. Karen had collided with the steering wheel in a space too narrow for a miracle to intervene.

The car might have been a loser dead in the pit after a demolition derby. Drew started to say something, but then realized how pathetic it would seem. The sight of the wrecked car brought an awareness of pain. He leaned against the wall and felt the coarse surface of the cinder blocks; tears began. He felt pressure at the back of his head and put his hands to his eyes.

A noise from around the corner startled them—the wind was rattling a drainpipe. They laughed sheepishly and walked back to the street. Wodka suggested they go find Jack Tice, the man on the phone who had told them about the accident. Tice was chairman of the 5–283 union local, and he was just about the last person to have seen Karen alive.

A short, scrappy man with a lean face opened the farmhouse door. "Come on in, fellahs," Tice said. He had been with Karen at the Hub Cafe and, unsettled though he was, he was willing to recall those minutes for his visitors. Recently Karen had been upset and alarmed, he said—"she was starting to think someone was out to get her"—but tonight she had been quiet, tense, purposeful and, in retrospect, perhaps a bit thrilled about going to an audience with *The New York Times*. "Though I myself didn't know where she was going till just now."

"We just told people on a need-to-know basis," Wodka said. He found it impossible at the moment to muster any tact.

Drew, in a fog of suffering, could not keep focused on the voices. He kept seeing Karen as he had seen her that morning, dressed in black and white, and he tried to remember those days when she wore bright sundresses and her hair was loose in the breeze of his red Sprite while a tape deck played the songs of Jackson Browne. Abruptly his own voice rang out. "Hold it, hold it. Just a minute. Jesus Christ, I've got to let Karen's folks know."

He went into the kitchen but came back in a few minutes, sad and resigned. "They already knew. The cops called them." He nodded at Tice. "I'll pay for the call." It had crossed the state line into Texas. Tice waved the offer away, and the three visitors left the house apologizing unnecessarily for the interruption.

It was late and there was nothing else they could do. But they felt a dread about returning to the Holiday Inn, as if that would declare their failure. Burnham headed the car toward Guthrie, at one time the capital of Oklahoma, but since reduced in size and importance. The undertaker lived there.

"You guys go ahead," Drew mumbled as they parked in front of the funeral home.

But the lights inside had been doused, and the undertaker had gone to bed. "Let's skip it," Wodka said in husky relief, and Burnham shifted into reverse.

Back on Highway 74 they came again to the culvert. Impulsively they agreed to stop. This time Drew nerved himself to get out. In a night turned even colder, all three hiked down the short ravine. Once more they picked their way among the tire tracks and the red footprints and the shards of glass and chrome. Wodka spied a rectangle of paper stuck to the ground, holding fast against a razory wind. He seized it. It was Karen's last paycheck from the Kerr-McGee Corporation.

Finally they returned to the Holiday Inn. Despite the temperature, sweat had spread secretly inside their shirts.

Drew manhandled the alarm clock without effect. The cacophony came from outside, the lonesome calls of geese in pursuit of southern marshlands. An early sun was lost behind black and silver clouds. Drew couldn't remember sleeping, but something had left an evil taste in his mouth. Over a basin he brushed his teeth, making foam out of anger and grief. He dressed in last night's clothes. At the motel he met again with Wodka and Burnham, and shortly after ten o'clock they began a second sortie.

The Highway Patrol office in Guthrie looked a little like a deserted army barracks and it smelled menacingly of gun oil. The walls were bare except for the harsh profiles on "wanted" posters. Rick Fagan was the trooper on duty. Just a few years removed from farm-boy chores, he had a towhead of brown hair, oversized hands, a premature belly. The extra weight gave him the appearance of authority. He had been the first patrolman to the culvert the night before and had supervised the dismal task of freeing the body; they'd had to use an air jack to pop open the door from its twisted columns.

"I'm here regarding the death of Karen Silkwood," Wodka said.

The trooper heaved himself to the counter, and the men stiffly traded names. Fagan had gone back to the scene early that morning to trace the Honda's flight from the road. He said, "From the looks of things, it's pretty clear she fell asleep at the wheel. She never woke up."

"Isn't that jumping the gun a little? I mean there are other possibilities."

"Sorry, sir, we got it listed as a one-car accident. My report is practically typed up."

The swift judgment only encouraged Wodka's suspicions. "Look," he said, "Miss Silkwood was on a special assignment for the OCAW. She had a folder full of documents, secret documents. I don't think it was an accident."

"Don't be giving me a hard time." Trooper Fagan appeared to be thinking of the extra paperwork. "She fell asleep."

"The hell she did."

"You're kinda grinding my axles, you know what I mean?"

"All I want is for you to go out to the culvert and take another look."

"Hey, I've looked!" The words were so fierce that Wodka took a step back.

That seemed to clear the air. Trooper Fagan became calm and correct. His superiors were aware of all the important facts, he said, and they considered it an accident, not homicide. As for Karen Silkwood's possessions, he had plucked them up from the mud and conscientiously placed them in the car. Last seen, they were being towed to Ted Sebring's garage.

Under a noonday sun the garage looked far less forboding. The Honda cast no shadow. It was sitting outside, away from the casual squalor of old grease and broken generators. Drew went in alone and found Sebring behind a squat desk. "I'd like to pick up whatever personal items were left in the Honda. I'm a friend of the owner."

Sebring looked at the young man; his shoulders and eyelids were sunk inward from lack of sleep. "Unless you're her husband or next of kin, I can't release anything," Sebring said. "That's the law." He was kind but firm.

Drew reached into a shirt pocket for a small address book. "Could you do it if I called and got permission from her parents?"

"Well, okay, I guess so." Sebring pushed the desk phone forward, and Drew dialed. He hoped Mrs. Silkwood would answer. Last night, over Tice's phone, he had sensed hostility from Mr. Silkwood, whom he had never met.

Karen's father had planned to fly in that morning to bring his girl home, but he had missed the only flight to Oklahoma City, so her body was still at the funeral home and he was still in Texas. He listened distractedly to Drew, then agreed to speak to Sebring. His words came few and muffled over the distance. "You can let the boy have her things."

Sebring withdrew to a back room and produced a cardboard box that had once held two dozen quarts of Pennzoil. It was sealed with brown masking tape. On signing a receipt, Drew sought the sanctity of Burnham's car. With Wodka and Burnham as witnesses, he stripped off the tape and rummaged through, taking a quick inventory. There was a snapshot of Karen, a first aid kit, a wide-brimmed hat of the kind worn on picnics, a warranty for the Honda, a postcard of a color-flooded mountain scene, a booklet called "Worker's Manual for Controlling Work Environments," papers from the OCAW contract talks, and miscellany. None of it was mud-streaked or spotted with creek water. Wodka stretched across the seat back and did his own sorting, heaping the contents onto Drew's lap. "Where the hell is her folder?" He swore in disbelief.

The snapshot was to have been artwork for a headline story in *The New York Times,* but there was nothing in the box to justify any headline. No manila folder of documents, no photomicrographs, nothing that was evidence of seven weeks of copying and purloining.

By two-thirty they were parked once more at the Holiday Inn. Wodka and Burnham were in a hurry to pack their bags: they had planes to catch. Wodka was due at an OCAW meeting in Las Vegas, and Burnham's editors had ordered him back to D.C. over his objections. Drew sat in the vinyl chair, his gaze locked in mute appeal on the phone, the agent of last night's news. He felt overwhelmed by a mystery that seemed to compound itself every few minutes. Wodka was repeating, for the fourth or fifth time, a feeling that he couldn't hold in, yet couldn't quite accept. "What d'you think? You think someone ran her off the road and grabbed her documents?"

Burnham put away his notes, which contained a story far different than the one he had come to Oklahoma for, a story he would have ridiculed in a spy novel, a story he could have scarcely imagined in the *Times.* He was disturbed by what they knew, and didn't know. As an excellent reporter, and therefore fastidious, he suggested, "Why don't you hire a private eye or somebody like that? Somebody who's independent."

LAS VEGAS. NOVEMBER 14, 1974. Rainbow neon, the fur coats that never come off no matter how hot the gaming rooms: this could only be The Strip. But Wodka didn't even glance sideways. Checking into Caesar's Palace that evening, it was just another town, another motel. After five years with the OCAW, and after two hundred or so such stops, they were all the same. Wodka put his bags in his room and then returned to the lobby. Inside a phone booth he set up camp. A sudden distrust of motel switchboards made him choose the pay phone over the one upstairs. First he dialed Tony Mazzocchi, his boss and senior partner in Washington, D.C.—he stayed in the booth while Mazzocchi phoned OCAW headquarters in Denver. Within a dozen feet the hopeful clacking of slot machines dueled with the yips and plaints of the players. After some minutes Mazzocchi rang back. "I went all the way to the top on this," he said. "You got the go-ahead."

Again Wodka dialed, this time a Dallas lawyer, a friend of the OCAW. "We need a guy to investigate a car crash," Wodka shouted over the din. "Yeah, preferably someone not from Oklahoma. . . . Sure, Dallas would be fine. . . . What's his name? P–i–p–k–i–n? . . . Yeah, got it."

OKLAHOMA CITY. NOVEMBER 16, 1974. A. O. Pipkin ambled down a ramp at Will Rogers World Airport and stopped with a quick shudder. Thick and stolid, Pipkin's parts seemed to move only when necessary. Scanning the crowd of passengers, Drew had no trouble recognizing him. He was wearing sunglasses and a Day-Glo orange jumpsuit, the uniform of grouse hunters and highway repair crews.

Pipkin's career dated back to 1951 and the police department of Albuquerque, New Mexico. Motorcycle cops had just been given two-way radios, and old-timers kept turning the gadgets off, which afforded the rookie Pipkin his big chance. Within a year and a half he was in charge of the traffic accident squad. By 1955 he had turned freelancer, selling what then was a pioneering specialty. For insurance companies, and against them, he reconstructed the final seconds of some two thousand accidents. He testified at more than three hundred trials; in dozens he was the pivotal witness. Hanging from his office walls in Dallas were framed mementos and a certificate of graduation from a course in Newtonian mechanics. One faded newspaper clipping told of his work in the gory death of actress Jayne

Mansfield; she was decapitated in 1967 when her Cadillac lodged under the chassis of a stalled truck. Until now, that had been Pipkin's most famous case.

At the culvert Drew watched him lay out his tape measure, unraveling it from a silvery spool. From a gray metal case, padded with foam rubber into which he had cut seven or eight odd spaces, he pulled out his other tools—folding tripod, stopwatch, transit compass, slide rule, camera clamp and Pentax camera. Pipkin made several calculations and diagrams. The road surface, black asphalt with intermittent yellow lines, was thirty-four feet across. There was a crown down the middle, and on either side the pavement slanted decidedly toward the shoulders, for runoff during a downpour. Two hundred and forty feet north of the creek there were furrows in the mud, three of them, and three tire tracks in the grass. With his camera Pipkin preserved everything on celluloid. The tire tracks. Skid marks. Culvert walls. The sluggish creek. The long empty highway.

Then Drew took him to see the sad-looking Honda. Pipkin jacked up each end and inspected the tires. He put his tape to further use and made a special note about the steering wheel. It had been bent almost in half.

Squatting on his knees, sunglasses in hand, Pipkin pointed to the left rear bumper where it curved around the fender. "You see those dents?" In the thick hard steel there was a gouge two inches long, three-quarters of an inch wide. Next to the bumper on the white field of the fender there was another dent, as if from an angry fist. "How do you suppose they got there?"

Drew took a close look. He frowned and peered some more. Compared with the damage up front, all that terrible upheaval of metal and wiring, the two dents did not seem like much. To Pipkin, though, they were full of meaning. "Yes, sir," Pipkin said, wiping grimy hands on the sleeves of his jumpsuit. "Yes, sir, I'd say they're mighty suspicious, mighty damn suspicious." A whistling noise came from between his teeth and his tone finally betrayed a certain fervor.

WASHINGTON, D.C. NOVEMBER 16, 1974. Tony Mazzocchi was trying to make sense of the past seven weeks, the seven weeks since Karen showed up in his OCAW office to tell him about dishonesty and disregard and fraud going on inside that Kerr-McGee building.

On the basis of her visit, Mazzocchi had sent her back to Oklahoma to get proof. He had liked Karen. She seemed raw, tough, savvy, with a reservoir for taking chances, a lot like him. She had volunteered to work undercover, a deeply ambitious task, but he had thought she was up to it. Now Mazzocchi wondered if he might have been wrong. Had he misjudged her? Some of his colleagues were saying that he had acted in haste. Of course, they were always saying things like that about Mazzocchi. But you did not grow up on the streets of Brooklyn without learning how to move fast or how to talk with your fists or be loyal to your people.

What some officials from Kerr-McGee were saying, however, had added substantially to his pondering. They were accusing Karen of being a crude liar. She never had any proof, they said, no documents of any value. And they claimed she had died in a drug stupor.

"I can tell you right now that's a lot of crap," Wodka said. Like his boss, he believed in loyalty.

Returning from Las Vegas on an afternoon flight, he had come directly to Mazzocchi's downtown D.C. apartment. At forty-eight Mazzocchi was nearly twice as old as his protege, though the difference was hardly apparent. Karen had put a coy nickname on him— "The Fonz." Mazzocchi had a young man's style and a cocky grin that could have been swiped off a street kid.

The grin, at this late hour, was a grimace. Mazzocchi poured a glass of milk for Wodka, he ordered his son away from the television, he hit fist into palm. He paced. How could Karen's car have ended up in a creek? How could her manila folder have vanished?

The phone jangled. It was Drew.

"You were right," Drew said. "Pipkin says it doesn't look like an accident."

"Where the fuck is Pipkin? When is he gonna call in?"

"Tomorrow. He's still running all the measurements through his slide rule."

Wodka and Mazzocchi got to their office early the next morning. Burnham walked the five blocks from the *Times* bureau so he could wait with them for Pipkin's call. It came as promised. Wodka motioned for Burnham to pick up on the secretary's extension. "Okay, let's have it," Wodka barked.

Pipkin presented his findings in the flat, knowledgeable style of a veteran courtroom witness. He wouldn't go so far as to swear that the Highway Patrol was wrong, but he had come to a different conclusion based on certain laws of Newton. If Karen Silkwood had fallen asleep, he said, the Honda should have drifted to the right, harmlessly, into a pasture. Instead her car shot left, up and over the road crown, and onto the left shoulder. There the car straightened out, indicating she was awake and trying to return to the pavement. Another thing: the impact of a limp, sleeping body against the steering wheel would not have so drastically altered its shape. The wheel had been concaved to the point of fracture, the halves shoved so far forward they almost overlapped. Obviously, Karen had braced her hands against it.

"You've seen the car?" Wodka interrupted.

"Yes, sir. There is considerable evidence to conclude that she wasn't asleep. Not one wink. And I don't think she was alone on the road either. She had company!"

"Another car?"

"Some kind of vehicle, yes, sir!" Pipkin was talking with increased energy.

"What's the evidence?"

Pipkin became the methodical investigator again. "There are dents in the rear bumper and fender that don't have any road film in them, which would mean they were made that night, the night of the accident. They were made by some sort of blunt object, maybe the knobby point of a bumper or a homemade cowcatcher. It's my conclusion that another vehicle came up from behind and hit her a good crack." The tracks and furrows were those of a car squirting over the center line and spinning off the road, not drifting. The rear left wheel actually spun off first, making three tracks instead of two in the mud and grass where it left the road.

It appeared that Karen's autocross experience had kept her from panicking and helped her regain control. She had managed to hug the shoulder, driving next to the road for two hundred and forty feet. Perhaps her assailant was hogging the road, preventing her return. In any case she was still on the grass when the culvert loomed. The car hit the short north wingwall and jumped. Karen's final act was to clutch the steering wheel as the car sailed with savage accuracy across twenty-four feet of creek bed into the south wall. "It was kind of a fluke," Pipkin said. "But it wasn't no *accident,* if you understand the difference."

Two

It was a Friday in the spring of 1972, and Karen had just put her three kids into clean clothes. From a closet she took out little fussy knickknacks and the jewelry box with roly-poly cherubs gamboling on velvet. These she put in new living-room niches, ready for a weekend of prominence, ready to please her mother. Cigarettes were Karen's big vice and the apartment usually smelled of them, but she had freshened each room with flowers. The furniture was dusted. Everything was spic-and-span by the time Mrs. Silkwood arrived from Texas.

Karen's kids used the last of the afternoon to wheedle a few games of ring-around-the-rosie out of their grandmother; then they all hustled to the supermarket. Going in, they ran into Kathy, coming out with her arms full. Kathy was a young woman with brown hair clipped pragmatically and a dumpling face. "She's my best buddy," Karen said in explanation.

Back in her kitchen, Karen peeled and sliced and cubed, trying to duplicate a *Better Homes & Gardens* picture. Karen's mother knew not to get in the way; she sat docilely, saying nothing about the lingering cigarette smell, marvelling instead at the blossoms sprouting everywhere from vases. "You must've had plenty of rain up here. Texas is all dried out and scraggly." These visits were no longer ordeals of suffocating advice. Karen had learned to listen attentively, encouragingly, to the family gossip. How else find out about her father?— the rugged, inward man who took his weekends in the Piney Woods, and who, if he could help it, would not set foot in the same room as Karen's husband.

For seven years, ever since Bill Meadows ran off with his oldest girl, Mr. Silkwood had given no sign of softening. He had warned her: "That boy's no good, he knows about the world a lot more than

you, he's lived in California and who knows where else." And hadn't
Meadows turned out to be a wastrel and vagabond? Okay, he deserved
credit for succeeding as a machinist's maximum at Mobil Pipe Line,
but was that worth the haggard odyssey on which he had taken
Karen? The Texas towns of Longview, Corsicana, Sweetwater, Mid-
land, Seminole, and now Duncan, Oklahoma. Look at her, the A
student, the only girl in her advanced chemistry class, the science
club leader, the winner of a Business and Professional Women's Association scholarship, the teenager who had imagined her future as
an assistant in some great experiment in a medical research lab—
what did she have? Not even that old weathered house, with its paint
eroding to dust and its equity mortgaged to the hilt. Along with
most everything else, the old house had been lost in the bankruptcy.

Towns and houses had changed during the seven years, but the
bankruptcy had been the only real breach in Karen's routine. Always
before she had to get a job, as a payroll clerk for the Adams Hat
Factory, a secretary for Flintkote, a receptionist in an insurance office,
work forced on her by their chronic need for money. Meadows was
paid well, but not at a rate to cover his debts to the motorcycle shops
and beer gardens. Karen always redeemed the checks he wrote and
always defended him. The arguments with her father were why she
had stopped coming home to Texas.

"Time to eat!" Karen shouted into the community backyard.
Chubby, dark-eyed Kristi and fair-haired Michael washed up. The
baby, Dawn, got a bottle that put her to sleep. On the dining table
Karen arranged pork loin, asparagus, creamed potatoes. A high-
pitched disdain greeted the picture-perfect meal. "Why can't we have
hot dogs like when Dad cooks?" Meadows was working overtime this
weekend, as he usually did when the in-laws were around. After
supper Mrs. Silkwood tucked in Kristi and Michael, then roamed the
living room picking up toys from the floor. The forced calm on her
face, the cloying in her hands—it was all too obvious. She couldn't
hold her worries in. Was Karen happy? Had the bankruptcy improved things?

"We're doing fine. I got a job, but it's only temporary, till we pay
off Dawn's doctor."

"I just wish you could take it easy for a while."

"Like you, Mama? I can't remember a time when you weren't
working at the bank." Karen sat with her feet childlike under her,
gnawing on her knuckles to forget the hidden cigarettes.

Mrs. Silkwood saw that her hectoring had displaced some of the good feeling; her voice became thin, placating. "Is there anything you need? Anything I can do?"

"Just sit, Mama. Don't worry so. I'm not overworked, honest. Kathy is a big help. She pops over and fixes meals. You should see her with the kids. She's wonderful. She builds them sandcastles at the beach so me and Bill can go water skiing." Karen had a mallard's grace on water, and she loved to have the cabin cruiser gunned to full throttle. "We might leave the kids with Kathy if we ever go on that trip to California."

"California—wouldn't that be nice! Remember how you used to come home from those movies and talk on and on? It could be like a second honeymoon."

"Mama, you know we never had a first one."

California didn't happen. On an evening a few months later, after bedtime, Karen knelt prayerfully and kissed her three children. She lifted a pressboard suitcase that had seen better days and shut the front door behind her. Dusty streets, some of them unnamed, took her out of Duncan. At the Bailey Turnpike she turned northeast, away from all those small Texas and Oklahoma towns, and two hours of steady driving delivered her to Oklahoma City. Bright happy lights defined the rise of skyscrapers. The city was more modern than any she had known: the state capital was the crossroads for politicians, ranchers, oilmen, and all those who could stand no more of Sweetwater or Corsicana or Duncan. Oklahoma City had been built on anemic red clayland alongside a shallow, island-strewn wash. The terrain was penurious, without timber, empty of grandeur, which once accounted for few pioneers among thousands of acres. For much of the nineteenth century this had been Indian Territory, a zone no one else wanted. Sixty-seven tribes from east of the Mississippi were force-marched into exile here in the 1830s. Mountain Cherokees, swamp Seminoles, thousands more traveled in terror into gritty, baking air; thousands did not survive. The harshness of the land held wonder only for the native Comanche and Osage, and for outlaws, Army deserters. But a time came when penniless men of the South, their caste doomed in the War Between the States, gathered twenty thousand strong, jostling hands on reins, strung out along a line drawn in the dirt. At noon on April 22, 1889, a Winchester was fired to signal the start of the largest horse race ever. Saddleless on cow ponies, aboard quarter horses, in buckboards, behind plow horses pulling wagons, and also on bicycles and afoot, they galloped across the sea of grass and laid claim to plots of their own. By nightfall they had settled an entire city. Oklahoma City was their frontier, their second chance, a lure it now held for Karen.

She stood at a strange doorstep in the middle of the night and bit her lip. A floppy black hat dropped off her head. Her friend Sally took her in. Karen was crying. "We've split up, Bill and me. He's been having an affair with Kathy. Can you believe it? My *good* friend Kathy? *My buddy!*" Karen's husband had left, a few weeks ago, not bothering to say good-bye. Then he had come back, heartsick, and they had tried to reconcile. But they were performing imitations of acts for which the love had gone. Their faces were stiff; it was no good anymore, none of it.

Sally poured coffee. Karen said, "He wants me to give him my kids. The bastard! He's screwing around, and *he* expects to get the kids." The words came ugly and bitter from deep in her chest. She sat in a rocking chair, in motion, chin in hands. "They're mine, aren't they? Let him and Kathy make their own. Why should I be the one to give up everything?"

Sally tried to be sympathetic. "When men get the itch, there's always some hussy around."

"Kathy's not a hussy. Oh God, I wish she was. I wish she was anything but what she is," Karen said. Toward dawn the rocking stopped. "I guess it's best for the kids. They need a father and mother both. And Kathy will be a good mother." Over the phone Karen let go of her seven years with Meadows. "Send me the divorce papers," she told him. "I won't stand in your way."

Their marriage was common-law. They had eloped when they were teenagers, spending a chagrined, unblessed night in search of a justice of the peace, and later they had never bothered with a ceremony. But after seven years together they were now legally a couple, and a divorce was necessary.

Karen gave up her three kids. All she asked for was the name that had belonged to her before she met the happy-go-lucky boy from California. In her twenty-sixth year Karen Meadows became Karen Silkwood once again.

Now hers was an independent fate, without love, without order, unconstricted. In a vastness where only one of 375,000 people knew her she could make another beginning or she could disappear. She was free, but it was a freedom that did not exhilarate. The vastness made her life seem more barren and narrow; each day began with an ache. She forgot to eat. Already thin, she grew thinner. "I got to make some money," she worried to Sally. "I can't sponge off you." Finding a job stole all her concentration. Oklahoma City was a huge place, second largest in acreage of all cities in the lower forty-eight. A walk around the whole of Karen's hometown would have been quicker than a drive from one side of Oklahoma City to the other.

On Karen's first few attempts it took all day. Rabbits still inhabited some sections that the land-rush settlers had staked out, but trees and water and oil had transformed the boulevards. She voyaged out onto wide smooth lanes graced by maples and cherry trees from the East. The gray State Capitol sat in among mansions with their swimming pools flashing emerald. South on Lincoln Street and left to Broadway lay downtown. Like Karen, it was in transition. Bulldozers and wrecking balls were the prevailing noise, knocking down fossils that had once seemed grand and permanent. New creations, tall and profound, were rising up, the triumph of ready-mix cement over quarried stone.

Most awesome of all was the Kerr-McGee world headquarters, a block square and thirty stories high, the biggest on the skyline. Even a small-town Texas girl like Karen had to be aware of Kerr-McGee. Begun humbly during the wildcatting boom, as an oil-drilling company, Kerr-McGee had turned into a conglomerate of energy investments: uranium, coal, helium, potash, asphalt. It became the best-known company in Oklahoma. Its headquarters was expensively done in granite, tinted glass filling narrow windows that did not open, heavy gun-slit architecture making it impervious to tornadoes, locusts, any fury that had been or might ever be.

Karen stopped to look. She always liked the new over the old. She left her car at the curb, went in and filled out an application form and then came out through the glass doors. She had been given a stenciled pen ("Keep it—we have plenty") and a compliment ("So many of our applicants are high school dropouts—it's rare we get people with even a year of college").

On the way back to Sally's apartment there was more frontier opulence: rows of splendid mansions, a bank's golden dome, a circus of boutiques with slinky dresses from New York, buildings shaped indulgently like gas pumps, restaurants with foreign names. It was all ordinary to the people here, but to Karen the city was a helter-skelter. There was so much to see, so much to buy. She had a salesgirl giftwrap a copper tea kettle. It took the last of her savings, or just about. Now did she turn right or go straight? The streets looked alike. She recognized the Praise-the-Lord bail bondsman's place but the profusion of signs played tricks on her and seemed to snicker at her. Her mood of confidence faded away. She was lost, adrift. When at last she reached the right driveway, she had her lower lip tugged in. "I'll never learn my way around here," she groaned.

"Tomorrow I'll give you lessons," Sally said, waving from the front door. "I was beginning to think you'd gone off and gone back to your old man."

"No, I'm done with that," Karen said, sounding certain. It was everything else that was in doubt. "I applied for a job at Kerr-McGee," she said. "They were real nice, but, you know, it's 'Don't call us, we'll call you.' "

"Oh, didn't I tell you?" Sally said. "I got good news. One of the transcriptionists at OK Med Center is quitting. You can have her job if you want."

"As long as it's not doing blood tests." Karen grinned and explained. "When I was a kid I used to dream about being a nurse for a brain surgeon; I would grab the scalpel and save the day. I made it as far as the Beaumont General Hospital. I was a Candy Striper there on Saturdays, emptying bedpans, changing sheets, you know the routine. But they wouldn't let me watch any operations—I was too young. Well, I had a little wart on my hand, so I decided to go to a doctor and get it removed. It was the funniest thing. As soon as I saw the blood, I fainted. Fell flat as a board. When I came to, my face hurt like the blazes. I'd broken my damn nose."

They both laughed, and Sally protested politely, "You ninny, you shouldn't have," when Karen ran back to the car to retrieve the tea kettle done up in ribbons and bows.

A secretary from Kerr-McGee was on the phone. Karen was to come in for an interview, not at the downtown headquarters but at Kerr-McGee's laboratory complex outside the city limits: the Cimarron Facility. Karen did not know what to say. She was about to start work as a transcriptionist for the Oklahoma City Medical Center. But it was a thrill to think she might have a chance to work in a lab. That had once been another of her dreams. She would imagine white-coated scientists all gathered in a cool white place, standing around a stainless steel table and gesturing at a tinker-toy exhibit of a chemical formula. Perhaps it would be a cure for asthma or diabetes and on a plaque there would be a filigreed inscription: *Dr. Karen Silkwood, Medical Researcher*! No one, except maybe her father and her chemistry teacher, thought it could come true. "Forget all this foolishness," her mother had scolded, "just do good in Home Ec." Long ago Karen had stopped dreaming.

But now she said, "Can you tell me how to get to this Cimarron place?"

"It's easy," the Kerr-McGee secretary replied. "Just get yourself on Highway 74."

The Cimarron Facility presented itself as three artificial rectangles. One building was a plutonium factory, another a uranium factory. There was not much to choose between the two, except that the plutonium factory had been painted a nondescript brown and the uranium factory a more flattering blue-green. The third building was an annex for administrators and visitors. The Cimarron name came from the lore of cattle drives and gunfights, and from the river, a quarter mile north, which churned and seethed and dispensed life through land that would otherwise be dust. Pin oaks, stunted survivors of the climate, clung to the riverbanks. A pasture flowed up from the banks and surrounded a promontory where the buildings sat.

Roy King had an office in the annex. He was the personnel director and he had Karen's application in his hand. His face was chubby and friendly, the face of a favorite uncle. He referred to Karen's high-school and college credits: advanced chemistry, physics, zoology, a summer seminar in radiology. "Very commendable," Mr. King said. "Not many girls get interested in boys' subjects."

"Science was just something I was good at," Karen said blandly. She still didn't know what to say. She had come to the interview out of a whimsy and curiosity; she figured she had been invited in the same spirit. Her hair was curly and shorn at the back of her neck. Karen had on a skirt and blouse, nylons and low-heel pumps, a costume much like those in her high-school yearbook pictures.

Mr. King began telling her about plutonium, how strategic it was going to be to the next phase of nuclear technology. Karen blinked quizzically. "God's truth," he said, handing her a booklet in emphasis. She skimmed the booklet. It was for new recruits, a simple history about "Energy" from wood to coal to oil to nuclear power. As the booklet duly noted, nuclear power had its beginning in the bomb labs of World War II.

There was a mention of Dr. Robert Oppenheimer, who became the "Father of the Bomb" and died a broken man largely as a result. But the booklet dwelt instead on Oppenheimer's work with uranium. Uranium has a quality that sets it apart. Left alone, underground in the desert, it is a crumbly gray or brown ore that is useless and, for the most part, harmless. In a refined state, though, after mining and milling, uranium turns the color of saffron—"yellow cake"—and its atoms can be divided in a process known as fission. The result is heat and, incredibly, the appearance of new elements like plutonium. For the Hiroshima bomb, uranium was used as the core. For Nagasaki, plutonium was substituted. Plutonium is more compact and more powerful and it would have been used earlier but you have to bombard a hundred tons of uranium ore to derive a teaspoonful of plutonium. After the war uranium became the fuel of the domed windowless reactors, turning the heat of nuclear fission into nuclear power. Plutonium and other radioactive elements (cesium, cobalt) and traces of dross were the waste from the reactors. There were now tons of plutonium, enough for all the bombs the Pentagon wanted, and much more. It filled up deep trenches and huge tanks at a government site in Hanford, Washington. Meanwhile, the uranium deposits of New Mexico and Colorado had begun to run low.

Mr. King had a speech. The Speech. All the new recruits, if they had anything on the ball, got to hear it. "At the current rate uranium will be mined out in thirty years, fifty at the most," he said. "That's like the day after tomorrow, as far as history goes. Which is why we have to be prepared. We need a new nuclear fuel. Plutonium."

Plutonium is even more special than uranium, he explained. Plutonium can't be destroyed and, under the right circumstances, it can even reproduce itself. A little quiz in the booklet put it another way. Question: What will you have left after you burn up three pounds of plutonium and one pound of uranium? Answer: Four pounds of plutonium. If that wasn't the ultimate alchemy, what was?

The Speech went on. "Plutonium is what we're working on right here. This is the biggest breakthrough since the forties."

Karen said nothing; she just listened in amazement.

"So can you come in tomorrow and get your picture taken for a security badge?" Mr. King asked.

"You mean I got the job?" After all the years of drudgery, was it possible?

"If you want it, you got it." Mr. King led her graciously to the reception area. Her silence signaled a rapt gratitude, unspoken because the shock had yet to wear off.

Mr. King bestowed a handshake and a final hovering attention. "Welcome to the team. From here on you're not just working for yourself, but for the whole country." It was his customary benediction, though sometimes he had to use it earlier in interviews if somebody had misgivings about the pay. Lab techs got only $3.45 an hour, which kept family men on the fringe of debt. But Karen made no complaint. This was more than twice what secretary's work had paid her—and now she was single. There was hope and bounce in her step. It had been a long time since anyone but her parents had fussed over her or treated her with such an assurance of worth.

"It's very dignified," she bubbled long-distance to her mother, "and it's full of fancy equipment. I can't describe it all because I haven't been inside yet, but maybe you could get a book that would tell you more about it."

Mrs. Silkwood intended to go by the library—the librarian was a friend from the pews of First Baptist—but the mission was neglected until it was forgotten. She was busy with her other two daughters: Linda, the youngest, just embarked on adolescence, and Rosemary, already a mother though still a teenager. Whatever the details of Karen's job, whatever its significance, what mattered to Mrs. Silkwood was that Karen be content, that she save her money, meet a good man, get remarried, and reclaim her kids.

CRESCENT, OKLAHOMA. AUGUST 5, 1972. At the Cimarron gate Karen proffered a shiny laminated badge, and the guard checked her name against the list on his clipboard. Karen Gay Silkwood, born February 19, 1946. He matched the face to the ID photo. Her hair was shampooed, creamed, bunched at the ends in thick curls; her eyes overcast with mascara and with the anxiety of trying to make a good impression.

Karen walked down a concrete pathway, through a heavy steel door, into a short hallway. This was the plutonium factory. The hallway was framed with two rectangles like airport anti-skyjacking devices. They were supposed to prevent nuclear theft. One was sensitive to the alpha rays of plutonium; the other would sound an alarm if someone tried to sneak plutonium out in a metal box. A health physicist ("They call us HPs") pointed Karen into the women's dressing room. It was like a locker room for gym class. Double-deck brown lockers, shin-high benches anchored to the linoleum floor, toilets, a shower, everything glistening and smelling of an acrid disinfectant. Karen was given a hairnet, white coveralls, taped-up gloves, protective glasses, and polythene booties over her shoes. In the outside world the outfit would have made her a woman apart; here it helped make her anonymous.

In an emergency, if plutonium dust got loose in the air, she was to dress even more circumspectly. There were windowed respirators, gauntlets, galoshes, and additional plastic raiment for emergencies. "Plutonium is radioactive," the HP said. "It has to be washed off immediately." The HPs were required to tell the bad with the good, but sometimes they forgot: they were overworked: it seemed as if they were training new recruits every other day. The HP crooked a finger, beckoning, and Karen followed him through a door emblazoned with a red-and-yellow admonition: "Radiation Area." They went past a laundry room and stopped at the metallography lab. The Met Lab. It was a big white enclosure. Beakers and other glassware were stocked on a bench against one wall. Long pipes ran along the ceiling. Shorter extensions dropped like the legs of a space ship into a series of boxes. The boxes had metal borders enameled a pale green and windows that were yellowing. On the Plexiglas surface Karen could see the shimmer of her face. It slanted up and away.

The HP motioned to three round holes at the bottom of each box. Black shapeless rubber things hung from the holes. Karen saw the man's hands vanish and pop up like genies inside one of the boxes. "They're called gloveboxes," he said. The nomenclature became clear. The rubber things were oversized gloves that ensheathed his arms up to his elbows. The third hole, with its glove, was spaced farther apart for extra maneuvering. "There's no air inside the gloveboxes," the HP said. "The pipes pull the air out and create negative pressure. A vacuum. Everything is airtight. The gloves are welded to the holes. The outside of the glove is sealed inside, and when you take your hands out, you pull the gloves inside out." He laughed at his tangled language. "Go ahead, put your hands in." Karen wiggled her fingers into the clammy material. Puppet fingers: they felt clumsy, disembodied, but she could move them. After a few days she would be able to operate nimbly in the gloves, to cut plutonium pellets into cross-sections and hold them against unexposed X-ray film, analyzing them for an even distribution of isotopes. She would be a technician in the Met Lab.

Karen's tour of the rest of the building continued in the footsteps of her guide. There were more white rooms behind other imprisoning walls. Three labs (E–Spec, Chem, General) and two areas for production (the "wet end" and "dry end"). And the vault. The precious bottles of plutonium nitrate went first to the vault. Each bottle was doubly protected. Each sat at the center of a steel drum four times its size: a wire cage suspended it there and plastic foam cushioned it. Steel-fingered forklifts carried the drums from the delivery dock to the vault where the plutonium was vacuum-pumped out. Then it was piped to the "wet end" and mixed with uranium nitrate in a ratio of one-to-five. The slushy gray nitrate went through a huge oven and was dried into yellow-green oxide, soft and powdery like talcum. The production workers stood before rows and rows of gloveboxes, tier on tier, a pageant of muted clangor, set up in the design of prison cellblocks. Karen watched from the safety of a catwalk. The oxide went to the "dry end" for shaping into pellets the size and texture of commercial rabbit food. With their hands in gloveboxes, workers stuffed the pellets into pencil-thin metal tubes about eight feet long: fuel rods. High-tensile welding locked the pellets into the rods. The weld had to be smooth and precise, done with pinpoint fire, a tedious procedure.

At each step, samples of the nitrate and the oxide and the pellets and the welds were sent to the labs for testing. The fuel rods were being prepared for the government, and the government had rigid specifications.

The Atomic Energy Commission, known by everyone here as the AEC, was paying Kerr-McGee $7.2 million to produce sixteen thousand fuel rods. But this money was only part of the deal. There was also the long-term potential, the future millions, perhaps billions, that came with the chance to be in on the beginning of the plutonium era. The AEC was building a new kind of nuclear reactor, an experimental one, at Hanford, Washington (not too far from the plutonium waste fields). The nitrate bottles came on flatbed trucks from Hanford, in caravans with armed guards, and the finished fuel rods were trucked back there, to be piled up, awaiting the reactor's completion in 1975 or 1976. Someone had given the reactor a nickname—the "fast-breeder"—from plutonium's ability to reproduce itself. "A fast-breeder, like rabbits?" Karen minced the words. "Like a big nuclear rabbit!" Two other fast-breeders had been attempted, a commercial one south of Detroit and one in the Soviet Union. Neither had had any luck: accidents had forced both into cold shutdown. But the HP, who might not have known, said nothing of them.

Later, talking about her tour, Karen was reminded of the fond urgency of the preachermen who had made her soul leap hither and fro at First Baptist in Texas. She liked the fact that the Kerr-McGee Corporation was a true believer in "the plutonium era," as if there were no doubt, like Judgment Day, about its coming.

That evening, in the flush of a glass of wine, she picked up her stenciled Kerr-McGee pen and was inspired to write a poem, her first since high school. She felt transported into the future.

Drew Stephens spotted her from across the Met Lab. Even with her hair wisping from a hairnet and despite the flat, ill fit of her uniform, the lady had pizazz. Drew sauntered over and gave a look that was the equivalent of a wink. "Are you lost, or did someone make a mistake and hire you?"

Karen was determined to play dumb. "What's the matter? Is something wrong?"

"Didn't they tell you? We have a rule against hiring beautiful specimens of the female persuasion."

"Are you for real?" In the white glare her cheeks were rose-brown. Perfume floated light and spicy on the sterile air.

Drew smiled roguishly, and he spoke in a lounging drawl. "Hey, give me a chance. I'll show you how real I am. I can eat, I can drink, I can jump up and down, and I can do things your Sunday School teacher never told you about." He had striking blue eyes full of invitation. He was tall, with a face young but not youthful, and hair like wheat. On first impression Karen liked best his directness, a bravado disarmingly expressed. Later she would come to rely on it.

They made a date and met after work at a watering hole in Oklahoma City. There was tough talk and heavy odors; rickety chairs had absorbed the reek of dead cigars; the floors were uneven and wet with slopped-over beer; the pool tables bore the scratches of errant gamesmanship. All of that was to be expected from a place named the Jail Saloon. Only the band on the corner stage did not seem right. Young whiskery men and their ladies were clomping about, not to the two-step or the Cotton-Eye Joe, but to an electric blare. The old culture, though, was still expressed in stirrup boots, skinny pants, tall hats. The new music had been made welcome here, but there was no rush to get into the new style of bell-bottoms and Earth Shoes.

Drew bought a pitcher of beer and sloshed it into mugs. The high white foam tickled Karen's nose. She hiccuped in protest and Drew teased her. "You gotta get half lit just to stand this place. Hang around here sober and you'll really get si-i-i-ick!"

In the next few weeks they went often, until they realized the loud background didn't excite them. It wasn't love music. On long drives in Drew's Sprite, that was when they found out things about each other. In her shy way Karen talked about her cheating husband, her seven years of marriage "gone down the drain," the children she had given up. Drew's face was all tenderness and sympathy. His own life was a span of just twenty-two years, four less than hers. He was embarrassed, but she laughed, kissing him, snuggling, nibbling his ear. She said, "I must be pretty good if I can get one as young as you." He saw in her brown eyes, below a few strokes of eyeliner, the faint flecks of gold.

Drew's early schooling had been in Kentucky and Missouri. "My father is an engineer, my mother is, well, my mother. We moved here my senior year of high school. I felt lost, kind of like you I guess, and kind of on display: the new kid on the block and all that. But Central State was okay—I was a chem major. I'd just be graduating now, I suppose, if I hadn't got married."

"Oh, God, you've got a wife." Karen's hand flew toward her mouth. "So what am I? A quick jump in the sack?"

"It's nothing like that."

"So then I'm a homebreaker."

"No, no. Honest to God! We were busting up before I met you. We were going, going, gone, shot to hell."

But Drew's revelation had the effect of a betrayal. It acknowledged an inkling Karen had not wanted to acknowledge, fixing in her shame and self-pity, quickly converted to rage. She pulled away, and when Drew tried to kiss her he got instead a cheek that tasted salty. "Leave me alone," she said.

"Don't be like that." Drew kissed her on the forehead. He talked some more, framing his desire in the most earnest and painstaking of terms, each word in its own candid space. He trailed his fingers down

Karen's face, along the lines of caress, clumsily, as a sightseer might touch sculpture in a museum.

The guards watched keenly as Karen marched out with the other workers. They lined up across the gravel driveway and raised "On Strike" placards in the air to make their purpose known. It was the beginning of the 1972 winter, a quiet time, too late in the year for the mooing of Herefords. Karen heard the diesel motor, the sound of the enemy, long before the truck came hawkishly over a rise in the highway. The driver shifted gears and a black plume steamed heavenward. He lowered his window and yelled for the crowd to disperse. Catcalls were the answer. But the truck kept moving, and the striking workers had to make a path. The gate to Cimarron swung serenely open.

The OCAW contract had expired on November 30, and negotiations had stalled under the union's demand for more money and better safety. Jack Tice was one of the leaders. Barely taller than Karen, Tice had a thick mustache and a sharp face, full of fire. The days became weeks, but he kept up a rousing patrol, pounding backs, trading wisecracks, reassuring those strikers who did not understand what good could come of this. He began to resemble a feisty coach attending to his team. Karen brought a thermos of coffee to share, and a few men covertly warmed themselves from pocket flasks. Everyone stamped cold toes on the hard ground and clapped cold hands over cold ears and grumped about weak flames in the tar barrel. "Get used to it," Tice cheered them on. "Let's show 'em we can take it."

They knew that Kerr-McGee would not be easily outlasted. The company had a history of taking a hard line. Coal miners had stayed out for six months in Stigler, Oklahoma, without a single concession from Kerr-McGee. And in Trona, California, a desert town of five thousand people who depend entirely on Kerr-McGee for their livelihood, the merchants had shut off credit to put a stop to a walkout of potash workers. Those two strikes had been attempted in 1970. There were not too many examples of strikes against Kerr-McGee before then. Until 1966, the company had kept the OCAW out of its factories altogether.

As the flatbed rigs went on hauling their special cargoes into Cimarron, the mood at the gate darkened, and some curses and stones were flung at the teamsters. Karen knew about strikes from the

OCAW's wars with Big Oil in Texas; her Grandpa Silkwood had belonged to an OCAW local. But what Karen knew was secondhand. She had never been part of any strike before and, if pressed, she would have had to admit she had not paid union dues anywhere else either.

It was not discontent with Kerr-McGee that had put her in among the picketers, nor avarice. If there was any one motive, it was Drew, who stood next to her and told her: "You want Kerr-McGee to treat you good? You got to get respect."

Karen had moved in with Drew. His divorce was final, his wife remarried. Life with him was a different kind of freedom: shopping sprees, weekend drunks, Steak & Ale dinners, long evenings with nowhere and everywhere to go. The evenings made the days bearable. Outside the Cimarron gate she let the winter bombard and bully her, let sleet sting her face, felt her collar become a stiff, cold ring, but she had time to talk to Drew. They were optimistic about themselves, less so about the strike.

One by one their group was dwindling. Rheumy, aching, most of the strikers slunk back inside. In mid-January, with the picket line down from sixty to twenty-five, an ultimatum came to them from somewhere high in Kerr-McGee. Either they came in or their jobs would be given away. That was more or less legal in the open shops of Oklahoma; there was no legal compulsion to join a union, and no tradition of strike solidarity. This was the first ever at Cimarron. Jack Tice polled Karen, Drew, the others: they bowed their heads. Their swagger was gone, fortitude had been frozen out, bank accounts had hit bottom, fatigue had become sadness.

The strike did almost nothing for them. The contract they had to sign, in fact, stripped away certain protections against getting fired or arbitrarily transfered.

"Have a nice vacation? You didn't get much of a tan!" The razzing came from farm boys and urban cowboys, many not yet out of their teens. They drove Firebirds and Camaros and bucked up the rear suspension with cinder blocks. Not long ago their older brothers had gotten a kick out of tormenting the much-ridiculed longhairs at the University of Oklahoma. A longhair out riding a bike would get sandwiched between two cars, wrestled to the ground and sheared to a military fuzz. But such prejudices were in passage. These kids at Cimarron now wore their own hair on their necks and made fun of the Fort Smith soldiers. Why stagger out for reveille when they could get a soft job that didn't tear muscles, with plenty of overtime to make up for the low pay? Yet they had no interest in walking a picket line to help improve the job. Next year they might have another.

Inside it was warm, and if there was boredom, there also were pranks. One worker, bending for a faucet, felt a pellet go down his pants. It was a uranium pellet, not as dangerous as plutonium, but he squirmed about, to great applause. Another worker rechambered an air gun and used uranium pellets for target practice. Harmless play, they assumed. Over brown-bag lunches, Karen heard all about the tomfoolery. Everyone guffawed, even Karen, who was inclined sometimes to act the schoolmarm. But when the room quieted, she asked, "You don't really mess around like that, do you?"

"Sure, why not? You ain't a Jelly Nellie, are you?"

She got up from the table. "Excuse me," she said, "I got more interesting things to do."

Drew lit the beeswax candles, then the incense. Wax trickled from a wrought-iron candelabrum onto a round coffee table. The incense smelled romantic. "People in Nederland would have a fit if they saw me now," Karen said. "I can't believe I grew up in that town. We were stuck in some other decade."

Drew gave an angelic smile. "Hey, I don't know how to milk a cow."

"I don't know why I ever told you about that." She smiled, but it was plain she wished there were more exciting things to tell. "We didn't really milk the cow," she explained. "Grandpa and Grandma Biggs just let us sit on her back and comb knots out of her tail."

"I'm impressed, I'm impressed. I never met a real-live farm girl before."

"Very cute. I told you, we only went to the farm for a few weeks every summer—that was our vacation. The rest of the time I babysat my sisters, went to church, fed our pets. Mostly, I'd try to hide out with a good book. My dad was all in favor of my getting an education, but not in Austin or Houston or any other big campus with strangers and strange doings. I had to live at home and go to Lamar University. No sororities for me, no wild parties, no dope. So what do I end up with? A hippie boyfriend." She pointed at the incense dish, the candles, his beard.

Against the whipsaw wind, Drew had grown the beard. Also, his white clapboard bungalow had taken on a new attitude. A discarded dentist's chair had appeared one day in the living room. From a Goodyear dealer came a showroom tire, a whitewalled Blue Streak Special that crouched in a mount on the carpet. The carpet was a mustard-gold shag, and it took a ninety-degree turn in one corner, shooting up to blanket the pine frame of a home-built bar, which seldom went unattended.

On the walls were pictures of sleek fine racing cars, pictures ripped from Drew's litter of magazines—*Stock Car Racing, Hot Rod, Road & Track, Motor Trend, Car & Driver*. One wall held a completed gallery. For Drew, cars went beyond the category of hobby: the red Sprite in the carport was his everlasting joy. He had been souping up hot rods since before he could legally drive. He had raced boxy, hell-bent stock cars when Richard Petty was his hero, and though he now drove in the less punishing, less expensive autocross, he still drove hard. Karen would kid him about hours lost fiddling in his carport ("If I had four wheels, would you love me more?"). But having ignored her ex-husband with his motorcycles—the challenge of the metal, the wanderlust, the handy excuses to get out of the house—she now made herself tag along to the dusty racetracks. Other girls might worry about grease under their nails; Karen learned the vocabulary of sparkplug gaps, carburetor intakes, rpms, manifold modifiers, and she talked of racing someday herself. From the way she handled a toolbox, she probably could.

"Sometimes I feel like I'm nineteen and starting all over," she would say, and Drew would nod in accord.

With his bachelor's quarters he had cut off his past. He was trying to help Karen do the same. Jeans and tight jerseys replaced polyester, and she unbound and uncurled her hair and let it grow down her shoulders, finding in this new look the fastest way to a new self. She began wearing bangled necklaces: teenage jewelry. But in spite of a strenuous effort to forget, the seven years were not forgotten. All it took was a mundane scene in a drugstore, a mother shepherding kids away from a candy rack, and everything came rushing back clearer then ever, everything about the three children who still knew her over the phone as "Mommy." She came home in tears and sniffled through the evening.

"Dammit, what's going on?" Drew insisted finally, and she told him.

"I got a great idea," he said. He grabbed her and lifted her out of her sandals. "Come Saturday, you pick up the kids from Bill and Kathy and we'll go make faces at the animals. I need a weekend away from the track. So the grime can wear off."

They had lunch at McDonald's. Kristi disassembled her burger and ate small bites from a smorgasbord of bun, pickles, meat, onions. Then she and little Michael took turns astride Drew's shoulders, playing horsie at the zoo, past the monkey cages and around the make-believe African veld. Karen thrilled through it all.

Later on she would bring out the memory and wonder aloud whether the reunion might be made permanent. But it was a wondering, nothing more. There was time—time for more visits, picnics with wicker baskets at Red Rock Canyon, sightseeing at the National Cowboy Hall of Fame where that giant black bronze horse pawed the air. "Let's see how things work out," Drew said. They had a good beginning: spontaneous, filled with cars, saloons, good times. The rest could come later.

OKLAHOMA CITY. SEPTEMBER 17, 1973. The three AEC inspectors accepted Ilene Younghein's iced tea and homemade cake. The one with red hair made an informal salute. Before this job, he had been in the military. "Glad to make your acquaintance," Red said.

"My husband and I belong to the Sierra Club," Mrs. Younghein said. Spirals of gray-brown hair framed a face that had been many years in the garden sun. There was a band of white at the top of her forehead that marked the reach of her straw hat.

Red and the other two inspectors sat down in the living room.

"I guess it was Dr. John Gofman's article in *Intellectual Digest* that got me started," Mrs. Younghein said. "I had no idea a nuclear plant could cause so many different kinds of accidents. It made me furious, to be frank. So I wrote an article for the *Observer,* which is one of our local papers. I can remember the day it was printed. It was blistering hot, like it gets, and I was on the patio trying to cool down. I remember I had to go in to answer the phone. It was a man. He wouldn't tell me who he was. But he said, 'Mrs. Younghein, did you know there's a nuclear factory just a half-hour outside Oklahoma City?' Well, I'd driven by the place. But it looks like a barn—I had no idea what it really was. Come to find out, Kerr-McGee was supposed to notify the public before you folks at the AEC gave it a license. But all they did was put a notice in a tiny paper that nobody reads. If you ask me, that's kind of underhanded. If not illegal."

"It's perfectly legal," Red said with exceeding patience. He was the chief inspector.

"Well, was it legal for them to put that factory right in the middle of Tornado Alley? I looked it up. We get an average of twenty tornadoes a year that hit down within fifty miles of where that factory is. If one of them hits dab smack, we'll have plutonium swirling around here like smoke from a fire."

Red appealed to his men for an answer. "There's a fail-safe system," one said. "As soon as a tornado alarm goes off, they move the plutonium into a big lead vault."

"Well, that's a relief."

Mrs. Younghein was a woman of prodigious dimensions: her letter-writing, her boisterous laugh, her size. She lifted a finger to indicate her cherrywood desk, the only cluttered spot in a tidy, spacious house. She said, "I hope you didn't think I was flying off the handle. Everything I told you was exactly as that man—I call him Mister Anonymous—said it to us. He said the gloveboxes have holes and there are all these spills. And this truck they had out there: the floorboards got eaten through with plutonium."

Ice cubes were all that remained of the tea, so Mrs. Younghein brought out a frosty round of beers. Red was grateful. He said, "We've just finished another inspection at Cimarron. Let me assure you, everything's in order. The accusations this man made, they're either overblown or outright falsehoods."

Mrs. Younghein's husband stirred on the couch beside her. He had a round, puckish face—the face of an accountant or, in his case, analyst. He worked for the Federal Aviation Administration. "Please don't feel we're putting you on the spot," he said. "But since the government is paying the bills out there, we'd like to be sure our tax money is being put to good use."

"The place is well run, as I said, but maybe I could be more specific if I knew a little more about your Mister Anonymous."

"He's a union man, that's all he said."

The AEC inspectors glanced at each other, as if a suspicion had been confirmed. "I don't want to insult you," Red said, "but this man could be trying to use you as a pawn in some dispute with management. I understand they've been having union trouble out there. Some people may be chewing on sour grapes." Red checked his watch. He seemed to be waiting for Mrs. Younghein to ratify his statement.

She was tempted to be a good citizen and go along. If Kerr-McGee didn't know how to operate a plutonium factory, who did? (Kerr-McGee had been the very first oil company to venture into nuclear power. The shafts it had sunk in 1951 in the uranium fields of the Colorado Plateau had given it, twenty years later, a forty percent share of the domestic yellow cake market: a virtual monopoly.) These inspectors looked like good men, too, and she could see they were anxious to get back to their office in Illinois. But as they moved toward the door, she stopped them. "I don't want to insult you either, but I like to think I can tell when people are lying. That man on the phone sounded truthful. You could hear the worry in his voice. I believe him."

"I've done my best to explain the situation," Red said, his manner now impatient, a little caustic. "Cimarron was designed so it doesn't pose a danger inside or out. All nuclear installations are designed that way, regardless of what some scientist writes in *Intellectual Digest*. The truth is, you can get dosed with more radiation standing under a pine tree than living next to a nuclear plant."

Karen notched the sirloin to keep the fat from strangling the meat. She scrubbed the potatoes for baking, and the carrots became curlicues of decoration. She showered and put on a dress that showed her legs to advantage. With cosmetics she worked on her mouth and eyes; she achieved prettiness, even if the fatigue showed through. Then she sat down to wait.

As fast as Drew had grabbed on to her life, he was letting go. Not that his disaffection was without cause. A shrill pique had become a habit with her, as regular as going to church. Sometimes her unhappiness was so great she swept supper dishes to the floor or kicked over the Goodyear tire. Other times she was lost in implacable moping. Drew would chance upon her, languid on their bed, knees tucked against her chest, eyes opened inward, pictures of Kristi, Michael, Dawn propped against one pillow, her face buried in the other. Karen had lived a year with her decision, but at times it was still agony. As much as Drew was glad to have the kids up, the visits seemed to leave Karen more pained and distant. "What am I supposed to do?" Drew would shout into her silence. He had begun to go alone to the

Jail Saloon. When she asked if he loved her, he would tell her she was reading too many junk novels. He didn't try to lie about his evenings that lasted all night. On his way out he would slap on cologne. He would ramble about in the Sprite for hours on dark rural roads, sometimes alone, sometimes not, and she would see the indelible wrinkles in his clothes and know.

Now he came noisily through the door, home from a Saturday car show. She kissed him directly, then stepped back for him to admire the dress. But he was soon plopped into his dentist's chair and in the spell of a TV show. She poured out a whiskey. "No ice," he instructed.

"It'll kill your appetite."

"I need it straight." There was a resigned shadow on his features. He saw little white grains in the well of her glass from an Alka-Seltzer. He raised his drink. "Join me?"

"No, thanks."

The meal was pleasant, and afterward Karen found an album of melancholy ballads. When the stereo breathed the last note, she thought the music had done its work. But Drew cupped big hands behind her head and gave a smile of exasperation, or maybe contemplation, the contemplation of a problem child. Her face grew empty beneath the lipstick and mascara. A sound came from inside her, rooster-crow piercing. She began hitting his chest and wouldn't let herself be held. "Damn you! Damn you men! So high and mighty! I'm through with you, all of you!"

She jerked away and ran. She slammed the screen door and Drew heard her slam the car door, heard her leave.

NEDERLAND, TEXAS. NOVEMBER 22, 1973. The house was the same as Karen remembered. A sparse, enduring structure, small enough to be a cottage, it gleamed green in the sun as an advertisement for the talents of Mr. Silkwood. He was a house painter.

Mrs. Silkwood had a job too. She was a loan officer at the Nederland State Bank, though at the moment she was fixing Thanksgiving dinner in the Hotpoint oven she had used for twenty years. She poked her fork experimentally into the turkey. "Get yourselves washed up," she said.

The Silkwood family outflanked the eroded white table. A card table had to be unfolded and a second oilcloth spread out. The prayer wobbled in the voices of three generations. From Karen popped a bunch of questions for her two younger sisters. Rosemary talked about enrolling in a correspondence course to get her high school diploma—she wanted to be a teacher's aide. Linda was in her first year at Nederland High; she talked about maybe going on a trip to California with the drill team.

The yams and fowl were soon gone, except for Karen's. She pushed away a half-eaten plate. "A couple more bites, honey—you're gonna blow away in the wind," Mrs. Silkwood said. It came out more tartly than intended.

"Let her be," Mr. Silkwood said. Karen clasped her father's shoulder. Presently he moved to the tiny living room. Rosemary's husband followed, and Mr. Silkwood began to grouse about his job. "It's the winter slump again. I'll never understand people. Everybody knows the worst weather around here is in summer. But when do people want their houses painted? July and August. You can't buck tradition, I guess."

"Lookit here, Frito. Look what you got." Mrs. Silkwood emptied a pan of leftovers out back for Frito, who was the last in a line of racoon pups from a failed enterprise by Mr. Silkwood. He had captured a pair of coons in the Piney Woods, thinking to breed them and sell the offspring, but he couldn't find buyers.

Frito also was the sole survivor of a menagerie of pets that had once thronged the backyard—coons and ducks and rabbits, every one a favorite of Karen's. Growing up, she had lived in the backyard with her pets, and her sisters. With Mr. and Mrs. Silkwood both at work, Karen had been the "Little Mother." Rosemary and Linda had preened about in her hand-me-downs and mimicked her every habit. They had adored her and still did.

Karen stationed herself at the kitchen sink while they carried and stacked. She got the suds going so the turkey juice wouldn't stick the plates together. "What's it like being a single girl in the big city?" Rosemary whispered, giving Karen a teasing jab. "You got all the guys climbing the walls?" Rosemary did not allude to Drew, though she had met and liked him on a trip to Oklahoma in the summer. Karen had called a few weeks ago to say they'd broken up; the subject was closed. "Things are better—I'm starting to like having a place of my own," Karen said. It was the first time she had ever lived by herself. For a day or so she had felt completely marooned, but a few posters (Waylon Jennings, Kris Kristofferson) and an ironwork planter of African violets had abolished the dourness and improved her outlook. "The best part is I get to spend all my money on me . . . and the kids. . . ." Karen's voice teetered, nearing a breakdown. She scrunched against the kitchen counter.

"You want to go Christmas shopping tomorrow?" Linda suggested. It was odd, looking at her short big sister from above. Linda and Rosemary had both grown up bigger than Karen, longer-legged and bigger-bosomed. Karen was six years older than Rosemary and twelve older than Linda, but right now she looked so young and vulnerable they might have traded ages.

"We can take my wheels," Rosemary said.

Karen brightened. "Guess what? My Christmas gift to myself is gonna be a little foreign car I can wrap up and put under a tree. I've really gotten into cars. Want me to teach you how to change points and plugs?"

"Wow. A mechanic in the family."

Karen laughed. "The trouble is, mechanics are gonna be obsolete pretty soon. The government is building a car that won't have points or plugs. Not even a gas tank." The summer of 1973, just past, had been the first one with long lines at American gas stations.

"You mean one of those cars you have to plug in? You gotta have a cord a hundred miles long." Linda smiled. She smiled a lot, as rehearsal for the Miss Photo-Flash contest she hoped to enter.

"No, a nuclear car. It'll run on nuclear pellets."

"Are they gonna make them at the place you work?"

Karen shrugged her bony shoulders. "I hope not."

"Don't you like your job any more?"

Karen shrugged again. "It's okay, I guess. But none of the supervisors are scientists. A lot of them don't know as much as me. It's more like a regular factory. It's not as special as I thought." In her long-ago radiology class Karen had been told that women were always supposed to wear slacks inside nuclear facilities. Otherwise, on the mirror-bright floors, they would be a sideshow of reflected legs and thighs. But at Cimarron the floors were a dull, scuffed white. Even the red-and-yellow heraldry was being eaten by rust, and on the gloveboxes the disregard showed as gray blisters and cracks. The cracks had been covered with masking tape. "Kerr-McGee is like everybody else, I guess. All they care about is getting their government money."

That night Karen slept in the bed of her childhood. On a closet shelf there was a box, tied with string, that still hoarded a few of her things. Isaac Asimov books. Mail-order microscope slides: pollen, fish scales, fungi. Sci-fi comics. She used to think science could do anything. Of all the fantasies (underwater cities, meals of steak-tasty pills, air-propelled trains) none had seemed more exciting, more certain, than those magical nuclear reactors. Their dimensions would be gargantuan, bigger than the Pyramids, of a scope that would call to mind visitors from outer space. Electricity would be so cheap it wouldn't have to be metered, and there would be no smell of pollution. Karen had saved a comic book that General Electric gave away free in the fifties. In the comic a young boy named Johnny was taken on a magic carpet to the future. "The potential locked inside the atom will provide power for everybody everywhere," he was told. "You're a lucky fellow, Johnny, to be part of such a wonderful generation."

A steamy sun revived mosquitoes that had appeared dead in the morning nip. They came winging in from Gulf marshes where they bred year-round. Karen slapped at them. Nederland is in the southeastern corner of Texas, closer to the Gulf and to Louisiana than to Houston. It hadn't changed much. The walkways to school and church were still grass, the driveways still white with mollusk shells. The library, in deference to the matrons of First Baptist, still had only a thin, moralistic selection.

The windmill museum was new, paid with dollar bills from a fund drive begun a few years ago. It was open three afternoons a week to any tourist who might wander this far from the superhighways. A dainty old lady with a small cheek mole tended the museum and showed off under glass her Tex Ritter scrapbook. Tex was a hometown hero, announced and pictured on a billboard at the town's western entrance, although there was still a certain bitterness from a year ago when he had snubbed Nederland's diamond jubilee. Today the museum was closed. But the double doors of the Rexall drugstore parted for Karen and her sisters. A fountain boy mixed syrup and carbonated water for colas. Oh, but she had had some good times here, side by side on the vinyl stools with her first true buddy, Karen Miller, who still lived two unpaved blocks from the green cottage of the Silkwoods. If the two Karens weren't at the drugstore, they were trying on dresses at the Dollar General Store racks or they were at

Drake's Drive-In, the only place that served you in your car. Usually they had to walk and eat—they had neither a car nor a father who would lend them his. Not that a car was needed; not in Nederland. Unless, of course, you wished to see a movie or wished to shop somewhere besides Dollar General. Then you had to go to Beaumont, fifteen miles north—which, after finishing their colas, was where Karen, Rosemary and Linda headed.

The road took them past Spindletop. It was another tourist attraction, a wooden ghost town of smithies, stables and oil derricks, rebuilt from ashes as a monument to the country's first big gusher, the one that started the Texas boom. It had hit on January 10, 1901. A spray of mud, sand and rocks had knocked the crown off a derrick. Then came a geyser, dark green. In quick order wildcatters also came, toting satchels of cash, paying up to a million dollars an acre for fallow land that previously had gone begging at eight dollars. The Garbage Lady of Beaumont, who collected table scraps from the gentry for her pigs, auctioned off her barnyard and joined the gentry.

Though that time had long preceded Karen, it was as vivid as yesterday to her. It lived on in a titanic stench worse than onions gone bad. The smokestacks of Texaco and Mobil might be poetic tall torches burning in the night, but by day all you could see was blue-black discharge. The Sierra Club had tried on several occasions to make them install filters, with not much success, and not much help from the Texas legislature. A local legislator, Billy Williamson, had put it to the Sierra Clubbers. "We're all willing to have a little crud in our lungs. We don't need do-gooders telling us what's fit to breathe."

In a pig's eye, Karen thought. She hated the refineries. From the time she was little she would hide in the bedroom when the stink rolled in with the heat, penetrating the house, gagging her like an awful hand over her mouth. Maybe, because of her asthma, she felt it more than others, or maybe they felt it but were afraid to object.

Today, at least, it was okay. The wind aimed it out toward the Gulf. The Silkwood sisters reached Beaumont and pulled in at J. C. Penney's. Karen went immediately to the section for Little Misses. With a mother's eye she held up frilly dresses.

"Ooh, get the red velvet!"

"No, the yellow with the cuffed sleeves."

"Get both, get them both!"

They did not realize Karen was crying until she tried to return the hangers to the chrome clothes bar and the hangers slid in a heap to the floor.

"What's the matter?"

"Nothing, it's nothing."

"It must be something."

"It's the sizes. Is Kristi still a six-X or is she a seven? God, help me! I don't know the sizes of my own kids."

Three

The sky outside warned of snow, but in the mall Karen had her coat on her arm. Her dress was pink and full of spring: the picture of an Easter girl. Karen did not see Drew when he saw her, did not see him cross the tile breezeway, did not notice him at all until he was next to her, out of breath, his smile winsome, his words all diffidence, charm. "Hi, lady. You aren't lost, are you?" After months without her, she was a hand's reach away, close and unguarded in the middle of Oklahoma City in the middle of a Saturday afternoon.

"I've got a date tonight," Karen said. "A nice guy."

"How about a deal? You break it, and I'll make it up to him," Drew said. "There's this little number I know."

"Cute, very cute."

"Yeah, she is real cute." He put on a grin.

"Everything has to be a joke with you, doesn't it?"

"I'm not joking. Break your date. Come back with me—I'll do up some ribs. Or tacos. You're still a nut for tacos, aren't you?"

"Stop it, Drew, stop it." She flung her coat over her shoulder, as if to move on. "I'm all cried out. I don't want to start up again."

He examined his cracked and dirty fingernails. He had strong hands and wrists, muscular beyond the requirements of his job. "I've missed you," he said. "A lot."

A subtle shifting: Drew's face pressed against hers. He was in his grease-monkey coveralls, and dirt got on her dress. But what did it matter? Nothing mattered. Racetrack groupies and barmaids were small sins, without meaning. Karen went with him back to his undomesticated bungalow. And stayed.

During the next few days, though, they stipulated new rules: dutch on expenses, split shifts in the kitchen, no jealousy over other occasional liaisons. Oklahoma City wasn't as dislocating as it had once been, and Karen wasn't as lonely for courtesy of any sort. In the bars where single women were welcome she had found poise; the strangers who picked her up had been of her choice. Even now, on a few ribald weekends, Karen and her girlfriends disappeared to Dallas, four hours south, to attend to libido in the giddy way of kids just out for the fun. Still, she always seemed glad to get back home, as Drew was to receive her. If everything was not perfect, it was familiar anyway, and there was enough between them to fill up those days of moping, days lost in a suffering spirit of love, when he ignored her and left her out of his pleasures. Karen did not say much on those days. But other times, mildly jubilant, she would brag to her girlfriends of Drew's little attentions, the surprise dinners he barbecued, the sudden lusty invitations on the couch.

Suzuki dirt bikes were on sale. Karen and Drew bought a pair, his a 250, hers a 125. "I know a place we can baptize them," he said.

Down dry creek beds and over brown bell-shaped hills the Suzukis got a tryout. Karen jumped the crests without slack, a hell-for-leather that seemed part of the metal. She flung away her helmet and let her hair whip behind her. "Let's get good enough to ride in rallies, okay?"

"I don't have the nerve for it," Drew said soberly. "You gotta start tooling around on these when you're a baby, before you know what fear is." Karen sprayed dirt and sped away, as though she no longer understood the instinct.

"You're outrageous!" Karen's supervisor choked on the exclamation. Karen had removed her underclothes and placed them in her locker. Her nipples and pubic hair showed defiantly through the white company uniform. "I'm just following the dress code," she replied sweetly.

The flaunting was not cabaret. Yesterday, with the heaters broken down, she had been reprimanded for wearing a sweater underneath. "Give me a break—I'm freezing," she had pleaded. But the supervisors had refused, and now she was getting even. She marched about the Met Lab in a know-it-all anger. Let everyone see what jerks they were! If they wanted to enforce rules, why not start with the safety manual? "You want to know what's against the rules? This is against the rules." She yanked open a desk drawer where a dozen sample pellets lay casually together. Karen's high, diligent voice raged, "We could've had a criticality, which you oughta know. And if you don't, you don't belong here." After a year and a half of being the quiet new kid, Karen was making herself known.

Karen had a strength about her, or perhaps it was a weakness. You did not get a lot of nonsense from her; but when she was in the right, the circumstances notwithstanding, you heard about it. One time at Lamar University, in her trigonometry class, the teaching assistant had overlooked a correct answer on her test. He chose to be obstinate about it, so Karen publicly and triumphantly went to the professor to get the grade she deserved. For the rest of the semester she did not let the assistant forget. More and more, that was her attitude at Cimarron.

But only part of her reputation was because of her spunk. In the lunchroom the men joked about her necklaces, her love beads. A man her father's age who had been to Africa told about a custom he had heard of. At birth the girls of a certain tribe (Ibo? Bantu?) are adorned with wide rows of golden neck chains. If they later commit adultery, the necklaces are snipped off, and their necks break at the spine where muscles had no room to grow. The men laughed crudely. What would happen if they took a pliers to Karen's jewelry?

During the strike there had been much jabber about Drew. Was he a malcontent or a champion of the workers? Now Karen was the subject of the debate. "Don't let it go to your head," Drew grinned. He was afraid she would feel picked on.

"Are you kidding? Let those cowboys have their fun. They don't bother me none."

CRESCENT. MAY 19, 1974. It was the start of a solemn day. A deluge of spring rain clattered on the concrete path and on the flat tar-smeared roof. Mud ribboned the pretty white of Karen's new Honda Civic. She drove into the parking lot alone. Drew had been put on the afternoon shift: punishment for them both.

In the Met Lab a woman with an ear infection fell from her stool. Karen heard the thud behind her. The stricken woman lay there, pale and tallowy, not responding. An HP rushed in and fumbled with a packet of smelling salts. Alertly, Karen snatched it and pinched it open. "You idiot! Don't you know anything? You got to let the ammonia out." She tried to revive the woman while the HP ran for a resuscitator. But that was of no help—the adapter for the oxygen tank was broken, and ambulance attendants finally had to wheel the woman away. A crowd had gathered, and Karen suddenly began preaching. "This is why we need a union. She could've died for all Kerr-McGee cares."

When the story was repeated to Jack Tice, he sought her out. "You were with us on the strike, weren't you?" he asked.

"Yeah, that was me. I'm sorry if I haven't kept up with the union like I should have. I keep telling myself to go to the meetings, but then something comes up."

"No need to feel bad about a couple of meetings." Tice peered at his feet and hitched himself up to his full jockey's height. On his right forearm there was a blue arrow that had found its mark in a red rose, a silly souvenir of a drunken Marine night. Karen thought he was about to ask for a date; she tried to remember if he was married. Instead he said, "Our contract's up in six months, and we're gonna be in for a tough ride." He took a deep breath to carry him to the punch line. "I was thinking, you might do real well on our bargaining committee. We need somebody who can stick to their guns."

Karen thought he was kidding. There was a lengthy, startled pause; then she said, "Are you sure it's me you want?"

"I'll be honest. Nobody's standing in line for this. It's a lot of hard work for no pay."

"Sounds wonderful." She laughed.

If twenty workers showed up for a 5–283 Nuclear meeting, it was a good turnout. But when word got out that Karen was a candidate, it began to look as if the Hub Cafe wouldn't hold the crowd. The latecomers had to push into the back room and bunch against a frail side wall through which they could feel the warmth of the cafe grill. "No smoking, no smoking," Tice said in alarm at a gray billow. Karen stubbed out her cigarette, but then quickly lit another. She smoked it down to her fingers.

The factory men, and women, had to choose three among themselves for the 5–283 Nuclear bargaining committee. Tice was the obvious one to head it, and Gerry Brewer was a popular second-in-command, leaving one spot in question. A middle-aged woman had her arm in the air. Jean Jung was her name, and she spoke up with spirit. "I say we elect Karen. She'll give the company what-fer." Karen saw another woman look timidly her way. In a room of forty the women were outnumbered ten to one.

A lean, strutty man yelled out, "Ain't we got enough trouble without some dumb broad—"

"You got no right to say that. You ain't never seen the inside of a college," Jean Jung shouted. She tucked the curls of her wig behind her ears. Tonight she was wearing the auburn one.

"Siddown, Jean. We've heard enough outta you."

"*You* sit down." Jack Tice clapped for order. The meeting came back to a decorous level. "I think it's time we pass out the ballots."

The workers scrawled out their choices on pieces of blue paper, using the walls and the backs of neighbors for writing tables. Two men had offered themselves as an alternative to Karen, but after a good deal of thumb-wetting, counting and recounting, the winners were Tice and Brewer. And Karen!

"Well, I'll be damned!" It was the lean, strutty man. "I don't believe you guys. You think she's gonna sleep with all of you?"

"Shut up, shithead."

"You guys are beautiful, really beautiful. It ain't bad enough we gotta listen to her all the time. Now she's gonna be our *official* bitch."

The researchers from *Consumer Reports* had written a cautionary note about the new Honda Civic. "With each blow from our bumper basher, the Honda bounded away more violently than any other car we've tested." But in autocross, that didn't matter. Karen wanted a car that could corner.

Drew went with her to the parking lot at the mall. They had to wait till night, till it was empty. Then she forced the Honda through a dizzying obstacle course of straw bales. The little car, the color of lightning, zipped and whined and laid down rubber as she worked the clutch.

She practiced until Drew was satisfied. "I think you're ready," he said finally. She unfastened the seat belt and hooked herself around his neck.

The autocross is a slalom on pavement. You need a boxer's reflexes and a feel for spots where the blacktop has gone soft under the blazing, hurting heat. At the track Karen was nervous, and her first two runs were not spectacular. But on her third weekend she accepted with wild pride a trophy. First place! Drew put the trophy in an honored place next to the Goodyear tire. Winning was wonderful— she hadn't won anything since the college scholarship she had used only one year.

KILGORE, TEXAS. JULY 3, 1974. Karen turned in at a mailbox. It rose atop a fencepost from deep in goldenrod and buffalo grass. The lid was closed, a red metal flag perked up for an outgoing letter. Karen's mother and sisters were in the shade of the porch, but her grandmother was already moving gracefully down the steps, taking them one at a time on slim, sturdy legs that needed no cane. Jewel Biggs had nut-brown skin, free of that common papery feel. "Ain't you a sight for sore eyes," she said, smiling broadly. "Your mom had about given you up, but I knew you weren't gonna miss blueberry pie because of some old car race."

Karen was damp and windblown from her long drive. In a tone anxious to please, she said, "I worked out a compromise—two days here and two days at the autocross. I'm gonna meet Drew in St. Louis."

"Well, half a holiday is better than none."

Rosemary had one toddler in hand. The other was by the flower garden, trying with ball and string to entice a cat that was more enticed by bees and nodding dahlias. She left them for Linda to watch while she carried Karen's suitcase upstairs. The bedroom shades in the old farmhouse had been drawn to keep out the sun. On a summer quilt Rosemary unsnapped the suitcase. "You didn't bring your refrigerator boxes this year," she said idly. Karen blushed.

"Hush," said their mother. She set down cold drinks. "Just help your sister unpack."

A year ago Karen had brought with her several plastic containers like the ones used to store dinner leftovers. These were bioassay kits. Because of an accident in the Met Lab, Karen's feces and urine had to be saved and analyzed to determine if plutonium had gotten inside her. She had been lucky. The tests had turned out benign. But the kits were the family's first hint that the Cimarron factory harbored dangers not quite ordinary.

Now Karen changed into a halter and shorts. She skipped outside, looking boyishly agile. She had hellos for the white Angus cow, the fat sniffing rabbits, the chickens with their heads under their wings. She made a circle from the barn to the pens to the coops, running restlessly, as if her feet needed the exercise. She grasped the hands of Rosemary and Linda. Head tilted back, Karen engaged them in a silly lawn dance. Mrs. Silkwood watched, thinking of the magical days from their childhood, and her own.

This was the Biggs homestead, a few rolling acres in northern Texas, which Merle Biggs had left in 1944 to marry Bill Silkwood in Nederland. But every summer she and the girls came for a visit. It was a place of exceptional delight. There was a deep pond that did not go belly-up with the summer sun. Pitched in, Karen had learned to swim in a splashing hurry, and on the green sward of lawn she had stretched out with her books and daydreams. Also, it was here, after high school graduation in 1964, that Karen had met Bill Meadows.

Meadows was staying down the road with his grandparents. He had wide burly shoulders, a mischievous grin, and he knew about chugging beer, hip-wiggling the Shimmy, all those basic improprieties denied to Baptist girls. He and Karen dated a few times, but then he had gone back to California and she to Lamar University. Over that winter she wrote him four letters, and he sent one. It was a lulling courtship, on the wane perhaps, or so her parents hoped. They much preferred her Nederland sweetheart, a boy intent on law school. But in Kilgore the next summer Karen and Bill Meadows got back together. Precipitately, on the last night of Karen's vacation, June 26, 1965, they began driving north, stopping here and there to ask for a justice of the peace. But neither Texas nor Oklahoma allows teenage boys to marry without the right signature—Meadows was eighteen—and the couple had to return, not yet man and wife. Rather than tell Karen's family, they concocted a story of a hurried, private ceremony, and not until the marriage broke apart did Mr. and Mrs. Silkwood find out it had no legal genesis. How much of the seven years had also been charade? Mrs. Silkwood wondered. She remembered one time when Karen brought the kids and her suitcases to Nederland, running from a bad quarrel. But then Meadows had sweet-talked her back, and Karen had not said another word against him. She must have pretended for so long to be happy, Mrs. Silkwood thought, that when the end came it had to be absolute.

A summons broke into her thoughts. "Suppertime!" After fried chicken and pie, the women rested on the porch. In the subsiding heat crickets began to whir; flies hummed out of the grass. A rainbow of scents, ripening berries and orchard fruit, fanned through the air.

Karen said good-bye late the next day, the others leaning over the suitcase at her feet to hug her. She drove through the night, following the Honda's bright beams northeast, and made St. Louis by dawn. She had no way to know the visit just completed would be her last.

CRESCENT. JULY 16, 1974. During the sixties, during all the protests, all the passions over war and race and ecology, Karen had been a housewife across Texas. Had you asked about her choice for President in 1968, she would have said Richard Nixon, and she would have told you she hadn't voted at all in 1972. As for Tom Hayden and Stokely Carmichael and the others who had turned emotion into political action, Karen had no opinion.

But a temper she had. All day she had been mad. The spill started it. It wasn't her fault, but she was assigned to "slurp it up." Arms vibrating, she guided a supercharged vacuum cleaner to everything that could be seen. Then, when she inspected herself, there were plutonium specks on her face and hands. Karen hadn't been sloppy; someone else had. Someone hadn't cleaned the vacuum after the last time it was used.

To be fair, certain things were working out fine. She had been transferred from Met Lab to E-Spec, which was a sort of promotion, and which let her see Drew more often. But on July 31 she got mad again. The air filter indicated a leak from Glovebox Z. And again the HPs had to place Karen on a routine of bioassay kits to measure the radioactivity inside her.

This time her anger did not evaporate with the next autocross or the next good movie. She stayed mad. She yelled at the supervisors. "It's getting to be one big spill around here." She nagged at them for a radical recognition of the problem, for a massive cleanup and overhaul. They merely ordered her back to work, and when a danger bell rang, they told everyone it was a false alarm.

During a coffee break Karen found Jack Tice and Gerry Brewer. Thin brown fingers italicized her flutterings of conscience. "Nobody listens to me."

"Or to me," Tice sighed.

"What about the AEC?" she ventured. "Okay, I know you said their inspectors are yes-men. But how about the AEC guys in Washington? The honchos. What if we went to them?"

Tice picked up on the idea. "It's worth a shot. You could put together a list. Write down everything that's not up to code."

For the next several weeks Karen circulated through the lunch-room, delicately amplifying her voice, insistently advertising herself, seeking out workers: making her list.

By law, the officials of the AEC had to set up a "public documents room" in Oklahoma for everyone who wished to read the Cimarron inspection sheets. But there was no law that made them tell anyone about the room or where it was located. Ilene Younghein discovered it only by accident, only because, as a former librarian, she was an addict of the stacks. The inspection sheets had been put in the Guthrie public library, in a musty space in back, where cardboard boxes sat in a bleached, horizontal heap. There was no index. The librarian brought forth a box with papers lying every which way. "Unless I'm mistaken, you're the first who's ever looked through these," she said. "Let's see—yes, the factory opened in 1970; that's when we started getting the sheets. We get copies, you understand. The originals stay in Washington. Never bothered to read them myself. But go ahead, take your time." Mrs. Younghein read one, then another.

At one time Mrs. Younghein had felt vaguely positive about nuclear power. She had no fondness for the way oil fouled the air, of course, or the way strip mining laid the land bare to annihilating rains. Indeed, when Congress created the AEC in 1954, most members of the Sierra Club were willing to give nuclear power a chance. They suspended doubt; some even believed in it. For unbelievers there were glamorous magazine ads and those free comic books and coffee-table books. The books had pictures of reactors made of tempered steel, three feet thick, the essence of invulnerability. Over time, though, some of the AEC's credibility had been lost. The agency had attempted to be both promoter and policeman, and its critics, eventually including the Sierra Club, thought it had not done well in the balance. There were too many AEC flacks and not enough inspectors.

In the library Mrs. Younghein continued through the papers, word for word like a scholar. Along with the inspection sheets, there were memos and other records. She was startled to see her own name in with all the jargon. It was in reference to Mister Anonymous.

"Can I get a copy of this?" she asked, unclear about the law.

The librarian had a perplexed look. "Legally, you can, sure," she said weakly. "But here you can't. We don't have a Xerox."

It took several hours of patient penmanship, instead, to reproduce the records. Mrs. Younghein's right hand felt gnarled and bloodless long before she was through.

Her husband had made beacons of the lamps in their house. "Where have you been?" He had been worried. The sheets were rolled up in Mrs. Younghein's hand. She shook them, as if holding a stick to chase away snakes. "They lied to us," she said, eyes wide in disbelief and fatigue. "Those AEC men sat right here in our house and lied to us."

"Have some supper. We'll talk about it."

Mrs. Younghein persisted. "They told us that place is perfectly safe, and all along they knew better. One of those Cimarron trucks did have an accident. Plutonium went through the floorboards, like Mister Anonymous said. Right through, right out onto the ground. Who knows where the wind blew it?" She sat at her desk and would not eat until she had tapped out an angry, fitful letter.

In a matter of days the postman brought a reply from the AEC. Whatever might have been wrong had been corrected. The truck had been buried. Mrs. Younghein need not trouble herself any further.

OKLAHOMA CITY. SEPTEMBER 13, 1974. Drew concentrated on his glass of Jack Daniel's, keeping his mouth close to the rim, lest the liquid escape. He was trying to sing himself into a better mood. "Steak when ah'm hungry, whiskey when ah'm dry, a honey when ah'm hard up, and heaven when ah die." Karen pried ice cubes from a tray and added them to the whiskey.

"You used to know exactly what you were doing," she said. "No one pushed you around."

"No one's pushing me around." Drew was a spurious king enthroned in his dentist's chair.

"They got you to quit."

When Drew hired on at Cimarron, he had figured to hang in for his gold watch. But since the strike his ambitions had gone downhill. A buddy, Troy Gooden, had knelt one day to adjust a compressor unit. It exploded; the handle ripped through Troy Gooden's hand and into his face, spitting tissue on the ceiling. ("They were washing the goo down the drain when I got there. The compressor valve had been put in wrong, but they acted like it was Troy's fault for getting himself killed.") For their part Drew's bosses had a lot to say about his beard, his coffee-break cuddling with Karen, his lobbying for new lab procedures, his muttering for a better union contract. In August they had transferred him to the General Lab, where conditions were in a bad state. He had filed a grievance, but because of a proviso in the contract the union had lost its say-so over transfers. Drew had made up his mind then to resign. Yesterday he had carried through with a letter.

"That's what they wanted," Karen said.

"I don't care what they want." His voice was thick. "It's what I want, and I want out. No more butting my head. Screw 'em." The whiskey acted not as a solace so much as an injection of truth serum. It made him realize how much the job had once meant. "Okay, so I thought the strike was gonna improve things. So I was a chump."

"We can win, Drew. This time we can win."

"Don't make me upchuck." He swallowed the rest of his drink.

"Damn you! You can be a real bastard," she said in angry sobriety.

"Gimme some air. I'm not telling *you* what to do."

"If you'd only come to the next meeting. Or talk to Jack Tice. Just don't give up. We'll get you transferred out of General. It could be an issue in our negotiations."

"You're dreaming. Jack too. All of you. You think Kerr-McGee is gonna change anything?"

"We can make it change." She sounded naive and seemed to realize it. "Maybe not everything. But some things: we could get a health-and-safety committee. That'd be a start."

"You think so? You really think it's worth all this bullshit? You think it's worth smoking two packs a day? C'mon, lady, you're turning into a nervous wreck."

Karen fidgeted with a burning Kool; the fidgeting became anxious, frantic. It was true: she felt like a wreck. She was worried about being fired—she had overheard a company man discussing it—and even away from Cimarron she could muster only a small, intermittent festiveness.

"When was the last time you felt good? I mean, so good you could reach out and kiss the whole world?" Drew puckered his lips in inebriated inspiration. "Or just one horny guy?" He hoisted himself up, intent on turning wish into antidote. Karen stepped back, hands on hips in mock retreat. He lurched swiftly toward her, and they both went sprawling on the carpet. Prone but still akimbo, she erupted in astonished giggling and tried to squirm away. Then she was still. If the closeness was not an aphrodisiac, it was a reminder of their good times. Her arms went around him in an emergency of love.

Karen and Drew no longer formally lived together; she had moved out again, this time because of the kitchen that always smelled of motor oil. But she kept extra clothes at the bungalow and stayed overnight two or three times a week. Tonight, folded limp and warm in bed, she lay awake. Tender images must have sailed before her eyes. She slipped away and padded in bare feet to the living room. Switching on a lamp, she took out a stenographer's notebook. She sat and composed, a satiny nude figure in the dentist's chair.

In the morning there was a piece of paper, torn out and folded on the leather seat.

> *If you still have the patience and*
> *the understanding you know it takes*
> *If you want to help mold a tangent*
> *to fit the curve of the circle*
> *Then I promise you no more willing*
> *pupil and lover in the world*
> *Your baby is no perfect lady,*
> *but I would lay my body down for you.*

WASHINGTON. SEPTEMBER 26, 1974. The Pick Lee desk clerk had to call Karen back for her key. She was out of her element. Forty dollars for a night's lodging! "What a hick," she laughed later, telling how she forgot to tip the porter and went around gawking at mahogany arches, potted palms. The Pick Lee Hotel had once been a grand red-brick establishment catering to foreign diplomats, and though its service and clientele had declined, its decor was still evocative, its location convenient. The hotel was around the corner from the Philip Murray Building, where Tony Mazzocchi had a fourth-floor office.

An airplane ride, Karen's first, had brought her here to see Mazzocchi, someone she knew only through correspondence. Jack Tice and Gerry Brewer had come too, constituting with Karen a secret delegation. Their supervisors at Cimarron knew that they had gone off on union business, but not where.

"What the hell's going on out there?" Mazzocchi was moving in his chair with restless energy.

Tice replied. "They've been trying to make do with secondhand equipment and a lot of untrained kids. We got a turnover rate of sixty percent a year. And now there's a panic because we're behind on production. It's gone from bad to worse. They got a bug up their butt to get them fuel rods done no matter what."

Mazzocchi hunched his shoulders. Though almost at an age for taking it easy, he was a bundle of energy, a guy on the move. After his Brooklyn boyhood he had passed through the turnstiles of a New Jersey construction company, the Hudson River Ford plant, the American Can Company, a Helena Rubenstein factory, and over twenty years he had moved up inside the OCAW, from shop steward to local president, on up. He was now the legislative director, a step or two from the top.

"To tell the truth," Tice went on, "the company didn't give a hot damn about our strike last time—they just waited for us to come in outta the cold. But this year they're real uptight. It's full speed ahead and screw anybody in the way, which is mostly us three. We got tension you could cut in squares. I go home with my guts aching. We had to sneak out to come here. The company don't know we're here, or what we're doing. It's that bad."

There had been petty harassments, embittered remarks, threats of strikebreaking violence and, of late, the transfers. Karen had been transferred from E-Spec back to Met Lab. She had appealed, then dropped it, writing formally in a letter, "I can see where nothing would be gained. It is not worth any further mental hassle." But despite taunts for her to join Drew in unemployment ("Why don't you wise up, honey?") she had decided to stick it out, through the crisis.

And there was a crisis. Karen and Tice and Brewer were pilgrims, in need of a strategy: in three weeks there was to be a vote on 5–283 Nuclear's continued existence. Some "company stooges," as Tice put it, had persuaded fifty workers to sign a petition, enough to force a decertification election. It would be a simple yes-or-no election. If a majority of workers voted no, Kerr-McGee would be legally rid of 5–283 Nuclear.

"What are your chances?" Mazzocchi asked.

"Like I said, they're desperate to avoid a strike. They're gonna lean on everybody they can. It'll be close. People are about fifty–fifty on this. Wouldn't you say, Karen?"

"Yeah," Karen said. She reached into her purse for a Kool.

Mazzocchi waved stiffly. "You've got to get in there and fight.

Your people need you, even if they don't know it. I'll tell you what I'd do, if it was me out there—"

"That's why we came. You've been through these decertifications before."

"Health and safety. Your best selling point is health and safety. That's the big area where a union is essential. You're offering people something they're not gonna get any other way."

It had taken Karen several minutes to adjust to Mazzocchi's fast, pungent, compassionate Brooklynese. Now she put down her cigarette and snapped off sentences as smart as his. "That's all well and good," she said, "but we got to have a strategy. These farm kids and cowboys don't care how dangerous plutonium is. A lot of them don't even know what it is. The supervisors don't tell them diddly—people are getting contaminated all the time."

"All the time? How often is that?" Mazzocchi knew how to play the tough guy too. He narrowed his eyes, measuring Karen. For a novice, she was far from bashful.

She said, "Our count is something like seventy cases. I got it twice myself. But I was lucky—mine was only a tiny amount."

"Just a minute," Mazzocchi corrected her, "even a speck is dangerous. It can kill you."

Karen's lips lofted. She thought he was being melodramatic. In her innocence she smiled at the statement, deflecting it.

"You can get cancer," Mazzocchi said. "Didn't they tell you? Plutonium causes cancer."

The word hit like a cudgel. He couldn't be right. Why, she had studied chemistry and radiology and she had read the Cimarron safety manual. "Nobody ever told me." She laughed—a terrible, bitter sound. "Nobody ever said anything about cancer."

"I'm sorry. But it's true."

"Oh, Jesus. Oh, God."

Mazzocchi saw he had let loose a small terror. Tice and Brewer had the look too. "I know these two professors," Mazzocchi said. "They're far more knowledgeable than me. I could ask them to talk to you." He had a sudden thought. "The professors might even be willing to go out to Oklahoma. We could set up a seminar. Your people ought to have this information. You're all working in a fools' paradise. That damn Kerr-McGee! No wonder you only got fifty–fifty support." Mazzocchi made a note in his daybook. "I'll call 'em first thing tomorrow."

He leaned back. His shirt was sticky from the summer weather that was hanging on, long past Labor Day. This was not an Indian Summer day, only a hot day—hot and muggy and vapid. On the wall there were autographed photographs of him with the Kennedy brothers, Jack, Bobby. He looked from the photographs back to his visitors and changed the subject. "Did you tell me you had a list of complaints for the AEC?"

"Yeah, Karen put it together," Tice said.

"Steve Wodka will go through those with you. He's in New Jersey this afternoon, at a chemical plant, but he'll be here by dinnertime."

Dinner was at a restaurant with linen tablecloths. Steve Wodka's welcoming grin was brief. He had about him an unexpected air of formality. Wodka belonged to the new breed of union leaders. He had come out of Columbia University and Antioch College, with a major in environmental studies, and aside from a college vacation spent in a paper factory, his entire career had been in white collar. For five years he had worked nominally in D.C., but much of his time was on the road, troubleshooting for Mazzocchi. He and his boss were both pugnacious, causing them to thrust out their chins, and they had eyes set in so deep you could tell only that the irises were very dark. And both of them, the younger one as much as the older, had been hardened a little by the constant seesaw of lives and dollars.

Wodka had a yellow pad with him. "Tell me what your problems are as precisely as you can."

Karen had gotten over her panic of the afternoon. She pulled out her stenographer's notebook. Raising her voice a trifle, with the pressure of eagerness, she described the contents of her list. In a general way the list had three categories. LACK OF TRAINING. Eighty percent of the workforce with less than two years' experience. Equipment cleaned with contaminated towel-wipes. Self-monitoring instruments not used, contaminations not recognized. Spills tracked from one room to another. FAILURE TO MINIMIZE CONTAMINATIONS. Dirty filters inserted in respirator mouthpieces. Pipes and gaskets corroded and leaking. Workers told to ignore emergency alarms and forced to work in respirators. POOR MONITORING. Air samples not counted immediately or results delayed. No repairman on duty at night. Plutonium storage that risked criticalities.

"Working in respirators, that's the worst," Tice threw in. "When the stuff gets into the air, see, they're supposed to stop production and decontaminate. But they got their own policy. They put us in respirators for the rest of the week and decontaminate on weekends." Tice worked in production, in the "dry end," and he'd lost track of the days spent with his head in a respirator. The devices looked ugly —black rubber and blue plastic—and they fitted tightly, squeezing into the soft flesh under the chin. Your air was cut off, except what came through the fluttering aluminum petals. Breathing became a sweaty, gasping labor, like breathing inside an oven.

"Fill me in on these leaks." Wodka's pencil was hovering over the yellow pad.

"It's the gloveboxes," Karen said. "Most of the time the leaks are from holes in the gloves, or from cracks around the glovebox windows. They bandaged the cracks with tape, but half the tape is peeling."

Wodka leafed through the notes he had written. "Let me go over everything once more."

Karen's list had been orderly and exact. Altogether there were thirty-eight specific incidents, with dates and names. "There's one more," she said. "We've found uranium dust in the lunchroom. Right where people eat."

At that Wodka grunted knowledgeably, the sound short, brusque. In the past year there had been two similar incidents. A waste pipe had been inadvertently hooked up to a drinking fountain in a Genoa, Wisconsin, nuclear plant, and every time workers drank from it radioactive water went down their gullets. The AEC inspectors considered that mistake over and done, with no real cause for alarm. But at an Erwin, Tennessee, plant, where radiation in the lunchroom had been measured at eight times higher than code, Wodka had gotten the AEC to order a first-ever scrubdown.

"It always takes a lot of pissing and moaning," he said, "but they will do things."

"Is it possible Kerr-McGee could have a special exemption?" Karen asked.

"What d'you mean?"

"I was thinking." Skepticism had reshaped her face. "If the AEC is so anxious to get the fast-breeder on line, like we've heard, maybe they can't afford to make Kerr-McGee clean up its act."

"We'll just have to piss and moan twice as much," Wodka said.

"Anyway you've got nothing to lose. I'll ask these guys to keep our meeting confidential so there won't be any fallout with Kerr-McGee."

Karen bartered with Wodka: she would give up breakfast for a tourist's walk around the neighborhood. Half a block from the Pick Lee she stopped to read the clean, vertical bronze script on the face of a squat building. *The Washington Post.* She and Wodka strolled on and loitered at the elegant Madison Hotel. Karen would have liked to see the White House and the Smithsonian too, but Wodka insisted on two more hours of briefing, followed by a hurried lunch and a twenty-minute drive to the AEC headquarters in Bethesda, Maryland. It was a modern fortress of poured concrete with the unfinished look of a child's experiment with Lego blocks. A blue-and-gold seal glittered from the foyer tile.

John Davis, the AEC deputy director of field operations, was their host. Actually, Davis was one of many. He had two assistants with him and four inspectors from the AEC regional office in Glen Ellyn, Illinois—two of whom had paid that visit to the Youngheins. The inspectors did not seem at ease, nor should they, for Karén's list indicted them as well as Kerr-McGee. But the way Wodka conducted himself they might have been furniture. He ignored them and talked directly to Davis. He asked that a new crew of inspectors be dispatched to Cimarron for new inspections, unannounced inspections, honest-to-goodness "surprise" inspections.

Karen made the thirty-nine accusations, and Davis managed a strained smile, nodding, talking appeasement. The AEC would cooperate, he said. Everything would be investigated. Different inspectors would be called in. And this meeting would be kept confidential. The role of the union would not be divulged. The ride back to D.C., a rush-hour crawl, was filled with confidence. "Everything's gonna work out," Karen predicted. "We did the right thing."

Back at the OCAW office, Mazzocchi had been thinking. He saw two battles, and he had devised two strategies, such as they were. For the first battle, the decertification election, he could not offer much beyond the seminar he had already offered. The more he considered the seminar, though, the more strategic it seemed. If nothing else succeeded with these workers, fear might. The first battle had to be won—or else there would be no second battle—but the second one seemed somehow uppermost: the contract negotiations. For that, he had a true strategy, clandestine and risky, but with the power of surprise. Karen had given him the idea. She had mentioned something yesterday about defects in the welding of the fuel rods. ("There are bubbles and occlusions and little hairline fractures, and they're all stress points, weak points.") Supposedly, technicians had been ordered to grind down the defects, disguise them, to circumvent the AEC code and sharply foreshorten production time. This accusation far outranked the others. If it could be proved, it would implicate Kerr-McGee in fraud.

But could it be?

"Sure, " Karen answered instantly when he proposed the assignment. He had diverted her into his office while Tice and Brewer were phoning home to their wives.

Karen was enthusiastic. "I could get you photomicrographs—they're like X-ray pictures. A *before* and *after* set. With all the defects showing, and then after they've been ground down."

"You're sure about this?" he asked. If she had any qualms, he intended to recruit Tice or Brewer.

"I can do it," she said stubbornly.

"How?"

She lowered her soprano voice to a soft tissue-paper rustle. "I'll steal the photomicrographs out of the files."

"Okay, fine, good. I'll have Wodka work out the details with you," Mazzocchi said. He had no problem with the ethics of rifling a file drawer. Hadn't the public been served when Daniel Ellsberg grabbed the Pentagon Papers and released them to *The New York Times?* The *Times,* as a matter of fact, was an important part of Mazzocchi's strategy.

OKLAHOMA CITY. OCTOBER 7, 1974. Mazzocchi had asked Karen not to tell anyone at Cimarron—not Tice or Brewer, no one—and she took this seriously. After prolonged and cautious reflection she did not confide even in Drew.

Happily employed again, as a dolly-and-hammer man in a Volkswagen body shop, Drew was lecturing her to find a new gig too. "Get out while the getting's good. Tell Kerr-McGee to cram it!" She was crouched over a radiator vent by the Goodyear tire, warming herself. Hand to ears, she squeezed her face into a facetious kindergarten gesture. "Make you a deal," she said, feeling uppity. "You lighten up, and I'll teach you how to win at autocross." She ran to him and tickled him till he groaned, then was out the door and into her Honda. "See you later, alligator."

Back at her apartment Karen phoned Wodka. She had a lengthy, technical report, and rather than take notes, Wodka attached a black suction cup to his phone and plugged in a Sony recorder. The conversation went onto a cassette.

Kerr-McGee had decreed another speedup, she said, from one pellet lot every three weeks to one every week; she was having to work six days out of seven. "And they're still passing all welds no matter what the pictures look like. I've got a weld I'd love for you to see, just how far they ground it down to get rid of the voids, the occlusions and cracks."

At Wodka's urging, she had begun a new list in a pocket-sized notebook she was never without, from which she now recited.

Room 124, 1st break, 3 Oct. 74. An HP had discovered holes in five gloves. "The room was hot, real bad, but instead of cleaning it up a supervisor overruled the HP and kept on with production." Karen had learned this from Jean Jung, her friend with the wigs. Mrs. Jung was a friend to all the girls, seeing them through spats with boyfriends; telling them when to squander thirty bucks on a silly seethrough nightie, when not to; being their housemother. But now the roles were reversed. Karen directed her to the HP office. "Jean, you gotta get a nasal smear lickety-split." The test revealed plutonium in Mrs. Jung's nostrils, from her shift in Room 124. Karen confronted the HP on duty, whose back went up at once. "He said, 'You don't have any business in here.' And I said, 'Yes, I do—check the contract. Besides, Jean wants me here, she's scared.' And she was, she was crying. I had hold of her hand, it was shaking like a leaf. 'Well,' he told me, 'I'm not doing any more talking.'"

Roy King's office, late afternoon, 4 Oct. 74. Karen had seen little of the personnel director since the day she was hired, the day of his still-remembered sermon. But he had summoned her, along with Tice and Brewer, because of the upcoming election. King had tacked a note on the bulletin board to stop the electioneering inside the factory. But right from King's office Tice phoned the National Labor Relations Board. The NLRB sided with the union. From now on Karen and Tice and the easygoing Brewer could campaign for votes during coffee breaks and lunch. King agreed to this policy because he had to; gone was all his old friendliness. Karen realized he would be rooting for 5–283 to lose the election.

CRESCENT. OCTOBER 10, 1974. A bearded man in a fleece-lined cap stood confused outside the American Legion Post 200 hall, a straggler. "Drew! You came!" Karen called out. But when the man turned she saw it was someone else. "Well, come in anyway." Coloring, she made her way to the front of the hall. Karen had put in many extra hours to bring out this skeptical crowd. "If it's a waste of time, I'll buy the drinks. Honest. Money-back guarantee."

They shuffled like schoolboys, pointed boots under cuffless straight-leg dungarees. A few promenaded, flirting with Karen, as she patrolled their edges. "Sit down, everybody," she said. "The sooner we start, the sooner you can leave." By now she was used to their gruff, profane ways, their masculine reek of hair oil and chew tobacco, their joshing and ribbing and roughhousing. She could get their attention, but she could not yet give out orders. The scraping of chairs over linoleum lasted until Wodka stepped up. He had a spring-knee gait right off the parade ground. Perfect, Karen thought. But Wodka's long dry sentences made everyone restless again.

Donald Geesaman and Dean Abrahamson stood next to him. They were professors and doctors. Dr. Geesaman was a doctor of physics. For thirteen years he had been an up-and-coming man of science, a researcher in an AEC lab, perhaps the one to head the lab someday. Then cancer cells ran amok in beagles and Rhesus monkeys that had been made to breathe a plutonium gas. He made an issue of it, asking for a review of radiation standards, and his AEC superiors fired him for insubordination. Now, at the University of Minnesota, Dr. Geesaman was a public affairs professor. Down the hall at the university was Dr. Abrahamson, a physician, ordained minister, fellow physicist. Dr. Abrahamson had resigned from Babcock & Wilcox because he thought it ran its nuclear operation with an eye for loopholes. The two professors were members with Mazzocchi in a scientific organization; its purpose was to push for better nuclear safety.

Karen chewed on her lip and strained over her shoulder, watching the reactions. She could sense a silent countdown. How long would these saloon boys listen to a pair of college professors? In their narrow-lapel suits, their lace-up shoes, there was no mistaking the professors. Dr. Abrahamson had a head of bushy hair and an abundant beard of the same. Dr. Geesaman was short and skinny, the absentminded type.

Dr. Abrahamson spoke first. He had a kindly pat-on-the-shoulder doctor's tone, but he wasn't describing mumps or chicken pox. "From your first day on the job, you should have been told pluto- nium is hazardous, and you should have been told that it causes cancer." Karen noticed an appalled imprint on one worker's face. Dr. Abrahamson quoted from Dr. Glenn Seaborg, the scientist who named plutonium. "If ever an element deserved the name associated with the underworld, it's plutonium. Plutonium is fiendishly toxic. It's a thousand times more deadly than nerve gas, twenty thousand times more deadly than cobra venom." A devil's brew.

A tall, gaunt man wondered aloud, "We all know we'd die if we had a criticality. But we ain't never had one."

"A criticality is a rare happening," Dr. Geesaman agreed. It occurs when too much plutonium is confined in too small a space; excess neutrons knock against each other and fission into a blast of heat and radiation. Three workers, killed in a 1961 criticality at an Idaho lab, had to be buried in lead-lined caskets to shield the cemetery from them. Their hands and heads had to go into a separate box and a separate cemetery: a nuclear dump. But, said Dr. Geesaman, criti- calities are not the only way plutonium kills. Tiny specks can do the trick as well. "A speck the size of a pollen grain can be immediately lethal. Much smaller amounts, invisible amounts, cause cancer."

There were more looks of confusion. "Think of it this way," Dr. Abrahamson explained. "Plutonium shoots off alpha rays like a sniper with a Gatling gun. If a bullet scores a direct hit on the brain, it kills you. Similarly, if an alpha ray hits the nucleus of a cell, the cell is dead as a hammer, and that's that. But suppose a bullet hits your frontal lobe, and instead of killing you, it leads to a drastic change in personality. A cancer cell is like that, one that's been damaged and goes berserk. A social outlaw. Or suppose the sniper killed half the people in this room. The dead ones aren't going to make trouble, but the rest of you might get riled up and become social outlaws. That's the kind of mechanism you have in cell communities."

Most workers were sitting up in an attitude gravely attentive, no longer smirking. Mrs. Jung raised a hand to inquire about her nasal smear. Did it mean she had plutonium in her lungs? "We'd have to look at the sample to say for sure," Dr. Abrahamson said. "If the powder was in big chunks, it might have caught in your nasal hairs and gone no further. But generally if it's in your nose, it's in your lungs." Mrs. Jung shifted in her chair, trying to shake off the answer.

Dr. Geesaman hastened to explain that they did not want to give a one-sided impression. Small amounts of plutonium are not a clear-cut death warrant, he said; sometimes they simply increase the chance of cancer. At truly minuscule levels the AEC presumes plutonium to be harmless, although both professors said they thought the AEC standards were rather optimistic.

"You guys are scientists," a young, hard voice called from the rear. "How come you can't tell us what's safe and what ain't? I mean, exactly."

Because, Dr. Geesaman said, all studies to date have had to rely on dogs and monkeys. A cancer in humans can take twenty or thirty years to develop, longer than the life of most nuclear facilities. "The human experiments are going on right now," he added drily. "You're the guinea pigs."

After the seminar Karen played chauffeur to the Holiday Inn Northwest, pushing the Honda over the speed limit, enjoying the ride. "It went well," Wodka said to the professors. "You have an effective approach, not too preachy, not too obtuse."

"A few guys still think it's a big joke," Karen said. "You know: 'Ain't no itty-bitty speck of dust gonna kill a big fucker like me!' But most everybody else seemed spooked. I know I was."

Wodka allowed himself a satisfied smile. "Sometimes you've got to scare people to wake up their instinct for survival." He had a devoutly calculating side which was well suited to his work.

"I wonder if Kerr-McGee sent anybody to snoop around?" Karen said.

"Doesn't matter," he said. "Even if they find out what happened, it'll be too late for a counterattack. The election is next week."

A bold, angry rejoicing flickered in Karen's eyes. At the motel she took out her pocket notebook and checked her notes with Dr. Abrahamson. "Size of pollen grain—lethal," she had written.

The whiskey that had given Drew comfort before bedtime woke him after midnight. Reaching for Karen, he felt coolness on the sheets where her resting warmth should have been. She was in the darkened living room, her back to him, one leg drawn up, the other tucked under her thighs, shoulders rocking. Drew watched her cigarette make a firefly trail in the night. She coughed in short, wasted hacks as if sending a distress signal. Since her trip to Washington there was a difference in her—not just the crazy-long hours and the sleeping pills, but something else he couldn't identify, something she obviously didn't want him to know. It was his home, but he felt like a stranger she barely knew, perhaps even an intruder. He groped groggily through the medicine cabinet and swallowed aspirin dry.

Wodka had left for other travels, and with him went Karen's exhilaration. The threat of cancer might be a strong way to motivate votes, she thought, but what did it mean to the people she worked with? Was the decay already inside some of them? Was it inside Mrs. Jung, the ginger-colored matriarch who could bear everyone's troubles but her own? Or inside pint-sized Jack Tice, a rare good guy who would least deserve it? Or inside one of those farm kids? And what about herself? What about that residue in her urine and fecal samples?

In Nederland, a jangling sound broke into Rosemary's sleep: three, four, five peals. She hurried to quiet it. Over the phone she heard Karen's voice, soft and poignant, as through tears. They had not seen each other since the Fourth of July and had not talked since Karen had cancelled out of the family's Labor Day affair—Karen had been too busy, too preoccupied with her strange missionary work. Now she unloosed a jumble of inscrutable words: alpha particles; rems, disintegrations per minute.

"Are you hurt? Should I call Mama?"

"No, everything will be fine. I was just a little lonely. I'll call you later. Go back to bed."

Rosemary did, yawning, undiscerningly obedient.

Four

Rumors spread, predicting opposite consequences. The place would have to close down if 5–283 won. Everyone would have to work full time in respirators if it didn't.

The National Labor Relations Board supervised the decertification election; the official tally was eighty to sixty-one. All but six of the eligible workers voted, making the outcome undisputed as well as significant. Jack Tice entered the lunchroom and swiveled on his heels. Seeing Karen, he waved and whooped in recognition. "We won! It's official!"

The union now had the right to demand a new contract. Or to go on strike if negotiations fell through.

WASHINGTON. OCTOBER 17, 1974. "Time for Phase Two," Mazzocchi said.

Wodka had anticipated the order. "I've already called Burnham," he said.

David Burnham had at one time been a director of President Johnson's Commission on Law Enforcement and the Administration of Justice. As a result, he was something of a cynic about heroes, especially cop heroes. But in 1970 in New York he had staked his reputation on Frank Serpico, a cop longing to be believed, and the two had produced headlines in the *Times* about heroin and bribes dealt out of precinct houses. *Serpico* became a movie, and Burnham, briefly, a local celebrity.

Currently Burnham was working out of the D.C. bureau, where he was not as well known. But over at the OCAW they knew him as the *Times* man on the AEC beat, and as someone who could keep a confidence. He agreed to meet Wodka for coffee. "We've got an operation going in Oklahoma," Wodka said. "One of our people, a woman, has access to the records at a fast-breeder factory. There are safety violations up the ass. Plus fraud. Who knows what else? Might be a helluva scandal."

Despite the Serpico success, or perhaps because of it, Burnham was always careful, always alert to a setup. He wouldn't commit himself to the story until he saw documents. But to get them he was willing to travel. "This woman needs another few weeks," Wodka explained. He checked his schedule. "I've got to be at an asbestos plant in Tyler, Texas, on Wednesday the thirteenth, which is a short hop from Dallas. Why don't I get her to fly down, and we can all meet in Dallas? That way she'll be less uptight about being seen with a reporter." Burnham agreed, and the rendezvous was set.

Karen welcomed the deadline and the knowledge that her days as a sleuth would soon be done. She was working overtime, lurking about the file rooms, staying into the graveyard shift when supervision was not so tight. Her union work had become a kind of parenthesis around her company work. Notice was taken of how jumpy she was, and she began to think her bosses could see through the great lie she was leading. In her pocket notebook she wrote, "the company knows something's going on."

CRESCENT. OCTOBER 21, 1974. Karen was not a horsewoman. Horses didn't obey the way machines did. But for an afternoon reprieve she went with Sherri Ellis to a broken-down ranch a few miles from the factory. It belonged to Sherri's grandmother, and Sherri kept a quick-footed roan in the barn. She yelled for Karen's attention. "Watch, watch!" Karen climbed the corral fence and straddled it. The roan had her knees slightly bent; Sherri's toes were in the stirrups, turned inward, her rump resolute in an old Connolly saddle, whip in hand. A whistling tap—Karen winced—and the roan was off, running left, then right, around one barrel, then another, kicking dirt, snorting to a stop. "It's just like an autocross race," Karen said.

Sherri patted the horse's neck. "Where'd you think they got the idea for autocross?"

Rodeos are nowhere tougher than in Oklahoma, but Sherri had a bedroom mirror bordered in ribbons and a shoebox of championship belt buckles, and next to her bed was a new saddle with her name and her highest success burnt in. Sherri was Karen's roommate, since August. They had met at the factory; Sherri worked with Tice in production. She was twenty-one, rawboned, lankily pretty, infatuated with being a cowgirl, and she was totally indifferent to the union crusade. Her vote for 5–283 in the decertification had been immensely halfhearted. ("Who needs it? Who needs another ten bucks out of your paycheck?") But give her time, Karen thought: she'll come around, just like me.

Karen broke open a bale of hay that smelled of summer inside. Sherri made the roan rear up on her hind legs in a burlesque of the Lone Ranger, and Karen threw the hay into the trough for a reward.

A gray cat with yellowing eyes came out of a hole in the barn. The old tom prowled about, surveying his domain, at one with the shadows. Cats, or pets of any kind, weren't allowed in Karen's apartment building; otherwise she would have brought one home, like the young tabby she met downtown one evening. But the tabby had a protector, as Karen learned. There was a Cat Lady who every night took bags of restaurant garbage to a vacant lot behind City Hall. Homeless cats—runaways and abandoned pets and ones born in the wild—they came meowing from everywhere, across rooftops, from under buildings, jumping through broken windows, forming a circle of eyes at the old lady's feet. They lived each day for her coming, but never let her touch them.

Karen had watched, thinking to turn the Cat Lady into poetry, but now, watching the old gray tom, she thought the cats would make a better poem. The old tom padded under the corral gate. A wooden oats bucket hung lazily from the fence. On the ground a flock of plump sparrows pecked at fallen kernels. The cat began to craft each step from instinct and memory; his creep suddenly became menacing. There was a pounce and a brown fury of dust and feathers.

Karen shuddered in the frosty silvered sunshine, and her gaze turned to an inner world. Later she talked about the barnyard tableau: how it must feel to be a hunter. That was the poem she was going to write.

Drew glanced complimentarily at Karen's slip of paper. "Cut coil springs to stiffen and lower car. Replace shocks (Konis are good). Put on header. Front spoiler. Thirteen-inch mags and radials. Disconnect controlled spark device. Reconnect vacuum hose to straight vacuum." As with everything she thought worthwhile, she had jotted down these ideas for tricking-out her Honda.

"What would it cost?" she wondered.

"Under seven hundred, or thereabouts. I could do most of the work myself. Buy the parts wholesale. We'll do it up right. Turn that buggy into a hot number."

Karen reflected pensively. "Guess I can't quit work yet."

"Hey, are you thinking of getting out of there? Finally?" Drew was very pleased.

"No, no, forget I said that." She shook her head in emphasis. "I don't want to talk about it."

Karen could feel the whole of the past two years; she felt it as a swindle. With a brown manila folder, each night growing fatter, bulging, she would get redemption and revenge. Once a week she was reporting over the phone to Wodka, assuring him about the folder. There were photomicrographs, other documents. The proof. "Great, great," Wodka would answer. Mazzocchi was counting on her, and a *New York Times* reporter was taking a chance, flying two thousand miles on his word. Wodka made sure Karen was aware of this gravity. "When you say you're positive, I want you to mean it. I don't want any foul-ups."

"I'm positive," Karen said.

Under her hard-boiled surface, though, there were sharp points of disturbance, worries like bayonets. Nothing in twenty-eight commonplace years had prepared her for this. She might be fired or blacklisted, maybe arrested. Even if all went well with the *Times* the plan was not without peril. Her supervisors might guess right off that she was the one who had snitched. And what if the AEC revoked the Cimarron license—might the factory hands call her traitor too? Somewhere she had read about Ernest Fitzgerald, the analyst who testified to Congress about $2 billion in cost overruns on the Air Force C-5A plane. Journalists had exploited Fitzgerald's information; then they had let vengeful military officers take his job and lawyers divvy up his savings. Would she end up like him? But Karen did not tell Wodka of her worries, her nights spent flopping in bed, sheets somehow warm and wet from chills. Wodka might take the assignment away, and more than anything she didn't want that.

Instead she was resorting to the pills she had used now and again since the final convulsing months of her marriage. She had prescriptions from two doctors for Quaaludes and other tranquilizers. The pills made her languorous, imparting a sense of well-being, instant soothing. But when Drew noticed her cabinet of near-empty bottles, he chewed her out. She had a lung infection, she said defensively, and it had given her a huge appetite for the pills. That much was the truth. Bacteria had invaded her lungs, aggravating her asthma, causing uneven breaths. Her voice was full of gulps and hissing exhalations. Also, when she was on night shift, she needed the pills to sleep in the half-light of her curtained bedroom. But it seemed to Drew that there was more to all the pill-popping—that she was trying to sedate a bad case of nerves.

OKLAHOMA CITY. OCTOBER 22, 1974. Suddenly it happened. As she chatted lightheartedly to a friend, a vision burst inside her. A nightmare, really: she was jimmying open a locked file drawer when footfalls sounded behind her; her hands turned feverish; despair seized her; she was frozen in place, unable to run.

"Oh, God, what's gonna happen to me?" she cried to her friend, James Noel, a slender young man who had left Cimarron months before to become a science teacher. He was a good listener, and Karen began blurting out the whole story. Would her risk ever be understood or credited?

"Get out of that place, Karen. You've got to think of yourself."

"There's just so much wrong," she said. Her eyes had the odd, burning look of unhealthy curiosity. "Every day I'm finding out stuff you wouldn't believe. I swear, you wouldn't believe it."

Afterward James Noel made notes, preserved in his daily journal.

The fact was, Karen had made up her mind to leave. By winter she planned to be in Nederland, outside the immediate reach of Kerr-McGee, but she confided her plan only to her mother and sisters. She asked Rosemary to fill an envelope with application forms. "Try that auto-parts distributor in Beaumont. And that ball-bearing place," Karen said. "I'll take anything." She was even willing to work temporarily at an oil refinery—her disillusionment with Cimarron was that complete.

Rosemary assumed the cause was another breakup with Drew. She pried a little, but it was altogether solicitous. "Come home tomorrow, why don't you? If there's nothing to keep you?"

"I just gotta finish one thing first."

CRESCENT. NOVEMBER 5, 1974. It was Tuesday, eight days before the scheduled appointment with David Burnham. The afternoon sky was shadily aglimmer. Thin argentine clouds scudded toward the horizon. Karen passed through the security airlock shortly after one o'clock. She stored a baloney sandwich in her locker and went to the Met Lab. For two hours she sat at a desk and filled out specimen reports. Three o'clock: time for a coffee break. She monitored herself the way the rules said, using a portable alpha counter. The counter had a dial marked with radiation measurements, but otherwise it resembled a hot-air hair styler, and seemed as innocent. She held the counter inches from her hands, face, clothes. Its silence pronounced her clean. Returning, Karen taped on gloves and worked with a lathe in Gloveboxes Three and Six. At the five-thirty break, the alpha counter again made no sound. Karen went to her locker and ate a sandwich, then resumed work in the glovebox.

Six-thirty: this was her real supper hour, but she had plans to spend it in the file rooms. *Rrrrit. Rrrrrit.* The sound was a diamondback's warning. "I'm hot! My hands are hot!" Karen's shout carried into an adjacent lab. An HP heard and came running. He took her to a darkroom and enlisted a woman clerk, who helped peel the layers of cotton and plastic off Karen. Polythene fingertips dropped everything into a bag for burial. A new smock got Karen down the hall to the first-aid station, a room small and white. Off came the smock, and Karen went into a tall shower, the nozzle turned to full pressure. Water sluiced down her body. She dried off with towels and hair dryer and retested herself; plutonium still lined her nasal passages. Dabbing with cotton swabs, flushing with a rubber-bulb irrigator, she finally showed clean.

The source of the contamination appeared to be Glovebox Three or Six. Guessing at a tiny fissure in one of the gloves, the HP had them removed. Karen meanwhile spent what was left of Tuesday developing radiographic film in a darkroom. She finished her shift an hour past midnight, and when she left she took along four bioassay kits.

Sleep, if it came at all, was short. Karen reported back at eight o'clock Wednesday morning. Today was special. Formal contract talks were to begin at nine. After nearly an hour in the Met Lab, she left to meet with Tice. But first there was the ritual. *Rrrrit. Rrrrrrit.* Alarm echoed in the room. "This thing must be broken!" she yelled. She gripped the alpha counter and waved it once more with deliberation from shoes to hair. *Rrrrit. Rrrrrit.* How could it be? After all that sanitizing, how could there still be plutonium on her face and hands?

"It must not have all come off," she said irritably to the HP.

He disagreed. "You were clean when you left last night. Did you go near Three or Six this morning?"

"I was at my desk the whole time."

"You're sure?"

"What d'you mean? Of course I'm sure." Karen's temper hurtled out of control. "I'm sure, dammit, I'm sure."

"Well, you got to go to first-aid again."

"Great, just great. I'm gonna be late for negotiations. You know, this better not be a trick to keep me out of there. If you guys are up to something—?"

At the negotiating table, which was long and skinny so that the two sides could face each other, Karen complained loudly about safety problems, flinging out her own contamination as the most recent example. Later, in a more agreeable tone, she invited an HP to inspect her locker. Perhaps a prankster had hidden a pellet there. No—nothing showed on the monitor.

"Try to think," the HP probed. "What other rooms were you in?"

"Just the locker room and the Met Lab," Karen said in an empty voice, between wheezes. Her lungs hurt from a day of talking too much. Her eyes looked faint, her skin blanched.

In a pitying gesture, the HP said she could go home if she would come straight to the HP office in the morning. "Mr. Norwood will be in. He'll want to talk to you."

Sherri was in pajamas, the TV tuned to a game show. Karen clicked it off. "Something's going on. I don't know what. But something."

They lived in a first-floor apartment. From the street their front door was hidden beyond a shoulder-high picket fence. Outside, the walls were brick, the color of medium toast. Inside, there were twin bedrooms and a living room, all done up with assembly-line furniture. The apartment complex was in the suburb of Edmond, a half-mile or so from Central State University. Most tenants were students at Central State, which university had thrived in the sixties as a draft deferment; now it was a convenience school. Sherri was taking classes twice a week.

Drew came over later, and Karen repeated her tale of distress. "My nasal smears were high," she said. "Maybe it's coming from inside me, from when I got dosed in July. It could be coming from my lungs because I'm coughing so much."

Drew waved away the puzzle with a flick of his hand. "Nah, it's gotta be from a spill. They'll find it. Don't worry."

"What if it's a trick? Would anybody pull something like that?"

"These cowboys might be crazy, but they're not out to lunch. It's a spill, you'll see."

"I wish I knew, that's all. It scares me." She fluffed out her hair. "God, I must look a mess."

"No. No uglier than usual."

Karen laughed then, a brave laugh, and Drew rallied her for a late supper of takeout pizza. Sherri ate with them, all three powwow style on the spongy carpet. Karen sipped from a bottle of Dr. Pepper and munched slowly on a solitary pizza slice, almost mesmerized by the pepperoni topography. Her spirit appeared to shrink with the pizza.

Sherri left for work about eleven-thirty. Drew volunteered to stay, holding Karen gently against her great inquietude. She burrowed under the crook of his arm and hid her face in his shoulder. But at every cough she blanketed her face with Kleenex, and seeing the litter of damp tissues, she got up to flush them down the toilet. She refused to kiss him good-night, for fear of infecting him, and later lay in bed with her face averted, arms flung up on her pillow as if to ward off a beating.

Karen rose on Thursday morning before there was any sign of dawn. The bioassay kits had to be filled first thing. While fastening the plastic lids, she spilled some of the urine; it was no big deal. She breakfasted on coffee and took baloney and cheese from the refrigerator to make sandwiches for lunch. Distractedly she carried the baloney package from room to room, at one point leaving it on the fuzzy cover of the toilet back. Then she decided against sandwiches and put the food back.

The sun was making a feeble show as Karen drove along Highway 74. Sherri, coming home from Cimarron by the same route, saw the Honda and honked.

At ten to eight Karen delivered her bioassay kits to Wayne Norwood. Norwood was the chief HP, a roundish, cheerful man who might have been a saloonkeeper. But he had tight lines at his eyes, lines that drew tighter at Karen's entrance. He had not been able to make sense out of her Tuesday and Wednesday contaminations. The gloves from Three and Six had been filled with water, a search for fissures, but there were none in any of the rubberized fingers. As far as Norwood could tell, the gloves could not be responsible for Karen's contamination.

He threw out an edict. "You better let someone monitor you." Karen obeyed, shrugging. But why bother? The cleansing procedure yesterday—Wednesday—had been nothing if not rigorous. From forehead to toes every inch of her had been washed with a liquid that was part Clorox, part Tide (for suds), and then with potassium permanganate. The permanganate is an oxiding agent that leaves no doubt about its coverage. Where it goes, the skin flakes white like a chain crystal of unseasonal frost. To remove it the HPs used sodium bisulfite with a vegetable brush. With it came a layer of skin. To be doubly sure, the HPs had put on extra permanganate and taken off extra skin. Her cheeks still hurt from the brush.

One of the HPs now moved an alpha counter near Karen's face. *RRRrrrrrittt. RRrrrrittt.* Karen went rigid with horror. A dirgelike groan escaped her lips. "It can't be!" But the metallic clicking contradicted her. For the third time in three days, her hands were contaminated. So were her forearms and her nose and the twitching skin around her mouth. "It must be inside me," she wailed. "I must be coughing it up."

"I don't think so," Norwood said. "Once it's in your lungs, you don't expel it like that. I'd say you're getting it on your hands and transferring it to your face."

"But where's it coming from?"

"I don't know. You tell me."

"I don't know either. We've checked everywhere."

"We haven't checked your apartment." Norwood seemed to have put considerable thought into his deduction.

"You think it's in my apartment?" Karen swallowed. "In my *apartment?*"

He nodded. "Is your roommate home?"

"Yes," Karen said tonelessly.

"You'd better call and tell her to stay put. She might be hot too. We'll have to go out there."

Before Karen could go anywhere, she had to be decontaminated again. They began with Clorox and Tide and water, then the harsher abrasives and the bristling brush. Karen held herself over a large laundry sink, tiny fists clenching the edge. She trembled; the brush spread pain and cascades of color across her face. She lifted her head for a second scouring, a third, a fourth. Her head slumped, but her fists held on, refusing to wipe away tears that went altogether unacknowledged.

Sherri had crawled back under the covers by the time Karen and Norwood and two HPs knocked on the apartment door. They carried portable alpha counters for a room-to-room hunt. Microscopic amounts of plutonium were on Sherri's hands and buttocks. Other flecks showed up on the toilet seat, the toilet back, the medicine cabinet, the phone table—everything touched by Karen. The trail turned hottest in the kitchen: radioactive "hot." Inside the refrigerator the alpha needle jumped. Standing back from the open door, Norwood slowed the hunt. He moved his counter from item to item. There was little to explore. Neither roommate currently had any inclination toward cooking, as the polychrome larder indicated: Budweiser, Dr. Pepper, mayonnaise, raspberry jam, eggs, bread, and baking soda kept in back for odors. Norwood stopped at the package of baloney. The tumult grew louder and the needle swung into the red. Four hundred thousand dpms! By any standard, a dangerous level. Alpha particles were radiating at a rate of four hundred thousand a minute, the metaphoric equivalent of a sniper's four hundred thousand bullets.

"Did you make yourself a sandwich out of that?" Norwood asked.

Karen ran a limp hand across her eyes. "No, I was gonna make one this morning, but I changed my mind." In her agitated state, she forgot about the baloney she had packed in Tuesday's brown bag.

"What about Sherri? Has she eaten any?"

"No, she doesn't like lunch meat." Karen peered closely at the package where it lay on the metal tines. "It's right where I left it."

Norwood drove the two women back to the factory—Sherri for decontamination, Karen for more tests. He took the baloney along for disposal. At Cimarron he ordered up a flatbed truck and a four-man crew. The four men dressed in "moon suits"—white hoods, oxygen tanks, layers of nonporous clothing, other life-support gear.

They drove to the apartment in the flatbed truck with a dozen yellow fourteen-gauge steel drums and a box of black garbage bags.

Karen and Sherri came later. What they saw was from science fiction, otherworldly beings in brigade. The "moon-suits" were emptying the apartment. Karen and Sherri were told to stay on the brown lawn, where their belongings soon joined them. Sherri wailed about her new saddle, but they refused to let her in to retrieve it. She fled to her car, unwilling to watch more. The contents of shelves and drawers went into the black garbage bags and the bags into the yellow barrels. Furniture and appliances became a separate hapless mountain on the flatbed. Within three hours the apartment was stripped of its modest worth: electric popcorn popper, eighteen-inch Magnavox, candle holders, wooden Indian busts, the book *I Never Promised You a Rose Garden,* sixteen Crayola crayons (for Karen's kids), a cement-block bookcase, eight bottles of nail polish, forty pairs of panties, Sheer Essence perfume, fourteen wall posters, Rock & Rye liqueur, vitamins, birth-control pills, iron-on knee patches, and more of the same, more nondescript items from the short, rather nondescript lives of the occupants.

It all went to the Cimarron warehouse, into the custody of Kerr-McGee.

Karen seemed in shock, a waiflike figure, face pale and indefinite. Moisture flooded her eyes and ran unchecked to the collar of her leather coat. A few homebound Kerr-McGee employees made a detour there and hovered about out of curiosity. One or two walked over to extend their hands in sympathy. The top man at Cimarron, Morgan Moore, came by with a company lawyer.

Drew threaded his Sprite through the honking delirium. Karen was in the lawyer's Oldsmobile, so he went up the sidewalk. The "moon suits" were prying open the ventilation ducts. They allowed him in and told him to undress in Sherri's bedroom. Drew had been with Karen the night before and therefore had to undergo the scrutiny of an alpha counter. His hands smacked together happily when the needle didn't move.

Back on the lawn, he looked about for Karen. She was gone.

Karen had parked the Honda in a U-Tote-Em lot. She was in a phone booth. As she talked, her shoulders slid down the length of the glass wall, were hauled upright, but slid weakly down again, a slow-motion calisthenic. At the other end of the connection Wodka was listening. He heard a mournful banshee roar. It came from a locomotive that Karen could see, crossing a trestle where the road hollowed. "Talk louder," Wodka shouted into the roar.

"I think I'm dying!" Karen shouted back.

Wodka is a man alienated by melodrama, and he is often hostile to those in its grip. He listened for a hint of jocularity. There was none. "I'll take the first plane out in the morning," he said. "Go someplace safe. Don't do a thing till I get there."

Karen went into the U-Tote-Em for more dimes and quarters. Long distance again. Minneapolis. Dr. Dean Abrahamson. She wanted medical advice from a physician. "Could I possibly be exhaling it?" she asked.

"I doubt it," he replied. "You probably got it on your hand and rubbed your nose. Or you're breathing it in. Either way, you need a full-body count. This is nothing to fool with."

Nederland was next. Mrs. Silkwood answered. "Is Daddy there?" Karen asked. "Or Linda?"

"No," Mrs. Silkwood said. "Linda's over decorating her boyfriend's house—they're having a big party after the game tomorrow. And Daddy's up at his cabin."

"That's good," Karen sighed. "I don't want to worry them."

"Honey, what's wrong?"

The voice on the line wavered. "I got contaminated. Three days in a row. It's all over my place."

"Honey, please come home. You can see one of the doctors in Beaumont. Or Houston—they've got good ones there."

"Regular doctors are no good. I've got to go to a specialist."

"Then I'm coming up there, girl. The bank owes me a couple days off."

"No, Mama, don't do that. Drew's here—he'll take care of me." Karen hung up.

As if racing an autocross clock, she jammed in another dime. Drew's number was busy. (Now he was the one engaged long distance with Wodka, taking down the time and flight number for Wodka's arrival tomorrow.) But Karen was in no frame of mind to wait. She dialed the neighbor next door, who came shouting for Drew, "Your girl's on the line over here, crying her head off."

The phone was dangling from the neighbor's kitchen wall. "Karen, where are you?" Drew tried to sound calm. "I'll come get you."

"I can drive okay. I just had to hear your voice. Oh, Drew, did you see the apartment? Did they tell you what happened? There was plutonium in the fridge. It was on our food. *On our food!*"

Two hours or so later, by now nearly eleven o'clock, Karen's car swung into the driveway. Drew led her inside. She talked brokenly about having gone back to the apartment. The windows had been dark, the doors sealed with quarantine tags. But the "moon suits" had inadvertently left the rear door unlocked. It had been a simple matter for Karen to break the wire seal, go in, look around.

"They didn't get the stuff," she told Drew, with mystery and exhaustion in her voice.

This car was a relic, fenders leprous from road brine, the front seat disgorging horsehair. The owner had brought it with reluctance to the Volkswagen body shop after giving up on homemade replacements for the grille and bumper. With force of muscle, Drew was holding a new bumper and firing a weld gun. Karen sat on a workbench where he could keep an eye on her. Her shoulders had fallen still and vague, but her face was a mayhem of emotion. Hand to mouth, she suddenly began coughing up yellow bile, spewing it out. She studied the discharge as if she didn't know where it was from.

Drew put down his tools and took her for lunch. But food had no appeal. While he ate, Karen found a phone booth.

Rosemary answered. "Mama told me you got poisoned. Are you gonna be all right?"

"Oh, Rosemary, it's awful. I might have cancer. I might be dead in five years. I wish to God you lived around the corner right now."

"If it wasn't for the kids, I'd come right up."

"Why don't you leave them with Mama? Oh, please, come up. I can't tell you how much I need to talk to someone."

After lunch, Karen and Drew drove to the airport. Headlong down the debarking ramp, Wodka shoved past the other passengers and pulled Karen into an embrace. Told she wasn't eating, Wodka ushered her into a coffee shop. Karen was a mute portrait of misery, down to under a hundred pounds—a loss of ten in the past week. Her hair was in snarls, not at all kept up. Her pretty face was dissolving. Her natural color had turned sickly; blue veins showed at her temples. Wodka made her remove a pair of big round sunglasses. There were whorls like smoker's fingers under her eyes, dark against the pallor.

It took some coaxing to get her to smile. "I've got to stop crying," she said with wan humor. "The tears burn my skin, it's so raw."

Wodka had no time to question her. They were already late for an appointment with the AEC at the Holiday Inn Northwest.

The AEC inspectors, when they came to Oklahoma City, always stayed at the Holiday Inn Northwest, a habit well known both to Kerr-McGee and to 5–283. Wodka had made a request to the inspectors to switch motels because he suspected that someone from the Holiday Inn was tipping off the company to the AEC's "surprise" inspections. This time, though, the inspectors were not supposed to be here on the sly. They had been invited by both the union and the company. Answers were wanted. The contamination of Karen's home, or anybody's home, was without precedent.

"I'm from the AEC office in Illinois," said Gerald Phillip. He reached a hand across a shabbily veneered table. Phillip had an agreeable face and elegant indented hair. His look and tone seemed to hearten Karen.

"Could you have accidentally picked up some plutonium at work and brought it home with you?" he asked.

"No. I always monitor myself before I leave," Karen replied. Besides, she said, she had not gone into areas marked with red-and-yellow signs on either Wednesday or Thursday.

"Okay," Phillip said. "Let's start with Tuesday. Tell me what you did, from the time you woke up."

"I got dressed and made myself a sandwich for work."

"What kind of sandwich? Was it from the baloney package?"

"Oh, my God!" Karen gave a muffled cry. A look came into her eyes, unblinking, the stare of a cornered animal. "I'd forgotten—yes, it was. I had a sandwich at work. And I had another sandwich that night. For a midnight snack. Oh, Jesus! I'm gonna die for sure!"

An encouraging hand like a doctor's was laid on hers; it happened to belong to a doctor; he was a consultant for the AEC. "Let me assure you," he said, "there's never been a single documented case of death or serious injury from this sort of accident."

She looked to Wodka. Impressive in a brown tapered suit, Wodka interjected, "Are you trying to say she doesn't need medical treatment?"

"I'm not saying that. But I don't believe this is a life-or-death matter."

"I'm not so sure. I've seen pictures of what happened to that New Jersey dockworker—Gleason—the guy who spilled liquid plutonium on his fingers. He got this ugly skin cancer. First they amputated his hand; then the cancer spread up his arm, and they had to amputate that. Then it went up his shoulder. They couldn't cut any more, so it went down into his body and killed him."

Karen's lips moved without sound. She coughed soggily into her hand, trying to clear out a flood of fears.

The doctor sat up in a scholarly posture. "I was a consultant on the Gleason case," he said. "Only about half your facts are correct. Gleason's arm did ulcerate and it was removed and he did die. *However,* there's no evidence that plutonium was the catalyst. Medically, the case is unresolved."

"It's unresolved because Gleason's widow settled her claim out of court," Wodka replied, getting hortative. "The industry got off the hook because there was no trial."

"There was no trial because no competent doctor would support your conclusion."

A hand went up: Phillip's. "Gentlemen, excuse me, but is this necessary? None of it pertains to Miss Silkwood."

The doctor shifted toward her. "Most of the plutonium inside you should pass through your digestive tract. Anything in your lungs might constitute a risk, but based on your nasal smears, I'd venture to say that the amount is within permissible limits."

"You probably have nothing to worry about," Phillip said kindly, endorsing the doctor.

Wodka did not accept that and gave them a baleful look. Being frequently in the company of medical people, he had acquired their sense of authority. The language of dpms and alpha rays and rems, once as unfathomable as a mountaineer's lingo to a sailor, had become his second language. But he said nothing more. Perhaps Karen would be all right. It might, in any event, be better for her to think so—until they could find out for certain.

By dusk, the men from the AEC knew all about Karen's movements for Tuesday, Wednesday, Thursday: the 5th, 6th, 7th of November, 1974. She told them everything she could remember, or almost everything. Left out, by oversight or purposeful omission, was her late-evening trip to the ransacked, deserted apartment.

Drew and Tice had been excluded from the meeting. They were waiting at a TG&Y store across the street, absorbing a TV medley on the display consoles. Smiling wearily, Karen and Wodka walked over. Someone mentioned pizza, and they went to find one.

In inflammatory circumstances, Jan Strasma was a "fireman" for the AEC. He was sent in not to contain runaway plutonium but to douse headlines and extinguish speculation. Nothing was amiss, he would assure local reporters. No one had been hurt.

Strasma performed well in Oklahoma City. None of Karen's neighbors realized she had just made nuclear history.

Jack Tice's brow was set in a frown, his thin, knotted body shaking with anger. "Lousy dumb AEC pinheads. They don't give a damn about Karen."

"They had you in there two hours," Wodka said. "They must've asked you something about her."

"Yeah, they wanted to know if she's stupid enough to dose herself."

"Dose herself? *On purpose?*" Wodka's voice was a harsh crack, an imitation of gunfire.

"I told 'em to open their eyes. Can't they see she's sick with worry?"

"What else did they ask?"

"A bunch of junk. Like who's been snitching to that Sierra Club lady, Mrs. Younghein. They got all heated up, ready to explode, 'cause I wouldn't tell them. Why *should* I tell them? It's none of their business. If it *was* me, why should I tell 'em? There's nothing worse for your state of employment in Oklahoma than to get known as a Sierra Club lover."

At the Holiday Inn in Wodka's room, jars of soiled Kleenex marched in a column across the top of a bureau. Karen was saving them—and all her other excretions—as indicators of the plutonium inside her. There was a quicker way to measure the little pinpoints of radioactive fire, but that was with an *in vivo* counter, of which there were but half a dozen in the country. The nearest was at an AEC lab in Los Alamos, New Mexico.

On Saturday, at Wodka's insistence, Kerr-McGee officials said they would put up the money for Karen and Drew and Sherri to fly to Los Alamos.

Wodka bought his own ticket for a schedule that was to shuttle him back to Washington, D.C., then to Tyler, Texas, for his asbestos meeting. Before leaving he talked privately with Karen. Phase Two of the OCAW strategy had been thrust into temporary panic. "I can have Burnham meet us here instead of Dallas," Wodka suggested. "Or I could postpone it? Or call it off?"

"Tell him to come," Karen said firmly. "We can meet right here. At the motel."

For comfort Karen was still taking Quaaludes, but her pallor had receded and there was strength in her voice. The AEC's offhand prognosis had been good medicine—she no longer talked of dying.

"You got the proof we talked about?" Wodka asked, wanting once more to be certain.

Karen nodded in assent and handed him two notebooks, the blue-green stenographer's notebook and the pocket one. "You can take these," she said. "The rest of the stuff is in a safe place."

Karen and Sherri and Drew had Sunday brunch in the air over the Texas Panhandle. For her drink Karen ordered a Tall Texan, whiskey over a single ice cube. "Let's take a lot of pictures to remember this trip by," she said.

"Why?" Drew countered gloomily.

"Los Alamos is in the mountains, and I've never seen real mountains before." Karen began fishing through her purse. "Oh, damn, I didn't bring my camera."

"You couldn't have. It's in one of those barrels, remember?"

"Oh, yeah." She sounded frail and plangent and on the brink of tears, though none appeared.

At the Albuquerque airport they rented a car and bought a bottle of red wine for the last hundred miles to Los Alamos. After an hour, Drew was swooned flat in the back seat. Karen kept swigging and driving. She followed a crooked gray-pink road, a crayon line in a mural of mountains and trees. The afternoon sun carved shadows from turrety rocks that had been thrust into the sky during ancient upheavals. Vultures rode the wind about an arid glitter. Somewhere around San Ysidro, Karen took a wrong turn. The road shot higher into ponderosa and aspen. Asphalt lapsed into pebbles and powder, flaring behind. Beauty turned quickly mean.

Drew woke up. "Where the hell are we?" he demanded crossly. Sherri had the map, but she also had been partying with the wine. Karen drove on, a jumpy breathless passage, and stopped at length below an American flag snapping and threshing on a pole. They were lost in a federal preserve that is seldom used except by Indians. They hailed a park ranger, and he pointed them back toward Los Alamos.

The sun was gone and it was the border of night before they spied a motel. Karen's vision was a little fuzzy, her bottle empty; but no fatigue, no drowsiness had descended on her.

"How d'you feel?" Drew asked.

"Better than you look," she said energetically, which cost her another coughing attack.

Five

Karen woke Monday morning in postcard wilderness. Forest fell away steeply below her motel window, and in the distance the Sangre de Cristos bulged up green and white and tall, mountains of a scale to put people in their place.

Los Alamos is built on a big mesa inside an even bigger canyon. Mule deer and bobcats drink from trout streams that form complicated patterns beneath big pines. At a certain angle the sun glints off a TWA plane that years ago fell from the sky in a brown smoke trail, screaming with useless power. The spot on the mountainside where it crashed is so remote they could not retrieve it.

It was the remoteness and isolation of Los Alamos, not the splendor, that the War Department was seeking in 1942. Asked to find a place beyond the range of wandering motorists, Dr. Robert Oppenheimer had remembered this canyon from youthful days on horseback. The War Department commandeered a boys' school, the only habitation, and threw up extra whitewashed buildings. For a while all the plutonium in the world was kept there in a storeroom, inside a cigar box. Armed guards in towers watched the Los Alamos perimeters, and at the front gate an Army tank was parked ominously, its cannon aimed against incoming traffic. The five thousand government people garrisoned inside could not vote, get divorced, file lawsuits, mail uncensored letters. On the birth certificates of kids born here in the forties there had been only a Santa Fe post-office box for their birthplace. Los Alamos had been a secret city. It was where Dr. Oppenheimer and the other fathers of the nuclear age perfected the bomb. Afterward, war correspondents had come back from Japan with photographs, keepsakes of a horror. Families lay together, gray with bomb dust, their shadows baked on walls from the strange heat.

In 1953, President Eisenhower had instituted a policy of atonement. "We will solve the fearful atomic dilemma and find a way by which the miraculous inventiveness of men shall not be dedicated to death, but consecrated to life." Thus began "Atoms for Peace." Talented, hardworking men, at Los Alamos and elsewhere, tried to rescue nuclear fission from damnation. The science of the A-bomb was transformed by commerce and hoopla.

Los Alamos was now open to visitors; the Army tank and the cloister rules had been done away with. At the BioMedical Building, though, the security was still in effect. "Bulletproof glass," Drew said, peering through. Its thickness bloated a view of laboratory walls. In the lobby he and Karen and Sherri were frisked, their photographs taken. Camouflaged eyes in the ceiling watched them, the eyes of closed-circuit video. A guard issued them electronic key-cards to register the opening and closing of every door as they passed through.

Dr. George Voelz, the director of health research, escorted them down hospital-style corridors. An odd aroma, a mix of antiseptics and feces, rose from racks of bioassay kits. Dr. Voelz motioned them to an atrium of light and space. "Our lab is equipped with the most advanced radiation counters in the world," he said proudly. He had his own little dithyramb about the white wonderland. "This is science at its best. As close to perfection as is humanly possible. Not just the hardware, but the people too."

But it was the gadgetry that Karen and Drew wanted to see, the counters that could foretell their future. Dr. Voelz showed them a wound counter, a pen-size metal rod used to probe orifices. For the *in vivo* they had to go to the main counting room. "The *in vivo* counts the scintillas as the nuclear material decomposes inside you," Dr. Voelz said.

"Scintillas—that's a fancy name for radioactive bullets," Karen whispered to Sherri.

Dr. Voelz gave a start as if for some reason she had scared him. "Scintillas are the dying flares of uranium. Or cesium, strontium-90, whatever it is that's decomposing," he said, no longer effusive. "Most nuclear materials become inactive in a few months or a few years." What he did not say, but what Karen knew from the two professors, was that plutonium is different. Its dying goes on for two hundred forty thousand years—*forever,* for all practical purposes.

Dr. Voelz looked up. An attendant had come for Karen. She

undressed behind a screen and put on white paper pajamas with buttons in front. The attendant stood next to a spoke-handled wheel, turning it. Air from inside made a sucking noise as the wheel was pulled outward. It created an opening in a vault. The vault was a green-drab cube about nine feet square, made of steel, with glossy, sanitized floors covered by brown paper like that from a butcher. Seven inches of armor plate formed the walls—armor from a pre-forties battleship. The date was important: with World War II came the alloying of cobalt in the manufacture of steel, which is radioactive enough to throw off the *in vivo*.

Karen went in alone. Sitting at a computer console, the attendant watched through a small thick window. Karen stretched out on a bed in a bath of light—huge, placid, clinical—from recessed fluorescent bulbs overhead. Two radiation counters like miniature flying saucers descended on a metal arm, pivoting from a universal joint, and landed on her chest. Numbers whirred into the computer. After thirty minutes the flying saucers withdrew. Obeying a voice over the intercom, Karen rolled onto her stomach. Again the saucers dropped to scanning range, counting the scintillas in her lungs. From the bed Karen moved to a padded chair, very much like Drew's dentist's chair, and another saucer came at her, from a horizontal angle. For a total of two hours Karen had the benefit of a magical exploration. (Dr. Voelz loathes this adjective. "There is nothing *magical* about nuclear science," he tells visitors. "That word is left over from a time of superstition and hobgoblins.") The attendant entered the vault and poked a wound counter into Karen's nose and mouth and vagina. Later, in another room, samples of Karen's blood, nail parings, spittle, urine, feces passed into an assembly line of test tubes and microscopes.

Meanwhile Drew went through an *in vivo* exam, then Sherri.

By late afternoon Dr. Voelz had news, preliminary but optimistic. Any plutonium Drew and Sherri had in them was below the threshold of detection. Karen was not quite as lucky—scintillas, like falling stars, were flashing through her lungs—but the numbers were within the AEC standard, about half the permissible dose. The overall effect would be as lasting as three-two beer.

Karen hugged Drew with wild relief. Outside, they raced with Sherri to the car. In the morning Dr. Voelz wanted them back for another "whole body" count, but tonight could be given over to Mexican food and dancing. A country-rock band was playing at a

Ramada Inn. "Drink up," Karen exulted. "We're on Kerr-McGee's expense account." By eleven Drew was played out, but Karen stayed past midnight, till closing time, till sleep overtook her.

Rows of stainless steel cages lined a long wall in one of the BioMedical rooms. The top of each box slanted so that the beagles inside could only sit. No pungent animal smell issued forth; these cages were as airtight as gloveboxes. The dogs breathed a hybrid of oxygen, nitrogen and plutonium oxide pumped in through black rubber tubes. Karen found the room and the doomed beagles after lunch on Tuesday. She began to cry.

"Hey, they're doing their bit for science," Drew said. "Better them than us." He cracked his knuckles.

"I know," she said. "I know."

When Karen was little she had had a favorite among all her pets. His name was Cotton, and he liked to rub his rabbit's nose companionably to hers. But one day during a heat storm Cotton's cage was left in the sun; his breathing came in gasps; he flattened himself to the wire mesh, and was dead. For a long time Karen grieved in the backyard, and years later she happened to see a newscast about rabbit roundups—ranchers were driving big jacks into snow-fence corrals and flailing away with clubs—she had written to her Congressman. "What great sportsmen they are. How proud they must be!" With sadness and anger she had written. It was how she felt a lot of the time now.

The *in vivo* tests of Tuesday duplicated the tests of Monday and reaffirmed the results. Karen and Drew and Sherri could leave knowing they were as healthy as the next person.

Karen phoned Wodka. "I'm gonna be all right. I didn't get a high dose after all."

"Did they tell you anything else?"

"Just how super Los Alamos is. It's funny. I always wanted to be a real scientist and work in a place like this. But after seeing it, I'm not so sure."

Wodka rustled up his datebook. "Are we still on for tomorrow night?"

"Yes, yes."

"Okay, see you then."

At a store in Los Alamos, before driving back to the Albuquerque airport, Karen bought a collapsible tote bag to hold souvenirs for her kids, and a Kodak Instamatic, fated for brief use. She got to try it out only from the car window on the mountains and on a mule deer that came bounding into view.

Drew stuck with the Almaden Grenache Rosé, a freebie on their Continental flight back to Oklahoma City—he was used to counting pennies. In the seat alongside, Karen drank Bloody Marys. She was speaking, the words low and controlled, but to Drew they flashed like lightning and brightened his face.

"Run that by me again," he sputtered. "What kind of craziness have you been up to?"

"I've been collecting everything I can get my hands on. Wodka thinks we can get it printed in *The New York Times*. This is gonna be our turn to hit on Kerr-McGee. Isn't it great?"

"It's off the wall."

"No, it's not. I've got weld numbers, photomicrographs, letters back and forth, all the shit. I'm making it public. If *The New York Times* won't print it, I'll give it to the devil himself. Drew, honey, I want those fuckers to fry."

"Sweet Jesus, why didn't you tell me?"

"I was under orders not to. It's been a big secret," she said quietly. "Anyway, I was afraid you'd talk me out of it." She looked at her hands in her lap, a thinker's pose. "There's something else. I'm gonna move to Nederland for a few months. Till everything calms down."

"That's the first smart thing you've said. Forget this union crap." He watched as she withdrew the last cigarette from a pack. "It'll do you good to spend some time with your family."

"Yeah," she said, but she seemed to be thinking of her other family, the three kids left behind. Christmas was coming; that was always the worst time. "But I'll be back," she said. "Maybe by spring." She smiled. "For autocross."

He kissed her and smiled too. But as their plane touched down in the cold of Oklahoma City he thought that spring seemed a faraway time.

This was Tuesday night. "You want to bunk in with me?" Drew tried to make it sound like a special invitation, even though he knew full well Karen's answer. Where else could she go? Her apartment was still under quarantine.

Everything in the bungalow was familiar—the tired furniture, the wall papered with race cars, the Goodyear tire—everything, it seemed, but her own face. Standing on tiptoes she examined herself for reassurance in the bathroom mirror, pressing so close the glass fogged in a damp circle. In the bedroom she set out for the morning a black turtleneck, plaid slacks, a silver necklace. The necklace was a favorite. It had shiny tendrils in rainbow colors, all the more shiny because of how her fingers exercised them whenever she was nervous or excited.

In the living room, at the carpeted bar, Karen measured out a shot of Smirnoff for her Bloody Mary mix. Upon consideration, she added a second shot. She was so tightly wound she needed the liquor for sleep.

OKLAHOMA CITY. NOVEMBER 13, 1974. An invisible morning sun gave the Wednesday horizon a sheen like the lining in an abalone. The air was deceptively warm. Karen put on her leather coat, a coat for early autumn. Another round of contract talks was scheduled for today, and she felt obliged to attend. If all went well the contract might be settled in time for holiday turkey in Nederland.

"Can you come to a union meeting at five-thirty?" Jack Tice asked over vending-machine coffee. "I've reserved the back room at the Hub."

"I was planning to do something else," Karen said.

"You're our health-and-safety expert. It'd be good for you to report on that part of the negotiations."

"Okay, let me make one call first."

Drew answered in a cavalier way, mocking the strain and strangeness of the past week. "Hi, babe! Wanna go hootin' and hollerin' tonight?"

"Drew, I gotta ask a favor. Wodka and this newspaperman are coming into Will Rogers at six or six-thirty, but I have to be at the Hub. I thought maybe you could go pick them up?" She waited for him to agree, but silence had reclaimed him. His pride was hurt, no doubt. She said, "I'm sorry I didn't tell you about this before. The whole deal, I mean."

"It's okay, it's okay," he reassured her with his old affection. "Drew's Chauffeuring & Catering is at your service."

"Thank you, Drew. I love you."

"Don't get sappy. I'm gonna charge the union for my gas."

Karen walked back to the negotiations room with a security guard trailing one step behind. The man had been assigned to watch her. This being her first day at Cimarron since the contaminations, her bosses had gone to the trouble, or so they said, of giving her the best protection they could. Her boots clacked staccato down the hallway floor as she hurried back, and the guard broke into a little trot too.

Morgan Moore, the Cimarron manager, was heading the company's negotiating team. From across the table Karen looked Moore in the eye, her face cold with distaste. The distaste was mutual. For some hours, until midafternoon, they went round and round on the 5–283 proposal for a health-and-safety committee. To the union's mind (that is, Karen's) the final word on the status of gloveboxes, respirators, emergency bells and the like should reside in this committee. But Moore was having none of it.

"It's criminal not to have a health-and-safety committee," Karen said.

"You're one to talk."

"What kind of crack is that?"

"Never mind. I'm not gonna quibble with you."

In an earlier conversation with the AEC inspectors Moore had been a good deal more blunt. It was his opinion that Karen was a zealot and a scheming actress. He had suggested to the inspectors that her contaminations might have been self-inflicted, perhaps to embarrass the company.

When negotiations adjourned for the day, there were two security men waiting to take Karen to the annex, separated by a short walk from the main plutonium building. The inspectors had been mulling over Moore's accusation. Had Karen heard of anyone sneaking plutonium out of Cimarron past the sensors? they asked. Had she ever done anything like that herself?

"No," she replied, quite emphatic. "If somebody's been stealing plutonium, it's not me."

Their interrogation was short, but it made her late for the Hub Cafe. Before joining the meeting she paused to call Drew. "Don't forget about going to the airport."

"I got it covered. You all right?"

"I'm fine," she said. "No, I'm better than that. Let's go hop some bars tonight, just you and me, like you said. After we take care of business—okay?"

"Sure. If you can handle it? How's your cough?" he asked, testing. "Drew's Chauffeuring & Catering can come get you too if you want."

"No, you go to the airport," she ordered. "I'll see you at the Holiday Inn."

The dozen or so Cimarron workers who had dragged into the Hub could smell a simmering pot of beef stew in the kitchen, which made them more anxious to get to suppers at home. Karen walked quickly past the cafe booths and tables and eased through a thin partition into the back room. On evenings when the Crescent Boosters or Kiwanians used the room it would be festooned like a private club. But without a flag or epigram, which were not in 5–283's budget, this rudimentary space was as inspirational as a monastic cell.

Jack Tice was trying in his own way to manufacture some esprit. "This year, if we go on strike, this year the front gate stays shut. Are you with me?" His voice pitched higher and higher, eliciting a short listless chorus of "Strike! Strike!"

Karen stood up and added a few words about Morgan Moore's rejection of the health-and-safety committee. From an adjacent table Mrs. Jung noticed that Karen had in her hands a manila folder and a russet notebook. She was hanging on to them as if they were the Scriptures. The meeting broke up around seven. Karen took a pasty white pill from her purse and gulped down a half-glass of tea in which the ice had melted. "Yecch!" she spat.

She came over and put a considerate arm around Jean Jung. "How're you doing? They haven't got you in respirators this week, do they?"

"No, it's been a good one so far." Mrs. Jung felt touched by the young woman's kindness. "How about you?"

"I'm not sure. Somebody's got it in for me, Jean. The way I got dosed was no accident. Somebody's out to get me." The light cast her shadow on a thin wall that had probably been built in one afternoon. "But those inspectors act like I did it to myself."

"That's the government for you. A pack of re-tards. Don't they know your place is ruint? And didn't you get about sick to death?"

"You're such a good friend, Jean, you really are. We ought to have you in on the negotiations too. All us ladies should be in there."

Mrs. Jung grinned and began moving for home—she had a daughter to feed. But Karen wasn't through. "See this?" With a finger Karen tapped the manila folder and the notebook. "Kerr-McGee is gonna get one big fat surprise. I got it right here. I hope to hell some of them end up in jail." A bright compulsion was on Karen's face. She had changed her mind about trying to stay anonymous. In her purse was a snapshot of herself, removed this morning from its place in Drew's bedroom. Karen intended to give the picture and her name to the *Times*.

Tice was lingering with two other men in front of the Hub, and as the ladies departed he hollered out, "Thanks for coming." Karen waved. "Need a ride?" one of the men asked.

"No thanks," Karen said. "I got my car."

She ran over to it. Inhospitable clouds obscured the last of the sun. A wind flew up, catching her hair, lifting the dark strands to reveal a ghostly silver necklace under a chin set firm and stubborn.

Wodka was nervous; irritated too. The Holiday Inn Northwest had lost his reservation and given away his room. He would have to bunk the night with Burnham. Burnham had a room, but the phone in it was dead. Slamming the beige instrument back into its holster, Wodka left to prowl for a pay booth.

The lobby downstairs is a wide Western court rich in dark wood and hearthstones and scarlet wallpaper. Wodka did not find a phone, but he ran into Gerald Phillip of the AEC. "It's the screwiest thing," Phillip said in a troubled tone. "How does plutonium get inside a refrigerator?"

Wodka said he didn't know and asked whether the inspectors were finding time to investigate the thirty-nine health-and-safety complaints from Karen's original list. "That's gonna take a while," Phillip said. "One thing at a time."

Back in Burnham's room the line issued a weak click and finally came clear. Wodka rang up Tice. "Do you know where Karen is?"

"Yes. I just talked to the police. . . ."

Within an hour the three men who had waited for her—Wodka, Burnham, Drew—were at the culvert on Highway 74. Karen had traveled seven miles from the Hub, a ten-minute drive. Her car had run off the road within sight of a landmark that sat on a low knoll under a floodlight aurora. Workers on the afternoon shift would be out soon. They would get into their cars, grind away at their starter motors, make eddies in the gravel under their wheels, and tool down Highway 74, down past the creek where rabbits often came to drink.

Paul Wayne Williamson, a graduate of the same high school class as Karen, was now a dispatcher for the Nederland Police Department. He was on duty when the teletype machine sounded three bells.

Karen's parents were at home watching television. Mr. Silkwood opened the door for the policeman. The policeman had a catch in his throat. A bad cold perhaps? "Sir," he said, "your daughter—uh, Karen—she's been in an accident."

Mr. Silkwood was gruff. "You sure you got the right girl? Our Karen lives in Oklahoma."

"Yes, sir. A Mr. Roy King—he's with Kerr-McGee—has been to the hospital and identified the body."

Rosemary rushed over as soon as she heard. Mrs. Silkwood stretched out her arms. A low moan, beginning in her throat, rose into a caterwauling scream that broke into sobs. "Karen told me she was going to be all right. She told me! She told me!" Mrs. Silkwood moved across the room, stumbling, her eyes closed, as good as blind, not saying anything more for a long, sad time.

Mr. Silkwood cursed phones and airline reservation clerks: Connections from tiny Nederland to Oklahoma City were not at all suited for his urgency. He could have driven to Houston in the morning and left from there, but his thinking was blurred. Instead he flipped to Western Union's number in the phone book. A funeral home in Guthrie subsequently received a telegram. "REQUEST AUTOPSY STOP DO NOT EMBALM." It came from the grief of a father and was a move of unknown importance, but years later the autopsy report would become part of a courtroom drama as odd and tumultuous as the death it analyzed.

KILGORE. NOVEMBER 17, 1974. Grandma Biggs had tried to reach Karen while she was still in Los Alamos. "Come down to the farm," Grandma had wanted to say. "Get out of the city, take your mind off all that nonsense. Come currycomb the white Angus and clean the rabbit pens."

Karen's final trip to northern Texas was in an unmarked cortege, back to the big, undiscriminating land that so often had given her peace. She was buried in a plot with Grandpa Biggs, dead a year, under sheltering oak and sumac in a little cemetery outside Kilgore.

The funeral was Sunday. There were few mourners. Mr. Silkwood kept a watch for someone from Kerr-McGee, but no one appeared. The undertaker had done excellent work with his cosmetics. None of the violence that had brought Karen here showed in her face, which seemed fresh and direct as always. Against the white pillow her coloring was vibrant. Light fell warmly on highboned cheeks. Karen's dress was new, from Texas; all her Oklahoma dresses were in the yellow barrels in Kerr-McGee's warehouse.

Among the gravestones across the way an old man was raking leaves. A Baptist minister read some words, and the gravediggers lowered a concrete slab with a dry, grating sound over the metal coffin. Red-brown dirt became the mantle.

Mrs. Silkwood knelt. The smell of unsettled earth mingled with the decaying fragrance of floral sprays. Because of the distance from Nederland to Kilgore, her future visits to the cemetery could not be as often as she would wish. She reached among the spilled petals and took up a flowerpot of lavender and yellow mums. How would the mums look planted in the backyard? Perhaps she could find a corner with half-sun, half-shade, not too far from Frito's cage. Flowers and a racoon, she thought—what else was there to remember Karen by? Not much had survived the past few days. Karen's car was junk, her apartment denuded as if she had never existed. Kerr-McGee had taken her letters, yearbooks, photographs, almost all her cherished memorabilia.

From Kilgore the Silkwood family drove north to Oklahoma City to recover what they could. At the medical examiner's office they were given Karen's ID badge, a Mickey Mouse pocket watch, seven dollars in bills, a dollar sixty-nine in change. A Kerr-McGee HP had saved from the barrels a pair of uncontaminated slacks, a few blouses, a set of dishes. That was it, except for what Drew had. More clothes, the wrecked Honda, her dirt bike. Also, her prized autocross trophy: a golden winged goddess on a pedestal of nursery-pink imitation marble. The inscription at the base in shiny bronze read "Fast Ladies Gymkhana—First Place."

"You might as well keep it. The car too," Mr. Silkwood said in a detached tone. He was standing uncomfortably between a dentist's chair and a Goodyear tire. Rosemary also was having trouble standing —it appeared she might faint—and Drew anxiously gave her a chair and a glass of water. Rosemary was definitely younger, with rounder cheeks and somewhat bigger bones, but in a shaft of afternoon sun her resemblance to Karen was obvious: the same remarkable dark hair, silky skin, strong nose, narrow waist.

Drew had not gone to Kilgore for the burial. Some time ago, in a mood common to lovers very young and very old, he and Karen had made a pact not to observe the formalities of death. However forlorn and doomed their memories might be, no preacher could change them.

But maybe I should have been there, he thought now, just to make her family feel better. "If you'd like I'll see if she left any odds and ends. Oh, yeah, there's a little Instamatic that she bought in Los Alamos. Would you like it?"

"Yes, thank you."

In the bedroom he rummaged through Karen's half of the dresser. He had seen the camera sitting on top with a spent roll of film. But now he couldn't find it among the unopened bills and old cosmetics. He tried the floor. Dust balls flew up and landed in new crannies. There was nothing else to see. The camera was gone.

It was meager booty for a thief, and its disappearance was a minor incident in a month filled with the bizarre, but Drew made a note, adding the incident to a list of "strange happenings." Foremost among these happenings was a brief unfulfilled foray by George Martin on the night of the accident. Martin was a tow-truck operator, the guy usually called upon in Logan County after six o'clock in the evening. The Code Two call that evening came in about eight. It started out as routine. Martin fell in behind the Guthrie ambulance, behind its clamoring siren, but halfway there something strange happened. He was radioed off and Ted Sebring was called to haul the wreck away. Why the switch? Was it to buy time, as Wodka suspected—time for someone to make off with Karen's manila folder and rust-colored notebook? Neither the folder nor the notebook had been in the Pennzoil box Sebring turned over the next afternoon.

Wodka had asked Drew to keep an account of every stray clue, every skittish rumor that might interest the FBI. Since the Oklahoma Highway Patrol seemed so lazy, Wodka and Mazzocchi were trying to interest the federal police. A good idea, Drew thought: professionals should be called in. And if there was anything he could do, he was ready and available. He had taken a leave of absence from the body shop. The bulk of his time he now spent trying to assemble the pieces of the life Karen had led after her trip to Washington, the life she had led to her death. Drew wanted mightily to do something, anything, though nothing he did was a cure for the torment at the back of his mind or for the shadows in the corner of a room that would catch him unaware.

Every night he phoned a motel in New Jersey or Louisiana or wherever Wodka was encamped. Tonight it was New Jersey.

"I can't imagine why, but somebody ripped off Karen's camera," Drew reported.

"Any sign of a break-in?"

"Nah. But, hell, I'm always leaving my front door open. Nobody has locks out here."

"You better get one."

"I just put in the best that TG&Y sells, a huge dead-bolt."

The camera reminded Wodka of the missing folder and notebook that had also disappeared, a mystery never long out of his thoughts. He said, "Remember what you told me about Karen going back to her apartment that night after the quarantine?"

Drew managed a wry smile. "Her back door was unlocked—that's how she got in."

"I realize Kerr-McGee carted away everything they could get their hands on. But I've been wondering: did Karen have a hiding place they might have overlooked? Where she might have kept special things?"

"Like a trapdoor? Jeez, let me think." Drew was lost in a tunnel of older thoughts, older times. "You know, you're right. There's a crawl space in the bedroom closet. Above the ceiling. Karen showed it to me once. She figured it'd be the place to hide her dope if a bust came down."

"That's got to be it. She must've kept the folder there, and she must've gone back to get it."

"I remember her telling me that they didn't get her 'stuff.' That must be what she meant."

"For all the good it does us now." Wodka had an inclination to kick the motel walls until the plasterboard swayed and burst, crumbling to pieces. If Karen really had proof, what had happened to it? "We know she went back to the apartment," he said, repeating himself. "Okay, let's say she grabbed whatever documents she had. That was the night of the seventh. The next day we did that long interview with Phillip and then you guys went off to Los Alamos. She must've found a new hiding place for those days. Stashed the documents somewhere, and retrieved them again on the thirteenth. Because Mrs. Jung says Karen had the folder with her at the Hub. Up to that point everything makes sense. But then what? I can't quite believe that cop, Fagan—saying he picked the papers out of the mud and threw them in the car and watched them go off to Sebring's garage. I mean, who would have known enough to go and steal them out of the garage?"

A. O. Pipkin had already called in his report to Wodka and Mazzocchi. But before submitting it in writing he wanted a second opinion. For that purpose Dr. B. J. Harris traveled from Dallas to Oklahoma City. He reinspected the Honda and revisited the accident scene and double-checked Pipkin's diagrams and slide-rule calculations. The conclusion of Dr. Harris, a structural engineer, was the same: namely, that Karen had been the victim of a strange hit-and-run.

Out by the culvert Mr. Silkwood found a road crew working on Highway 74. A tractor-grader had sliced soil and dead grass from the highway shoulder, obliterating the Honda tracks. The culvert wing-walls now jutted above the skinned earth, stark like a tombstone.

A steamroller was repaving the road's west half. It was strange, because all the remodeling was being done in the few miles on either side of the culvert. The steamroller had altered the slant of the pavement, smoothed the road crown, made it flat as gravity.

"Regular maintenance," a police lieutenant said when Mr. Silkwood asked.

"What if the FBI wants to take measurements? Isn't evidence being destroyed?"

"No, sir, I wouldn't call it that." The lieutenant showed a small trace of exasperation, but pity overcame it. The man standing before him was surely a good American. His appearance testified to that— the rustic, muscular face, the girth overflowing his belt, big hands that seemed sad and clumsy without a tool. You had to feel sorry for him, hundreds of miles from home, his eyes washed-out and empty, unable to sleep because he had yet to accept his girl's being dead under these circumstances.

The lieutenant felt a helpless kind of pity. Probably any father would be doing this, but he wished he could urge Mr. Silkwood toward home. Before someone in Oklahoma let out something they shouldn't. It was a shame, a damn shame. Mr. Silkwood was after the truth; but from what the lieutenant had heard, the dark, terrible truth would break the man's heart.

Hiding as best they could in the Sprite, which was tiny and a brilliant red, tomato-red, Drew and Rosemary held hands. They were watching a phone booth. Inside the booth, to the bottom of a triangular ledge, Drew had taped an envelope with photographs of the Honda.

Karen had been dead two weeks, and this still was very much a time of uncertainty—Drew might be next—and Wodka had instructed him not to put himself in danger, to be cool and casual and keep a low profile. Somehow that had been translated into this spy-book delivery. The envelope was for the *Daily Oklahoman*. A copyboy was supposed to pick it up.

The time dragged, as it always did now, and Drew reached under the seat for the feel of his new .38 Special Chief, loaded and ready. His nerves were shot. And why shouldn't they be? Ever since that night, that awful night, he felt sure he was being watched and followed. Maybe he was just imagining it. But maybe not. A week or so ago one of Tice's union buddies had been chased at awesome speeds by some sort of heavyweight vehicle, chased madly down Highway 74. And poor Sherri—on her first night in her new apartment burglars had broken in and ransacked the few things she had left. The cops only shrugged. Drew sure as hell wasn't counting on them. The power of .38 slugs you could count on. You could feel the shiver of the saplings where the bullets hit in target practice. Perhaps the feeling of power, like the gun itself, could be turned against you, but wasn't it better than the other feelings—those sick feelings, the nausea, the wet on his ribs, the pulsing at the back of his head that tried to crush his brain?

Nothing in his face ever revealed the inner pain. Rosemary was the only one who seemed to notice it. She had stayed behind when Mr. and Mrs. Silkwood and Linda left town; she was staying at Drew's bungalow, held there in exile by thoughts of what might have been, or should have been. Late into the night Rosemary would sometimes sit in the sanctuary of the dentist's chair, rocking her shoulders like Karen, her voice like falling feathers. "I should have come when Karen asked. She was an angel to me. The best big sister in the whole world."

Yeah, Drew would agree. I should've done more for Karen, too, he thought. I should've made her quit. She should've been baking pies, yeah, and singing to her kids. If only I'd been more . . .? More what? He felt the sickness coming on again, and he concentrated harder on the gun and its cylinder of shiny brass bullets.

Cars were racketing by. "Hey, look ou—!" Drew swallowed the yell. A station wagon went racing under the stoplight's fading amber and a low-slung car jumped out ahead of the green, both in the same second. There was a loud freight-yard sound, then a funny quiet. The silence shriveled Drew's stomach and set his heart pounding. The cars had met and were joined in the gutter next to the booth. One driver struggled to the phone. A traffic cop came and made a call. Drew and Rosemary crouched lower. Could they be arrested for "improper use of a phone booth"? But the police and the crippled cars departed, leaving behind only a pudgy pedestrian. He rubbed his back against the booth and sent it into spasms. Finally the copyboy approached. He circled the booth twice, worried his hands, looked sideways, reached in, and tore loose the tape.

Back at the bungalow Drew and Rosemary laughed—laughed at themselves, at their ludicrous, artificial drama. They couldn't remember ever being moved to such laughter.

"Did you see that guy itching himself?" Drew hunched his back in mimicry.

"Like an old cow. I thought he was gonna knock the thing over."

"What a comedy. Better than TV."

"The way that copyboy went around and around. I nearly died holding my breath."

"You were wonderful, Karen."

"I'm *Rosemary*." Her laughter drained away.

"Christ, I'm sorry," Drew said. He took her hand. From irregular eating, her cheeks had thinned in attractive melancholy, and when her index finger was poised for emphasis, she might have been Karen come back to life. "I'm sorry," he said again, but it was an image he couldn't suppress.

A TV news helicopter chuk-chukked overhead. Except for the sparkling skies, a deviation necessary for the aerial cameras, the conditions along Highway 74 seemed to match up pretty close to those on the evening of November 13. There was a slight blow out of the northwest. The pavement was dry as chalk.

A white Honda identical to Karen's and an ABC network truck caravaned to a spot a half-mile north of the culvert. The man in the Honda was a former race driver. He accelerated to fifty miles an hour, the approximate speed at which Karen had left the road; then, about a hundred yards from the culvert, he let go of the wheel like a driver asleep. Fifteen times he repeated the simulation, and fifteen times the Honda followed the slope of the shoulder and angled lazily into a pasture, as A. O. Pipkin had said it would. But fourteen times it went left, across the road crown, contrary to Pipkin's theory. The slant of the crown did not keep the car on the right half of the highway.

Not until the ABC newspeople were back in New York did they realize why. The pavement Karen had traveled, the pavement Pipkin had measured, was not the pavement the ABC cameras had filmed. The helicopter footage showed how the highway had been repaved and the road crown flattened.

OKLAHOMA CITY. DECEMBER 8, 1974. Jack Taylor of the *Oklahoman* was an investigative scourge, arguably the best reporter in the state. Assigned to an influence-peddling affair or a realty-kickback scheme, he routinely brought about resignations, indictments, prison terms. But the case of Karen Silkwood was not one of his successes, as he conceded in the first paragraph of his Sunday-morning article:

> Investigations into a series of radiation contamination incidents and into the death of the central figure in the incidents may never resolve some crucial questions. . . . The most difficult of all is how plutonium, one of the world's most dangerous substances, could have left a Kerr-McGee factory undetected and reached an Edmond apartment.

Even so, Taylor did have one scoop. He had talked with someone inside Kerr-McGee about the thinking going on there. Although the Kerr-McGee higher-ups were rejecting all questions about the case, Taylor knew his way around the Skirvin Plaza, the Sheraton, the Quail Creek Country Club and other prime watering holes. Over a dimly lit drink, a brash junior executive had described the company's reaction. "All we have to do now is get rid of the rest of the trouble-makers," the exec had said with colicky good humor. He had described a plan whereby Kerr-McGee would find an excuse to close Cimarron temporarily while lie-detector tests were put to the workers. "Then we'll tool back up slowly and hire people who are trustworthy and aren't involved in the union." As for the hotheads of 5–283? "You don't have to tell them anything. You can just say, 'You didn't clear security.' "

Taylor's scoop, however, wasn't printed in the *Oklahoman*. Taylor and his editors believed the exec was blowing smoke. With an employee dead, and Christmas at hand, it didn't seem like the time for the company to try to break the union.

PART TWO

Six

Across the country it could not properly be said that the Silkwood case was forgotten. The case, a mystery of many parts, had not become known, not in any real way. The *Times* gave it attention for a while, because of David Burnham, but even among the people of Capitol Hill, that mighty concentration of *Times* readers, it didn't catch on. Not that Burnham was a dull writer or that more sensational writing would have mattered. This woman's death, unusual and unhappy though it may have been, was a statistic of Oklahoma. Geography condemned it. *The Washington Post*, flush with Watergate, mentioned it only in passing, as did most of the other media giants. Oh, there was some parochial interest. The two U.S. senators from Oklahoma, Henry Bellmon and Dewey Bartlett, thought it might be worth investigating—investigating Burnham, that is. The senators did not like what his articles implied about Kerr-McGee.

Their little witch hunt, which amounted to a few speeches, was in a sense Burnham's highest compliment. He tried for higher. He tried hard to solve the case—all of it, any of it. Without being asked, he came early to his desk and stayed late; he let his coffee go cold, spent hours on the phone. From the D.C. bureau he wrote of the case as long as there was anything to write. Then he asked to be sent back to Oklahoma. But the request was put aside by his editors, and eventually so was the case.

On the Hill, in a certain congressional office, the coffee smelled hot. A pair of old skates lay under a desk in a tangle of laces and freshly sharpened blades. Their owner, Peter Stockton, was a moonlighting hockey goalie: for fun and bruises. He also had ten years behind him as a government investigator. A dimpled, slightly creased face, brown unstyled hair, a barbershop cut usually overdue—Stockton gave the appearance of a family man with four kids. He was that too.

He put down his copy of the *Times*. Not even the sports pages distracted him this morning. "Hey, Stockton, what's bugging you?" It was another investigator, one of his counterparts from the Joint Committee on Atomic Energy, stopping by for coffee. The man helped himself to a cup. "Listen," he said. "I've been scoping out that Silkwood case. Believe me, the lady was a real mess, a weirdo. Do yourself a favor, Stockton, and forget it."

"Thanks," Stockton said. He looked up with real interest. "You just made up my mind."

Later he put in a call to the AEC. On the strength of his boss's name, Congressman John Dingell, twenty years on the Hill, Stockton was granted an appointment. Taking along a congressional aide, he drove to the AEC offices in his yellow VW, rattling past the slower cars. A junior official greeted them, and striding ahead briskly, arms stiff with authority, he made sure they got to the correct inner sanctum. Six men stood in welcome. It is often a practice of bureaucrats to present themselves in a group, as if greater numbers somehow adds to their arguments, but to gather up six men, all from the top rank of the AEC, just for a briefing—that was overdoing it. Damn unusual, Stockton thought—an opinion privately recorded.

"You must be Mr. Stockton. Glad to meet you." The AEC officials were at his service, eager to prove themselves as his benefactors. In a room hung with pictures of past nuclear achievements, a room now of modern headaches, they made Stockton feel an insider: honored chair, open chatter, a rolled-up-sleeves mood. Do they think I'm one of their cocktail crowd? Stockton wondered. He wasn't—he drank beer.

The briefing was thorough. The AEC men spoke openly. They spoke of things that might have been more appropriate over martinis, if appropriate anywhere. Apparently they didn't want Stockton to think they were holding anything back. With heads down, almost in unison, they told him what they knew about Karen. "She was really offbeat." "A little kinky." "A pervert." "A wacko."

"I guess you've done your homework," Stockton said. "But, well, I don't need to know about her sex life." The rebuke sounded mild. As a habit he is unemotional and easygoing—a calculating throwaway style that often gives his targets the illusion that they're in control.

"I'm telling you," an AEC man said, "she was one screwed-up girl. Came here and told us nonsense; told even worse to Mazzocchi and Wodka. Still don't understand why they were so gullible. But then, she did have her ways with men. Women, too. If you follow my meaning?"

"Well, I guess so. But I think I'm missing the point."

"The point is her reliability. You can't expect someone like her to be reliable. It's just too bad she was able to raise the ruckus she did. We wouldn't want you to make the same mistake Mazzocchi and Wodka did." The AEC men all nodded, smugly patronizing. They seemed to have worked on their routine. "Don't get us wrong. We're not moralizing. But this girl was way out, as you can obviously appreciate. I mean, who are you going to believe? A four-square corporation like Kerr-McGee? Or some kook?"

In their show of openness Stockton sensed the opposite at work. It was all the fussing, the exhorting, that made him suspicious.

The next afternoon, reporting to Congressman Dingell, he was able to inspire a sort of congressional investigation, albeit the most indirect sort. Dingell agreed to refer the Silkwood case to the General Accounting Office (GAO), which is a repository for complicated, unpopular problems. A few days earlier, as it happened, Winston Turner had also forwarded the case to the GAO. Turner was chief counsel for Senator Lee Metcalf. Turner didn't know Stockton, but like Stockton, he was a man with a great defiant curiosity. Elsewhere on the Hill, the men and women who had never broken from regular business continued with it. If anyone asked about Karen, the GAO had them covered.

Stockton was at home in suburban D.C. From an adjoining room came the noise and delight of kids playing with still-new Christmas presents. It started him thinking about his departure. The thoughts were a reflex; he had been all through the decision.

Trained as an economist, Stockton had made a career of finding mistakes and corruption in areas where millions, sometimes billions of dollars are at stake, for the Budget Bureau, the Joint Economic Committee, the House Banking and Currency Committee. He could whiz through government accounting sheets, zeroing right in on the discrepancies. In another circumstance, though, he might have been a gold-shield detective. The hunt for answers, not just numbers, was what excited him. It made for a quixotic streak in him, like an exclamation point in a column of figures, and it was linked with an even stronger stubborn streak. So when he informed his friends he was taking a sabbatical and going to Oklahoma—in the dead of winter—they knew it would do no good to tell him he was out of his mind. (That did not stop them, though. "You don't need to go out there to get yourself in trouble. We can get you into plenty here.") But Stockton's decision to go, tossed about for days, had become firm a week before. Barbara Newman, a reporter for National Public Radio, an ace reporter, had bought him lunch in the fancy dining room of Jacqueline's. Barbara Newman had some news. She was sharing it with Stockton, ahead of the rest of the country, because she also had a proposition.

First the news. "I called Westinghouse," Newman said. "There's a new twist." She had chess player's eyes and a fondness for bright lipstick. Her manner was abrupt.

"Go on," Stockton said.

"I guess you know Westinghouse is working on the fast-breeder in Hanford—the actual construction. Well, I got through to Ersell Evans, one of their veeps. Guess what? Kerr-McGee has been having trouble with its inventory. According to Evans, forty-four pounds of plutonium are unaccounted for."

Stockton understood the implications. As little as ten pounds of plutonium will suffice for a crude bomb; this was four bombs. "Dingell has to be told," he said.

"Go ahead, but Dingell will only kick it over to the GAO, and who knows how long that'll take? Look, if you're really serious about this case, why don't you go out to Oklahoma with me next week? Take a leave of absence. We can do the case top to bottom. C'mon, you're always complaining that reporters get all the good assignments."

"I've never said that." He had laughed.

But with a grant from the Fund for Investigative Journalism, he was about to buy a plane ticket. The scoffing from his friends made the decision all the easier.

OKLAHOMA CITY. JANUARY 2, 1975. After the gossipy, glad-handing style of the Hill, Stockton had to adjust to "out there." The way he saw the big holy prairie city was not how Karen had seen it. It was practically empty. Except for the breakfast buffet of sausages and pork chops at the Skirvin Plaza (where Stockton and Newman took rooms), the downtown held little enticement. Sidewalks were treacherous from patches of ice left for nature to remove, and the restaurants closed at dusk. Also, the bars were not really bars at all; they were membership clubs. To drink liquor you have to pay yearly dues for a decanter kept in storage; then you rent a bar glass at your club. Almost everyone is in the habit of ignoring the law, but this was an election year and lately the police had been active. Bartenders were selling a lot of beer, which is the only drink regularly legal. Stockton felt strange sitting in smoke and furnace-heat with everybody drinking his drink. He wasn't part of this crowd either and didn't wish to pretend.

At the Skirvin, in his room, he was going one by one through a directory of Cimarron workers, phoning them up. Their responses took him by surprise. At the mention of Karen's name, he got unrehearsed excuses and other ungallantries.

The problem was that a week before Christmas, these workers had been thrown out of work, at least temporarily. "You want to know why? I'll tell you why," Jack Tice said when Stockton called. "It's union-busting." Five workers had been contaminated on the job— but their supervisors said it was a deliberate masochistic act—and for this ostensible reason Cimarron had been shut down. Everyone was being sent instead to a room with a Stoelting Deceptograph. "Lie-detector tests," Tice said. "They got us over a barrel. We can't go back to work till we take a lie-detector test. We got to pass a security clearance."

Initially, after Karen's death, several workers had chipped in for a special grave marker. But now the mood had reversed—the collection was being refunded. The shutdown had reminded them of what it was like to stand in unemployment lines, and they had taken to blaming the dead. "Damn right I'm bitter," said one worker. He had been at the factory four years. "You'd be bitter too if you had to scratch to make your payments every month. You people come in here and raise hell, but we're the ones who get it in the neck. Karen Silkwood was just as bad. If she'd of kept her nose to herself, she'd still be alive. And we'd still be working. There's a name for people who don't mind their own business. I won't say it, but there's a name."

Stockton had not known what to expect, but he hadn't expected Karen to be so disagreeably remembered. "Wasn't she doing worthwhile things? Didn't she try to alert everybody to the danger of cancer?" he asked.

"Don't talk to me about that. That's twenty years down the road. Right now, my family's got to eat, and Logan County is the poorest county in the whole damn state."

Stockton shut his notebook and went down the hall to knock on Newman's door. She opened it, stretching the phone cord to its limit. She was having no better luck. "Want to get a beer?" he asked.

"I bought some California wine. It's not bad." She unwrapped a glass from its swathing of plastic and poured in the topaz color. It helped lift his depression. Glass in hand, he walked back to make more calls.

Seated in a booth, Stockton took a good look at the Hub Cafe. There were half a dozen booths, a line of round stools, a Formica counter. A hollow unvarnished door closed off the back room, but he could hear overwrought voices through the flimsy wood. He ordered tea for Newman and a milkshake for himself and waited for the 5–283 meeting to end.

The shouting stopped, and white light broke through the door, catching the orange of the Formica. A dozen workers came barging out. "Got a minute?" Stockton asked. He stood, blocking one man's way. It did him no good. The man's shoulder flung Stockton aside. "Forget it," Newman called out. But Stockton was out the door, huffing after the interview as if after a hockey puck.

"Buddy, you can go straight to hell." The man had one foot into his pickup, a wide-body machine that accommodated his size; he was a behemoth. He opened the door, using it as a wedge. There was a rifle on a rack across the rear window.

"This'll just take a few minutes," Stockton said stubbornly.

The man spun around, his voice grown to a bellow. "Get the hell out! You and your jackal pack. Or you're gonna get your ass shot off!"

The engine's roar filled the street. Stockton headed back to the cafe. He was in good shape from hockey winters and softball summers, which was fortunate, because he had to lunge sideways, barely in time to avoid two tons of truck.

Against the black sky the windows in the old house were golden chinks of lamplight. Stockton and Newman unlatched a gate in the wrought-iron fence and went up the porch steps and knocked. The lights indicated a presence inside, but no one came. They walked around to the back and rapped on the kitchen door. Only then did Tice give them entry. "I've had my fill of trouble," Tice said, by way of apology. The house was large and shingled; it held everything dear to him. He pulled down the shades as a precaution, and the kitchen took on the look of a cave.

"Ain't this a hell of a thing?" Tice held out a typed sheet. "This is their so-called *security clearance* test." The typing was rough, capitals leaping above the other letters. He had composed it from talks with the workers who had submitted to the Deceptograph. They were being asked a number of odd questions.

> Have you ever talked to Karen Silkwood? To Drew Stephens? To Steve Wodka? To Ilene Younghein? To the news media?
> Are you a member of the union?
> Have you been involved with anti-company or anti-nuclear activities?
> Have you ever had an affair with another employee? Do you know anyone who has?

"What's any of this got to do with security, I'd like to know," Tice demanded. "Maybe I'm not the most educated guy in the world, but it seems like we ought to be able to talk to who we want. Isn't it in the Constitution?"

"Mazzocchi would know what your rights are better than us. Or a lawyer," Stockton said.

"We've got a lawyer. Mazzocchi got us a good one. But lawyers jest throw paper back and forth like cusswords. It don't mean a good goddamn. Meanwhile, the company keeps slapping us down in that lie-detector contraption."

"What happened when *you* took it?"

"I didn't take it," Tice said. "Wild horses won't make me. I object on principle." In particular he objected to the question about Mrs. Younghein. Tice cared deeply about the factory environment and was, in strict terms, an environmentalist, but for all that he was still leery about being known as a Sierra Club lover.

Tice moved to a window and pulled back the curtain for a quick peek. He said, "Kerr-McGee has got us playing musical chairs.

Everybody's shoving everybody else out of the way to save themselves. Divide and conquer, that's what they're doing. Jim Reading's the one behind it. He's the one drew up these questions. You should watch him operate at Cimarron. He's got his own personal stooges. He can start a rumor at the front and it don't take ten minutes for it to get to the back. He had rumors about Karen flying fast and furious —she wasn't even buried."

"What can you tell us about what Karen was doing?" Stockton asked.

"Well," Tice said. He knew they had come to talk about Karen, not the security test, but his disappointments and resentments kept feeding each other. "We're not gonna strike, you know. The membership ratified the contract yesterday. Even though it don't gain us one iota in health and safety." His face was swamped with defeat. "Course, health and safety ain't worth spit if you don't have a job." He had not moved from the window; he might have been talking to himself.

"What sort of documents did Karen have in that folder?" Stockton probed.

Tice left the window for a chair. "I know she had the goods on what a sloppy ship the place is. She knew something about them faking records, too. I don't know what else. That part of her project was secret."

"So you never actually saw her documents?"

"Not actually." Tice's face clouded. His tumble of short exact phrases came to a halt. From his brief experience with reporters, he did not trust them. They seemed to favor the company, as if everything it said were gospel. These two strangers from National Public Radio had pushed their way into his home—why should he confide in them? He sighed, though he was not the sighing type. "There was a woman, a union woman. She saw Karen's papers at the cafe that night," he said. "But I'm sorry, she don't want her name given out. She's scared, like everybody else." He sighed again, a dreadful sigh. If folks wanted to think that Karen's folder was a phantom, there was nothing he could do.

Stockton sat with Newman at a restaurant table and totted up their stingy encyclopedia of innuendos and gossamer facts. They had phoned thirty, maybe forty workers. They had solicited comment from townspeople, civic leaders, the police, local reporters. Interviewing George Martin, the tow-truck driver, they thought at first they were on to something. "Peculiar, damn peculiar, pulling me off that run," Martin said, "specially since it was a Code Two, which means someone was pinned inside a car."

"How long did it take for Sebring to get there? Could someone from Cimarron have gone over and grabbed Karen's folder before Sebring arrived?"

"There would've been time, yeah. But I don't think anybody did that." Martin scratched a spot on his head. He had a kind smile and considerable heft from his face down. "Most of these cops are straight —they won't shoot you in the back—and they tell me there were plenty of witnesses out at the scene. There was the truck driver who found the wreck and two riders with him and a couple passersby who stopped. Nobody from Kerr-McGee could've taken the folder without being seen."

"Why'd you get pulled off the run, then?"

"Oh, some yokel decided it was Sebring's turn to get a run, not knowing I do most all the ones in the evening. So they rousted Sebring outta his party and made him go mudding in his shiny new clothes. Just a typical screw-up."

After a week of interviews Stockton and Newman were probably the most recognized Easterners in town, but they might as well have stayed in D.C. for the little they had learned. They kept hearing about Karen's folder. But had she really had a folder? And could any of her accusations about Cimarron really be believed? Were any fuel rods defective? Were there bad welds? Had photomicrographs been falsified? Tice didn't know—he was a production man—and no one else was saying. Nor would anyone say what might have happened to the forty-four pounds of plutonium. Was it actually missing?

Back in D.C. the *Times* had published a report by Burnham that as much as sixty pounds had been misplaced or lost. Or stolen. By itself the possibility of nuclear theft might have created a sensation. But Burnham's sources were unidentified—they were AEC inspectors and the like, unwilling to go on the record—and Newman's source, the man from Westinghouse, had suddenly recanted. The story of "missing" plutonium went into the same bag as everything else, a bag of accusations, unproved. The closest Stockton and Newman came to proving the story was another story they heard from a barkeep at a roadhouse near Cimarron. The barkeep bragged about a regular customer who, on a dare, had spent a night hiding inside the factory fence while guards patrolled artlessly. Even so, smuggling out plutonium was a good deal more difficult than scaling a fence.

At the State Capitol, where Stockton and Newman also went, the politicians had been as friendly as politicians anywhere. But from politicians how much candor could you expect? All they would say about Kerr-McGee was that it had considerable gumption and civic pride. It had holdings worth more than one billion dollars. It ranked high in the *Fortune* 500 and owned parts of thirty-three states and five foreign countries. But its home was here. The company paid a heavy share of state taxes and employed several thousand Oklahomans.

The Kerr-McGee name was vestigial. For seventeen years, until his death in 1963, Robert Kerr had been Oklahoma's biggest politician. He had been the governor and a U.S. senator, and at the end of his career he was as powerful as the President—more powerful, according to some. Dean McGee had been his partner and then his successor as chairman of the board. McGee, an industrialist known for integrity and philanthropy, had stayed largely in the boardroom. But by reputation and deed both men were of the caliber that had civilized the West. The humble homes where they had grown up would someday be Oklahoma shrines. A short drive around town gave you a glimpse of the legacy to date: the Robert S. Kerr Boulevard, the Dean A. McGee Eye Institute, Kerr Park. And topmast at almost every intersection, or so it seemed, the bold K-M trademark, on gas-pump signs of red, blue and white, staking out a claim. A deskman at the Skirvin Plaza carefully cleaned his fingernails and said, "Ask anybody. Kerr-McGee runs this state." Currently in the local newspapers there was a full-page ad declaring that Dun & Bradstreet had named Kerr-McGee one of the five best-managed companies in the United States. "People here look at the Kerrs and the McGees the same way people in New York look at the Rockefellers—they look up," beamed a city councilman.

"Could you get us in to see Mr. McGee?" Newman asked.

"Oh, he never talks to the press," the councilman said, laughing at the absurdity of the ambition.

That was their largest frustration. The most inventive posturing —the loose-bull charge, the wall-eyed touristy amble—could not get either Stockton or Newman past the armed guard in the tall windowed lobby at Kerr-McGee's world headquarters. They had to settle for a phone call between Stockton and James Reading, the security chief.

Reading had authority over all security operations and reported directly to Dean McGee. He had a suite high up at headquarters, padded chairs, heavy carpeting, a view lofty but spartan. The city below was revealed mainly as gray-skinned trees and rooftops spiked with lightning rods and TV aerials.

"Understand that Barbara Newman is a tough li'l lady—got a tongue that can hammer nails," Reading said.

Stockton was aware of the overdone banter; he used it often himself. He said, "We're trying to find out about Karen Silkwood."

"I don't like to speak badly of the dead, but you got to understand about that lady. She was *no lady*. She was a good-timing girl. Liked to party and bunk around. You'd be making a mistake to take her say-so for anything."

"But she was hired for a pretty responsible position."

"That was before she got hooked into the union. They put her up to a lot of nonsense."

"Mazzocchi and Wodka say she volunteered."

"What if she did? Six of one, half-dozen of the other. She was bad as them, out to get the company. Between you and me, I could destroy her reputation flat out. Not that I want to, but I could."

"You're denying all the accusations she made?"

"Absolutely."

"But you concede that Cimarron is a dangerous place to work?"

"What's everybody so upset about? The world's overpopulated anyway." Reading let out a hearty laugh. "Hey, can't you take a joke? I swear to you, Cimarron is perfectly safe. The AEC will tell you the same thing!"

A big snow had smothered the black-and-gold countryside, barricading city streets, frosting the trees. The horizon was lost to a sky peculiarly flat and white. Into this quiet came Mr. Silkwood, and with him a suitcase, a pistol, a slow anger. And a shadow: Rosemary.

Rosemary had been back in Nederland for a month, back to the confinement of housewifely chores, but not to any peace of mind. When her father left for Oklahoma again, she had to follow him. She couldn't let anything happen to him as it had to Karen. "I'd like to make him come home, but I know he won't," she said to Drew. "Next to Karen, he's the most bullheaded one in the family."

"So what're you doing?" Drew asked.

"I sort of tag along after him. But I keep out of sight. He doesn't know I'm here."

"He'll blow a gasket when he finds out."

"Please don't tell him. I'm staying at a motel. I won't get in your way."

"You're not in the way. But—oh, hell, Rosemary don't you think it's time we all started acting normal again?" After two months of daily conferences with Wodka, rehashing and rehashing the events of last fall, Drew had gone back to work in the body shop. It was that or eat beans. He'd had to borrow six hundred bucks just to pay the phone bill.

The next day Rosemary followed her father to the culvert. She parked on a rise and watched him walk along the creek in snowbanks up to his knees. A wind was sweeping the open fields; it added to the drifts. She could not see clearly, but she could tell by the way her father stood that the distress in his heart was cold and deepening, like the snow. After he left she walked down and tried to fit her short stride into the frozen footprints. She fell and lost a glove. She was suddenly angry about her clumsiness, her father's grief, Karen's killer getting away. On the highway back to town Rosemary began to speed. A state trooper sirened her over. He gave her advice instead of a ticket, but the the rest of the ride her hands jitterbugged on the wheel.

She found Drew at the body shop. "It was a young cop, sweet-looking," she said. "He asked me what I was doing, and before I knew it I'd told him I was Karen's sister. You should have seen him jump, like I was having a baby in the car or something. 'You best get yourself to Texas and stay there'—that's what he told me." Had it been Karen interrupting his work to tell him about a policeman's tight-lipped warning, Drew would have laughed at her. But such nonchalance belonged to the past. He held Rosemary till her shaking stopped, then she went home to Texas.

At his bar Drew mixed drinks for Mr. Silkwood. The old man looked around. The last time, immediately after the funeral, he had not stayed long enough to sit down. CORVETTE: ANOTHER WINNER—a magazine proclaimed the liturgy of sports-car sales-manship. As a young man Mr. Silkwood had sold cars and later insurance, jobs he had been happy to leave. Picking up the magazine, he sat down. So this was where Karen had "shacked up." The words were of his generation, but they weren't his. Karen had said nothing to him of Drew. What he knew of "the boyfriend" came from whispers between the missus and the girls. He hadn't wanted to know more. Mr. Silkwood was not a churchgoer, but even without the faith he had a father's strictness about his daughter. Now he was glad there had been no hard words. Drew gripped his hand in understanding. They talked of Karen, keeping their emotions flat and slow like a monk's flagellation.

Back in November, over at Kerr-McGee headquarters, the company men had been solicitous. Mr. Silkwood could have a thousand-dollar check, they said, to compensate for Karen's soiled belongings, the same as they'd offered Sherri Ellis. Flushing, stammering, Mr. Silkwood had had the urge to shout. Didn't these bastards see the difference between his Karen and that other girl? Karen was dead, and he wanted an explanation. A reason. They could take their thousand dollars and shove it.

Across the street in Kerr Park he'd seen trees lit by holiday bulbs. But there had been no Christmas for him this year; not in Nederland, nor in Kilgore, where no snow had fallen to cover the bleak scar in the ground. For two months Mr. Silkwood had been shaking a bare-knuckled fist in the air and mailing letters to Kerr-McGee and to the Highway Patrol and to Congress—a waste of time. So he had come to do his own detective work.

"You should talk to Jack Tice," Drew suggested.

Mr. Silkwood rested his hand on the Goodyear tire. "I don't hold much with unions."

"No problem." Drew forced a laugh. "There's not much of a union left."

"But I thought everybody was back to work?"

"Oh, sure, the factory's running. But Gerry Brewer got the big boot. Along with three other union people—good people. Like that, out on their ass."

"Did Tice get it too?" Mr. Silkwood made the inquiry to be courteous. But he found it hard to care about someone like Tice who was still alive.

"They kept him on. It might've been sticky with the Labor Relations Board if they'd fired him. But they did the next-best thing. They restricted him to the warehouse. Nobody there but a couple of forklift guys. It's Siberia. No way can Tice keep tabs on how they're treating people in production."

"Can't he get somebody else to do it?" It was beginning to register how isolated Karen had been.

"You could go to hell and back looking for somebody. The union's a whipped dog. Jim Reading put out this rumor that Tice and Karen and Brewer were in cahoots to get the AEC to yank the operating license. There's no sense to it whatsoever—why would they want to screw everybody out of a job, themselves included?—but you know how a rumor is once it gets started."

"Would the AEC do that? Take away the license?"

"I wouldn't hold my breath. Wodka says the AEC is happy as a clam. The fuel rods are coming in faster than ever. It's worked out fine for the AEC. For Kerr-McGee too."

Mr. Silkwood half-raised his head. He looked tired and strangely impassive. The loneliness and long rides—everyone in Oklahoma seemed to live an hour from everyone else—were absorbing his anger. He had not been able to do here what he had set out to do. But how could he? He was one man.

Drew had been trying all morning to bolt a muffler under his Sprite. The wrench twisted and slipped in fingers thick from cold. Warming them, he bent over a kerosene heater.

From the street there was the approach of steps, slow and heavy, across dry snow. Drew looked up. A hand was extended, hard and pale with red, irritated knuckles.

"Mr. Reading! You working Saturdays now?"

"I was in the neighborhood. Got a few minutes?" Years of deep-fry cooking were bunched at Reading's waist and across a broad face. But in his bristling stand-up hair you could see he was still a tough cop.

"If it's car trouble, I'd rather you brought it to the shop on Monday," Drew said.

"It's about your girlfriend. Different stories keep coming my way. They tell me she had a twat like you couldn't believe." Reading attempted a grin. It did not go beyond his mouth.

Drew swung the wrench in a hostile rhythm.

"Take it easy, fella," Reading said. "All I mean is, we got a lab test from Los Alamos. There were traces of plutonium all through her vaginal area."

"So?"

"So? What's it look like to you?"

"You tell me."

"It's just that it makes her look bad. Like she was shoving plutonium up inside her to sneak it out. Don't you think?"

Drew was on his feet now, wrench in hand. "You don't want to
know what I think," he said.

WASHINGTON, D.C. JANUARY 11, 1975. It would do no good to
read Burnham's article again. Wodka knew every paragraph by heart.
Yesterday the Highway Patrol investigators, still insisting Karen was
asleep when she died, had issued a rebuttal to Pipkin's theory of foul
play. It was only a partial rebuttal—there was no explanation why
the car had not wound up in a pasture or how the steering wheel had
come to be so concaved—but the state cops seemed to have cleared
up the most critical of all the points Pipkin had raised. How was it
that there were two dents, fresh dents, in the rear bumper and rear
left fender? Pipkin regarded the dents as *prima facie* evidence of foul
play. But now the cops were saying the dents were the fault of Ted
Sebring and his tow-truck assistants. Supposedly they had jostled the
Honda against the south concrete wingwall as they winched it from
the creek; a pointed corner of the wingwall had caught the bumper
and the fender.

Until now the police had treated Karen's death as a bother. They
had shown neither initiative nor logic. But this Highway Patrol
report had both. Wodka was at a loss; he had no patience for puzzles
of any sort. Could it be possible that Pipkin's hit-and-run mugger
was no more sinister than an uncoordinated winch operator? Wodka
drummed his fingers. Why didn't Pipkin call? He had left three
messages with the answering service.

"Dallas, line one," Wodka's secretary called out.

In his thorough way he told Pipkin the news, quoting from Burnham's article. "See if there's anything to it, will you?" Wodka said.
"Take that car apart. Run whatever tests you have to."

MANASSAS CROSSROADS, VIRGINIA. JANUARY 17, 1975. Thirty
years before, in the French winter of 1945, Mazzocchi had been a
machine gunner at the front of the American invasion. It was the
campaign to pierce the Siegfried line, and he was a kid of eighteen.

He had bounced along in a half-track and slogged through dirty snow. Over his uniform he had only a light field jacket, torn, grimy. A lot of GIs had begun to scavenge for clothes among the bodies that were accumulating too fast to be buried. One day, at a river crossing, Mazzocchi came upon a captain, face and torso half-hidden in a snowbank, shot through the stomach, dead several days. The captain's coat was brand-new, perhaps issued the day he was killed. It was long and woolen and warm, the sort of coat to save you in a blizzard. In theory the rules of the Army did not permit scavenging, and Mazzocchi took a while to make up his mind. The freezing cold won out. He brushed away some dried blood and rolled the captain over and eased the coat off stiffened arms. Then he locked the incident away.

Now it came rushing back. Now it was Mazzocchi lying on wet ground, belly down, bleeding, disoriented, and there was a stranger kneeling over him, tugging at his coat. Holy Jesus, he thought, if this guy gets my coat, it means I'm dead. He clutched the coat around him. "Get outta here! Lemme alone!" he said in panic.

The stranger—the thief—shifted around and got a better hold. "You're hurt," he said. "I'll get you to a doctor." The stranger continued to pull on the coat—not an Army issue but a stylish brown mackinaw from Mazzocchi's recent vacation in France. The stranger was a motorist who had stopped to help. He was trying to drag Mazzocchi away from a puddle of spilled gasoline.

Slowly, achingly, Mazzocchi recovered his senses. He remembered going to a Church of Christ conference to give a talk about worker safety. Afterward, sitting around and jawing, he had drunk two martinis with ice. Extra ice, in fact. About six o'clock he had started back toward D.C., driving east on I-66 through low-forested Virginia meadowlands. The last he remembered was an exit sign for Manassas Crossroads. The rest was darkness.

Twenty minutes into his ride home he had blacked out. His new Chevrolet Impala yawed left, bounded down a lumpy median, climbed an eight-foot dirt barrier, hung briefly in the air, then fell forward, landing on its roof, facing two lanes of oncoming traffic. Mazzocchi's head bashed against the windshield. The roof buckled around him. His nose broke and the rearview mirror cut into his scalp. But the heavy French mackinaw cushioned his neck and his spine and kept him alive.

Could he have passed out from the martinis? In his whole life he had never been drunk—never stumbling drunk or falling-down drunk, certainly not passing-out drunk. Hell, he had made it through the Army—he knew he could handle two martinis. Somebody must have slipped him a mickey. On the road there had been no warning, no cold-sweat jerks, no meandering off and on the pavement. Unconsciousness had attacked like an assassin.

At George Washington Hospital he demanded a blood test. A doctor ordered one, to humor him, and gave him the sample. He sent it to a lab for analysis. The results that came back revealed an alcohol content well below the level of drunkenness, as he had known, but there was no trace of a knockout pill. And a brain scan found him in fine shape neurologically. It was another mystery.

Not wishing to appear paranoid, he tried to forget it. He tried, but couldn't. In New York a week later he conducted a test of his own. Following the annual board meeting of an insurance company, which he served as a consumer rep, he took up an unobtrusive seat in a hotel bar. A waitress brought Beefeaters and a friend kept count. Five, six, seven. Mazzocchi gulped them till his stomach rebelled. He felt nausea, but he could walk and he didn't pass out.

It was not a test that could be a courtroom exhibit, nor did it explain why anyone would want to murder him. But he was sure now that murder had been intended, and he felt it was related to the Silkwood case. From the time of the Pipkin report Mazzocchi had been lobbying for the FBI and the Justice Department to get involved. He had sent telegrams to FBI Director Clarence Kelley and Attorney General William Saxbe, and he had tried in a variety of other ways to put pressure on them. For the most part it had been a one-man campaign in the face of a great indifference. Because of the French mackinaw, though, Mazzocchi's telegrams and bombardments did not stop, and shortly thereafter he heard from a Justice Department emissary. "The FBI has got a good man on the case," the emissary said. "If there's anything to find, he'll find it."

OKLAHOMA CITY. FEBRUARY 7, 1975. Ilene Younghein's arms chimed from bracelets of shells and silver beads bought on a visit to her son in California. Settling ponderously at her desk, she delved into a cache of papers. She pulled forth a thin volume bound in see-through plastic. The AEC inspectors, the experts, had produced this report under a meek and indirect title. "Do you believe it? They're letting Kerr-McGee get off scot-free," Mrs. Younghein said, not believing it. "Scot-free."

Peter Stockton nodded but made no reply. He had his own copy in his briefcase. The report said that twenty of the thirty-nine items on Karen's original list had merit, but only three were violations of the nuclear code. And these were violations in the way tomatoes are fruit: technically. According to the report, Karen had been alarmed about matters that didn't matter. No fine, no penalty—just a rebuke without sting, easily ignored—was the punishment. It was this leniency which had called up Mrs. Younghein's scorn.

"You probably know the AEC better than me," she said. "Do you trust them?"

"I don't know them that well," Stockton said mildly. "Anyway, they're in a state of reform."

"Oh, yes. What a big to-do over nothing!" After twenty years in which the AEC had tried both to regulate and to promote nuclear power, Congress had finally tried to end the contradiction. From now on the functions would be divided between two new agencies: the NRC (Nuclear Regulatory Commission) and the ERDA (Energy Resource and Development Administration). The old AEC was a thing of the past. Someone at the Sierra Club had suggested they celebrate. But no one had. On closer inspection the reform seemed to be only on paper. The acronyms had changed, but not the people or the policies. "Whatever they call themselves, AEC, NRC, XYZ," Mrs. Younghein said, "they're shutting their eyes to what's going on at the factory. Maybe they can fool some people. But not me. Not on your life!" If she had been a man, she would have spat.

"From an investigative point of view, you're right," Stockton said, pointing to the report. "It's an inept job, extremely inept." Every point of controversy had been glossed over. Health and safety conditions at Cimarron (a vaguely worded conclusion that everything was okay). The contaminations of Karen in her apartment (a one-sentence speculation that they were self-inflicted). The alleged defects in the fuel rods (a declaration that all fuel rods were up to snuff, though there had been some "irregularities"). The "missing" pounds of plutonium (no discussion of any sort). "It's an F report," Stockton said. "They flunked."

In fairness, he didn't give himself much higher marks for the hour long broadcast he had put together with Barbara Newman for National Public Radio. The broadcast had been bold and dramatic—one listener wrote and said she had mistaken it for *Mystery Theater*. But the listener also wondered about "all the questions that cry out to be answered." That was it in a nutshell, Stockton thought. No answers. He had been thinking exactly that last week in D.C. when he went by Newman's office. She was slicing open the mail. He had sat there, thinking and reading the letters—a flurry had come in—and thinking some more. His wife was gently encouraging him to come to his senses; his friends were being less gentle. Yet the Silkwood case nagged. Like a poorly mapped island it challenged the explorer in him, and the accountant in him wanted it to add up. "I've got a few bucks saved," he had said on impulse to Newman. "If your editor will pitch in a few more, I'll go back to Oklahoma with you."

So here they were in Mrs. Younghein's living room on her chintz couch. Stockton was not sure what to make of her. She couldn't sit still. She moved back and forth, always like a pheasant bursting from cover, from her desk to the coffee table to the magazine rack, her arms full of handwritten notes and odd clippings.

"What about the politicians out here?" Stockton asked. "Is there anyone who'd help us?"

"Try Tom Bamberger. He's about the only one with backbone. He's an old populist. Been in the state legislature quite a while. Sticks up for the Sierra Club. Doesn't have a real high opinion of corporate morality. He's made a few noises lately. Wants to hold a public hearing. I'm supposed to be the lead-off witness."

"Was Karen Silkwood telling the truth or not? One way or the other, I'd like to find out," State Representative Thomas Bamberger said. He pulled up chairs for Stockton and Newman. "A public hearing might be just the ticket."

The hearing was a rash idea. It implied that Bamberger didn't have much faith in the AEC inspectors, or more to the point, in the owners of Cimarron, and it had inspired some off-color condolences. ("Poor Tom's got his pecker in it this time.") But Kerr-McGee's official reaction had been to invite Bamberger to tour the factory. He had gone through and come out unconvinced. ("It wouldn't be bad if you were making ball bearings. But for plutonium? I just don't know.") The hearing was still on his schedule.

Stockton glanced around. The State Capitol is an elegant old place with tall, beamed rooms as capacious and dignified as those on the Hill. "I've been trying to get hold of you," Bamberger said. "Is there anything more you can tell me about this missing plutonium? I don't understand why more people aren't concerned about it. To me it's the big issue in this case."

Stockton concurred. "It's one of the reasons we came back. Unfortunately, there's nothing new. Everybody seems to be as close-mouthed as ever. Particularly out at Cimarron."

"Welcome to Kerr-McGee country." Bamberger laughed, a soundless old man's laugh. He had a brown weathered face. "I'm having trouble just getting anybody to come to my hearing."

"Have you tried to subpoena the company records? That's where the proof would be."

"It's not as easy as that. With the local judges and all, they'd get a subpoena quashed and never miss a beat. When you go against Kerr-McGee, all you get is resistance. Rock-hard." Even as he spoke of such realities, though, he managed a wry edge. "The hell of it is that my best witness is not only dead, but she turns out to be a sex-crazed pothead."

Stockton watched the gas pump's spinning digits. The attendant, a bloated man with creased pant legs, talked on. "Yep, that Silkwood broad musta been a real dope addict. Musta been. You gotta be real stoned to run into a culvert at fifty miles per."

Public comments about Karen, evasive and deferential while she was newly dead, had acquired a nastiness with the passing of time. Even local reporters from the *Oklahoman* and the *City Times* and the *Journal* were beginning to accept the theory that Karen's misfortune had been the result of her own frenzied zealotry. Others said this with spite; the reporters didn't. What they said was that Karen had had a kamikaze plan. Sneak out plutonium, poison herself, blame the country, then commit suicide and hope that that too was blamed on Kerr-McGee. But how had she got the plutonium past the Cimarron sensors? "I know it's crazy," said one reporter, "but it looks like she slipped it up her vagina. Of course, that's not something we'd print. Why make her parents feel bad?"

The *City Times,* however, did print some disturbing and rather incoherent comments from Sherri Ellis, who from the time of the

accident had kept largely to herself. One of the few times she had
been seen around town was at the Broadway Motor Inn with two men
from Kerr-McGee, her face all red-eyed and screwed into a grimace.
Sherri's comments to the *City Times* reporter had come a day or so
later. Asked if Karen might have taken plutonium out of the factory
to embarrass Kerr-McGee and get the union a better contract, Sherri
had said, "It's something to be considered." This was widely believed, and when Drew questioned her lack of loyalty, Sherri said
hotly, "Dead's dead. It's the living that got to get from one day to
the next. Me, I'm one of the living." But she was having nothing
more to do with reporters, as Stockton and Newman discovered.
Sherri had hired a lawyer to keep reporters away, and to negotiate a
payoff from Kerr-McGee for any harm the plutonium in the refrigerator might have done her.

Snow draped the dead grass. The creek was rimmed with ice. Stockton felt obliged to inspect the culvert again, though there was nothing to be learned, nothing beyond what he already knew. By walking
the two hundred and forty feet from where the Honda had spun off
the highway to where it had hit the north wingwall, you could see
why Pipkin had ruled out homicide in the first degree. Karen's death
couldn't have been intentional, bumper-banging or no. With the
flatness, the treeless fields, you could not reasonably have expected
her car to end up here, between the wingwalls, in the creek bed. It
was conceivable that someone had tried to scare Karen or forced her
to stop so her documents could be stolen. But the crash itself most
likely had been an unforeseen "fluke," as Pipkin put it. Her assailant
might well have panicked and fled and left the documents blowing in
the mud. But the men of the Highway Patrol were positive that no
assailant had fled because no assailant had ever existed, that the dents
and the steering wheel—all the signs of foul play—were part of one
gigantic tragic accident. A freak accident, but an accident nonetheless.

Looking up, Stockton saw a crack appear in the frozen clouds,
releasing a flow of sunshine. He got back into his car. From the
culvert he drove with Newman to Crescent, to Ted Sebring's garage
and then back to Oklahoma City and the main Highway Patrol
station.

"You're from out of town," Lieutenant Lawrence Owen said, as though it were evident from their handshakes. The lieutenant had a workaday, thoroughly functional police face, with a small grin at the corner of his mouth.

"I guess you've had some trouble deciding what caused Ms. Silkwood's death," Newman said offhandedly.

"I wouldn't call it trouble."

"Didn't you claim that she drove six hundred miles the night before, from Los Alamos to Oklahoma City, and that she was so exhausted she couldn't stay awake?"

"We corrected that. I know she flew back from Los Alamos and got her regular sleep. But as I'm sure you realize, we did find traces of tranquilizer in her system." The balance sheet of foreign substances in Karen's blood and stomach had revealed fifty milligrams of methaqualone: the Quaalude swallowed at the Hub Cafe. "Our local medical examiner, Dr. Chapman, tells me the drug acts as a hypnotic. It can put a full-grown man to sleep. And if I'm not mistaken, Miss Silkwood was . . ." The lieutenant pulled an official paper from a flat metal box. "Let's see, yes, five-four, ninety-five pounds. She was a very skimpy girl."

Newman said, "It might interest you that I sent the same statistics to six different toxicologists back in Washington. They all say fifty milligrams is not necessarily enough to induce drowsiness."

Lieutenant Owen gave an exaggerated shrug. "It's not uncommon for experts to disagree."

"There are other factors, Lieutenant, which I think are persuasive." The voice was Stockton's, modulated, but bright as a silver dollar. "We know Ms. Silkwood had built up quite a tolerance to Quaaludes —she was a pretty liberal user. It's highly unlikely that she'd have gone into a stupor from a single pill. Just consider the circumstances. She must've been shivering—it was cold as the devil—and with all the excitement, her adrenaline had to be pumping like mad. She was on her way to the most important meeting of her life. Plus: she only drove seven miles. I clocked it. It takes ten minutes. I just can't buy the idea she'd fall asleep in ten minutes. Not under those circumstances."

"You can believe what you want. I'm not going to sit here and argue."

Newman jumped back in. "Are you saying that six independent toxicologists are wrong, and your medical examiner is the only one who's right?"

"Yes, ma'am." The lieutenant's small grin stayed fixed.

"Have you had a chance to drive along the road shoulder?" Stockton asked.

"No."

"It's like a washboard. And it's on an incline. You have to be a helluva driver just to make a car stay straight. You've got to really hang on to the steering wheel. Nobody could do it if they were asleep. Never in a million years."

Lieutenant Owen leaned back and exhaled. He said nothing, as if hoping for a recess bell. But Stockton again met his gaze. "How do you explain the steering wheel? It's bent so far forward it's almost doubled over. Your arms have to be braced for that to happen. You can't be asleep or in a stupor."

"It's true that Miss Silkwood should have been in a relaxed state. Methaqualone is a depressant drug. . . ." The lieutenant's voice trailed off. He seemed sort of befuddled, which was unexpected because he personally had been handling the case.

"We've interviewed Ted Sebring," Stockton said to change the line of questioning. "He admits that he was a little preoccupied keeping his shoes out of the mud, but he doesn't think his men caused the dents."

"What do you mean?"

"He doesn't think the car hit the wingwall when they were winching it out. It would've made a scraping sound or a jarring sound, and he didn't hear anything like that." On his lap Stockton had the Pipkin report, thirty-seven pages of diagrams and photographs that evoked other sounds, other images: headlights in the rearview mirror, zooming up, flooding the Honda; tension at the wheel; the smack of metal against metal, a jolt along the drive shaft; the panic of the car out of control, skidding onto grass; a rush of relief, the car straightening; hope, trying to regain the road; then seeing the culvert wingwalls which a second before could not be seen: the final trick.

Newman checked her notes. Wodka had told her that the new Highway Patrol report—the rebuttal to Pipkin—was badly off the mark, perhaps even a put-up job. She addressed the lieutenant. "You're aware that Pipkin has now run chemical tests on the fender and bumper?"

"Yes."

"Did you know there are metal fragments and rubber smudges in the dents, but no concrete?"

"No, I didn't. I haven't seen his results."

"Okay, let me ask you this. If Sebring's men bumped the car against the wingwall, as you say, shouldn't there have been traces of concrete in the dents?"

"I suppose so."

"Was there any concrete in the samples you took?"

"Well, we decided not to take our own samples." Sweat mustached on Lieutenant Owen's upper lip. His cheeks grew taut, jerky.

Stockton noticed the signs and guessed their meaning. "Has anyone from the Highway Patrol examined the car since the accident?" he asked.

"No, sir, we haven't." Suddenly the lieutenant looked defiant. "If you have any more questions, you should ask the FBI. The case has been turned over to them."

They agreed to protect the woman's identity, and under this agreement, Drew surrendered it. The woman lived in Kingfisher, yet another of the tiny rural towns that ring Oklahoma City. Her name was Jean Jung.

They drove an hour in darkness. They passed only a scattering of farm lights. The roads were raw, desolate. Headlights created ghostly patterns that raised bumps on Newman's arms. Although Mrs. Jung's trailer was no bigger than a wilderness shelter, it was a warm oasis. A chubby teenager at a gingham-covered table was dawdling over a bowl of chili. The smell wafted through the trailer.

Mrs. Jung was recognizable by Drew's description: a rouged, powdered woman who had improved herself for the occasion with a streaked blond wig. "You gotta promise not to use my name. They'd come after me for sure," she said anxiously.

"You'll be a confidential source."

Mrs. Jung was not sure of the term, but understood its meaning from Stockton's handshake. "I seen Karen's folder, I sure did," she said. "It was about an inch thick. Karen was holding it real close, but she flipped through. I saw some pages with those big K-M initials. You can't mistake them."

"Did she have any photomicrographs?"

"Yes, I think so. And there was a notebook too, the spiral kind that students use. It was red-brown, a rusty color." Mrs. Jung reached out suddenly to restrain Stockton's busy pencil. "You did promise not to use my name, didn't you? Ever since that night I don't know what's gonna happen to me." Her composure broke and she put her face in her hands. Those few suspended moments with Karen had plagued her and plagued her until she wished, shamefully prayed, for her memory to vanish, like the documents.

Seven

Winter-thinned geese were parading north, and Drew had thoughts of fleeing with them. He would get himself a van and dress it up with carpet, portable fridge, fishnet hammock, tape deck, fog lights, heavy-duty shocks. Maybe a handpainted insignia: "To Hell and Back." Other worlds were reaching out from across the borders of his own—the California that Karen dreamed about, the million-acre dimensions of Alaska, the Kentucky farm his parents had retired to. And Washington Dee Cee. Wodka had invited him. ("Stop by anytime. We'll do up the town.") Of course, Wodka probably wouldn't even be there; he was always on his way somewhere else. But Stockton might be. Among the out-of-towners who had come through, Stockton had been the most like a real private eye, conscientious, casually inquisitive, the farthest thing from a dummy. He had a crafty, mild-mannered act, but you could tell about him from his eyes. When they blinked they were like lights on a pinball machine reflecting the points totaling up. It might be worthwhile to talk more with Stockton—the guy was a pro. Of all of them, he was the one to put money on to bust open this case. A lot of the other reporters had been honorable enough, poking around to flush out murder suspects. But mostly they were from less established journals like *Ms.* magazine, *Rolling Stone, New Times.*

The network crew from ABC-TV had been in and out so fast Drew hadn't got a fix on them. He had heard their report was a good one, hard-hitting, incisive. But he hadn't seen it; the local ABC affiliate had chosen not to air it. For that matter, he had had to send away to get copies of *Ms.* and *Rolling Stone* and *New Times.* These magazines were not the most ordinary commodity on Oklahoma City news-stands, but the particular issues featuring Karen had been conspicuously unavailable, as if someone had hopscotched through town buying them all up.

In his new atmosphere of flight, though, Drew wanted not to read any more or hear any more. Or care any more. What was that old aphorism? You can't move into the future until you let go of the past? A man should try to move through life in a straight line, he thought. Of course, there would be zigzags, but you had to avoid the loops.

Anyway, it was the right time of year for moving on. The snow-bound countryside was coming out for spring. He would sell off the Honda for scrap. His Sprite too. Forget about autocross. It was time to get out and see the rest of the world. Time to visit that VW dealer over by the Northwest Expressway. Start pricing vans.

NEDERLAND. MAY 2, 1975. After the funeral neighbors had come by the green house, callused hands bearing casseroles, clanking voices offering to do more, begging to do more. Karen had been such a good girl, they said—she didn't deserve this sad ending. Merle Silkwood thanked them, holding herself tearless, and asked them to go. They went, taking no offense—the family had always been private.

It had ended for Karen, but not for her family. After six months Mrs. Silkwood was still trying to return the house to normal. Her own suffering was not visible, except for the creep of sadness in her eyes, or lips sometimes set in a tired, spinsterish line. The Baptist minister felt no necessity to call on her. At the Nederland State Bank she counted out fresh stacks of twenties and fifties to men in sweat-stained overalls. She smiled if they asked for a recount. She did not know how to be tiresome or insufferable. Folks made note of her quiet nature and took pride. Here was a lady, without airs, face thin and brown like a gypsy's, but with refinement. They felt deep sorrow for her. She had lost Karen for good, and Rosemary to a long depression.

On trips to the cemetery Rosemary was always happy to come along. Perhaps not happy—she looked most unhappy—but eager, eager to escape her house across town.

One morning Rosemary had appeared at the green house with suitcases and pajamaed kids. "Come in, come in, don't just stand there," her mother had said, and by noon Rosemary was settled back into the room she once had shared with Karen.

Mr. Silkwood seemed lost too. He would sit and chew on a pen, laboring over words, words of fury to everybody he thought should be doing more to see justice done. After church on Sunday—his wife's morning of peace—she would edit out the excesses and correct the spelling in his letters. This campaign was consuming him while his house-painting business fell apart. "I get so mad I can't see straight enough to paint" was how he explained the stiffened brushes and rollers, unused since Karen's death. They managed well enough with Mrs. Silkwood's job, and she didn't mind the work. At times it was a blessing, at times he was off by himself, alone, not with grief, but with a terrible rage. There was something rootless about him now. No square of earth seemed to give him peace. He would relax at his cabin in the Piney Woods, but then he would drive farther north to Oklahoma City. He had even gone to see A. O. Pipkin in Dallas.

Pipkin's office was in an old warehouse. Mr. Silkwood had parked and gotten out hesitantly. He thought he had mistaken the address. Doorways along the street had been boarded up; tumbleweeds grew in the sidewalks. Young toughs were lazing against a storefront. One chucked a bottle in an arc that ended with a splatter near Mr. Silkwood's car.

To his relief, he found inside the warehouse a broom-swept room. Pipkin had a system of tags for the banged-up auto and truck parts in back. The system was something of a luxury. Pipkin knew precisely the location of the rear bumper and the left rear quarter panel that had been sawed off Karen's car.

Holding up the fender panel in the halo of a shiny bulb, Mr. Silkwood had felt somehow disappointed. "I thought the dent would be bigger."

"A bullet don't make much of a hole going in neither," Pipkin had replied, displaying his flat wit. "It's where it hits that counts."

"What did the FBI think? Could another car have caused the dents?"

Pipkin had shrugged. "Nobody from the FBI's been here. Nobody's even called. I have no idea what kind of investigation they're doing."

After yesterday, of course, it was pointless to ask.

WASHINGTON. JUNE 10, 1975. The chalk questions were hard to make out. Mazzocchi's longhand was not the best, and after seven months the white squiggles had faded from the top right corner of his office blackboard. *Who knew about Karen's folder? Who knew she was going to the Holiday Inn? At what point was her folder stolen? Who took it?* In all this time Mazzocchi had not erased that corner of the blackboard. Or rewritten it. What was he to do with questions for which the FBI had found no answers?

Next to the blackboard, David Burnham's latest article about the case had been tacked up. It would probably be his final one. The case had been officially closed. The Justice Department, relying on the FBI's investigation, had ruled that Karen's death was an accident.

Mazzocchi rotated his chair toward the two women in his office. The frizzy-haired one had a baby over her shoulder. Mother and daughter looked as fragile and white as alabaster curios. They had pale eyes, liquid reflections of blue wax. The mother was Kitty Tucker; the baby, Amber.

The other woman was Sara Nelson. She had arms and legs polished brown and bright sunflower eyes; a face open, radiant, immediately likable, bursting with health. The sun had calicoed her chestnut curls, a California sun. Sara was in D.C. temporarily to work for NOW (the National Organization for Women) and for the Coalition of Labor Union Women, but in sleeveless sundress and sandals, she still looked very much the Californian.

"I was the one who called you," Sara said.

"Yes, I remember." Mazzocchi also remembered the muggy autumn day of Karen's visit. But now it was summer, when the central air conditioning was on, and he couldn't feel the weather outside.

Kitty pointed to the clipping on the wall. "How can they do that? It's like they don't care."

"Have either of you spoken to the FBI?" Mazzocchi asked.

"No. But we've read everything that's come out. The government reports and the stories in the press." Kitty's voice was a girlish singsong, but up a decibel it could rage. It fitted her face. The face and the voice were both lifting. "It seems to me that Karen was the only one willing to stick her neck out. Now that she's dead, it's back to business as usual."

Mazzocchi was not sure what she meant by that, and he might have dismissed her out of hand except for her enthusiasm. He liked enthusiasm. "If you mean that everybody in the government's rolled over, you're right," he said. "The FBI, the Justice Department, the General Accounting Office, they all have."

"That's why we're here," Sara said, hastening to explain their plan.

"We think a petition drive might pressure Congress to reopen the investigation. We're sending the petitions to NOW chapters around the country, and we'd like to mail them to your locals if it's okay with you." As the Labor Task Force Coordinator for NOW, Sara's job was to help bring feminists and unionists into the same political camp. Karen had been a rarity among union organizers: a woman.

Mazzocchi was staring at his photographs of the Kennedys. The one of Jack was from a campaign crowd in the rain. In the other, Bobby was shaking hands with Mazzocchi, their fingers clasped in solidarity. There was a third picture, from 1950, of Helen G. Douglas. She had run against Richard Nixon for the Senate, a dirty, dirty campaign in which Nixon had made her out to be the "Pink Lady." She had lost. But what if she had won? Sometimes Mazzocchi would sit and wonder how different things might have been. No Kent State. No Watergate. But also, no Nixon–Kennedy debates. What if it had been Rockefeller–Kennedy? Kennedy might never have been President; that bright moment might never have been.

Mazzocchi was an idealist, a tough, pragmatic, hopeless idealist; he always imagined things being better. "Sure," he said to the two women. "I'll be happy to help in any way I can."

"Thanks," Sara said.

Mazzocchi held out his hand. "I should be the one thanking you. We need an organization like NOW to pick up the ball on this." He stood up, then sat down, as if he were suddenly absentminded. "You can count on my support, and I know Steve Wodka will help any way he can. But I have to tell you, you're gonna need one helluva lot of signatures to get anywhere. Congress is a tough crowd. I hope you're not harboring any illusions."

Sara put out a cigarette burning awkwardly close to her fingers. Kitty smiled and spoke for both of them. "We don't have time for illusions."

Petitions spurted from the old mimeograph. Kitty had the handle cranked up to a furious whirlwind.

"That's just the way you looked the morning you came over. A blur," Sara said, laughing gently. She was folding and stacking the petitions.

"You mean you weren't impressed?" Kitty pretended to be hurt.

"Oh, I was impressed. You were a *vivid* blur."

Kitty had called ("You don't know me, but I have something important to show you") and an hour later had shown up at Sara's doorstep in jungle humidity, stars of moisture beneath an electric hairdo, an impossibly beautiful baby squirming in a backpack. Tofu and vegetables were ready, and Sara had set out an extra plate, being meticulous about all courtesies, but Kitty had passed it up. Veggies. Her idea of a good lunch was a roast-beef sandwich and potato chips, even after living in communes east and west for a decade. Instead Kitty had gotten right to the point ("I think NOW's help is absolutely essential on this"), bringing out a packet of tattered clippings from *Ms.*, the *Times, Rolling Stone, New Times,* even an offensive one from *The Washington Post* that suggested Karen had poisoned herself. With a quick hug, Kitty and baby Amber were gone. Later that night, propped up in bed, Sara had read the clippings, and had gotten angry and sad, just as Kitty had. Sara's hands had felt clammy, her face hot and cold.

"It was a very strange feeling, very powerful," Sara said now. "It was like I was in the car with Karen, seeing what she saw—the road, the headlights, the culvert; feeling what she must have felt. I knew I had to do something. Something had to be done."

"It was Bob," Kitty said, meaning her husband. "He was the one who thought of getting NOW involved. And I came to you because it seemed to be perfect for the Labor Task Force. And *you* seemed to be perfect."

"I'll tell you the truth," Sara said. "While I was sitting and reading, I was trying to wriggle out of doing it."

"Because you thought it was hopeless?" The mimeograph had begun to cough from overwork. Kitty stopped, and with a funnel she poured in a smelly violet ink.

"No. Because of the problems it might cause within NOW. A certain number of NOW members don't want to be aligned with unions. They think unions have been more of a hindrance than a help to women. It's the same old argument. Feminists should stick to feminist issues. Otherwise we'll dilute our effectiveness."

"Then why does NOW even have a Labor Task Force?"

"Because there are a lot of feminist issues that deal with jobs: equal pay, child care on the job, fighting the layoffs. Women get laid off first because they were the last ones hired. But not everybody in NOW considers health and safety a feminist issue. I've got to work on changing their minds and, meanwhile, keep up with all the other projects, and there's just Jerry Stoll and me on the Task Force. So the Silkwood case has to be done in my spare time. No more movies, no more weekends off."

"I guess I didn't realize what a major decision it was for you to say yes," Kitty said.

"It would've been a lot harder to say no," Sara said. "I believe completely in what Karen was doing. In California I once worked at a dinner house and tried to organize the waitresses into a union, so I feel like I know a little of what Karen was up against." She paused and began sliding the petitions into envelopes. "I stayed up till three that morning, reading and thinking about everything, and I suddenly felt a presence. As if someone had come quietly into the room. My bedroom's in the basement—old bricks, tiny, cement floor; kind of ghostly. But this wasn't a ghost. It was more like Karen's soul hovering there, at the foot of my bed, about eight feet off the floor, completely invisible. I closed my eyes and told myself I was imagining things. But I could still feel her there, just watching, urgently watching. I knew that if NOW didn't do this petition drive, no one would. And I knew we had to do it, whatever it takes. Even if it turns into a big flop."

"It's not going to flop." Kitty stood there cranking away, not knowing what to think of Sara's "vision." Kitty looked out across the room, which also was a basement, the basement of the Butternut Commune, and looked into a corner as if to see something in the weak light, and repeated herself. "It's not going to flop. Don't say that. Don't even think it."

The ink on some pages had run and blended; the mimeo was coughing again. And then there was a racket on the stairs. A man came tramping down carrying Amber.

"Hi, Bob," Sara said. A dark ponytail hung loosely over Bob's three-piece suit, a sight as incongruous here as on the Hill, where he was an aide to Senator James Abourezk.

Bob gave his handful to Kitty. Unbuttoning her dress, she went upstairs with Amber nursing away.

"You're just in time to stuff a few envelopes," Sara said, thrusting them at Bob. "Put a petition in each one, and a leaflet."

"Quite a little production line you've got down here," Bob said. He fell to the task: fold, slide, lick. The address labels were already on.

"Kitty invited me to move into Butternut, at least while we're doing the petition drive," Sara said.

"I second the motion. There's an empty room next to ours."

Bob and Kitty and Amber lived in the Butternut Commune with Shawn, Kitty's eight-year-old son from her first marriage, and with three unrelated adults all recently turned thirty. The house itself was advancing on old age. Rot was in the wood on the windward side. Neglect showed in the gap-toothed porch railing. The ivy was dusty; the scabby portico had been a while without paint. But in certain ways the house was touched with elegance. It had been built when fashionable people still lived inside D.C. There were archduke moldings, a procession of twin sliding doors, a tall mahogany staircase. The furniture, of course, was strictly make-do. In the drawing room where gentlemen callers once waited for the swish of ladies on the stairs, there were now a fold-out bed and a cheap desk. The living room had a crushed-velvet chair turned from ivory to gray. The stereo case was a jerry-rig of orange crates.

"I suppose I should warn you," Bob said, tugging on his ear. "Two people moved out because Kitty was pinning notes to their pillows. She gets upset if you don't follow the duty chart." It was the lack of concern that Kitty minded. To think that her housemates, so happily recruited, would not care enough to make the commune work.

"A set routine is what I need—I've been sleeping and eating on the run," Sara said. "And everybody here seems so nice." In just three weeks she and Kitty had become friends, and now family. But Sara did have one small hesitancy. "It's just that sometimes I wonder if I'll ever get back to California. I've been in D.C. for six months already, and no end in sight. There's so much to do."

Bob's voice fell to a level of concern. "This Silkwood project isn't going to be a huge hassle for you, is it? I realize Kitty sort of shanghaied you."

"No. I've thought it through. I'm committed. It's one thing to fire a person or harass her; it's quite another to kill her."

Had Sara and Kitty ever met Karen, they might all have been friends. They were about the same age, and they had all come from the villages of Middle America. Sara had grown up in Stanley, North Dakota. Population: seventeen hundred. Her grandfather ran the bank, then her father. After high school Sara was a follower of Goldwater's Better-Dead-than-Red speeches. At Cornell she was into miniskirts and painted smiles and Kappa Kappa Gamma. Kitty's hometown was Clear Lake, Wisconsin. Population: five thousand. Her father was a teacher, her mother a postal clerk, one brother a priest, a sister married to a Lutheran minister. In high school Kitty was a Betty Crocker Homemaker of the Year and wore a Hearth pin to school every day. The University of Wisconsin had radicalized Kitty; Berkeley had done it for Sara.

"Kitty and I do have slightly different perspectives on the case," Sara said. "Her mind's made up that Kerr-McGee is the villain. I'm not so sure who the villain is, just that there is one." Sara had shoved out of her mind the worry that they might be careering on a fool's crusade, that Kitty might be full of wishful thinking.

The whole thing, after all, had been Kitty's idea. All through last fall and winter, through her rotund months and her first months cooped up with Amber, Kitty had scissored out the stories and kept them in a file marked *Injustice.* All winter she had pestered Bob. ("You've got all those big-shot connections—why don't you do something?") Restless, trapped at home, Kitty had turned archivist and bibliophile, reading a shelf of nuclear books. Her instincts were those of a political soldier. For years there had always been one cause or another demanding the pleasurable pains of lost sleep and unpaid labor—segregation in the South, Vietnam, Kent State, Jackson State, the Free Clinic movement, Impeach Nixon. In muggy Alabama she had been arrested for sitting with black teenagers at the Orange Bowl Cafe.

Kitty had read everything she could find about the Silkwood case, trying to reduce it to its elements as a lawyer would. (Her application to law school was presently pending.) She was a great admirer of logic and order, and the Silkwood case was first and foremost a matter of fairness. It wasn't fair; not fair that Karen Silkwood had given herself to a greater good and gotten what in return? An unpitying obituary in *The Washington Post?*

Sara had talked to Mazzocchi and Wodka, and read Pipkin's reports, but when she thought about *why* she was doing this, it went beyond the reports and the press clippings, beyond the political points that could be made. Strange as it might sound to Kitty, who was very literal, there was no other way to say it: she was also doing this because Karen had asked her to.

Kitty gave Win Turner the once-over. He had a grooved face, but he looked younger than his age—approaching retirement—and he was one Senate staff man who thought younger than he looked. One in a thousand. At least in Bob's opinion.

Bob and Kitty squeezed into Turner's cubicle in the Richard Russell Building. It was somewhat bigger than Bob's office, but just as paperlogged and as badly lit.

"This is my wife, Kitty Tucker," Bob said. Turner seemed not to notice the difference in last names. (Bob's was Alvarez, but Kitty had kept her own.)

"Does it seem like a cover-up to you?" Kitty asked, being blunt to draw him out.

"Well, that's an interesting question, Mrs. Alvar—uh, Kitty," Turner said. "Have you seen the GAO report?" He began shuffling papers on the gray metal shelves behind him.

"I gave her my copy," Bob said. "But we may be the only ones who'll ever read it. Plus you and Stockton, of course."

"Was Stockton the other guy who put in the request to the GAO?" Kitty asked.

"Officially, Senator Metcalf and Congressman Dingell made the request, but Stockton and I put them up to it. In our capacities as hell-raisers. Our *separate* capacities. I didn't even know who Stockton was then."

Bob had spotted the GAO report stuck between two thick green volumes. "Here's their peerless prose," he said, retrieving it.

"The problem is that they relied on Kerr-McGee and the AEC for almost all their information," Turner said. "The report reads like concentric circles."

Kitty smiled. Even with all Bob's praises, she had not expected to like Turner. He had been a cop when he was young, and in the Senate he had made his reputation as a Mafia-hunter for Senator Estes Kefauver. He had stuck around and become chief counsel for Senator Lee Metcalf, a cop glorified by a law degree. He was dressed like a cop, in a narrow-lapel suit and a skinny army-olive tie. But what a cop! Kitty thought. He was great. He sat up straight and direct, showing none of the slump that usually comes with twenty-five years on the Hill. And he talked just as straight.

"Is it true, like Bob says, that Congress almost always goes along with whatever the GAO tells it?" Kitty asked.

"Yes, almost always. Although with this case, the GAO isn't quite finished. They've still got to tell us about the so-called 'missing plutonium.' "

"I guess what I really want to know is whether you could get Metcalf to do a completely new investigation, starting from scratch."

Bob waved to someone passing by in the wide waxed corridor—a distraction, perhaps, to take Turner off the spot. "Did you put your wife up to this?" Turner teased. He could tease because he and Bob were friends, the former cop and the former hippie; good friends.

"I told her that Metcalf would have jurisdiction," Bob said. "Since he's on Government Operations."

Kitty was off on a new tack with Turner. "What do *you* think happened? Do you think somebody ran her off the road?"

Turner was evasive. "I probably don't know the facts as well as you."

"But you've been in law enforcement. You must have an educated hunch."

"Well, I do have a cop's nose." Turner rubbed it for effect. "You want my opinion? The case smells. It smells to high heaven. This lady was set to blow the whistle on Kerr-McGee, and they're trying to say she nodded off on her way to do it? I don't buy it. Even if her stomach did look like a drugstore."

"It was only one Quaalude," Kitty said, politely correcting him.

"See there, you do know more than me." Turner had no hang-up about giving people credit. It was why Bob liked him so much. "Anyway," Turner said, "I don't see how you chalk this case up to a drug OD. Not automatically. The circumstances are too damn irregular. I wouldn't go so far as to say the GAO or FBI is covering up, but they sure as hell haven't done a thorough job."

"Has the FBI released its report yet?"

"The FBI doesn't write reports," Bob spoke up. "The FBI turns over its evidence to the Justice Department, and the Justice Department writes a report."

"Okay, has the Justice Department released a report?"

"Not yet," Turner answered, adding a fine sarcasm. "Maybe they don't have anyone who majored in creative writing."

Kitty laughed affably but not long. "The official investigations are over with—that's my point," she persisted. "They've all done their thing—the FBI, the Justice Department, the GAO. We need somebody new to come in. Like you and Metcalf."

"I'm willing, but you'll need more than me." The sarcasm fell away, along with the fierce cop slang, the fierce enthusiasm.

"Won't Stockton help? I hear he's terrific."

Bob interrupted again. "Where *is* Stockton these days?"

"He's back from sabbatical, back with Dingell," Turner said. "Actually, I've been meaning to give him a ring." Locating his *Congressional Directory*, he flipped through. "No time like the present, I guess." He scrunched the phone receiver in the cavity between neck and shoulder blade. "Hello? Hello, Pete? . . . Yeah, I'm here with Bob Alvarez from Abourezk's office. And Bob's wife. It's about the Silkwood case. . . . Yeah, me too. . . . well they'd like to get us involved. . . . That's what I told them. . . . Yeah, thanks for your candor. . . . Look, how about lunch sometime? I'll buy if you walk over—the Russell cafeteria's better."

Turner replaced the phone. "Stockton is willing to work with me. But like I said, it'll take more than that. We'd need authorization, and I know I can't just walk in to Metcalf and get it. The fact is, I've already tried. And Stockton's already tried it with Dingell. This case is too controversial."

"But if you get the authorization, the two of you will do it?" Kitty said, sorting out the good from the bad.

"*If* we get the authorization." Turner straightened the knot in his tie. "Stockton has the impression there's a really powerful force that doesn't want the truth to come out."

The tan Plymouth Valiant that half a year before Sara had driven across the country now pulled up outside Butternut.

"Can I carry anything?" Kitty yelled.

"No, just hold the screen door open." Sara was a little embarrassed; she had so few things to move in.

The laundry basket of clothes went first, with Sara's arms stretched underneath and her chin nestled on top for balance. Upstairs, her room had been aired out, the baseboards dusted, the bed whitened with clean sheets.

"Welcome to Butternut," Kitty said.

The air shimmered, and sunshine pooled on the hardwood floors. Kitty was opening the mail. Suddenly she hurrahed, "I'm in! I made it—I'm gonna be a lawyer!"

In the kitchen, Bob laid down his cleaver—the green peppers, chard, mushrooms, round steak were all chopped for the wok. He began whirling an opener on a can of bamboo shoots. Kitty found him and threw her arms around him like angel wings, laughing and kissing. Then, taking a scarlet pen to the revived and once-again-respected duty chart, she circled the date: a red-letter day! She held aloft a letter from Antioch Law School as irrefutable. proof.

"Let's celebrate! Sara can baby-sit and we can go to the Magic Pan." A small frown; then Kitty's huge smile reappeared. "If they don't have champagne, I'll settle for piña coladas."

"We can make it a double celebration," Bob said quietly. "I got fired today."

"Oh, no! Not today, of all days." She let the Antioch letter fall to the floor and brushed the hair out of his face. "Are you all right?" she asked.

"I'm okay. It was bound to happen sooner or later." The problem was not any incompetency or disloyalty, not even the double image Bob presented with his ponytail and business suits. It was simply that he would not play the game.

One afternoon this past winter seven men had filed into Bob's cubicle. They were Navajos; their faces proud, enduring; their moves sober, unhurried, the moves of people who are outsiders. Momentarily they mistook Bob for one of their own, with his midnight-black hair, his strong, coppery features, exuding patience. The Navajo leader had a scrapbook. Discolored pictures of Navajo uranium miners stared from the pages; gaunt men, they stood erect in a scrabble of ochre rock, their backs to corrugated-tin shanties. The shanties were so flimsy the roofs sank under the weight of big desert birds. For as little as $1.60 an hour the Navajos had been digging uranium from below parched land at Shiprock, New Mexico, hauling the precious metal out in wheelbarrows. Ventilation was poor; uranium dust hung in stifled, scratchy air. Of a hundred miners at Shiprock, eighteen were dead of a rare lung cancer and twenty-one more were terminal. Kerr-McGee owned the mine. ("Our people are dying, but the company refuses to pay compensation to our families.") Bob looked again at the scrapbook. The men had crinkles at their eyes. Were they squinting in the sun or enjoying a private thought?

After the Navajos left, Bob had gone to one of Senator Henry Jackson's staff men. On Jackson's say-so, a small fund could have been set aside for families of the dead miners. But a renewal vote for the fast-breeder was coming up; and more to the point, Jackson was about to run for President. He didn't want to antagonize Kerr-McGee's friends on the powerful Joint Committee on Atomic Energy.

The timing was bad, but Bob wouldn't accept it. He kept going back to Jackson's office, and to the offices of other senators, rasping bitterly in his overused voice. The Jackson staffer had begun to avoid him. ("Give it up, can't you? Indians have been killing themselves with cigarettes and booze for two hundred years. Have you ever seen how they live?") Up to this very afternoon, Bob had still been working to get money for the Navajos, and to get the Silkwood case reopened, and to carry through on half a dozen other do-gooder requests. But he had worn out himself and his welcome.

Kitty squeezed closer, caressing his hair. "We can skip the piña coladas," she said. "We probably shouldn't spend the money."

"Don't be silly. It's not every day you get accepted to law school."

"But we owe Amber's doctor, and now there'll be tuition . . ." Kitty broke off. Her conscience was at work. "I don't have to go to law school," she said. "I can get a job."

"Absolutely not. First thing tomorrow, you tell Antioch you're coming. We'll find the bucks. The only question is whether you're gonna have time for those petitions now."

OKLAHOMA CITY. JULY 25, 1975. "It's time to get cracking again," Ilene Younghein called out. She was out of breath. Her large burlap purse was loaded with her morning's work at the library microfilm machine. Too agitated to sit, she stood in the middle of the *Oklahoma Observer* city room.

It had once been a living room. The *Observer*, a small semiweekly, was published out of an old brick house. Frosty Troy was the editor. Before anyone in Oklahoma had ever heard of Karen Silkwood, he had been running essays about the madness of building a plutonium factory in the middle of Tornado Alley. Mrs. Younghein had written them. Of the *Observer*'s five thousand readers, though, the only response had come from a Kerr-McGee man. He had likened Mrs. Younghein to a lover of horses at the time of the Model-A.

From her burlap purse she extracted a white-on-black sheet. "Look at this story by David Burnham," she said. "It goes to show what I've been saying. Nobody has ever cracked down on these nuclear companies, no matter how many code violations there are. There were over three thousand violations in 1973 and 1974, but all the AEC did was hand down eight tiny fines. Eight fines for three thousand violations!"

"How many did they find at Cimarron?" Frosty Troy asked in his editor's voice.

"The article doesn't say. But there were thirty-nine on the list Karen Silkwood gave them."

"But a lot of those were minor violations."

"I don't think there is such a thing as a *minor* violation when it comes to plutonium."

Frosty Troy was used to Mrs. Younghein's outbursts. With her children grown, her husband at work, time on her hands, she had at first seemed like another busybody nagging him for free space in his paper. But she wasn't. Her essays had been uncommonly accurate and studded with footnotes.

"I'd be happy to write an editorial asking the State Health Department to inspect Cimarron," he said. "Not that it'd do any good."

Mrs. Younghein pulled more microfilm copies out of the burlap. "Maybe you could reprint something by Dr. Gofman. He's done a lot of research, and he's really outspoken." She pursed her lips, remembering someone else. "What ever happened to Tom Bamberger and his public hearing? I've never been called to be a witness."

"That's dead in the water. Bamberger couldn't get any support."

"I suppose Kerr-McGee twisted a lot of arms."

"No, as a matter of fact, they didn't. They just purred some. They can purr real nice when they want."

WASHINGTON. AUGUST 10, 1975. It had been eight months since Karen's death. The Butternut Commune was one of the few places where it was still an ongoing topic of conversation. But tonight Kitty and Sara and Bob were slow getting around to it.

Bob was lolled on the couch, long legs crooked to fit, earphones over his head, probably descended into Mozart, Haydn, some music from before 1820. Kitty came in and blew him a kiss. No reaction; he was lost in time. With her fingers Kitty began snipping the ends of a lavender coleus in the bay window. The window was shut despite the heat. Careless painters had sealed it permanently. Outside in the sky there was a thin wafer of moon.

Sara was going through a checklist at the dining table, a solitary figure at the pine longboard built for twelve. The longboard was the centerpiece of the house, stretched across ten feet of hardwood floor. Sara tipped forward uncomfortably in the chair. "We've hit a thousand," she announced, shunting away the silence. "A thousand

NOW-Alerts have gone out with the petitions. Every NOW chapter knows what the case is about."

Bob came back from wherever he had been. He disconnected the earphones and turned the radio to a soft murmur. "Have any petitions come back in?" he asked.

"A few. They're coming slowly but surely," Sara said. She lifted and spread her arms.

"It's hard," Kitty said. "It can take ten minutes of explanation to get one signature. Either people haven't heard of the case, or if they have, it's something from last year. They don't remember it." She advanced on the refrigerator and uncapped a giant green-brown bottle. Whenever she got revved up, her addiction to Coke returned.

Sara was drinking orange juice. "I think people will respond, though," she said. "I think we can even get people to write letters to Senator Metcalf."

"The more the merrier," Kitty said. "Metcalf's a politician. He'll do whatever he thinks is the most popular."

"I hope he turns out to be the best choice," Sara said.

"We chose him mainly because of Win Turner," Bob said. "But as senators go, Metcalf's above average. He's a Democrat from Montana, sort of a Wild West populist, which sometimes makes him a good liberal. He's gone after the coal companies on strip mining and on the thirty-inch black-lung tunnels. The Sierra Club has supported him, and so have the coal miners. I think he'll respond if NOW can get the signatures."

"The big push is going to be August 26: Women's Suffrage Day," Sara said.

"Oh, no!" Kitty said. "I just realized that's the first day of my law-school orientation." She shrugged. "I guess I'll start off as a truant."

Sara talked past her. "There'll be rallies all over the country. We'll have mass circulation for the petitions."

"It'd be even better if we could get the media to cover it," Bob said. "But I suppose a petition drive isn't news. They want confrontations."

"We've got a plan for that too."

WASHINGTON. AUGUST 26, 1975. They made their way through a warren of rooms, each with a closed door. Kitty's eyes were a hot blue, the blue that issues from blowtorches, blazing a trail.

The mammoth Justice Department building is designed like a

giant square doughnut, and by this arrangement, the center translates into the top. At the periphery are young college grads and lifers waiting to go to Florida to die. A few lifers, by dint of service, reach the center. John Keeney, chief deputy of the criminal division, was one of these. He had supervised the Silkwood investigation.

Keeney was behind a magisterial desk. "Please, sit down," he said generously. A smile hung on a jut-jawed face. Two assistants, smaller and wiry, already had the best chairs. Sara did the introductions: herself, Kitty, and two NOW officials: Karen DeCrow and Kathy Irwin, who had come as a favor to Sara.

Keeney made a few casual comments. Talking to these women was all in a day's work.

"We find it difficult to understand why you dropped this case when you haven't come up with a single answer. Not one," Sara said. "Plutonium couldn't just grow in Karen's refrigerator. The dents in her car couldn't have happened by themselves."

Kitty said, "The public knows this case is being covered up—there's been a tremendous response to our petition drive." She was exaggerating, but she didn't care. Nor did she care one whit about protocol, which made her seem nerveless and somewhat uncouth. "We're taxpayers, and we feel shortchanged. All we've gotten from the FBI and Justice Department is a big fat zero."

Keeney was watching her with the detachment of an old man watching frisbee players. "I'm sure your intentions are good," he said, "but your assumptions are wrong. Every feature in Mr. Pipkin's theory was examined. Mr. Olson from the FBI did a thorough review. The dents were caused by the tow-truck men, and as for the car going off the wrong side of the road, I believe a very strong crosswind was responsible."

The words sounded final enough, but Kitty thought she detected an evasiveness in his tone. "Do you have a report we could see?" she asked.

"We have a report, and I'd be happy to give you a copy. But in cases where we don't prosecute, we're not allowed to make our investigations public."

"That strikes me as a rule that you can either ignore or enforce to suit yourself."

Keeney flushed. For a few turgid moments the two of them jousted over the government's right to privacy. "Excuse me," he said severely, "but it's not the government I'm trying to protect, it's Miss Silkwood's family. Certain things should be left buried with her."

Kitty was not to be outshouted. "If you mean that Karen Silkwood liked to get high or liked to have sex, so do two hundred million other Americans. I don't see what that has to do with anything!"

Sara put up her hand. "Can you tell us what happened to Karen's folder of documents?"

"Let me ask *you* something. Do you watch a lot of TV?" Keeney hunched forward, not bothering to act charming. "Real life does not imitate TV. We don't always find a Colonel Mustard in the library with the candlestick. We don't know what happened to Miss Silkwood's documents. I don't even know that she had any. But if you should find them, or if you find any other evidence, we'll be happy to take a look."

The four women got emphatically to their feet. The meeting was over. "Gentlemen, you should know that this meeting has been most unsatisfactory," Sara said. "But this will not be the end of it."

That evening Sara and Kitty twiddled with the dials on an old black-and-white portable TV upstairs at Butternut. The lines wavered and the voices were crackling, but they easily recognized themselves under the klieg lights on the Justice Department steps. "The FBI and the Justice Department are engaged in a cover-up," Sara heard herself saying. "It's up to Congress to get to the bottom of this." Her comments made it into newspapers all over the country.

Kitty was burrowed into the *Post*. She was still in her nightie. Mornings exposed a different Kitty, basically shy, unsettled, less radiant. It took the newspaper and two cups of herbal tea to make her normal.

"I thought you had to go to orientation at Antioch," Sara said.

"They're letting me skip. I'm getting credit for Life Experience."

The law school is huddled among tenements and blind pigs in a tough section of D.C., and as a rule, new students are asked to spend a few days living with a neighborhood family. But Kitty was already oriented. Living with her first husband had seen to that. "My parents were furious, their daughter living in a ghetto. Of course, they were mainly furious because their son-in-law was black. They stayed furious till Shawn was born. Funny how grandchildren can bridge the generation gap—the great conciliators."

"I've never met a man I'd want to have kids with," Sara said.

But Kitty wasn't listening. There was a story about the Silkwood case in the *Post*. An unidentified Justice Department official, Keeney perhaps, was quoted: "*Only* by conjecture is there a suspicious overtone to this case." Kitty flung the paper to the table. "They think Karen was a kook, and they think we're kooks too. Well, screw 'em. We're gonna prove them wrong." In seconds her fury was spent. She sounded bleary. "We have to, Sara. We have to."

"I've been thinking: maybe we should take a whole delegation into Metcalf's office. That way he'd notice us," Sara said. "I could ask Karen DeCrow to go with us, and Mazzocchi might be able to get some union people."

"How about Ralph Nader, or at least a Nader Raider?" Kitty said, seconding the idea. "Nader has a very detailed position against nuclear power."

"You know who else should be there? Karen's mother and father."

"You really think so?" Kitty made a gesture as if testing Amber's bathwater. "They're probably real straight, real conservative. You want to bring them into this den of iniquity?"

"Which den do you mean?" It was Bob, coming in from outside, sweaty from mowing the lawn. "Congress? Or Butternut?" He smiled.

Kitty did too. "I guess it would be nice to meet Karen's parents," she said, changing her mind. "Why don't we invite them to the NOW convention?"

"We could get NOW to award Karen an honorary membership," Sara said.

Eight

With deft thimblework Merle Silkwood was patching a pair of work pants. It was a chore she welcomed, now that her husband's days were again spent on paint-spattered scaffolds. Rosemary was back where she belonged too, back in her own house, though without her husband. Their separation had ended in divorce.

Mr. Silkwood had the phone to his ear in the kitchen. He had been talking and listening for ten minutes at least, for him a long conversation. "It was two young ladies from Washington," he explained, settling again into his easy chair.

"From the government?" Mrs. Silkwood's words quavered slightly; she prayed for good news.

"Nah, they're with a women's group. N–O–W. Whatever that is," he said.

"What'd they want?" Irritation crept into her voice, overcoming the tremor.

"They got some kind of award for Karen. They want us to come to Philadelphia to accept it."

"Oh, I—" Mrs. Silkwood slumped in her chair. "I don't think I could." The ambit of her life was the church, the bank, the green house. She left it only for the Beaumont shopping mall or the Kilgore homestead.

Mr. Silkwood felt the same way. To go to Philadelphia, to get suited up, shuffle onto a stage, mumble a thank-you speech—it would be an awkward, afflicting showcase of their grief. He was a man of solitary doings. When he was younger, his salesman years, he had gotten on better, pumping hands, putting on a public face, spiffed up in coat and tie. But for a long time he had worked outdoors in a cowboy hat and shirtsleeves. Retreating to the Piney Woods, he could go for days without seeing a single soul, without reading newspapers or magazines, without any and all extensions of people. There was no way in hell that a man like himself could go to a convention of feminists. He could imagine the expectant faces staring up at him, smiling artificially as he stood tongue-tied. No, it was not for him.

But the words that came out were at odds with his thoughts. He said, "I kind of let on like we'd go."

"But why?" Mrs. Silkwood looked up from her sewing.

"It's not that I want to go. Lord knows I don't."

"Why then? Why not let things be?"

"Because Karen wouldn't have! She wouldn't have let them be!" He lumbered to his feet and went outside to feed Frito.

WASHINGTON. AUGUST 28, 1975. Bob might not have ingratiated himself to the Senate, but his grin and his happy eyes, richly colored like dawn through stained glass, always declared him warmhearted. He had a Ph.D.'s grasp of technical material. People took it for granted that he was one, though his education had actually stopped far short. "You're exactly who we're looking for," Joe Browder told him. Browder was director of EPC (the Environmental Policy Center), a third-generation offspring of the Sierra Club. In 1964 David Brower had left the Sierra Club to form Friends of the Earth. David Brower had hired Joe Browder. But they had had their differences, and in 1972 Browder had set up the EPC. EPC used a direct approach. Fifteen lobbyists, operating out of two austere floors above a Roy Rogers hamburger joint, trooped the four blocks to the Hill every chance they got.

Browder spoke with an educated accent, Texan perhaps. "Up till now nuclear power's been a low priority for us. We've done strip mining, air pollution, white water, all the problems that people can see. Radiation is invisible. It's hard to convince people that radiation can kill them."

"I'm not sure I'm convinced myself," Bob said. They were between the EPC offices and the Hill, walking through an orderly timberland that long-dead gardeners had planted. "I know about uranium mines, of course. But that's something you *can* see. The air is yellow with dust. As for nuclear power, all I know is what I've picked up from my wife."

"Well, think it over," Browder said.

The floating notes of a lullaby led Bob upstairs. Kitty kissed his upturned face, and he kissed Amber's. They walked softly to their bed, a king-size rectangle of foam rubber. They sat on it, using the wall for a backrest, and Bob told her about the EPC job. "Take it!" she cried in joy. "Take it! Don't even think about it. Well, okay, I suppose you should think about it. But why wouldn't you take it?"

"Because I've had this city up to my eyeballs. Every time I ride an elevator half the people in it are figuring out what they have to do today to be president in twenty years—and the other half are comparing notes on IBM and Exxon, wondering if it's time to sell out to the highest bidder. I want to get away from all that."

She was startled by his vehemence. "How far do you want to get?"

"Oregon, maybe."

"But we've done that." They had met in Oregon. Kitty was living with Shawn in an old school bus that she had painted lavender and curtained with lavender bolt-cloth. She was a volunteer at a walk-in clinic for dopers, runaways, unwed mothers. She had a hundred times more vitality than the girls Bob had known back home.

Bob's route to Oregon had begun in Youngstown, Ohio, a steel-mill town. He hated the mills and dreamed of Broadway. He played Lorenzo in *The Merchant of Venice,* but his talent was strictly local. He went to South America for the Peace Corps and built chicken coops. Then the Army taught him to be a medic, which is how he came to work at the clinic and meet Kitty. She had become his supreme passion.

She was stepping around diapers that lay in a damp heap. From a cement-block bookcase she took down *Poisoned Power* by Dr. John Gofman and Dr. Arthur Tamplin. "You should read this," she said.

"Not now," Bob said, treating the comment carelessly. He had no idea what the book was about.

"Gofman and Tamplin used to be AEC scientists. But they've been —what's the word—enlightened? Their book is scary, Bob. Nuclear power is a very unforgiving technology. One mistake and zap!"

"It can't be that bad," he said. "They've used X rays for years, and where would you be without those radiation treatments they gave you? They saved you when you had Hodgkin's."

"That's different." The subject of Kitty's disease, usually avoided, was a threat, as awful as the disease itself. "I'm talking about radiation that isn't kept under control. Sooner or later, there's gonna be a huge accident."

"You want me to take the job, don't you?"

Kitty smiled. "If you don't, I will."

He hurled a pillow at her, but she ducked. Retrieving it, she jumped on the bed and pretended to smother him. They hugged each other and felt happy. Bob regarded her haloed head under his arm. So much worry inside that head, he thought; so much worry as great as its cause.

"All you need is a brown snap-brim and you'll pass for the FBI," Win Turner said, laughing at Bob's haircut.

"Yeah, I've gone respectable." The ponytail had been shorn. An eco-lobbyist had to look like any other lobbyist to get anywhere on the Hill.

Bob sat on the edge of Turner's desk. "I thought I'd check in with you. Is Stockton still with us on the Silkwood case?"

"He'll clear his decks when he gets the word. But you know what the chances are. Slim and none."

"We have a new plan," Bob said. "We'd like to bring in a delegation. Sara is running around trying to get people."

Turner put his hands behind his head. "Might as well give it a whirl. But—"

"Like you said." Bob roused himself, getting to his feet, shoving hands into his pockets. "That and fifty cents will buy us cotton candy."

PHILADELPHIA. OCTOBER 25, 1975. Bunting drooped from a ballroom stage at the old Ben Franklin Hotel. Placards jabbed the air. Hands were busy with buttons and leaflets. The chairwoman shouted out rules of order above an insistent roar.

Kitty waited until the NOW delegates lined up for lunch. Then she hailed them with clipboard and white plastic bucket. If she could get them to sign her petitions, the bucket might automatically fill with fives and tens like in church. She had placed a few crumpled bills at the bottom to give everyone the idea. Six hundred dollars she was hoping for, enough to pay off Bob's American Express which had been used for the two round-trip fares from Texas.

In response to inquiries Kitty had a sloganeering answer. "Karen Silkwood was a woman ahead of her time." But was she a feminist? "No, not the way you mean," Kitty would reply with a steady smile. "But she had more courage than all the men she was working with. I think she was as much a feminist as any of us." Some members refused to subsidize that opinion. If Karen had been trying to get equal pay for women, fine and dandy. But health and safety? Those weren't feminist issues. Still, a great many other members scrawled their names and parted gladly with their money. Kitty was glowing with success. After lunch she grabbed up everything and ran to show Mr. and Mrs. Silkwood in their room.

They had ventured out only for breakfast and were happy to have a visitor. There had been short, half-swallowed exchanges of biography during the ride in from the airport, but now Kitty exuberantly laid out the plan to recruit Senator Metcalf.

"I wouldn't mind seeing Congress," Mr. Silkwood replied carefully. "I got a few things I'd like to tell our congressman."

Kitty beamed. "If you can come to Washington, I'm sure my husband could arrange it."

Downstairs, outside the ballroom, Sara was pessimistically sucking fire into a Winston. A business-suited woman had just surged through, pushing into everyone's hand a high-gloss flyer, a piece of propaganda. *Women need nuclear power. Our electric kitchens—our dishwashers, vegetable dicers, orange-juice squeezers—depend on nuclear power.* Along with the flyers, the woman was circulating some harsh words. "This Silkwood petition is a mistake. It's going to put mud on our faces. Karen Silkwood was just a union whore."

Sara's thoughts whirled; she felt punchy, dazed. To hear such malice from a clean, matronly type—God forbid Karen's parents should overhear!

Sara tried to reason with the woman, but the woman was beyond reason. Kerr-McGee had been in the right! Defective fuel rods? Impossible! There are stringent controls. Missing plutonium? There are too many safeguards. Dangerous working conditions? Impossible! Impossible! Read the government reports! The woman went on as if Sara weren't there, handing out her flyers, hurling her words like stones.

You picked this fight, so get in gear, Sara scolded herself, jumbling her metaphors. Her biggest ally was Karen DeCrow, the president of NOW. Ms. DeCrow had been elected last year with the campaign pledge to move NOW "out of the mainstream and into the revolution"—women shouldn't be satisfied just to make it in the system, they should change the system as well. By general policy NOW members were in favor of change, but some more than others. A split had developed. The "traditionalists" versus the "gate-crashers," the Chicago Machine versus the Majority Caucus. Ms. DeCrow was a leader of the Majority Caucus, but on the NOW board of directors the Majority Caucus was in the minority. Already there was going to be a fight between the two factions when the vote for new directors came up Sunday. Now it looked as if the flyers woman was also going to turn Karen's honorary membership into a fight. If Mr. and Mrs. Silkwood came two thousand miles to be made into laughingstocks, I'll die, Sara thought.

She calmed herself with one more cigarette, then strode through the ballroom doors toward the tumult within. A pretty, willowy woman with a helmet haircut was in an aisle, a banner held high. Its calligraphy spelled *"Lesbian Rights."* Sara glanced about. Kitty was by the far wall, clutching her clipboard. Who were those people with her? Sara looked again and waved—a slight, shy signal. Mr. and Mrs. Silkwood were a tight step behind Kitty, faces blank, eyes riveted on the banner. Kitty was oblivious. That was her way: she had very little concern for the right place and the right time. There was nothing for Sara to do but walk over and give them hugs. Karen's parents returned to their room soon after, without any real understanding of the mumbo jumbo. Kitty went along, chattering about the Capitol Hill doors they were going to break down.

The next morning the convention regrouped. Mr. and Mrs. Silkwood sat near the front, with Sara and Kitty alongside. The flyers woman was nowhere in sight.

Up on stage appeared Ms. DeCrow, a lawyer by profession. With the lights dimmed she gave a tough, flourishing off-the-cuff speech, asking for a clear mandate in the election. Then she picked up the text that Sara had written. Ms. DeCrow hesitated, seemingly at a loss. The lights went up and down—the woman at the control switch was in suspense. "Sisters and supporters," Ms. DeCrow said, barely audible, "we have a chance today to honor a very rare woman."

Mrs. Silkwood's face began to tingle. She felt suddenly conspicuous, and filled with a glorious pride. Then somehow she was at the podium, the clean dry feel of parchment in her hand. Sara and Kitty had wanted both parents to go and accept the certificate, but Mr.

Silkwood stayed in his seat, leaving it to his wife. Taking hold of the microphone, she knocked static from it. "I don't know what, uh, how to thank you." Behind her glasses, tears began to overflow. "If Karen were here tonight, she'd be so happy. In her heart, I think she was one of you. God bless you all."

All the heaviness of political discord that had hung over the convention seemed to lift away with Mrs. Silkwood's simple words. An older woman began dabbing at her eyes. Tears glistened on cheeks throughout the room. People were on their feet. The applause was loud and genuine and went on for some minutes. Only Kitty was in motion, moving her buckets swiftly down the rows.

Sara was in an urgent huddle. The registration list had been stolen: an old trick of ward politics. Without the list, whoever lost the election would be certain to yell foul. "But if we cancel, we're stuck with an unacceptable status quo," Ms. DeCrow said flatly. Her solution flew down the halls and into the ballroom. They would remake the list. With a lot of grumbling, everyone stood in line and registered again. At the sight of the line, though, Kitty's face erupted in a smile: one more unforeseen chance for her clipboard.

When the election was finally done—about eight the next morning—Ms. DeCrow was again president and the Majority Caucus was a true majority. The outcome ensured that NOW, under the control of its most determined element, would lead the delegation that went calling on Senator Metcalf.

NEDERLAND. NOVEMBER 13, 1975. Pellucid skies. The humus smell of autumn. Unmowed verges of dewy grass. On the first anniversary of Karen's death the purple and yellow cemetery mums, planted lovingly in the backyard, came into bloom: a small phenomenon, a small comfort to her parents.

In the evening Rosemary came to visit. The flowers were a table bouquet. The trip to Philadelphia and Washington must have gone well, she thought. "Was it winter back there?" she asked, trying for a neutral topic.

"Indian summer, like we got," her father said. "The convention was real nice, but it was a big waste going to Congress. Especially that Brooks—what a yella-belly." With hope Mr. Silkwood had sent letters to Congressman Jack Brooks, a politician he had voted for, a man who had grown up in the next town over. But seeing Brooks had made all the difference. "He hemmed and hawed, real stiff like, and said he didn't have authority to do nothing. Bob, that's Kitty's husband, spoke up straight away. 'You could get subpoena power,' Bob told him. 'You could *make* those Kerr-McGee people talk.' But Brooks didn't want to hear no more. Before I could say 'Remember the Alamo' he had us out the door."

"Did you and Mama see that other congressman, um, Metcalf?" Rosemary asked.

"He wouldn't give us an appointment," her mother said. "And, anyway, we couldn't wait. I'd told the bank I wouldn't be gone more'n a few days."

"Oh, Mama, the bank wouldn't have cared. You've been dependable for twenty years."

A mosquito flirted with Mr. Silkwood's warm hairy arms, daring him. Whap! He was quick for a big man at rest. "Washington ain't much of a place," he said, "Just big gray monstrosities. I wouldn't bother going back, except for Bob—he's a real gentleman. And Kitty and Sara too. They showed us around, treated us good. They're gonna try to get Metcalf situated."

Kitty called the next evening to say Senator Metcalf was willing to meet four days hence. "Can you come? We'd like to have a memorial service on the Capitol steps the night before. Sara has been organizing it. Ralph Nader's group is sponsoring it, and Bella Abzug will be there."

The names meant nothing to Mr. Silkwood. "I got a storage shed to undercoat," he said. "But I guess I can do it later. I'll come, long as I don't have to make a speech."

"Can Mrs. Silkwood get away from the bank? It'd be good to have both of you along when we see Metcalf," said Kitty.

"This ain't gonna be another runaround, is it?"

"This is the best chance we'll ever have," came the answer with an inflection of certainty.

"Okay, then. But here's the what-fer. My wife don't hold with this raking over the coals, so to speak. She appreciates it, but, well, it wouldn't do to give her false hopes. That'd go hard on her."

WASHINGTON. NOVEMBER 17, 1975. It was a tribute to Karen Silkwood, sponsored by Critical Mass, one of Ralph Nader's organizations. A crowd of folks, three hundred or so, paraded from the White House down Pennsylvania Avenue to the Capitol. They huddled on the steps and declared their presence with long white church candles. They sang folk songs and heard Bella Abzug's thundering statements and Sara's open, direct passion. Kitty had a speech too, but she had come down with a sore throat. (If the truth were known, she was terrified of speaking to big crowds.) Then, incredibly, there was Bill Silkwood at the microphone, straight-armed and soberfaced. His anger suddenly found expression, the hurt shining through like the flames below in the wet, drizzling night. As he stepped down, the missus had her arm through his, and in her eyes a brave, baffled look.

Out in the crowd Mr. Silkwood saw an Oklahoma face. "Mrs. Younghein? You came all the way for this?"

"I heard through the Sierra Club they were having a memorial service, and, well, a body can't sit around Oklahoma all her life." Mrs. Younghein was holding a candle from which wax had congealed on red, rough fingers.

Later another hand reached out, uncertain and shivering. "I'm Sherri Ellis; I was Karen's roommate." She was a tall girl in a Western blouse. "I wasn't sure I should introduce myself. Mebbe you don't want to talk to me." Mr. Silkwood didn't—he had read her quotes in the paper, how she said Karen might have gone fanatic and poisoned herself—but Mrs. Silkwood thanked the girl for coming. Sherri seemed sad, an abject supplicant.

When the candlelit vigil was over Sara went with Sherri to a bar, then ducked away to call Kitty at Butternut. "Don't bring that turncoat here," Kitty whispered frantically.

"Then come to the bar," Sara said. "I know you're sick. But I think we should hear her out."

After Sherri had told her story, Kitty was willing to reconsider, and Sara, who succeeded better at being Christian, was saying, "There's no way you could've stood up to them."

"I've growed up about ten years since then," Sherri said, though she looked, and was, hardly more than a teenager. "If you've ever been locked up, you'd know what it was like. There were two of them, company men in white shirts; they took me to the Broadway Motor Inn. They didn't rough me up. But they kept me there a long time and made me believe I'd be the scapegoat if I didn't say Karen did it to herself. After a while I would've told them anything."

"Since you cooperated, how come Kerr-McGee ended up firing you?" Kitty asked in a mild cross-examination.

"That was after I got my lawyer. See, the company paid me a thousand dollars for all my stuff getting ruined. But I had to agree not to sue. Then I got to thinking, 'Whoa, girl, they oughta pay more'n that for what you been through.' Some plutonium got on me too, and even though they told us in Los Alamos we were okay, my gums got to hurting, and I had aches in all my muscles and couldn't keep solids down. So I told the company I was going to sue anyway. The next thing I knew I was pink-slipped."

"Didn't your lawyer do anything?"

"He lost interest real fast. Just like the police. My new place got broke into twice the first two weeks I was there, but the police acted like it was a big joke. They said it didn't count if nothing was taken."

"How'd you know someone broke in?"

"All my stuff had been gone through. The first time I thought mebbe they were looking for Karen's documents. But the second time—I didn't dare tell this to the cops—but I swear somebody planted dope in my closet. A set up. It was after that . . ." The next thought seemed to elude Sherri and it took several swallows of coffee to bring it back. "That was when I started to go a little crazy. One day I got in my truck and drove on out to Cimarron. My .22 was behind the seat. It wasn't loaded, and I don't know what came over me, but I grabbed it and went right for the fence, hollering and screaming, 'Kill me, kill me, please kill me.' I was lucky they didn't 'cause I climbed all the way over the fence. But the guards saw how crazy I was, and they just tackled me."

Temporary insanity might have driven her over the fence, Sara thought, but what drove her insane? Guilt? Rage? Fear?

"I could've been charged with a federal crime," Sherri said, finishing her story, "but they said they'd go easy on me if I kind of disappeared. So I did."

The next morning Sara sang out in her usual cheer, greeting the latecomers. She had kept warm the breakfast of eggs and Cream of Wheat.

"Yckh," Kitty said. She went to the porch for the *Post*. The gray parliament of clouds overhead promised rain. "Yckh," she said again.

"Everybody is on board. They'll meet us at the Russell Building,"

Sara said. "I called the whole list. Which reminds me, the long-distance phone bill came." Sara was this month's "money fascist," a title and job created for balancing the Butternut budget. "I must've run up a hundred and fifty bucks just calling all the NOW chapters." She unpinned the bill from the bulletin board and trailed a tanned finger past the numbers.

"It may be all for nothing," Kitty said tensely. She cleaned egg from around Amber's mouth. Aiming a kettle, she watched a tea bag rise in her cup. "There's a clipping on the board that I saved for you."

Sara located it. The article, from the *Christian Science Monitor,* told about the Price-Anderson bill coming up for renewal. In the history of Congress there had been no other bill like it. Originally passed in 1954, Price-Anderson had granted nuclear companies a special exemption from liability. Should the worst happen—should a tornado hit Cimarron, say, before all the plutonium could be locked safely away—Price-Anderson would allow a nuclear company to pay pennies on the dollar to anyone damaged or killed.

"What's this got to do with us?" Sara asked.

"Keep reading."

To prevent defections on the Price-Anderson vote, the article said, industry lobbyists had been working overtime to head off bad publicity of any sort: *For instance, if reopening the Silkwood investigation disclosed culpability on the part of Kerr-McGee, it might have an adverse effect on this legislation.* In all likelihood the case would stay closed, the article said.

"You were the one who was so positive," Sara said in a short descent toward anger.

"I wasn't *positive,*" Kitty defended herself, her mouth tight. "You know this is pressure politics. Kerr-McGee knows it too."

Bob came into the room. An easy smile announced his confidence was still intact. He grabbed the two women in a simultaneous hug and made cooing sounds at Amber. "Your mommy's gonna strike a blow for sisterhood today," he said playfully, trying to melt the intensity on Kitty's face.

"We are, we really are," Sara pledged. What did the media know? After two years of producing a TV news show in California, watching scattered, incomplete reports go on the air, she believed only half of what the media said anyway.

In the end, Sara had been the one to get the appointment with Metcalf. Actually, it was with Metcalf and Senator Abraham Ribicoff. Ribicoff was chairman of the Government Operations Committee, and Metcalf was chairman of a subcommittee. Most everyone in NOW knew of Ribicoff; they had rung campaign doorbells for him. In the past two months they had swamped his office with letters. "Yes, I've been hearing about this Silkwood case," Ribicoff had told Sara. "Bring your delegation over and I'll have Senator Metcalf here."

Now, with Kitty holding on for support, Sara navigated the porch steps, frostbitten and slippery. "Don't worry," Sara said brightly. "I have a special feeling it'll all work out."

Oh, God, not another "vision," Kitty thought, looking skyward. As clearheaded as Sara was, as pragmatic and well reasoned, there was a part of her that reveled in special feelings, unseen enlightenments, unverifiable guidance from above. Kitty had given hundreds of Sundays to St. Anthony's in Clear Lake, Wisconsin, but her belief in guardian angels had long ago ended. Tireless organizing, petitions, telephone trees—that's what brought justice and success. Of course Sara understood about hard work; she worked harder than anyone. It was just that sometimes she could act so . . . so cosmic.

The humid cold had settled in Kitty's bones. The approach of a rainstorm was blowing through leafless trees. She did not believe in omens. But if there were such things, she thought, today's were all bad.

Bill and Merle Silkwood took a taxi to the Richard Russell Building. The heavy rain had held off, but it was too far from their motel to walk. The fare was less than two dollars. The cabbie explained nastily how Congress keeps the D.C. taxi rates unnaturally low, as if it were a privilege to ferry such a high class of passengers. Mr. Silkwood sensed an insult. In his second look at Washington he was finding more things not to like. He and the missus were cooped up in a dreary little motel. The soda machine was broken, and there were tiny crystalline hobnails instead of cubes in the ice vendor. Come sunset, they had to be inside and the door locked. Outside was the effrontery of street ladies, so thick their perfume clouded the air, and pimps, dark lithe gangsters in ambush somewhere. Mr. Silkwood felt totally out of place. The brief visit to Butternut had not helped. Was it possible the boy with the Afro was Kitty's son? Perhaps, with this new generation, it was better not to know. Seeing the orange-crate furniture, though, he had begun to doubt seriously whether two U.S. senators would listen to people like these.

"The taxi must've left us off on the wrong side of the building," he grumped. "There's no door on this side."

"Hush, don't complain so much," Mrs. Silkwood said.

Kitty glanced up with worry around the lobby. "Where is everybody?"

"They've probably already gone up," Sara said.

Bob pressed the elevator button. Upstairs, they walked three abreast down a long, echoing hallway. They turned where the hallway did.

Ribicoff's outer office was filled with desks. Kitty banged her knee on a desk corner. Behind a large, dark door they saw another desk, a huge, gleaming one, and a seldom-used leather couch. On it sat Bill and Merle Silkwood, and on the chairs next to them were Stockton and Turner. "Oh, thank God," Kitty said.

The room was rich, formal, imposing; high ceilings, dark furniture. So this is what power looks like, Sara thought. She had never been in a room that made her feel so small. Her heart was racing, the blood hammering against her eardrums.

Senator Ribicoff came from behind the desk. His silver hair was neatly brushed. He introduced himself and Senator Metcalf, who was a big man, stooped, not as neat.

Within a few minutes, the rest of the delegation arrived—Eleanor Smeal from NOW, Frank Wallock from the United Auto Workers, Pat Ganzi from the Coalition of Labor Union Women, Jim Cubie from Nader's Congress Watch. Sara was relieved to see how distinguished they looked. She wished that Kitty had trimmed her hair, that exploding hippie frizz, but it was too late.

"All we're asking for is simple justice," Sara said to the senators. She took a deep breath. "If that's a radical request, so be it." She had a speech to give, and she gave it. Ribicoff and Metcalf kept their eyes forward, listening, sitting there with dogged courtliness, legs tightly crossed.

"Thank you," Ribicoff said. "We share your concern."

Metcalf nodded. He addressed Mr. and Mrs. Silkwood. Hands in their laps, they had not uttered a word. In a measured voice Metcalf said, "You have to understand that a traffic accident is not normally a concern of the U.S. Senate."

"This wasn't a normal traffic accident!" Kitty interrupted.

Stockton shook his head. Like tart apples she set his teeth on edge.

To look at her, in a soft dress with a red smudge on her lips, he would not have predicted such a strident, peevish voice. A signal in Sara's eyes guided Kitty away from the argument.

How did I ever get mixed up with this crew? Stockton wondered. He sat in a small uncushioned chair he had deferentially taken. He was someone who accepted protocol even when he didn't believe in it.

Kitty stood up, unclasped her hands, and laid out dozens of petitions like an ellipse over the desk. "We have eighty-five hundred signatures."

Neither Ribicoff nor Metcalf seemed to care. They didn't even look at them.

"A lot of people believe there's been a cover-up," Sara said.

Bob started to say something about the shabby way Congressman Brooks had treated Karen's parents.

"Your points are all well taken," Ribicoff said, rising partway out of his chair. "I might as well tell you: Senator Metcalf and I have already discussed this, and we're both aware that several federal agencies have looked through this case. However, we do feel the agencies themselves need to be looked at—the Justice Department, the FBI, the NRC. Senator Metcalf has agreed to undertake this. Mr. Turner will be in charge of the investigation, and he'll be borrowing Mr. Stockton as his chief investigator."

There were happy tears on Kitty's cheeks.

"One more question," Bob's voice flew across the room. "How about subpoena power?"

Metcalf pushed himself up with the help of a wolf's-head walking stick—he walked with a limp because of Nazi shrapnel in his leg. "If I have to subpoena witnesses," he said, "you can believe I will."

Kitty went over to him. "Thank you very much!" she said, expressing a gratitude not easily inspired. Ribicoff was shaking Sara's hand. "And thank you, Miss Nelson, for bringing this to our attention."

In the hallway, Stockton waded through locker-room hugs and soul-shakes, returning a few despite himself. He came up to Sara and Kitty. "I don't know how you did it, but you did," he said.

"We were in the neighborhood," Mr. Silkwood said lightly. He looked the way he always had, broad face in repose, dark hair holding its color. Karen's mother had a healthy pink touch of autumn in her cheeks.

"How long has it been? A coon's age," the young man said. Once he had been Karen's high school sweetheart. Now he was a Justice Department lawyer. "I read about your good news."

"Yep, we're gonna get to the bottom of this," Mr. Silkwood said. "I hope they kick some Justice Department butts. Uh, no offense."

"That's okay. I wish I could've done something." The young man shrugged. "It's not my division." He tried to imagine Karen as he had known her: the musky scent of car leather, the rustle of blue silk on Junior Prom night, hair piled in a beehive; the sweet, untouchable virgin, her nose in a book, only a hint of wanderlust in the arch of her head.

"We finally got some good men on the case," Karen's father was saying. "They're not gonna get buffaloed."

The old sweetheart surveyed his unfrilled office. Almost as an afterthought, he said, "I hope you're right."

Nine

Mr. Silkwood noticed the plaster cast on Rosemary's foot and tried to drag out an explanation in that stern way of his. "It's nothing," she said, red warmth on her face. "I got clumsy and dropped my iron."

He gave this momentary thought. Rosemary was not prone to accidents. No, it had to be something else. "By the way," he asked, "how come you didn't pick us up at the airport in your car?" She confessed then. Her car was in the shop for grill work, wheel alignment, suspension work, new radiator, new rocker arm. "I had a smashup," she said. It had happened late one afternoon while Mr. and Mrs. Silkwood were in D.C. A whiskey-colored sun was sinking behind her. She was on an access road over by Beaumont and did not see the other driver until he shot out of a dead-end street, blindsiding her. Her reflexes were fast, fast and smart. She hit the accelerator and twisted the wheel hard right. The two cars passed close enough for the bumpers to make sparks. Otherwise he missed her. She had been lucky, although not completely. Coming out of the spin, her car banged head-on into a phone pole. Her right foot hit the floor instead of the brake. The large foot bone and all five toes were broken. "But it could've been a lot worse," she said. "I'll be fine in a week or two."

The other driver had kept going, never touched horn or brake, never looked back. That was what bothered Mr. Silkwood most of all. An innocent driver would have stopped, would have made sure the pretty woman didn't need an ambulance. The man might have panicked, sure, but you had to consider the peculiar timing. The accident, if it was one, had come the day before the meeting with Metcalf and Ribicoff, had come like a clear, brutish warning.

"No, Daddy, don't say that," Rosemary pleaded. "Don't scare me."

WASHINGTON. NOVEMBER 20, 1975. A cold mist dripped off the trees and onto Stockton's beer-drinker hat. The hangdown brim, old and supple as chamois, soaked up the moisture. Feeling foolish, he wrung it out and ran the last two blocks. A Justice Department guard stopped him inside the door. Stockton had to submit his briefcase to the customary inspection for guns or explosives. There was nothing at all in his case.

"Do you think it'll hold the files?" he asked Turner, who was standing by a bank of elevators, his feet apart as if under arrest.

"Let's see what the Justice Department gives us. Keeney was very noncommittal on the phone."

Stockton would have liked to meet Keeney on a more casual basis, but the files made this formal appointment necessary. Keeney was at his desk. His jaw jutted out, probably more from self-control than from heredity. Three associates were around him in an arc. One had a look like a mousetrap closing. "Your request has been denied," the associate said. "Our files can't be made available to you. This may seem arbitrary, but truthfully it's not. Part of the case is still under active investigation—"

"Since when? Yesterday the whole kit and caboodle was closed," Stockton said.

"—and part of the case is restricted because of national security."

"What part is that?"

"If we could tell you, we could give you the files."

"I see. Catch-22, updated to 1975. How'd you like to test that in a courtroom?" Stockton was bluffing, as they probably realized. Court action would keep the Senate inquiry in the backwaters, slowing it like a huge barnacle.

At length Keeney permitted a rather unique sharing. Stockton and Turner were given a small room to which a guard brought files that a censor had okayed. Anything pertinent to the "active" phase or pertinent to "national security" was kept back, and nothing could be copied or removed from the building. Each day for a week, Stockton and Turner sat at a small table in the small room. It had an unpleasant, neglected feeling. While the guard watched they read aloud from the files, enunciating with drama-school care: gobbledygook oratory. The guard gaped. Suspicion entered his eyes. He looked closely at the sport jacket that Stockton wore all day even with the thermostat in the high seventies. Below the lapels the jacket bulged away from Stockton's shirt. Was the pocket weighted with a revolver? The guard had the authority to inspect briefcases, but not jackets, and therefore Stockton's scheme worked. He had a miniature tape recorder concealed. Each evening, after the guard reclaimed the files, Stockton was exiting into trench-coat weather with the best passages preserved by Sony.

WASHINGTON. DECEMBER 10, 1975. Cleaning up tomato stains and French-bread crumbs, Sara and Kitty talked about boyfriends. "I've been going with a guy who's great to talk to and he plays a beautiful guitar," Sara said. "But he's completely political. Just once I'd like to meet a man who was spiritual too."

"You should meet Danny Sheehan. He's a lawyer who refuses to take a case for money."

"That's a contradiction in terms."

"He went to Harvard, Wall Street, F. Lee Bailey, the ACLU, and came out the other end," Kitty said. "Now he works with something called the Ministry for Social Justice. He'll be at our meeting tomorrow night. To advise us on the SOS charter."

SOS was new to the city's popular alphabet shorthand—Supporters of Silkwood. It was an expanded version of the *ad hoc* coalition Sara had put together to lobby Metcalf. Kitty had formalized it, as SOS, to keep the pressure on. Meetings were held in Bob's office over the Roy Rogers restaurant. The treasurer's report and the minutes had been read when Sara arrived late the next evening. Steve Wodka had the floor. "Let's keep Karen in perspective. She was trying to reform the nuclear industry, not do away with it, as some of you are." He meant Kitty.

A stranger sat at attention on a chair near the coffeemaker. Sara sat down next to him in the only available chair. He had watchful eyes, curly black hair, a rakish curl of lips: rugged, declarative looks, exemplar Irish, dating to Finn McCool and Wolfe Tone. But he was out of place in his black suit. He must be the lawyer, Sara thought. The formality of the suit had turned shiny with age, implying a different past for its wearer, like the decayed robes of royalty in exile.

She saw him watching her. He smiled. She smiled. But the meeting was into overtime, and Sara had yet another on her schedule. She had to leave. It was a day or so later before she asked Kitty, "Was that Danny Sheehan, by the coffee machine?"

"Yes. Did he say anything to you?" Kitty asked. "I couldn't tell if he agreed with me or Wodka."

"I couldn't either. He just sat there like a coiled spring."

A week later Sara was late again, this time for a meeting of a civil-liberties group at the National Council of Churches building. The elevator was poky, so she took the stairs, the belt of her coat tagging behind like a tail.

The curly-haired man in black was presiding over the meeting. Listening to him, Sara liked the way his mind worked.

"Hello, Danny Sheehan," she said afterward. "I'm Sara Nelson."

"Yes, you were at the SOS meeting," he said. "Tell me, are you always like this? An hour behind everybody else and running to catch up?"

"I'm a Californian," Sara said, "I'm actually two years ahead of everyone else."

He laughed, as she had hoped he would. He reached with light-hearted gallantry for the door, to let her go out first.

A large wooden cross hung on a leather strap around his neck. "I didn't know you were a Christian," she said.

He scratched the back of one hand. His voice got garbled. "I'm working with the Jesuits," he said. "But I'm more into spirituality than religion. Buddha as much as Jesus. I call it universal perception."

They walked out in tandem. "Can you come to a birthday party next week?" she asked. "Amber's a year old."

"Your little girl?"

"Only in a universal perception."

Stockton shrugged off Kitty's compliments. "I'm not doing this to save Oklahoma City from Armageddon."

"It's not Oklahoma City that's in real danger. It's Hanford, Washington," Kitty said implacably. "That's where the fuel rods are gonna be *used*." She had broken unannounced into Stockton and Turner's workday. They were in Turner's cubicle behind walls that ended shy of the ceiling.

"I've been reading about how a fast-breeder works," she said. "The rods will be under unbelievable pressure. The tiniest hairline crack could be trouble. If plutonium leaks out of just one rod, the others could blister and swell, blocking off the coolant. And if it's blocked, the rods overheat and fuse together. In seconds you'd have a criticality! A big one! A mammoth, mammoth blowout. Everybody in Hanford could be killed."

"So you don't believe the new Rasmussen Report?" Stockton said in mock surprise.

"No, I don't. I know Rasmussen supposedly calculated all the variables. I know he says the odds against *any* major nuclear accident are a million to one. But who does he work for? The same people who are building all these damn reactors."

Turner rubbed a ring on his left hand. He said, "You may be right, and Karen might have been right, but first let Stockton and me find out, okay?"

Kitty put her coat back on. "I almost hope Karen wasn't right. But I know she was. You have to stop them from using those rods."

"For that, we have time," Turner said. "They're having construction delays in Hanford. The fast-breeder won't be ready till 1977 or 1978."

A rueful rumbling escaped from Stockton. "At the rate we're going, it may take us that long."

"What's the matter?" Kitty asked in a fresh gust of alarm. "Is Metcalf trying to renege?"

"Not Metcalf—the Justice Department. They won't get nitty-gritty with us."

Stockton was diverted by a friend in stocking cap and mittens, waving a hockey stick. In an aside Turner said, "I don't mind you coming by, Kitty, but right now we're in the thick of it. When we're through, you and your SOS group can make whatever political hay you can. Not before."

WASHINGTON. DECEMBER 19, 1975. Beneath a crisscrossed decor of red and green streamers Bob led "Happy Birthday" in his rich stentorian voice. Pink gobs of ice cream vanished greedily. In the kitchen Sara was talking to Danny Sheehan. "I like your outfit," she said.

Danny's gleaming suit and black eye-hole oxfords were somewhere else tonight. He wore a light blue shirt and jeans. "My Idaho clothes," he explained. "That's as close as I've come to California."

"Idaho?"

"I did a few cases there for the ACLU. We sued Idaho State University for firing a professor who'd started a union."

Danny and Sara regarded each other across four feet of kitchen floor. The space between them was vibrating, Sara thought: something is happening here. His eyes ruled his face, and a smile softened the corners, sheltering his privacy. Without it his features were predatory, as though they had been formed early, having to grow up fast. Sara had the feeling he had never been young and would never be old.

"Was Idaho before Wall Street?" she asked.

"After. Right out of Harvard I started at Cahill, Gordon, a muckety-muck firm, working on the Pentagon Papers case. But the senior partners thought I was spending too much time on things like the Panthers and prison reform, so they canned me. In a hundred years I'm the only one they ever canned for 'excessive *pro bono* work.' I wish I had the letter so I could frame it."

"A badge of courage?"

"An emancipation proclamation. It made me realize I'm not cut out to work *for* anybody. With someone okay, but not for."

"How do you pay your bills?" Sara demanded curiously.

"The Jesuits let me have a desk at the Ministry for Social Justice. And I live cheap. Who needs a closetful of suits?"

A small puddle was inching across the linoleum: melted snow from Danny's boots. "You don't suppose the Jesuits would sponsor me?" Sara asked in a half-joke.

"Well, they do rather cater to men. Why do you ask?"

"It's just that NOW can't pay me, and I don't have the money to stay here," Sara said. "My mother called today. She wants me to come to Texas. My father died a few months ago, and it's been very difficult for Mom, so . . ."

"The prodigal daughter goes home." Danny's smile tapered into a mute ponder, willfully remote. He didn't understand his massive disappointment.

From the living room the sounds of Amber's party mixed with Christmas carols on the radio. Shawn came into the kitchen—a happy boy of nine, skin a creamy brown, delicate like Kitty's, but the color was from a half-forgotten father. Shawn held out a birthday plate: cake and ice cream. Sara accepted with a profusion of thanks.

"Whatever you do," Danny said, "money is the worst reason in the world to do it." It was a platitude he utterly believed.

CRESCENT. JANUARY 1, 1976. The winter stillness at Cimarron was strangely complete. The factory sounds were no more. As of yesterday there were no more three-a-day shifts, no more trucks, no one to make noise except a skeleton security crew. Cimarron was in cold shutdown. After six years Kerr-McGee had dropped out of the plutonium business. Unlike last year's temporary closing, this one had every appearance of being permanent.

Company officials said in a press release that the factory had not been as profitable as they had wished. But there were other explanations. An official of the NRC legal division said Kerr-McGee had decided to close down rather than make certain improvements that the NRC had asked for. That conformed to what Stockton heard elsewhere: that the NRC's high command, for whatever reason, had forced the lockup. Did they think it would make the Silkwood case moot? Stockton wondered.

WASHINGTON. FEBRUARY 8, 1976. "Welcome back, Sara—we didn't think you'd make it," Bob said. He lifted a shovelful of snow and found the sidewalk. Snow and shovel went onto the lawn. "Let me take your bags. All your stuff is in the attic. I'm sorry, we had to rent out your room. We thought you'd be moving to Texas. But you can have the attic. Rent-free."

"I'll take it," Sara said cheerfully, "and don't worry, I can pay now." Inside, Bob struggled out of his galoshes. The attic was the entire third floor: warehouse-size, drafty, and barren. Under the eaves Sara saw a mattress, a roll of tar paper, some beat-up posters, her few, nomadic belongings. From far away they heard a pounding on the porch, low on the front door. Kitty was kicking away, her hands occupied with grocery bags and a satchel of law books.

Back downstairs Bob took the load, and Kitty rushed to Sara with possessive hugs and tonic exclamations. "Welcome! Welcome! It's so good to have you back! You *are* back? For good?"

"Yes, yes. Oh, I missed you. I missed everybody. Though I sure didn't miss the snow."

"Here," Kitty said, pulling tattered bits of paper from the bulletin board. "Here are your messages. About half are from Danny Sheehan."

"Danny?"

"He says he doesn't have anyone to take to the movies."

During the next few weeks, finding time when they could from horrendously busy schedules, Sara and Danny sat together through

movies and long conversations in her attic. They balanced on the
edge of the waffled mattress, a blanket over their knees against the
draft, rows of warped two-by-fours around them like bars. Sara had
tried to make the attic homey, but if anything, it was grubbier. She
looked with regret at wrinkled clothes pushed into a corner. She had
no hamper or dresser, not even a desk to hide them behind. But it
didn't matter. They had eyes only for each other.

"Is this what I think it is?" Sara said.

"I think it is." Danny's hand touched her, a quiver on her arm.

Sara had entranced him at first encounter, and Danny could prove
it by the details he remembered—the blue wraparound skirt, her hair
curled and bouncy, her bustling exit, the mugging smile.

Sitting on the bed he inquired about her past (a divorce), her
health (excellent), her feelings (gauzed over). Of late, though—well,
beginning last spring with "the vision"—a sense of destiny had settled on her, Sara said. From Texas it had guided her back here.

"My mother left it up to me," she said. "I could stay or leave. I
was undecided, so I prayed to God, got out my mother's Bible, and
said, 'Thy will be done.' The Bible fell open to the first chapter of
Jeremiah. I read verse seventeen: 'Therefore gird up thy loins, and
arise . . . be not dismayed . . . they shall fight against thee, but
they shall not prevail.' The next day I flew back here. I went straight
to the NOW office. A wealthy woman was on the phone. She was
willing to endow me with four hundred bucks a month to do my
NOW work. I'm rich!"

Danny straightened his spine, sucking in his stomach. A laugh
that was half a yawn came out. "From now on you buy the popcorn."

Sara's look was sobering. "I had another revelation when I got
back," she said. "I realized that my deepest political concerns date
back to Sunday school—stopping injustice and war and oppression.
And it's also why I'm bothered so much by cutthroat politics. I
realize now that I'm a Christian first, and everything else—feminism,
unionism—everything has to spring from that."

"I went a year to Divinity School and I'm still trying to understand
the world," Danny said. "I know I don't want the money-grubbing
Wall Street life, or the F. Lee Bailey life, pigging out at fancy
restaurants, getting shit-faced. They took me to a topless place once
—all these poor women grinding away and the men drooling—and
I couldn't stand it. I walked out. They started kidding me: 'Maybe
you should be a priest.' And I started thinking, maybe I should. Not

because I'm into being a prude. But I want to be grounded in something besides money. So I've applied to get into a seminary in Oregon. I'm a candidate for the Jesuit Order." He reflected a moment. "I guess I didn't tell you that."

"No, you didn't." Sara was hurt, but not startled. It explained a lot. She lit a cigarette and drew deeply, swathing her emotions in smoke. "Father Sheehan—it's a good solid priest's name. Wasn't that Bing Crosby's name in *Bells of St. Mary's?*"

"Bing Crosby isn't my model," he said. "Counseling the wives of drunks, setting examples for kids—that takes a real Irish heart. My plan is to be a social-justice advocate."

"Do you have to be a priest to do that?"

"Well, I've never planned to get married or have children," Danny said. "I've always felt marriage should have gone out with the Middle Ages. It gets in the way of relationships."

"Exactly," Sara said. "That's exactly what happened when I was married. I felt trapped. I was suffocating. And I had to break out."

"But you think a seminary would be just as suffocating?"

"I didn't say that."

Danny glanced at his feet and then out across the room, noticing for the first time the dirty clothes and the harsh surroundings. It was like a monk's room, and very like his own bedroom, which was also in an attic in another part of town. "Look, I won't pretend I want to be a *monk*," he said. He looked at the fanfare on Sara's face. Her sense of goodness, he thought, was total and lasting.

This is crazy, she thought, as he bent to kiss her.

WASHINGTON. FEBRUARY 13, 1976. The tires of Stockton's yellow VW yelped around a corner. He aimed it up an urban hillside created by the zigzag of a new highway. Bargain hunters like him used the sod for a parking lot. Jammed into a guardrail, the car lost a thin strip of paint: another tattoo. "Damn," Stockton said. "Double damn." The second damn was for Keeney and the other Justice Department men. After three months they still were denying him full access to the files.

Turner's reaction had been stoical. "It's an old syndrome."

"Yeah, the old hunker-down-like-a-jackass-in-a-hailstorm syndrome." But was that the extent of it? Stockton's suspicions ran deeper. At his desk he dialed for the FBI bureau in Oklahoma City. The phone rang in an empty office. Stockton let it ring, forgetting that the prairie morning was an hour behind his. He was lost in a maze of disagreeable, dispirited thoughts. One held his attention: had Kerr-McGee, in fact, managed to "lose" forty to sixty pounds of plutonium? Company officials had ridiculed those MUF figures when Newman and Burnham reported them months ago, and none of the official agencies had found any corroboration. But had they looked for any? Nowhere in the files, those that had been made available, was there any discussion of MUF. About all the Justice Department was willing to explain was the jargon. MUF was the government collo-quialism for "material unaccounted for."

Sighing, Stockton set down the unresponsive phone. Turner served him a steaming cup of coffee. "Thanks," he said. The day-old taste cleared his throat. Stockton was fingering a notebook that looked like it had been fingered before. "Okay," he said, "we know it's possible to smuggle out a little chunk of plutonium, a milligram or two. You put it in a metal capsule and you put the capsule in your mouth, or vagina, to get past the skyjack sensor."

"Not just possible," Turner said. "Somebody obviously did it." He was referring to Karen's baloney package. A match-up of electrons and neutrons, a test as reliable as fingerprinting, had traced the plutonium on the package to Lot 29 at Cimarron.

"Anyone could've done that," Stockton said. "A tormented Romeo, a woman-hater, any deranged person."

"Including her."

"Okay, sure, the field of suspects is wide open. But let's forget her refrigerator for a minute. Suppose there was a huge MUF. Suppose someone took home forty, fifty, sixty pounds. You couldn't do it by shoving it up your cunt. At a milligram a day it'd take you several hundred years. Forty pounds is big time. One flunky couldn't manage it. I don't think ten flunkies could. You'd have to be high up in the company to pull it off. And you'd have to be able to peddle it somewhere."

"There's the Mafia, of course. Or, with the right contacts, you could sell it to a foreign power."

"So why didn't the FBI jump all over this? As far as we know, they never even checked it out."

Later in the day Stockton put the same question to Lawrence Olson, the FBI agent in charge of the case in Oklahoma City. Olson's accent sounded more Dixie than Okie. He was unstintingly cordial. "But," Olson said, "I can't comment about the MUF. I'm not at liberty to discuss certain particulars of the case."

"Didn't I explain myself? I'm with the U.S. Senate," Stockton said loudly.

"Yes, suh, I understand. But my orders are not to talk to anybody. Not even the U.S. Senate."

The next morning Stockton let his coffee go cold; adrenalin was fueling him. He handed Turner a handwritten column of numbers. "That's air fare, motels, incidentals," he explained. "I'll go to Oklahoma City first, to see Olson, then to Chicago to interview the AEC/NRC inspectors. Face-to-face is the only way."

Turner agreed to the plan, but for the next several weeks it was held up by red tape. Stockton's travel voucher was for less than a thousand dollars, a routine expenditure, but for some reason it was not being treated as routine. Two ranking Republicans, Senator William Brock of Tennessee and Senator Charles Percy of Illinois, would not sign off. On March 25, after the excuses had worn thin, Stockton marched with Turner over to Senator Brock's office. An aide received them with seeming indifference.

"No more dickering—we need this voucher approved," Turner said. "Metcalf wants to hold hearings in two weeks, and Stockton has to get out and talk to the witnesses."

"Talk on the phone," the aide said. "You don't need to fly anywhere. Planes are expensive."

"A thousand dollars? It's chicken feed!" Turner was obstinate. "A thousand now might mean we save millions. If it turns out the fast-breeder is in real trouble."

"Come off it. All you want is a media show. You want to make dummies out of guys who've just been doing their job."

Stockton spoke up. "Give us a little credit. This isn't your typical dog-and-pony act. We're dealing with the possibility of murder, fraud, and smuggling. And everybody's been rolling over and playing dead. We want to know why."

"You've been told national security is at stake. You're both old enough to take a hint. The case is out of bounds."

"We're not hurting national security, and you know it. It's bullshit!" Stockton's mild manners deserted him. "Yes or no, are Brock and Percy gonna sign my voucher?"

"No."

"And you won't tell us why?"

"I've already told you."

Busboys at the Richard Russell cafeteria were scraping margarine pats and chicken bones from the spindly tables. "Why do we always come here?" Turner grumbled.

"Because it's cheap," Bob said. The table they had picked was slippery with corn oil.

Having shed the bluster of young men on the way up, Turner was comfortable talking to Bob, who had never had it. Turner gestured with his fork. "They named this place after Senator Russell because he was better liked than Kerr or LBJ. But those two were something to watch, Kerr and LBJ. They ran the Senate like they'd paid cash for it. LBJ was tough and Kerr was tougher. They took on everybody and pounded them silly. When LBJ got out, to run for vice-president, Kerr took over as undisputed king. That's what the press called him: the 'King of the Senate.' "

As an aide to Kefauver, Kerr's chief rival, Turner had had a catbird's seat for the making of the king. On Kerr's arrival in the Senate's damask-lined chamber, however, he had looked anything but royal. It was 1948, and Kerr was a big hayseed. He wore baggy pants, red suspenders, and a shirt that he claimed had once been a feed sack. By way of publicity he passed out autographed pictures of himself in a yodelling duet with Gene Autry. Many big-state senators wrote him off with a smile. "They were," he crowed later, "the dumbest collection of college graduates I ever saw all in one place." Kerr's actual political skill later inspired the irreverent biography *He Buys Organs for Churches and Pianos for Bawdy Houses.* In 1952 Kerr ran against Kefauver for the Democratic presidential nomination. Both lost to Adlai Stevenson, the quiet candidate, but Kerr came out of the campaign with national stature. His homegrown populism had delighted whistle-stop crowds. "Son," he told one reporter, "I'm agin any combine I ain't in on." For his convention headquarters at Chicago's Conrad Hilton he had constructed a replica of his childhood home: a log cabin, about four strides square, with no windows, no plumbing, no electricity and, as he was fond of telling, only a fireplace to read by.

"But he never ran again," Turner said. "After a while the White House would've been a step down." There was a story about Kerr that had been popular when John Kennedy was President. Kerr singlehandedly and singlemindedly was standing in the way of Medicare, open housing, and a dozen other of Kennedy's bills. Then, toward the end of his first year in office, Kennedy announced he would help Kerr snip a ribbon for a desolate stretch of macadam in the Kiamichi Mountains. Oklahoma Governor Howard Edmondson called the White House to be sure he had heard right. "Why the hell is the President of the United States going to such a bush-league event?" he asked. Kennedy's reply was to the point. "I'm going out there to kiss Bob Kerr's ass."

Listening to Turner tell the story, Bob gave a head-shaking snort. "Now they want us to do the same for Kerr's ghost," Turner complained. A querulous expression had turned down the corners of his face. "It's like we're back in the old days. Things aren't supposed to be done this way any more. Not without a by-your-leave."

"It is funny. Funny-peculiar," Bob said. "It's hard to believe Brock and Percy would feel any lingering courtesy toward Kerr." He reflected a moment. "Somewhere in the woodpile, I'd bet, is the Atomic Industrial Forum. Remember that woman Sara told us about, the one at the NOW convention who was bad-mouthing Karen? Well, afterward Sara found out that she's a Forum lobbyist. And I've had my own hassles with the Forum. They're a serious bunch."

"But why should Brock and Percy go along?"

"They're from Tennessee and Illinois, the two states with the largest investment in nuclear power. Tennessee has five reactors on line, seventeen on order, and TVA is the biggest buyer of uranium outside the Pentagon. Illinois was among the first to commercialize the atom, the Chicago area alone has seven reactors." Bob carried these statistics and hundreds more in his head. "Look, Congress has been babying the industry for years. Nobody ever gave it much trouble before you and Stockton. You two are real troublemakers."

Turner grinned; he hadn't been called that since his Mafia-hunting days. They walked back to Turner's office through a wide subterranean tunnel that always smelled moldy. "At least we've still got Metcalf in our corner," Turner said. "We can still hold the hearings. And if I have to, I can get Metcalf to subpoena Olson's little ass. Keeney too. The whole herd."

"Too bad you can't subpoena Kerr's ghost." Bob laughed. "It must be roaming around somewhere in these catacombs."

Back at the EPC office Bob spiked his messages. From a secondhand cabinet he pulled a folder titled "Care & Feeding." In it was the blue-ribbon Parkinson report. Written for Congress in 1952, two years before "Atoms for Peace," it had recommended equal federal subsidies for solar, geothermal, and other untried energy sources. Bob had made a project out of counting up the actual appropriations over two decades. The nuclear total was more than five billion dollars; the ratio of nuclear to all the alternatives combined was five thousand to one. The reverence for the atom, of course, went back to World War II. Bob had heard any number of variations on the theme: "We won the war with the atom, now we're winning the peace." The reverence was ongoing. At the moment, public money was paying for Operation Awareness, a blitz of TV ads and doorstep pamphlets in California. Very simply, Operation Awareness was a government move—executed by ERDA, funded by Congress—to defeat Proposition 15, an anti-nuclear ballot proposal. That was in the normal course of things. Not so normal was what the Watergate special prosecutor's dragnet had revealed. In Bob's folder was a *Post* clipping that told how an industry lobbyist had made cash payments to three members of the Joint Committee. The reverence, it seemed, had been corrupted.

Hunched over his electric typewriter, the only item on which the EPC had splurged, Bob pecked away. The two letters that issued forth were bluntly written. Why had Brock and Percy prevented Stockton's trip? Had they intended to obstruct justice? From Percy days later came back a stony denial; he defended his reasons without identifying them. Brock sent silence.

Ordinarily a visitor who called on such short notice would have been put off for a day or two. But Dean McGee was no ordinary visitor. One of Metcalf's secretaries, who saw important people every day, thought Mr. McGee made an exceptional figure; flinty features and unbending posture encased in a dark blue suit. The distinction of the Old Man was the distinction of power and place. He was on first-name terms with congressional chairmen, Joint Chiefs generals, think-tank experts. President Eisenhower had appointed him to the Arms Control and Disarmament Advisory Commission, and President Ford had invited his advice on long-range energy plans. Nonetheless McGee was not the political extrovert Kerr had been. McGee had not gone after elective office, and he did not often mix with those who did. He was a private man. It was a private audience that he now wanted from Senator Metcalf.

The secretary chaperoned McGee to a chancel of darkly burnished wood. Metcalf was at his desk, an arm's reach from a sliding panel that opened to a cache of bourbon and Scotch. The senator had red cheeks with broken veins. Booze was his weakness.

Had his days stopped at noon, Metcalf might have been a senator for the history books. But by the late afternoon his handshake was often a limp gesture, his eyes wandering, his words elusive. *Post* reporters, when quoting him, had taken to inserting the time of the interview. Anyone aware of his habit could judge Metcalf's quote by the lateness of the hour.

It was now going on five o'clock. The secretary closed the door and left McGee and Metcalf to their talk. If the senator had a drink or two, McGee almost certainly did not. Like Kerr, he was a teetotaler.

The next morning, in the enlightenment of hot coffee, Metcalf gave his staff the briefest of summaries. It happened that McGee had been in Denver to meet with OCAW officials. The Silkwood case had come up. Everyone in the OCAW hierarchy, according to McGee, thought it was time to put the unhappy story to rest. The young woman had been an unreliable Cassandra of loose sensibilities and looser morals. Why put her parents through more shame?

"Now I've heard everything," Stockton said when Turner delivered the deflating news. "McGee was here? The Old Man himself?" He made Turner repeat it once more.

Over at the National Public Radio offices, Barbara Newman was thumbing through her Oklahoma notes of a year ago, prepping for the hearings, when she got the call from Metcalf's office. For the next few hours she was on the phone nonstop, calling Stockton, Mazzocchi, Wodka, everyone.

WASHINGTON. APRIL 6, 1976. On this, birthday number thirty-three, Sara bobbed through twice that many sit-ups. She did them daily in the optimism of early morning.

A party had been organized. Danny's gift was the promise of a two-hour massage—he didn't believe in store-bought presents. The sheet cake was homemade, with honey and raisins. Pink icing spelled out the occasion, pink candles the arithmetic. "What did you wish for?" Danny asked when Sara blew out the candles.

Karen Silkwood

Drew Stephens: Karen's boyfriend and one of the last people she talked to.

Karen's family: from the left, her mother, Merle; her two sisters, Rosemary and Linda; her father, Bill. They are standing outside the federal courthouse in Oklahoma City.

Kitty Tucker

Karen's car ran off the left side of Highway 74 and ended up between the wingwalls of a culvert (above). The car was wrecked (left) and she was killed.

Steve Campbell

Steve Campbell

KAREN SILKWOOD
1946~1974

DEAD BECAUSE SHE KNEW TOO MUCH?

A poster distributed by the Supporters of Silkwood (SOS)

The founders of Kerr-McGee were self-made men of the caliber that civilized the West: (left, Dean McGee; right, Robert Kerr).

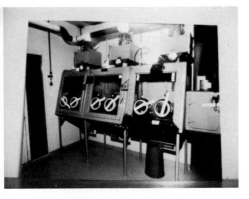

Karen worked at the Cimarron plutonium factory (below). The factory contained a number of gloveboxes (above) in which plutonium was processed. Karen felt the sign out front (right) concealed the true nature of what was happening inside.

Steve Campbell

From the left, Kitty Tucker, Bob Alvarez (holding Amber), Sara Nelson (holding Danny-Paul), and Danny Sheehan. "If it hadn't been for these four people, the trial would never have happened," Karen's father said.

Tony Mazzocchi: the union official who approved Karen's plan to work undercover.

Peter Stockton: he took a sabbatical from Capitol Hill to investigate the case and found out about the missing plutonium.

Steve Wodka: he was waiting at the Holiday Inn for Karen and her documents.

James Reading: the Kerr-McGee security chief who compiled a dossier of Karen's activities.

John Seigenthaler: the newspaper publisher who discovered a spy in the cityroom.

Congressman John Dingell: he held public hearings after U.S. Senator Lee Metcalf dropped the case.

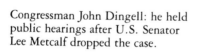

Jackie Srouji (shown here with her son): she worked for a newspaper, but had a secret life as an operative for the FBI.

Howard Kohn

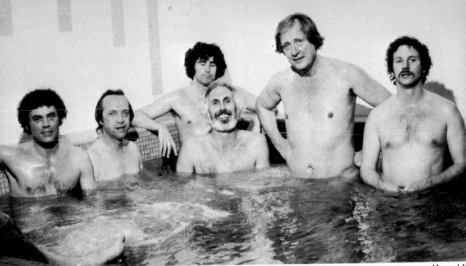

Howard K

The trial was the longest in the history of Oklahoma civil litigation, but there was a reprieve in the late afternoons at the YMCA whirlpool. Standing in back, from the left, are Danny Sheehan, Gerry Spence, and Art Angel; sitting in front are Father Wally Kasubowski, Father Bill Davis and Jim Ikard.

Howard Kohn

Bill Paul: the bar association president who defended Kerr-McGee in federal court.

Gerry Spence: the courtroom gunslinger who was recruited to take on Kerr-McGee.

Doug Magee

Dr. Thomas Mancuso: his study revealed that the radiation standards were at least ten times too lax.

Howard Kohn

Dr. John Gofman: he testified that Karen "was married to cancer."

Kitty Tucker

James Noel: the surprise witness who had something new to say about the missing plutonium.

Jim Smith (at left): the only company supervisor to testify on Karen's behalf. He is talking with Bill Silkwood.

Howard Kohn

The Team: (standing, from the left) Father Wally Kasubowski, record keeper; Rob Hager, attorney; Buzz Hirsch, movie producer; Father Bill Davis, legal investigator; Bill Silkwood, plaintiff; Jim Ikard, attorney; Robyn Petty, legal secretary; Gerry Spence, trial counsel; Bob Alvarez, lobbyist; Ilene Younghein, housewife activist; Art Angel, attorney; (sitting, from left) Howard Kohn, reporter; Kitty Tucker, political organizer; Danny Sheehan, chief counsel, with Danny-Paul; Sara Nelson, chief fundraiser; Pat Austin, legal secretary, with her son Jacob.

May 17, 1979. A wooden marker is planted next to the culvert on Highway 74 where Karen was killed.

Karen with her children: they were the beneficiaries of her estate.

"If I tell, it won't come true." A champagne bottle popped; the cork ricocheted off the ceiling. Butternut glowed with harmonious conviviality.

"Kitty—the phone." She answered it upstairs. Bob sought solitude from the noise. Enclosed by his chair, he tuned in National Public Radio. The news was run-of-the-mill. President Ford was denying aid to postwar Vietnam. Wooden junks of refugees were attracting escorts of sharks from the dead thrown overboard. Senate hearings in the controversial Silkwood case had been canceled.

What? Surely he was daydreaming. *Silkwood, Metcalf, McGee.* The names were so familiar Bob couldn't connect them to the radio. "This is Barbara Newman reporting to you from Washington," the newscaster said. What else had she said? Had she really said that Senator Metcalf had canceled the hearings?

Sara and Danny were gathered in the archway. A ribbon dangled brightly from Sara's hand, but the mood was shattered. "Did I hear what I think I heard?"

"I don't mind telling you it gives me a red ass." Mr. Silkwood's anger could be felt across two thousand miles of wire. Kitty and Sara, at upstairs and downstairs extensions, tried to stay calm. Keeping Mr. Silkwood informed over the months had meant unforeseen brinkmanship. His small-town skepticism ("Why is it taking so long? Why are they giving us the runaround again?") had forced Kitty and Sara into defending an erratic, red-faced old goat, an old goat who now, at the eleventh hour, had deserted the cause.

"Karen's dead and gone," Mr. Silkwood said. "Nobody gives a damn no more." Sara and Kitty could hear a swallowing back in Nederland. "You're the ones that got me into this. What're you gonna do now?" He talked as if they owed him another option, another hope. Perhaps they did.

"What would you like us to do?" Kitty asked.

"Dammit to hell, you're the ones with all the ideas." They heard a noise they couldn't distinguish. "Why don't you call Wodka or Mazzocchi."

WASHINGTON. APRIL 7, 1976. Today was to have been the first day of hearings. Instead Al Grospiron, the OCAW president, assembled a press conference. "The cause of Karen Silkwood's death remains unsolved, as do certain events leading up to her death," he said. "I don't know why Senator Metcalf decided to withdraw these hearings, but it certainly wasn't our wish."

Hours later Metcalf apologized. Still he would not reinstate the hearings. It was as if McGee had given him an additional message he would not or could not reveal.

At his borrowed desk Stockton was emptying drawers. He extracted a pile of white sheets, memos of an orderly mind. He had been forwarding copies of them to Congressman Dingell every few weeks. "Do you think Dingell ever bothered to read them?" Turner asked.

"He's read them," Stockton said. "He's conscientious like you wouldn't believe. Loves minutiae. Ask him for Ty Cobb's stats sometime." Dingell was a fan of the Detroit Tigers and also followed with humor the roller-coaster fortunes of Stockton's teams.

An intern gave Stockton a solitary cardboard box. He began packing. Turner helped. "I know Dingell is something of a maverick," he said. "But will he really take this case on? After all that's happened?"

"Well, it would fit under one of Dingell's subcommittees, Energy and Environment, and he definitely gets the willies from the fast-breeder. There was a commercial one, the Fermi plant, built outside Detroit, practically in his backyard. It's the only fast-breeder that ever went on line in this country."

"That's the one that almost melted down?"

"Yeah, there's a new book about it, *We Almost Lost Detroit.* Kitty gave me a copy. It's damn convincing."

"What about hearings?" Turner pressed. "Is Dingell interested enough to hold hearings?"

"I'm about to find out," Stockton said. He stuck out his hand for a farewell. He left with Turner's good wishes and the box under his arm. He was glad to get into the air. He broke into a little trot, the box jiggling at his side. Slowing down, he made himself think honestly about Dingell. Plainspoken, headstrong, tenacious—there was much of the bulldog in the congressman. The plain speaking Dingell had learned from his father, who had preceded him in the House of Representatives and whose seat he had held since 1954. The elder Dingell had once engaged Senator Kerr in a name-calling debate, matching him caption for caption and getting in the last word: "horse thief."

Dingell's district was Downriver Detroit, a name that told its geography and hinted at the brown waters and lumpy air that came with its famous business. You had to use soap and water to clean the soot off windows and windshields, and on heavy summer days even that was not enough. Dingell had attached several amendments to the Clean Air Act, but the afternoon sky had not noticeably improved. His amendments were half-measures, reflecting the half-will of GM, Ford, Chrysler. Ralph Nader had named Dingell one of Congress's "Dirty Dozen." At the same time, though, Dingell had made himself unpopular with the energy companies by pushing for stiff price-fixing laws, and the drug companies were upset with his bill to outlaw untested, unnecessary medicines.

Dingell could use a little more consistency, Stockton thought, but he liked the man. Maverick was a term appropriate to them both.

Dingell was expecting him. "Something's got to be done," Dingell agreed. "I can't let six months of your work go to waste." Tall, suntanned, the congressman had a face gone happily cherubic, and not much hair.

Stockton presented a duplicate set of memos about the case. Dingell browsed through. "I've read these. Is there anything new?"

"No. That's why I need to go to Oklahoma and Illinois."

"Oh, yes, your trip." Dingell squared the edges of the memos.

"I don't see any value in Oklahoma. That trail's cold," he said. "But Illinois might be worth it. Why don't you just pop in on the NRC. See what they have to say for themselves." Dingell was willing to take the FBI's word about the car crash but not Kerr-McGee's word about the "missing" plutonium, the MUF.

GLEN ELLYN, ILLINOIS. APRIL 9, 1976. The drive from O'Hare Airport passed by rows of tract houses. Old cornfields had become subdivision streets slick with rain. At the NRC regional headquarters, however, the changes were less graphic. The same inspectors worked out of the same offices as when the NRC was the AEC. The old AEC regional director, James Keppler, was the new NRC regional director.

Keppler chanced to be out of town. Instead Gerald Phillip introduced himself, as he had eighteen months earlier to Karen. Even in a padded suit Phillip's shoulders were thin. His eyes looked troubled, his long trim fingers jittery. He said, "I felt that Miss Silkwood was generally candid and honest, but having said that, I still think our report is justified."

"Well, I'd like to go through it with you, page by page," Stockton said.

The AEC/NRC report contained few hard facts and no hard conclusions. But it did suggest that Karen had eaten a radioactive sandwich on purpose: *The most reasonable explanation seems to be that the gastrointestinal contamination was caused by self-administration of Employee A.* Karen was "Employee A." In Stockton's copy, outlined in red and yellow felt-tip, he had changed the appellation back. It seemed the height of contempt to reduce her to a letter of the alphabet.

"I can't swear she contaminated herself, but she had the best opportunity," Phillip said. "It was her apartment, her refrigerator."

"Horse puckey," Stockton replied. "Anyone could have waltzed in. The back door was always unlocked; that's the custom out there. I'd like to know why you didn't dust the apartment for prints?"

"Everything had been cleared out by the time we got there. The Kerr-McGee people had pretty well concluded she did it to herself."

"Right from the beginning? That soon?"

"Everyone knew she was a troublemaker. It was logical for her to come under suspicion."

"It's just as logical that someone from Kerr-McGee did it. In fact, it's more logical."

Phillip threw out a weak hand. He seemed most uncomfortable. "It could be I was a little naive," he said. "But it wasn't my job to separate the good guys from the bad guys. That was up to the FBI."

For the official word about MUF, Stockton had to go to an inspector down the hall. The man had an attitude more prosaic than arrogant. He said, "As I recall, Cimarron did have MUF problems in 1974. We had to do two reinventories. But they were completely separate from this Silkwood business."

"What's a reinventory?" Stockton asked.

"Companies do inventories, we do reinventories," the inspector explained dully. "An inventory is done every month at every nuclear facility. If there's a major discrepancy, we go out and do a reinventory. Every ounce has to be accounted for."

"How major were Kerr-McGee's discrepancies?"

"I can't give you the numbers, but I can assure you we found it all. Here, I'll explain how we do it. A reinventory is an extremely sophisticated procedure. You can't run plutonium across a scale like a cow. At Cimarron they had fuel pellets, lab samples, warehouse drums, the trash, plus the slush in the plumbing. There's a mile of pipe in that place, a real spiderweb. You have to assume a certain distribution per centimeter—"

"*Assume?*"

"Yeah, assume. We couldn't very well rip up the pipes. We assumed a certain amount of plutonium over a certain length of pipe."

"How did you calculate that?"

"Kerr-McGee ran a test on one section, and we used that as the common denominator."

"I see." Out of habit, Stockton was taking notes. He shook his pen. The ink had turned faint. He edged forward in his chair. "Isn't that one hell of a loophole?"

"I don't see a loophole."

"But when it's all said and done, the amount in the pipes is a guess. You're at the mercy of the company. If they decide to jerk you around, there's no way you'd know."

The inspector did not like the inference. Grudgingly, he said, "You're assuming Kerr-McGee would have a reason to do that."

WASHINGTON. APRIL 26, 1976. Popcorn and cigarette butts tempted the pigeons scooting along the sidewalk. They kept a narrow distance ahead of Bill Silkwood, as if playing tag. He had set out walking from his motel, and he felt warm from the effort. Dampness had collected at his hairline. Outside the Rayburn building Bob and Kitty, heads together, came into view. Mr. Silkwood also recognized Sara, but not the man with her. "This is Danny Sheehan," she said, once the greetings were out of the way. "His job is to keep us from getting nervous."

Kitty managed a smile. Her suit was robin's-egg blue with gathered folds. It was brand new. The dresses in her closet were all too short for current fashion and had not matched her sense of triumph. So she had taken her mad money to a Capitol Hill department store. In front of a mirror, swirling about, she remembered the pastel blossoming of distant Easters in Wisconsin, the parade of finery into St. Anthony's.

Mr. Silkwood had exhumed a checkered salesman's jacket, his version of being decked out. He said, "I have to hand it to you folks. I'd flat given up on these hearings."

"It wasn't us," Sara said. "Stockton's the one you should thank."

In the hearing room Stockton and another aide hastily consulted Dingell on the agenda. It lacked many of the witnesses they had wanted, but that was no surprise. Dingell did not have subpoena power. That was vested much more in Thomas Steed, a powerful committee Democrat from Oklahoma and friend to the Kerrs and McGees.

Dingell called for order. The eight other subcommittee members sat with him at a long elevated hearing bench, a backdrop familiar from the Watergate hearings. Stockton nodded curtly to Mazzocchi, Wodka, Mr. Silkwood, the Butternut gang, some others. He sidled into a chair, harried, the unpolitic investigator. He tilted back. His feet flew up, putting him in danger of toppling over.

At the witness table Mazzocchi spoke into a bouquet of radio mikes. Hearing rooms were his turf. Four years earlier he and Wodka had helped get the Occupational Health and Safety Act through Congress. Mazzocchi looked up at the dais, punching his hands through the air, shadow boxing. "The Silkwood case points up a new kind of Washington cover-up." Lips synchronized with the hands. "In Watergate we saw people actively trying to cover their tracks. In the Silkwood case we see a pattern of nonresponse. By refusing to look for a scandal, the federal agencies have ensured that one will never be uncovered."

After Mazzocchi, and after Wodka, the witness table was given over to Kitty and Sara. They planted their elbows on the felt table-cloth, apple-green. It was fuzzy against their bare skin. Around them flashbulbs blinked. In yawning hours at the longboard they had prepared twenty-six pages of testimony—a synthesis of press clippings, union files, public records. Kitty had stolen time from Antioch, Sara from NOW. Kitty read the first half, her throat so tight Dingell had to ask several times for her to speak up. But Sara's words rang out hard and loud. She said, "We've never been to the scene in Oklahoma, but we've seen what's been done here in Washington to squelch inquiry. Are we to assume that women who take on leadership roles in this society can be harassed and intimidated and maybe murdered while the government simply stands by?"

The final witness was Jackie Srouji. She was about Kitty and Sara's age, but she was more demure, more matronly—prim, really, in a high-necked blouse and pink suit. Srouji was a copy editor for the Nashville *Tennessean* and author of an unreleased book about nuclear

power. Also, she was Stockton's gamble. Last December, late on a
blustery afternoon, she had dropped by the cubicle he was then
sharing with Turner. In explaining herself, Srouji said she was including a chapter about Karen Silkwood. "What can you tell me
about the case," she had asked.

Not as much as she already knew, it turned out. Stockton had been
amazed. Srouji was airily, impertinently familiar with the quaran-
tined apartment, the names and habits of Karen's friends, the singu-
larities of that November week. "It's all from the FBI files," Srouji
had explained. "I've got a thousand pages of documents in a safe
deposit box." On request she had produced a few. The FBI letterhead
looked genuine, and there were no censor's slashings. When Stockton
asked to see all thousand pages, though, she had turned cagey. Until
her book was ready, Aurora Publishers of Nashville wanted her to
keep the documents exclusively hers. Stockton had not made an issue
of it; the First Amendment was on her side. Not until Keeney,
Olson, and the other federal witnesses refused to honor Dingell's
invitations had Stockton thought about inviting her. Turner was
against it. ("Let her stay in Nashville. She's a publicity hound. She
just wants a big splash for her book.") But two days ago, almost by
chance, Stockton learned she was conveniently in D.C. He drove his
battered VW to the Naval Research Laboratory. While he was sifting
through his wallet for his top-secret pass, Srouji had breezed out. She
was in a blue and white uniform. She saluted smartly. "Second-class
Petty Officer Srouji at your service." After a couple of quick calls,
presumably to her publisher, she had agreed to testify.

Now Srouji coughed gently, her nerves magnified electronically.
Her face was a powdery moon.

Michael Ward, the lawyer for the subcommittee, asked the key
question. How had a lady reporter, whose only passport was a soft
Tennessee accent, gotten into files that had been denied to Congress?

She answered, "Let's see, how can I say this without violating any
confidences? I was able to see, unofficially, the substance of the FBI
investigation. By lucky coincidence one of the agents working on it
had known me for some ten years when I was a reporter in Nashville.
He kind of shared the Silkwood material with me. It was a ton of
material, a thousand pages at least."

"Did you Xerox the pages?"

"Certainly." Srouji leaned into the mikes, smiling. "I didn't want
to end up in a ditch outside Nashville."

"How many times did you have access to the FBI records?"

"I would rather not answer that question."

"On what grounds?"

"I'm not here to put the Bureau in a bad position."

But Srouji was willing to tell how she had heard about Karen as a "female Don Quixote who'd perhaps gotten mangled by jostling one windmill too many." Srouji told how, like Karen, she had gone to Oklahoma and Washington and Los Alamos. It was a dull recitation. Two subcommittee members left their seats to talk in a corner. Others stared vacantly, sluggish as turtles. One had hand to chin, looking as though it was expected that he be bored.

In a smoky voice Srouji was saying, "Not to cast aspersions upon Karen Silkwood, but I found out she used marijuana, and she attempted suicide on at least one occasion that was attributable to a drug overdose. I've got the documentation right here—the drug use and the suicide attempt."

Stockton lifted up from his chair. Dingell was irritably rapping on the wooden lectern. He said, "We are not interested in the personal affairs of Miss Silkwood."

"Excuse me," Srouji said, appearing to repent, "I don't want to knock someone who's dead."

"You just did!" The rejoinder came from the left of the table. Kitty was on the edge of her chair, face flushed.

Srouji twisted in her chair. Her eyes chilled over, and she plucked up a handful of papers. "Well, if I *really* wanted to, I would read all of these." She tugged her skirt back over her knees, as if her modesty had been somehow violated. Reasserting herself, Srouji said, "The question we have to ask is how many other Karen Silkwoods are ready and waiting to go off? Do we need a better screening process for workers in the nuclear industry? Do we need to do background investigations or psychological profiles on these people? Is this a matter we need to address?"

The hearing ended on this suggestion. As the onlookers shambled away, reporters were immediately in a ring around Srouji. Suddenly Sara broke through. "How could you do that?" she yelled. "How could you say those things about Karen?"

Ten

With his saturnine step and long dark coat the man had the look of a bear just out of his cave. He announced himself with certainty, "Nicholas Callahan." He was one of the Old Guard that had ruled federal crime fighting for forty years; with his last promotion he had become the number two man in the Bureau. His coming here to Congressman Dingell's office, even on this gentle spring day, was an unusual stirring.

Stockton took it as a good sign, as he did the way Dingell was fiddling impatiently with an engraved wooden gavel. Dingell would not be taken for a fool. He confronted Callahan. What's so special about this Jackie Srouji? Why does *she* rate favors from the Bureau?

Callahan seemed to expect deference and was plainly unhappy at this reception. His profile moved vertically. It was an aristocratic profile, like those struck on old Roman coins, but the voice was back-alley, roughened by the years. He said, "I'm surprised to see you involved, Congressman. The people behind this are misguided fanatics. They see conspiracies everywhere. You have my word, the Bureau has given this case as much attention as anything since the Reverend King killing."

"You're evading my question, sir."

"Congressman, I'm trying to save you a lot of trouble. Forgive me for reminding you, but, if I know Tom Steed, he's not going to like your badgering the most important corporation in his state. I think Steed would agree with me—a car crash is pretty far afield for the Energy and Environment subcommittee."

If intimidation was Callahan's intent, and it clearly was, it did not succeed. Dingell's immobile, understated face blazed a bright red. For a moment Stockton thought he might fling the gavel across the room. Callahan cleared his throat and began again in a different octave. Perhaps the congressman hadn't been told about the character of the woman whose cause he had taken up. "For instance, I think you should know—"

Here it comes, Stockton thought. Here come all the pieties about sex and dope. But Dingell slapped the gavel into his palm. "I'm not interested. We heard this same character assassination the other day from Mrs. Srouji."

"I'm simply trying—"

"What I want from you, sir, are those thousand pages the Bureau gave Mrs. Srouji."

"I have no idea where that woman got her information."

"Well, the first person we're going to ask is your agent—what's his name? Olson?"

"Olson is way the hell out in Oklahoma."

"Well, get him here! Tomorrow!"

WASHINGTON. APRIL 30, 1976. Lawrence Olson came into the Rayburn Building with FBI men on either side. The two extra agents were restless, measuring shadows. Stockton was not sure of their role, whether as advisers or guards.

Olson was forty-four. He had flaxen hair an inch long and a tall athlete's body with no hint of a paunch. Olson's face had a hard brown hue, barren of humor, and yet it showed none of the discomfort he must have felt. It was unfamiliar, being the target of an interrogation, but his answers were businesslike to the point of aloofness. He had spent four months on the Silkwood investigation, he said, and he had no apologies to make.

Stockton was reading Dr. Seuss to his kids that evening when the phone interrupted. The caller's voice was unbusinesslike, and unidentified; Stockton had to think a minute before he realized it was Olson. "Now I know what it feels like to be captured by the Gestapo," the voice said.

The following evening Olson called again, pleading in an anxious drawl. "Please, please leave Srouji out of this. She's just going to get hurt unnecessarily. The FBI will never tell you the truth. They can't afford to. Forget the whole thing. Give it up. You're in over your head. This thing is so complicated you'll never figure it out. You'll go crazy trying."

Stockton tried to get Olson alone the next morning to ask him privately about the tortured late-night calls. But Olson was never without his escorts. They were always at his side, even at the urinal. They must be here to keep him in line, Stockton thought, to keep him from saying too much. Stockton and Michael Ward, the subcommittee's chief lawyer, had delayed asking Olson about Srouji. By merely alluding to her, they had kept Olson on edge, letting the omission work on him, making him sweat. Finally, Stockton's shoulders rolled suggestively and he framed the question. "Do you know a reporter named Jackie Srouji?"

In Olson there was a visible stiffening. "I used to know her. I met her in Nashville in regard to a national security investigation."

"Did you ever talk to her about this case?"

"I can't answer that."

"Why not?"

Olson stole a sideways look. "It would violate regulations."

"You'll have to be more specific than that."

A haunted expression, like a matador's, came into his face. "Mrs. Srouji has a special relationship to the Bureau."

"A special relationship? What the hell is that?"

Though this and other questions pursued him for several more minutes, Olson would say no more. A great fatigue slowed his words, and the other FBI men grimly closed off the pursuit. Stockton wondered if they were only worried about the Bureau's image, as when J. Edgar Hoover used to juggle the Most Wanted List statistics. Was Srouji's "special relationship" a code word for adultery? Were these moralistic agents merely trying to conceal some tawdry romantic urges?

Olson was free to go. There was no way to coerce more answers; he was protected.

Srouji also had protection, the protection of being a journalist, but that did not seem as impenetrable. John Seigenthaler, publisher of the Nashville *Tennessean,* subsequently received a call from Dingell's office. "You have an employee who claims to be in possession of secret FBI documents," Seigenthaler was told. "She's either lying or she's in tight with the FBI. We'd like to know which."

NASHVILLE. MAY 3, 1976. As a newspaperman and a Southern gentleman, Seigenthaler's first instinct was to put a protective arm around Jackie Srouji, although all he knew about her was that she seemed pleasant. Srouji had started at the rival Nashville *Banner* in 1963 as a reporter. In 1969 the *Tennessean* hired her away. It was during Seigenthaler's big push to end sex discrimination in his newsroom. In 1970 Srouji quit—to be with her children, to try her hand at free-lance writing, to enlist in the Naval Reserve. She had returned to the *Tennessean* only a few months ago, after finishing a book for Aurora Publishers.

She was working three evenings a week at the copydesk rim, fixing grammar, editing copy. But on checking with his editors, Seigenthaler learned she was regularly doing more. A few months back, after three reporters had flunked out trying to track down an FBI sweep of Nashville's back-room casinos, Srouji made one call and came up with the addresses and sequence of the raid. "Come to think of it," one editor said, "we don't have anyone with better FBI connections."

"You want to tell me about it?" Seigenthaler asked, having summoned her to his office.

Although Srouji was only on nodding terms with her publisher, he reminded her of another tall man with hypnotic clear eyes, a man named Lawrence Olson, someone she greatly admired. Seigenthaler smiled, encouraging her to lay down her burden of secrecy.

Over the next three days Srouji told her story in frantic, broken snatches.

After the Dingell hearing, she had reported back to the new J. Edgar Hoover Building. The FBI men were not as glad to see her as they had been in the past. Congressman Dingell was upset with them, and they were upset with her. She was put in a small room reserved for white-collar criminals. Homer Boynton, associate director of the External Affairs division, gave her a paper. Would she sign it? It wasn't a question. Boynton and the other FBI men sat there until they got her signature. The paper was like a sworn statement. It stated that she had never "officially" received the Silkwood files from anyone in the FBI.

Now, in Seigenthaler's office, Srouji reached for a sleek feminine briefcase and sorted through for two handwritten letters. They were from Lawrence Olson in Oklahoma City.

Srouji had known Olson for twelve years, since the day she became an informant for the FBI. Olson had been her control agent when he was assigned to Nashville. She had been nineteen and a cub reporter for the *Banner* in 1963 when it began. The *Banner* publisher, James Stahlman, a personal friend of Hoover's, had put her in touch with the FBI. Soon she was traveling to New York and Berkeley and mingling in the angry scenes of campuses and ghettos. When she went to Michigan for a Students for a Democratic Society (SDS) conference, the FBI reimbursed the *Banner*. After each trip she filed an article for the newspaper and a longer, more detailed memo for the FBI. "I thought it was my duty," she said.

When she left the *Banner,* she claimed, this two-timing had lapsed. But last year she had interviewed Dr. Sergey Zaitsev for her book. Zaitsev was a nuclear physicist in the Soviet Embassy. A few days later an FBI agent contacted her. He told her Zaitsev was in actuality a KGB colonel under an Embassy cover. "We want you to get close to him," she was told. "We think he'd like an American reporter for a friend." The FBI rushed her to the Defense Language Institute in California for a refresher Berlitz course in Russian, the better to understand her mark. Zaitsev took naturally to courting her to the KGB. He made friends with her children and lent her money. Srouji played along—going to an energy conference, visiting a U.S. military base—all the while taking orders from the FBI.

"Now the FBI is threatening to tell everyone I'm a Soviet agent," Srouji said.

Seigenthaler gave her a look of disbelief.

"They'll do it," she said. "They see Communists everywhere. They're always asking about the radicals at the *Tennessean*."

"*What* radicals? Who do you mean?" His voice took on a slicing edge; his face flashed red.

Hers faded to gray. She was crying. A weak sound came from between two lines of lipstick. She tried to pass off her remarks to the FBI as coffee-break conversation, a little loose talk about a couple of colleagues. "Who?" Seigenthaler repeated. Well, one was news editor Dolph Honicker. He made the FBI itchy because he had spoken out against nuclear power.

"I didn't tell them anything bad," Srouji said. She had only tried to appease the FBI men, which was something she could not now do to her employer.

The nephew of a Nashville policeman, Seigenthaler might easily have had an FBI agent as a drinking buddy or tennis partner. People were always surprised when they found out he was the type that required a search warrant to let FBI men into his house.

Early in Seigenthaler's career, he himself had been part of federal law enforcement: special assistant to Attorney General Robert Kennedy and editor of *The Enemy Within*. It had been a near-idyllic time, idealism fed by dinners at Hickory Hill. In 1961 the President had asked Seigenthaler to go with the freedom riders through the South. In Montgomery, Alabama, things had turned ugly. A Klan mob had attacked the riders. Seigenthaler's skull was laid open with an iron pipe. FBI agents stood idly by, taking notes. But Seigenthaler raised no cain about it. Nor, in making the *Tennessean* a top paper of the South, had he let any resentment interfere with news lines to the FBI.

Lawrence Olson was a familiar name. In the sixties Olson had been known around Nashville as the FBI agent to see if you wanted to hear the Martin Luther King tapes. In the right company Olson could always get a chorus of hilarity from King's bedroom moanings. But that was a while ago. Olson had been out in Oklahoma City five, six years.

Seigenthaler knew nothing about Olson's work out there and only a little about the tangled tragedy of Karen Silkwood—that was eighteen months and four states away. It seemed only happenstance that a phone call related to the Silkwood case had led to the unmasking of Jackie Srouji.

With a sense of loss Seigenthaler announced in a front-page article that he was firing Srouji. His anger, though, was reserved for the men who had so eagerly used her. "The FBI has been guilty of a terrible exploitation," he said.

WASHINGTON. MAY 13, 1976. With his lawyer, Seigenthaler returned to the square of cement where he had served the Kennedys. He had to ask for directions to the Office of Professional Responsibility, on the Justice Department's far-flung periphery, where he went to make a formal complaint about the FBI's infiltration of his newsroom. The action was largely symbolic, but Seigenthaler felt a balance was being restored.

Within an hour or two Homer Boynton of the FBI ambled into the *Times* D.C. bureau with a complaint of his own. Why hadn't the *Times* given a bigger headline to Clarence Kelley's speech? Kelley, the new FBI director, had been at Westminster College in Missouri, promising kids no more abuses of authority. Boynton's tone was goodnatured, suggesting he was fulfilling a trivial duty. Unlike others in the Old Guard, despised for the arrogance of their press releases, Boynton was known to be forthright, gregarious. For a year he had been nursing along a friendship with John Crewdson, the *Times* reporter on the federal police beat. The two got into a conversation, and Bill Kovach, a news editor, came over to listen. The topic changed to Jackie Srouji, and Kovach sensed this was the true purpose of the visit. Boynton said, "I don't want to tell you how to run your business." But he evidently did. His manner turned confidential. "There's a lot more to this Srouji stuff, and it's not all anti-FBI. Seigenthaler isn't entirely pure himself."

There was a message waiting for Seigenthaler at the Jefferson Hotel. It was from Kovach.

Years before, Kovach had been a prized reporter at the *Tennessean.* The publisher dialed, anticipating a few minutes of nostalgia. Instead he was told of Homer Boynton's strange, vicious declaration.

"What the hell—? Is this what you *Times* guys consider a joke?"

Kovach convinced him it wasn't.

Seigenthaler swallowed. There was a raw clench in his throat. "What did this Boynton say?"

"That you aren't pure. He thinks Crewdson should go to Nashville to check you out."

"I stand accused of being *impure?!*"

Kovach chuckled hoarsely. "It's probably just to get you to back off."

"J. Edgar would be proud. Old ways are always easier, I guess."

"John, we have to follow through on this."

"You know damn well what the FBI's trying to do. Print *that* in your paper."

"I'm sorry."

Kovach's voice sounded far away, at the bottom of a well. There was a crackle on the line. Seigenthaler wondered if an intercept was being hooked up. He swore again, sinking further into despair. "Okay, tell Crewdson to come to Nashville. Tell him to investigate me till hell won't have it."

Homer Boynton—hadn't Srouji mentioned that name? Wasn't

Boynton the one who had bullied her into signing a statement about the Silkwood files? Seigenthaler tried to puzzle it out. Did the FBI want him to back off because of the Silkwood case? How could a dead woman, someone he had never known, put his life in upheaval like this?

WASHINGTON. MAY 19, 1976. Wire grille protected the windows. The irony was not lost on Stockton, that he should be billeted in an old FBI building. The cracked-plaster archive at Third and D, left for the vandals, had been salvaged in an unusual act of congressional prudence. Stockton had been given a nook among the bleak interrogation cells and restrooms as big as gyms. At one time millions of fingerprints had been stashed in the basement. And a hundred thousand dossiers—though not, of course, the best ones. Hoover kept those in a private vault. The best ones: the ones of presidents, senators, generals, even, it was rumored, of CIA chiefs. Everyone knew about Hoover and his dossiers, which was why he seldom had to take them out of storage. The threat was enough. Only his most trusted aides knew what was in the dossiers exactly, but it was assumed to be all manner of sexual and financial indiscretions.

The subject had come up because of the article about Seigenthaler in the morning *Times*. "I thought they shredded all the dossiers when Hoover died," Kitty said.

Stockton smiled halfheartedly. "If you believe that, you better watch out for door-to-door salesmen."

A large round voice: "I'm serious."

No doubt of that, Stockton thought. Kitty's manner seemed dictated by an emergency that had no end. She would be at his desk one moment, quizzing him to bothersome excess, then be gone suddenly for the law library or an anti-nuclear meeting or Amber's day-care center. Kitty was not someone he could invite out for an afternoon beer, even if he had wanted to.

Her starched face tipped toward him, squinting in the fluorescent gleam. She held out her copy of the *Times* and quoted from the article: "The FBI believes that Seigenthaler has a diabolical mind and is involved with a criminal syndicate."

Stockton said, "I've read it. It says there's no substantiation."

"Yeah, but in such a half-assed way. Where there's smoke, there's fire—that's the way people think. I feel sorry for Seigenthaler. He gave the FBI a little trouble, so they smeared him good."

"It's a time-honored tradition," Stockton agreed. He cleared junk mail and some crayon drawings off a chair and handed Kitty a galley proof about thirty pages long. "While we're on the subject, you might as well look at this. It's the Silkwood chapter from Srouji's book." Kitty put down her worn leather satchel. Ink-stained fingers pulled off a lavender shawl. She sped through the galleys, stopping at underlined portions. "I knew it! Srouji is working for them! Look at this—she has no right to call Karen a junkie." Kitty looked up. "She doesn't, does she?"

"No," Stockton said. "It all boils down to a syringe and a few glass beakers recovered from the apartment. *Alleged narcotics paraphernalia.* But the beakers are nothing more than cooking utensils, and the syringe has a hog-nosed needle. Karen would've looked like a small-pox survivor if she'd ever jammed that into her skin."

"Did she have any needle tracks at all?"

"None."

Kitty read some more and soon was agonizing aloud again. "Damn her! I can't believe a woman would write this . . ." She read farther. "Oh, now I see." Kitty had come to the unnamed male collaborator.

Smoke drifted over to my side of the table as my faceless companion shot back, "You don't understand. The girl was a lesbian. A queer. If she was any kind of human being at all, do you think she would have left her three children? Lesbies don't care. They'll do anything, and that is a significant factor in this investigation."

Kitty gave back the galleys with a sense of revulsion. "I don't know who's more despicable: Srouji or her *faceless companion.* Do you have any idea who he is?"

"Probably Reading."

The name of James Reading, the Kerr-McGee security chief, was scattered through a modest collection of documents the FBI had reluctantly released. From the papers, and from the interrogation of Olson, there now existed a partial narrative. Stockton began to tell it. "Olson's first move, once he was assigned to the case, was to go see Reading at Kerr-McGee headquarters. You can just picture the backslapping, the dirty jokes, Reading being delighted with the chance 'to clear up some rumors.'" With a grim laugh Stockton unwrapped a health-food candy bar and broke it in two.

Kitty examined her half for coconut which always stuck in her teeth. She asked, "Did Olson ever officially regard Reading as a suspect?"

"Olson claims he did, but it's obvious from his own memos that all he did was kowtow and kibitz. Basically he tried to prove Kerr-McGee's side of the case, and he got all excited about Reading's dossier."

"Reading kept dossiers too?"

"From what I gather, Reading put this one together after Karen was killed. He's an ex-cop, so he's got a built-in network. I interviewed him when I was out there with Barbara Newman, and he knew everywhere we'd been. As you'd expect, he really tried to do a number on Pipkin. He got a friendly New Mexico cop to pull Pipkin's old personnel records, and the Pinkertons gave him what they had—I don't have to tell you how much the Pinkertons love anybody connected to a union. It turned out the IRS had audited Pipkin back in 1955 and he later had some trouble with his P.I. license. Nitpicking stuff. But every nit found its way into the Oklahoma papers— they made him look sort of like a shady hotshot. And now Srouji is doing it to him again in her book."

Nothing was left of the candy bar except the crumpled label, and Kitty thought hungrily of dinner. She hoped that whoever was responsible for cooking tonight had remembered. If she could manage to put dinner on the table once a week, despite her hectic, unhinged schedule, why couldn't her roommates?

Stockton went on. "Most of the dossier is about Karen, of course. A regular rumor mill of information. How she kept dropping her pants in the broom closets at work. Which Olson swears is true. He acts like he knows chapter and verse."

"But it's all from Reading?"

"No. Later on, Olson did his own investigation. He devoted himself to finding everyone Karen had slept with."

"How can grown men be so warped?"

"It's being shrewd. At least in Reading's case. The dossier is Kerr-McGee's insurance. Karen's family will never sue—not unless they want her private life dragged out in a lot of grotesque headlines," Stockton said. "Srouji's book is just a sample of what could be done."

"Like preventive bombing." Kitty's screaming eyes went again to the galleys. "Who put her up to it? Olson?"

"It's still unclear who did what and who said what to whom. Olson claims that Srouji came out there unannounced, that she was in her role as journalist, and he didn't cooperate. But at a minimum he introduced her to Reading, and it's pretty clear Reading was her *faceless companion* with all that lesbo talk." Stockton hadn't intended to go on in such detail. Not that Kitty was a prude, but he distrusted the emotion with which she perceived Karen, her vision of Karen as a Joan of Arc. "Just so you know," he said, "Srouji's book isn't all twisted facts. Karen was no saint."

Kitty seemed not to hear. "I hope her family does sue," she said in a voice coldly exalted. "Let Reading and Srouji do their worst. It'll blow up in their faces."

"Isn't that a little naive?"

The comment was unforgivable, the more so because it was true. It stung. Putting out a hand as if to catch the sting, Kitty threw it back. "Nobody would've ever heard of Srouji, or her book, if you hadn't let her waltz into the hearing. *You* gave her a forum!" Too late Kitty curbed herself, pulling back her hand, pressing it to an ache in her forehead.

Stockton let it pass. "We knew Srouji would use us to plug her book," he said. "But we were using her to get at the files." He had said "we," speaking in a chary, remote plural, like a bureaucrat. Oh, hell, he thought. "Srouji outfoxed me," he said, rephrasing his answer. "I never suspected she was anything more than a journalist."

"At least you blew her cover." Kitty wanted to make amends.

"That was a lucky break. Dingell made it happen. If you get him mad, he's like a bulldog with his teeth in your cuff."

"They must not have expected that, the people who put her up to it."

"Well, she almost pulled it off. If Dingell hadn't stopped her, she might've convinced everybody that Karen was a hopped-up suicide case waiting to happen. That could've been the end of it. You'd be back peddling your petitions, and I'd probably be in Alaska."

"Alaska?"

"Yeah, I might have to go there anyway. As soon as I'm free, Dingell wants me to figure out how much money they wasted on the pipeline."

Stockton was getting ready to lock up. He switched off the lights and the Xerox machine. He locked the door as they left, and they walked to the elevator, Kitty with a satchelful of anti-nuclear literature from Ralph Nader's office, her night's reading. Stockton carried rubber-cleat shoes and his softball glove in a canvas bag. The thought of his last game, his wild throws from third base, made him hurry. A few knee bends and his legs would be ready, but this spring he could feel the age in his arm. He needed extra time to warm up.

"Coming to the hearing tomorrow?" he asked.

"I'll be there. But it won't be the last one, will it? I mean, Dingell is gonna stick with this till we get some answers?"

"Oh, absolutely. I told you, he's a bulldog."

An unseasonable temperature added to the pressure-cooker feeling in the Rayburn Office Building. At the witness table, Seigenthaler wiped the sweat from his face, as after a hike that has gone on too long. From a prepared text he told about the confession Srouji had made to him. How Olson had given her the Silkwood files for her book and how the FBI had taken an interest in his newspaper apparently because one of his editors didn't like nuclear power. Also, there was the grim coincidence of Seigenthaler's own reputation under attack.

After listening and expressing sympathy, Dingell let the other subcommittee members have a turn. Republican Congressman William Cohen read an excerpt from a book, *FBI: An Uncensored Look Behind the Walls,* which described Seigenthaler's beating in Alabama when the FBI stood by.

Cohen asked, without much charity, "Do you have a grudge against the FBI?"

"No," Seigenthaler said woodenly. He realized how it seemed.

James Adams of the FBI was the only other witness. He was Nicholas Callahan's chief deputy, a man of some age, with a solemn, lethargic look.

Adams was asked about Srouji's "special relationship" to the FBI. He glanced over to where she was sitting, motionless, by herself. "I can't discuss that," he said. How often had Srouji been to FBI headquarters in recent weeks? Adams claimed not to know, but he promised, with effort, to find out. (Under Dingell's imperative, he later confirmed that she had met thirteen times with FBI officials during the three weeks from before her testimony to the day after her firing.) Had the FBI done more than give her files? Had it sponsored her book? Was Aurora Publishers a front for the Bureau? "No," Adams said, "we have no proprietary interest in Aurora Publishers."

But in a general way, wasn't the Bureau engaged in a campaign to protect the nuclear industry from criticism? "There is no such campaign." Yet you have collected material for your files about people who oppose the use of nuclear power? "It's possible that we have." Why have you done it? How do you justify it? "All right, I'll tell you." Adams signaled with a finger that he was about to reveal a hard truth. "The Communist Party of the United States, which is dominated and controlled by the Soviet Union, has a program to try to discourage the use of nuclear energy in the U.S."

A strangled sound came from someone in the audience. Seigenthaler's wife had a hand to her mouth. She had come to Washington to stand with her husband and to mark his accusers. Now, out of nowhere, an accusation had been aimed at her and others like her. Mrs. Seigenthaler was not a political radical, nor a gadfly, but a year ago she had lent her name to a legal fight against a TVA nuclear reactor going up thirty miles from her home. To her it was the sort of thing a mother bear does when hunters are around.

"The FBI has just put me in league with the Russian Communists," she snorted to her college-age son, sitting alongside.

Adams apparently heard her, but his expression stayed as distant as if beamed by satellite. "We're always investigating the Communist Party," he said. "We're interested in the Communist Party's program in the United States today, tomorrow, the next day." He paused for water.

"Is that a hypothetical statement or is the Communist Party truly trying to stop the growth of nuclear energy in this country?" a congressman asked.

The FBI man's certainty faltered. "I would have to check. Uh, the last time I saw the Communist Party program, it was several years ago. . . ." His old throat grew parched again and his answer gave way to atrophy.

In the anteroom an air conditioner whirred and vibrated, and John Seigenthaler felt its cooling calm. "My mother the Red," young John said drolly. His father laughed, experimenting with the sensation.

Stockton came in, and the talk got serious again. "The FBI looked pretty damn silly, trying to lump housewives and newspaper columnists in with Stalin," Stockton said. "But I'm afraid we didn't do much to clear your name."

Seigenthaler was acutely aware of the public uncertainty. People wanted to know: was the FBI making up tales or *did* he have a darker side? "I have a few friends left over at Justice," he reported, "and they've found out what they could. On the day I fired Srouji, FBI headquarters asked its Nashville bureau for whatever it had on me. Nashville sent a two-page telex: some crap about my being involved in white slavery." (The FBI later divulged one line from the telex: "allegations of Seigenthaler having illicit relations with young girls." In the *Times* article it appeared that the Bureau also was inferring "impurity" from Seigenthaler's lifelong friendship with the Nashville sheriff, a man accused of consorting with prostitutes.) "Nobody ever considers what happens to the family in situations like this. The sideways looks on the street, the remarks at school. I've got a kid, and I've got seven brothers and sisters who've got kids. We're a big family, and we're a family that's always been respected. It'd probably go easier on them if I didn't pay attention to this mud-slinging. 'Just duck,' people tell me. But I can't. I'm a newspaper man. I have to print every word in the *Tennessean*."

"At least you're putting the FBI in a position of having to put up or shut up," Stockton murmured.

Seigenthaler felt he could be candid. "I went cluck-cluck when the FBI was smearing the radical left. But I let it slide, like everyone else. So the FBI is still trampling on whoever they feel like trampling on. Except now they're trampling on me. Well, the Seigenthaler family is drawing a line that should have been drawn years ago. We had a family council in Nashville last week. My mother, a fine Southern lady—crinoline and violet sachet—gave her blessing. 'Hew to the graven line,' she said. 'Let the chips fall where they may.' That's why I'm here today."

"We tried to get Homer Boynton to come," Stockton said, "but the Bureau said he was 'unavailable.' "

"Yeah, I know. I've had my lawyer write and demand an apology. No response."

James Adams had set off Dingell's temper, not for his shortwinded remarks at the hearing, but for what he had done secretly beforehand. He had tried to prejudice the Republicans against Seigenthaler by telling them about the Alabama incident. As a fling at sabotage, the action was rather trivial, but Dingell's anger subsided only into resolve. He dictated a letter to the Justice Department demanding a complete rundown on the affairs of Olson, Srouji, Seigenthaler, and copies of any FBI dossiers on Karen Silkwood or similar "anti-nuclear persons" and anything else pertinent.

Dingell's letter was more or less an ultimatum. Either the FBI came clean, or it would be in contempt of Congress—at least the piece of Congress that Dingell controlled. He set a deadline of June 14.

WASHINGTON. MAY 28, 1976. Sara's latest acquisitions were two old floor lamps with bare globes. Walking over to Danny she intersected the twin glints, splaying out the light. It bounced off her new pyramid walls. The character of the attic had been altered. Sara and a downstairs roommate had been hard at work, struggling with a power saw too big and two-by-fours too long, mortising old rectangles, chiseling, hammering sheetrock, stripping over cracks, making the attic tight. They had placed woven rugs on the floor, oiled the secondhand furniture, painted the walls a gaudy white, brightening everything. The enamel and the pine studs, still raw, were acrid in Danny's nostrils.

"What do you think?" Sara asked. Someone else had declared the scantling off kilter and predicted buckling in the first freeze.

Danny was not smart with his hands and knew little about tools or proper design. "It looks like the inside of a refrigerator," he observed.

"Yeah, and feels like an oven," she said, swinging around with an overdone laugh. No matter. In winter the hot stuffy air would be cozy. Sara was settling in and planned to stay.

Danny was languorous on the bed. Lawyer's lunches had rearranged the athletic form that once ran up and down his high school football field. He had the untended, carefree waistline of the courtroom, not the monastery.

Every morning, though, he would meditate cross-legged on the floor, knees out flat. The meditation cleaned out his mind. Day after day, he started fresh, and yet he wanted to get away, to read and study, to get his head completely straight, to spend time in the Jesuit seminary, however long it took.

"I can see you taking time off," Sara said. "But I can't see you in a seminary. It's not you." She could not see him lost in a world satiate, chaste, cold as a stone floor at midnight. "We have such exquisite times together," she said. "You're as sensual as anyone I've ever known. More sensual."

"I'm kind of swoony about you too." Danny kept his tone light.

"I just don't see how you can make love one minute and talk about celibacy the next."

"The seminary is in the future. We'll work it out."

"How? I'm not going to sneak myself into your room in a janitor's cart." Sara smiled at the thought, smiled despite herself. "Get this through your head, Daniel Sheehan. If you want to live with me, it will have to be in broad daylight."

NASHVILLE. JUNE 4, 1976. At the unemployment office the line had burgeoned onto the sidewalk. A Channel 5 news team, assigned to film the unfortunate procession, discovered Jackie Srouji there. Much of her past, and all of her future, was a mystery. For eleven days she had been incommunicado on a Florida beach—a *Times* headline reported her as "missing"—and she had rebuffed all questions at the second Dingell hearing. She had hired a lawyer to help regain her old status with the FBI, though it seemed quite out of reach.

Srouji had suffered a fate that shadows all undercover agents. With her double life now revealed, who would trust her? Not Seigenthaler, nor Sergey Zaitsev at the Soviet Embassy, probably not even her FBI pals, whom she had also let down, if not betrayed.

Yet she was not without a certain bargaining power. She had gleaned a few secrets in her work—"I can take some of Hoover's finest down with me," she told Seigenthaler. At the Bureau this was taken seriously. How else explain their schizoid behavior? The same week that the Bureau was subsidizing her Florida vacation, Callahan was putting the evil eye on her in D.C. If you use Srouji to make a liar of Lawrence Olson, Callahan told Stockton, I'll make her out to be a KGB spy. Stockton had laughed that off—she might be a red herring, but not a Red one. In his judgment Srouji was what she had confessed to be, a lowly FBI operative charmed by the intrigue. She would bomb in a James Bond movie; she was too plumped out. But in the drabness of real life, she did okay. She had a Mata Hari glow that made you forget she wasn't very pretty.

She could have stayed forever in Florida for all Stockton cared. And yet he was being drawn unwillingly into another consideration of her.

Srouji's present situation made her valuable. If she was ever to tell all
she knew about the Silkwood case, it would be in this unattached
state, and over the phone Stockton had widened ever so slightly her
estrangement from the FBI. He told her of Callahan's private moves
against her, how the FBI was protecting Olson but not her. "Time is
your enemy," he said. "The longer you wait, the less your credibility."

"I'm sorry, I can't say anything," she had demurred. "My lawyer
feels it'd be a big mistake."

But now in the unemployment line, with a mike thrust in her face
and a videopack aimed at her, she began to talk. "They're trying to
discredit me," she said bitterly. "There's a massive effort going on
right now. The FBI's afraid of what I might say."

The Channel 5 reporter perked up. "What don't they want you to
say?"

"I don't know." An inner struggle went on. "Okay, I'll tell you.
That nuclear worker in Oklahoma, Karen Silkwood, she had figures
in her possession which not only pinpointed how much plutonium
was missing, but also who took it. They had forty pounds at least,
enough to sell on the black market."

"The black market? Is that where it went?"

Srouji hesitated again. "I can't say that for a fact. But it was
definitely stolen. I saw the MUF figures that Karen Silkwood had.
That poor girl—she didn't know what kind of time bomb she was
carrying."

The interview with Srouji was telecast on the Channel 5 evening
news. An AP reporter saw it and called her up. She repeated her
accusation that Karen had been killed after coming across skewed
figures in the Kerr-McGee inventory, numbers that added up to
nuclear smuggling. The AP sent the story across its national wire,
and it made the morning papers around the country.

But, in D.C., Callahan dismissed it scornfully. "Nothing to it,"
he told Stockton. "Srouji's cuckoo. Always has been. Did you know
the Army discharged her for mental instability?"

Eleven

Turner had to detour up the stairwell. The elevator in Stockton's section, bulky and balky like the cages in mine shafts, was now the private transport of carpenters. New walls were going up in the old FBI building. The carpenters with their heavy lumber wagons seemed not to care about the load limit stamped on a sign inside the elevator. They were as nonchalant as the mice roaming the sawdust with open stealth.

"Next time let's meet at the bar," Turner said.

"How about a tire store?" Stockton said, wishing for the bar. "I had a flat this morning. Want to come shopping with me?"

"I guess I can stand the excitement."

They pounded down the steps like six-year-olds and ran at jogging speed to the no-man's-land by the freeway. It was a summer afternoon with a sky of fat, dumpling cumulus. Stockton had left the windows down in his VW to catch the breeze. Thieves wouldn't look at it twice with all its dings and scratches. The sun slanted through a dusty windshield, turning it glittery as mica. They had to pull the visors for shade.

"So you think Srouji has the smoking gun?" Turner asked, breaking the solitude of the ride.

"I don't know." Stockton's face was in a loose frown. He had heard the low, concerned murmurs of his friends, wondering if fatigue had settled into his thinking. He was dumb to believe Srouji, her of all people, a dime-store author out to hype her book.

Turner had another fear. "She could be trying to sucker you. Maybe she wants you to believe something so melodramatic no one else will believe it."

"I've thought of that too," Stockton said. He braked hard for a stop sign.

"Kerr-McGee denies flat out that any plutonium is gone?"

"Yeah, and the NRC people pretend they're just as positive. Though, when you read some of the letters they wrote back and forth, you can sense a few doubts." In November of 1972 an AEC official had written to Kerr-McGee: *We are particularly concerned about the superficial treatment you have given to measurement problems.* A March 1974 letter from the AEC again warned Kerr-McGee about its MUF and its lack of security. A month later there was a third letter. It was during this period that inspectors from the Glen Ellyn office had to fly to Oklahoma for a reinventory. In January 1975, after the mitosis from AEC to NRC, the new NRC commission ordered three new inspectors to Cimarron. The commission's memo held a hint of breathless worry, requesting reports on a day-to-day basis. One commissioner went along for a firsthand look. Within days, however, the commission's attitude was curiously transformed. The inspectors were recalled and Kerr-McGee was given sanction to continue operating. "It was like somebody sat them down and told them the facts of life," Stockton said.

"It's a touchy subject: plutonium smuggling," Turner said, being objective. He understood about need-to-know circumstances. He didn't like them, but he understood.

"Don't you love their logic, though? If they admit plutonium is missing, they think some nut will try a phony blackmail scheme. Fine and dandy. But what if some nut actually *did* get his hands on forty pounds? We'd be blissfully ignorant till we got blown to kingdom come."

"You think the NRC is covering for Kerr-McGee?"

"I don't think the NRC knows whether there's a MUF, one way or the other."

"Which makes it likely Karen Silkwood didn't either."

"Well . . ." Stockton looked unhappy. That was the blind spot in Srouji's tale. Karen had never mentioned anything about missing plutonium, not to Mazzocchi or Wodka or, as far as they knew, to anyone else. The very suggestion made the union men uneasy. They saw a flip side to the imperfect security at Cimarron. If smuggling was proved, the company might pass the blame to the workers and thereby justify more lie-detector purges, more union-busting.

Stockton pulled in at a discount tire store. The air held a subtle whiff of vegetation and fresh rubber.

"Has Srouji shown anybody these MUF papers?" Turner asked.

"No. But she insists they're locked in her safe-deposit with the rest of the thousand pages."

"The pages she showed you in Nashville didn't mention MUF?"

"No, she showed me FBI-letterhead memos, which is what she showed Seigenthaler. Chances are she's reading MUF between the lines. But who the hell knows? I'll give her this much: she's put the fear of God into Callahan. He's got his agents beating the bushes to get back whatever it is she has. They've been hassling Srouji's folks, even her grandmother."

"Srouji would just be a lot easier to buy if the Army hadn't certified her."

A suspicion blurring at the edge of Stockton's mind came into focus. "That Army business," he said: "that's what's almost got me believing her. It's too pat. She was sane enough for the FBI all these years, and sane enough for the Naval Reserve—they even had her assigned to that hush-hush Project Seafarer. Then what happens? She mouths off to this TV reporter, and right away Callahan is telling us how the Army decided she was weak in the head fourteen years ago." Stockton turned and got from Turner a noncommittal shrug. "Well, yesterday, I called the Pentagon to get a record of her discharge. The Army doesn't have it. Her whole file is missing. And that's not all. Guess who happens to have a photostat? Callahan! He brought one over for Dingell."

"You think it's a fabrication?"

"Srouji swears it is."

Turner stiffened at the impact of the sentence. "You better look sharp—they'll be out to smear you next," he predicted quietly.

Stockton had a flash. In Nashville he had gone to the offices of Aurora Publishers, where Srouji's book was being edited. The offices had a peculiar feel; they looked temporary, ready to be abandoned. And the editor, Dominic de Lorenzo, had the look of a Foreign Legion officer, not an editor. De Lorenzo had assigned a secretary to drive Stockton to the airport. That had been most peculiar of all. On the way there the secretary had tried—well, she had tried to get very friendly.

But Stockton laughed it off. "They won't come after me," he said. "Dingell is much more interesting."

The laughter reverberated in the VW's small chamber.

SOUTHFIELD, MICHIGAN. JUNE 14, 1976. It was midmorning when Lois Herman got out of bed—earlier than usual. The time in jail had disrupted her internal clock. She combed her long raven hair and painted an alluring mouth on peregrine features. Her clients wanted a face that was an alloy of sweetness and eroticism, and thighs soft, experienced. But nothing lewd. They were all men of taste, none of them vulgar or reckless, none willing to tomcat in Detroit's combat zones. Lois Herman was thirty-three years old, a divorcée in need of money. An old friend had introduced her to the men, told her of spacious unpatrolled motels in the suburban corridors south of Detroit. From her window she could see a radiant sign inviting travelers in for a "happy rest," mocking her misery. She was in trouble. The Southfield police had been abnormally stern. No fine, they said. They had booked her for running a bawdy house, for which she could get twenty years of hard time.

In the *Detroit News* city room a call was routed to Mike Wendland, a crime reporter of some distinction. It was a tip. Wendland scribbled down the information. A Lois Herman had been arrested in Southfield and a shoebox confiscated, a shoebox filled with the names and preferences of her clients, Mafiosi and politicians, on index cards: Sam "The Mustache" Norber, Michigan Attorney General Frank Kelley, Congressman John Dingell.

From the Southfield vice squad Wendland got verification. Yes, Lois Herman had been booked, and yes, they had her shoebox. Quite a classy clientele: All the names checked out, all but Dingell's. Taking along another reporter, Wendland went to see Mrs. Herman. "Oh, Congressman Dingell wasn't a regular," she said. "It was a special arrangement. It was a present for him. Somebody else paid me."

For years it had been improper journalism to write about the sex lives of politicians. But Judith Exner had pretty well abolished the taboo a few months earlier with her memoir about Sam Giancana and John Kennedy. The front page story in the *Detroit News* on June 20 was of this new tradition: how Mafia capos and public-office holders sometimes take their recreation with the same companions.

Stockton heard about it on his car radio. A fast synopsis: Prostitute, Mafia, Dingell. "Damn," Stockton swore out loud. "They've gone and done it."

Dingell tried to make light of it the next morning; the story was cheap and malicious, he said. But his advisers were less indifferent.

They thought Dingell should do some emergency campaigning in Downriver Detroit to avoid another nasty surprise on Election Day.

Stockton read through a copy of the article. Guess I was hasty, he said to himself, reconsidering. Nothing conspiratorial about a hooker trying to negotiate a plea bargain in the press.

But one thing, a minor coincidence, disturbed him. Lois Herman had been arrested on April 25. Two months had gone by before the story broke, and it happened to break the week Dingell had set as the deadline for the FBI to make full disclosure in the Silkwood case. But now Dingell was going to be busy tending to reelection chores—probably too busy to make the FBI comply. Which, perhaps, made it not so minor a coincidence after all.

PINEY WOODS, TEXAS. JULY 3, 1976. The morning sun had gilded the leaves of pin oak, black gum, sweet gum. Thickets of wild grapes, shrieky-green against summer grass, pushed through the trees almost to Mr. Silkwood's castaway cabin. It was still his refuge, now more than ever.

Ahead of a rooster tail of dust, an old van burst through the scrub mountains northwest of Nederland. It slowed for a silt-packed shallow. The sandy road to the cabin lay, in this spot, at the bottom of a flat river. In spring, with the water up, Mr. Silkwood would park on the bank, wade across, and hike the last mile in. With legs as sturdy as his, the fording was no hardship, and since, by mute consent, the missus and the girls did not come here often, he had never bothered with one of the portable Army-surplus bridges that downstream neighbors used.

In their holiday custom the Silkwood women had gone to Kilgore, taking the garden trowel to weed around the simple gray stone. Mr. Silkwood had not been there since the funeral, and his wife knew better than to ask. Although his preoccupation with Karen's case was now almost total—trips to Oklahoma, daily calls and correspondence, sessions with lawyers—he was no less burdened. Talking about it, he still felt inarticulate, unfacile. Long-distance with Kitty and Sara, he would sometimes refer to Karen without benefit of her Christian name. They thought this oddly impersonal, unaware of the wretched face at the other end of the line.

Safely reaching his cabin, Mr. Silkwood took off his shoes and padded about, careful of splinters; the floor was rough, in need of more varnish. The air inside was close and hot, and it soon drove him outside. Unraked leaves crackled under his feet. He found a familiar stump in a copse of trees and watched the sun sink in a red trembling. A breeze cooled his face; stars spun slowly up from the horizon; thunder muttered far away. Still he sat. Patience and impatience washed over him in waves. Dingell had announced another public hearing for later in the month, though Stockton said it might be postponed till fall. So what? So frigging what? Those Congress people had lost sight of the objective. Why hadn't they nailed Kerr-McGee? And why, f'r chrissakes, had they let Srouji spout off about Karen's personal life? He had felt hapless that day in the hearing room, having to listen to those lies, as he believed them to be. Gall had risen at the back of his throat. The girl that Srouji described was not the daughter he knew, or wished to know. He wouldn't deny that Karen had used marijuana; the medical examiner had found two "joints" in her purse, and in her penciled monthly budget she had listed "dope" as an expense. But the rest—everything else in Srouji's book—was *trash*. He had hidden his copy of the galley proofs away from the girls, as parents do with household poisons. If it was in his power, they would never see the actual words, never have to feel what he felt. He was grateful that the library at home did not often replenish its shelves; the book probably wouldn't appear there.

In a style that was basically straightforward, and thus more virulent, Srouji had turned gossip into journalism. If the FBI was doing the same to her now, it was no less than she deserved. He had no room for forgiveness. Let her try to atone, gush out forbidden secrets about plutonium smuggling. Let the FBI cannibalize her. To hell with her. He would sue her too—Srouji and Olson and Reading and Dean McGee. All of them.

That was his latest intention. In the past he had despaired of a lawsuit as too ambitious. But through the Butternut gang, he had obtained the services of Michael Kennedy, a fighting lawyer from San Francisco. Kennedy had helped him get appointed administrator of Karen's estate, rather than her former husband, which gave him standing to sue. "Don't get me wrong—I'm grateful for what Stockton and them have tried to do," he had explained to Kennedy. "But dang it, their deal hasn't worked out. We got to try something else —if we're gonna get the buggers that done it." The British obscenity was one he had picked up during the war.

WASHINGTON. JULY 25, 1976. They ran through the night in plunging, headlong strides that steadied into an uphill climb. Sara got to the Butternut porch and flopped down. "You're getting old," she taunted. Danny, lagging behind, wobbled from overheating.

"I let you win," he replied slyly. "To build up your ego."

"That'll be the day."

They were back from another evening at the movies. The cinema was Danny's sole relaxation, if you didn't count Socratic dialogue. It was the one happy ritual left from a lot of unhappy weekends growing up. Starting on Friday evenings Danny's father would finish off beer after beer, and his mother would take the kids to the movies and keep them there till the binge was leached dry. They might see five, six showings on a single weekend.

When Danny was ten his father walked home in snow from Great Meadows prison in upstate New York, walking miles and miles, leaving his car and guard's job behind. His father had watched a prisoner slash his wrists and die that day in a red spectacle before the cell could be opened. The family moved to San Diego, escaping the prison, but things didn't work out. His father left, going back to New York, and Danny was sent along. Danny was twelve, a street-gang leader, one foot in the reformatory. His mother bought him new corduroy slacks and a flannel shirt for the Greyhound ride. Aunt Agnes met him at the bus station in Glens Falls, New York. It was Christmas Eve, 1957. His father left to go get drunk, and stayed drunk into the new year. This was no proper upbringing, Aunt Agnes said; she called a taxi and sent Danny to his mother's relatives. It was an hour's ride, a snowy wait on a strange porch, then another ride. Aunt Gladys and Uncle Jim didn't know they were about to get a new son. Shivering in his corduroys, Danny had wondered if they even wanted one.

Ever since, Danny's life had been full out. He had never considered what might hinder him. He had made his way on his own. Telling his many stories, he would carom one off another, assuming always that Sara's interest was total: Danny as a college student, rising up during Mass to denounce a priest, then befriending the priest; Danny as a community-relations liaison in Boston, standing up to police brutality, and nearly assaulting a cop himself; Danny as a lawyer, learning savvy, baffling his associates with bottomless enthusiasm and discontent.

The heroes of the screen were Danny's models and accounted for his tendency toward melodrama. His ideas of the courtroom had come from Spencer Tracy at the Scopes monkey trial and from Henry Fonda in *Twelve Angry Men*.

"I won't take a case unless I'm right, and unless I can win," he said.

"Winning isn't everything, it's the only thing?" Sara asked. "Is that your motto?"

"No, if I had a motto, it would be: 'Losing is nothing.' The cases I work on, the people can't afford to lose—Wounded Knee, the Panther Twenty-one, the Berrigan brothers." Danny had assisted on a dozen such successes and, by degrees, had acquired the nerve and adamancy of an improbable winner. "Take the Cortright case," he said.

"Cortright?".

The story was a favorite. "David Cortright was a drum major at Fort Hamilton. He got some general all bent out of shape with an anti-war petition. Next thing Cortright knew he'd been transferred to an artillery unit. So we went to court, me and Fred Cohn from the Law Commune. In trotted the general, crew-top hair, spaghetti all over his chest. Fred Cohn is a huge guy, six-three, walrus mustache. He leans over and starts quoting from this letter. See, Cortright's friends had gone through the waste bags, fished out the used type-writer ribbons, got some stationery and retyped the transfer letter verbatim. It was all there: how the general had sent a noncombatant band guy into a combat unit. When the general saw the letter, he turned green. The judge had Cortright flown back first class, and Fred Cohn was ecstatic—he was so used to losing. The Law Commune was always taking cases to make a political point, not to win. I kept telling him, 'I don't have anything to do with losers.' "

Danny's rollicking memory was a stimulant, picking up and launching new subjects. Inevitably the Silkwood case came up.

"Did you talk to Michael Kennedy?" Sara asked. "Is he going to file a lawsuit?"

"I did what you wanted," Danny said. "I went to New York to see Kennedy. He was very straight with me. He can't do the case right now. He's strapped. He just moved east from San Francisco. He's got to get into the New York bar and all that rigamarole."

"Well, can you do it, then?" Sara asked straight out.

Danny rested his weight on the porch railing and winced at the outcry of old wood. "I don't know if it's such a good idea," he said.

"It's not worth it just to harass a corporation. Or just to make Kitty feel good."

"That's not fair," Sara said loyally. The hint of disunity upset her.

"I don't have anything against Kitty," he said. He knew he was treading on friendship. "More power to her. I hope she makes it as a lawyer. But I know she resents it when people ask me legal questions instead of her."

"You're wrong. She made you vice-president of SOS."

"And she made herself president! She likes to be the one giving orders."

"That's not as important to her as the lawsuit." Sara looked woeful. "You're the one who said it's getting down to the wire with the statute of limitations. And you know a lawsuit is our best hope. Dingell's running scared because of that sex scandal."

Danny pushed away from the railing; the wood shook, then relaxed. "I just don't think there's a reasonable chance of winning it." He paused. He was in sympathy with the motives in SOS—union solidarity, eco-politics, mystery-solving, retribution, mythmaking —though there had been a time when he wouldn't have felt even sympathy. The classic overachiever in high school, Danny had scored highest in his district for the military academies, and with his sights on the moon, he had selected the Air Force astronaut program. But the appointment went to a mayor's son, rated seventh, and Danny became instead a college Green Beret. Vietnam was his destination until the day a sergeant tried to show him how to decapitate with a wire garrote. It came so easily and virtuously to Danny's hands that his mind knew it was wrong. He dropped the garrote and left the drill field. When the Berets tried to get him back, Danny threatened court action, and so began his legal career. Still, for a political lawyer, Danny was not very ideological. He saw himself as an inheritor of eighteenth-century libertarianism, the lawyer defending individual liberties, righting institutional wrongs. His professors, of course, had warned him that such piety was useless—no, worse than useless: it would destroy his legal skills.

"Okay," Danny said. "I'll sit down and look through everything Kitty has, every scrap. If the facts are there, if I can tell a judge, to a moral certainty, that Kerr-McGee or the FBI broke the law, then I'll do it. I'll file the suit."

"All right!" Sara grabbed one of Danny's hands. "Let's go tell Kitty. She'll make piña coladas for the whole house."

Danny restrained her with a light touch. "I'll try to get the suit done in a year. I'd rather not put off my entrance date . . ." He felt a vacuum move between them, in which he couldn't speak.

". . . to the seminary." She finished the sentence for him. "I understand, Danny. However it works out."

Kitty's head hurt from the radiated light. She felt tempted to start a wholly personal crusade: the banning of fluorescent tubes. Everywhere she went they droned overhead, just at decibel level, pulsing, flickering, hardening eyeballs to marbles. These offenders were in the NRC reading room, three blocks from the White House. After four days at a reading table, Kitty had a cramp that started at her eyes and went down her spine.

Piled before her were perhaps six thousand pages of turgid, coded AEC/NRC prose, the Cimarron records open to the public. She had been through them once before, like a scythe through grass, when she wrote her testimony for Dingell's subcommittee. Now she was trying, insatiably, to find meaning in every page. The records were far from conclusive. A great many specifics were missing, blanked out by law, so that rival nuclear companies couldn't plagiarize Kerr-McGee's methods. Selecting the most revealing pages, Kitty had photocopies made. Then she walked to a subway stop, staring dully at a black Continental that glided up to the White House—a dinner guest for President Ford.

At Butternut, after her own dinner, Kitty luxuriated in the downstairs tub. Bubbles sprang along the surface and floated leisurely over the side. Slowly she began to feel normal. In the living room, with a towel folded around her, she went through a limbering-up routine learned from Sara. She spread her fingers wide, then her arms, stretching muscles in sequence. She arched forward, touching her palms to the floor, a minor feat recently mastered. Trying to imitate her, Amber fell chin first. "Upsy-daisy," Bob said, piggybacking her upstairs for bed.

Danny had come by. He was at the longboard, engrossed in the photocopies.

"You can see that Cimarron was having trouble all along," Kitty said, breathing hard from the exercise. "In 1971 several workers got internally contaminated because of a defective valve, and it got worse after the 1972 strike. There's a letter to the Sierra Club. This woman,

Ilene Younghein, was up in arms, but they told her the only problem they had was these untrained kids hired during the strike."

Another letter had a red margin comment from Kitty: *What gall!* Danny held it up. "What's this?"

"It's a letter from Kerr-McGee."

"I can see that."

Ignoring his curtness, she said, "After Mrs. Younghein got upset, the AEC decided the people around Cimarron ought to be inter-viewed to see if they wanted to live next to a plutonium factory. Kerr-McGee sent this letter to the AEC, saying the interviews weren't 'a proper subject of inquiry.' "

"Kerr-McGee told the AEC to fuck off?"

"Almost. A public survey was finally done months later. Suppos-edly everyone liked the factory. The Crescent City Council sent a letter to the AEC saying that Crescent people liked it. The Guthrie City Council said the same thing—exactly the same thing, word for word. So did the Logan County commissioners. All three letters were identical. The Guthrie city manager later admitted that Kerr-McGee had written the letters."

A door slammed and Shawn came in. He was taking big juicy licks off a grape popsicle. "You're not supposed to eat junk food," Kitty scolded. He hid the sugared ice in his mouth. "And you're supposed to be home by dark."

Slurp. Slurp. "Honest, Mom, it isn't dark yet." There was a pale glimmering of light behind the trees.

"Okay," she relented, "go and say good night to Amber." Kitty went upstairs with him to get a bathrobe.

Sara was in the kitchen, shelling peas into a colander. Danny kissed her on the cheek, a hesitant little-boy kiss, and she kept on tumbling the fat spheres out of their pods. Danny scrounged in the refrigerator. His dinner had been an ice cream cone. He made a sandwich of bread, mayonnaise and beefsteak tomatoes plump from the garden. Mulch and a compost bed had made the vegetables plentiful all summer.

Back at the longboard, Danny and Kitty put the photocopies in order. "You've done a good job," he said.

"I added up the airborne contaminations," Kitty said. "Seventy-three. One guy got hot his first day there. He quit the next day, and no doctor was ever sent to diagnose him. Another time the company waited a full day to call in a doctor for seven workers who were hot, and it was four days before they were checked for lung damage."

"We'll need witnesses like them. To demonstrate wanton and reckless disregard."

Kitty was making a different point. "Don't you see?" she said. "Karen had no reason to contaminate herself. Kerr-McGee must have done it."

"You're jumping bases. Even a thousand contaminations wouldn't prove that Kerr-McGee put plutonium on her baloney."

"Let me play devil's advocate," she said sharply. "Let's say Karen did want to make Kerr-McGee look bad, to get leverage in the 5–283 negotiations, and let's ignore for a minute the fact that getting contaminated made her scared stiff. It still wouldn't have made sense for her to contaminate herself. There was no leverage to be gained. If Kerr-McGee didn't give a damn about the first seventy-three contaminations, why would it care about number seventy-four?"

Danny's brows lifted. "Good point," he said. The soles of his tennis shoes kneaded the carpet. "Another point: if Karen had really wanted to embarrass Kerr-McGee, she'd have done it at the factory, not in her apartment."

"So are you convinced? To a moral certainty?"

He gave her a thin smile. "We've got a long way to go. We'd have to convince a jury that Karen's manila folder was worth stealing, that Kerr-McGee had a reason to stop her."

"I'll go to Oklahoma if you want."

Again the smile: "Better leave that to a professional. Incidentally, have you talked to Mr. Silkwood?"

"Yes. He doesn't care who does the suit, as long as someone does."

"Have him give me a call. I'll talk to Stockton. We'll see what happens."

SOUTHFIELD, MICHIGAN. AUGUST 26, 1976. The professional spectators were about to get their first look at the body that went with the mug-shot face already seen in the *Detroit News*. If they expected centerfold superabundance, they had to be disappointed with the diminutive shape going into the Forty-sixth District courthouse. Lois Herman had donned large sunglasses and a pantsuit for her pretrial exam; she looked like the housewife she had once been.

The Oakland County prosecutor called two witnesses. Most reporters regarded Sylvia Western as the more newsworthy. A former kindergarten teacher, she was Mrs. Herman's associate; it was funny-sad to hear her tell the judge that a stingy school board had put her in this fix. The other witness was Hugh McMartin, Southfield police intelligence officer, a member of the Red Squad; he described Mrs. Herman's arrest. How had *he* come to make the arrest instead of a vice-squad officer? Well, Officer McMartin replied uneasily, the FBI had tipped him off.

The FBI's involvement in a prostitution case is not the usual run of business. Call girls generally were beneath the attention of the Bureau, except as titillations in Hoover's old dossiers.

A *Detroit Free Press* reporter was alert to Officer McMartin's strange footnote, and Stockton read about it the next day. He drew in a hard breath. It gave him the creeps. I don't want to find out any more, he thought. But he had to, and with some research he did. Mrs. Herman's best friend, the woman from whom she had purchased her shoebox clientele, was an FBI informant. The friend had informed the FBI, the feds had tattled to the Southfield cops, and someone had tipped off the *Detroit News*. It had advanced like dominoes. That was not so unusual. But the dates were. Mrs. Herman's friend had informed on her at least a year ago. But the FBI had not mentioned it to Officer McMartin until this spring, a week or so after Metcalf abdicated and Dingell assumed control of the Silkwood case. Then, after Dingell got tough with the FBI, the press had been told.

Dingell had admitted meeting Mrs. Herman at a restaurant party ("I meet lots of people"), but he had denied taking her to bed. Stockton believed him. So did the Oakland County prosecutor. But that did not mean the incident was forgotten, not by reporters or voters.

On Labor Day weekend Stockton went with his wife and children to the ocean. They were buying a cottage near a beach. He walked the sand at tide's edge while gulls dived and screeched rusty-hinge epithets. He might as well have stayed in his office, he realized, along with his thoughts, thoughts of a conspiracy.

WASHINGTON. SEPTEMBER 10, 1976. Stockton's calendar was attached to the top box in a cardboard stack that stood by his desk like a sentinel. "Damn, I did it again." The adhesive hook had come off with the calendar.

Stockton turned the beach scenes ahead to November. "It's gonna be close," Danny said, looking over his shoulder.

The statute of limitations for a civil suit would run out either November 5, two years from the first day of Karen's contaminations, or November 13, the date of her death. Election Day was November 2. Dingell planned to resume the Silkwood hearings, but only after he was reelected. "No, that's too close," Danny decided. "If we sue, it'll have to be before then."

Stockton compared his watch with the wall clock. He said, "Let's talk over lunch." From a metal rack he grabbed his beer-drinker hat. They walked across a baked-dirt plateau and across a freeway bridge; the canyon below echoed with the hot whiz of wheels. A good-smelling basement cafe beckoned them in. Stockton had a lean-fried chopped steak. He was counting calories for hockey season. "It's either take a few pounds off now or those kids will skate them off me." Danny had the appetite of someone who starves between free lunches; his stomach growled like a jungle beast. He ordered extra rations of salad and every vegetable on the menu.

"I figured Kitty for the vegetarian, not you," Stockton said.

"Why Kitty?"

"Living in a commune and all." He laughed. "Though now that I think of it, she's not mellow enough for a vegetarian." He exchanged a knowing look with Danny, teamed up, as they were, with a woman as substantial and aggressive as themselves.

Danny got down to business. "What can you tell me?"

Stockton said, "Mostly I've been investigating the investigators. It's screwy. I don't care how rumpled a detective Olson is, you can't be as incompetent as he was without doing it deliberately. On everything crucial Olson fell down on the job. He'd like us to think the dents were the result of the car being winched out of the culvert, because that's what the Highway Patrol told him. But he never checked it out; he didn't even talk to Pipkin. Like with the autopsy, he didn't bother to consult any independent toxicologists. The local medical examiner said the Quaalude knocked Karen out, and that was good enough for Olson. Same with the missing plutonium: he simply took Reading's word that it was all accounted for."

"Is smuggling a real possibility here?" Danny asked. "Or is it a smoke screen?"

"I wish I knew. I feel like I've been chasing my own tail for damn near two years." Stockton stabbed a bite of steak; he had almost forgotten his food. "At one point an Oklahoma radio station got an anonymous letter, full of names and dates, all about how Kerr-McGee was selling plutonium on the black market. A bank cashier from

Dallas and a Tel Aviv Aviation official supposedly were the middle-men, and if you can believe it, Karen supposedly was a courier for Kerr-McGee. Supposedly she was paid over a hundred grand in Odessa Pipeline stock, then tried to double-cross Kerr-McGee, and they killed her."

"What a weird twist that would be."

Stockton put down his fork. "Yeah. But all the details turned out to be phony. There's no bank cashier by that name, no Tel Aviv Aviation official, no Odessa Pipeline. So it's back to square one."

"There's still the plutonium in her apartment."

"That was a microscopic amount, not nearly enough to sell."

"But does Olson have a theory on how it got on the baloney?"

"That's a story you should hear over a beer. Want one?" Stockton signaled the waiter.

"No, you go ahead." Danny was foraging for the last morsels on his plate.

"First, you have to understand Olson. He gets real jacked up on the sex angles. 'AC-DC girls,' 'switch-hitters.' On and on, every squad-room idiotism. Reading sold him on all the nympho and per-vert gossip, and how she'd snuck the plutonium out in her vagina. As soon as Olson heard that, it was obvious. Deductive reasoning: she must've been abusing herself with the baloney, using it like a dildo: that's how it got hot. You can imagine Olson's chagrin when he found out the baloney was in slices; it wasn't a ring sausage."

"Typical. Trust the FBI to move the crime out of the kitchen and into the bedroom," Danny said drily. "What happened when you confronted Olson on all this?"

"It wasn't an ideal interrogation. The FBI sent along extra agents; they had us outnumbered, and they had the guns, poking out over their belts. They held Olson together." The waiter brought a Hei-neken, and Stockton took several quick gulps. "Olson was real proud about tracking down a thermos of red liquid that'd been in the Honda. It'd been sent to Idaho for radiation testing, and he hoofed all the way to get it back. He thought the red liquid was a Bloody Mary and Karen had been sipping it to get warm."

"Could that have caused her to lose control?"

"No, the thermos was under the seat with the top screwed on. And it wasn't a Bloody Mary, it was spoiled tomato juice. There was only the smallest trace of alcohol in Karen's bloodstream, probably from the night before. The thermos has no meaning at all. The whole Idaho excursion was a wild-goose chase."

"Idaho! What a place! But that's another story. Excuse me."

"There's not a lot more I can tell you that you don't already know. Unless you haven't heard about the sixty-mile-an-hour crosswind?"

"Sara mentioned it. I think she heard about it from that Justice Department guy, Keeney. It's the official theory, isn't it? That the wind made Karen's car go off on the wrong side of the road?"

"That's right. But guess where it comes from? An old lady in Dallas! She phoned the FBI with this story about a howling crosswind and Olson took it as gospel. You know what the wind speed actually was? Fifteen miles an hour. And it wasn't a crosswind. It was from the northwest, behind the car. You can check with the U.S. Weather Bureau."

Danny motioned to indicate his amazement. "How'd you find out about the old lady?"

"It was in the files, the ones we finally got."

"No wonder they didn't want to turn them over." Danny grinned. "I guess they made Nixon's mistake. They didn't stonewall long enough."

"What they did was underestimate Dingell. As long as Metcalf was in charge there was no pressure." Stockton made a derisive noise. "Turner did his best—I've never worked for anybody better—but all Old Man McGee had to do was show up and, splash, Metcalf went overboard. I'm not saying that Dingell is willing to go down with the ship, but he's got a modicum of courage."

"I hear he's losing it."

Stockton was suddenly irritated. He swallowed the rest of his beer and looked at his watch. Danny noticed and changed the subject. "If Olson did such a hack job, why hasn't he been busted to private? Why is everybody in the FBI and Justice Department covering for him?"

"A damn good question." Why hadn't the checks and balances worked? It was not difficult to see how Olson could have been side-tracked—he and Reading were buddies. But for the Justice Department to have seen and countersigned everything he did—that was a cover-up on a grand scale. Sighing, Stockton said, "The files we got are a crazy quilt. But there's a very curious memo that was sent to Keeney. It's from Phil Wilens, the labor and management section chief. He wrote it in February of 1975, at a point when only three of eleven FBI field reports were done. With less than one third of the evidence in, Wilens had already made up his mind there was no foul play. Then he assigned Thomas Goldstein to compile a Fact Memorandum, which normally runs a hundred pages or more. Goldstein should have spent weeks sifting through all of Olson's evidence. At most he spent a couple days. The Fact Memorandum he compiled was four and a half pages long. But none of his superiors said a word. They obviously didn't want a thorough job. If they had, they wouldn't have assigned the case to Goldstein. He was on his way out; he'd already given notice; he was moving to Miami. He had two weeks to close out some litigation in New York and clean out his desk. And write the Fact Memorandum! They treated the case like the final decision was preordained."

The waiter deposited the bill, and Stockton got to his feet. Lunch and his narrative were at an end. All summer he had had a sense of being at the end of things. He had been wrapped up in the Silkwood case for the better part of two years. His wife wished he were back hunting wayward decimal points. One more month, he kept telling her, two at the most. Outside in the cool air, he imagined himself emerging from a great cocoon.

Danny was mumbling under his breath. Mr. Silkwood and Kitty had wanted to sue almost everybody, and that no longer seemed so unreasonable. "If we could get a Deep Throat or a John Dean, someone on the inside," Danny mused. "Somebody like Olson."

"Did I tell you he called me up at home? Twice. It was very strange. His attitude was half bully, half little boy. Wanted us to lay off Srouji. He sounded like he was sincerely concerned. But he also threw in a new dodge. Blamed the cover-up on the OCAW. Said he had been blocked from going after the union."

"What was he trying to imply? That the union set up Karen to be killed?"

"Something like that. I think it's the FBI's fallback position. It hinges on the fact that Mazzocchi, Wodka and Drew Stephens were the only people who knew Karen was going to the Holiday Inn that night," Stockton said. He adjusted his hat. There was a wind. Autumn had come in ahead of schedule.

"Is there any way Kerr-McGee could've known about the Holiday Inn?"

"One theory is that someone at the motel could've tipped them off. But Srouji let something slip once. She was trying to impress me, and she started telling me about these transcripts Reading has. Apparently he had Karen's phone bugged. He had transcripts of dozens of conversations."

Danny whistled. "So that's how they knew! A wiretap!"

A class of pubescent Catholic girls, eyes shining, maroon skirts flapping at their knees, marched into the crosswalk. They were in the city for an afternoon at the Capitol. Danny almost collided with them. He was lost in thought. Already he had the look of commitment. The girls went on up the Hill, and fat squirrels gobbled cookie crumbs in their wake.

Danny was reading Rousseau and thinking of Idaho. It was a clear cold space in his memory, that day two years ago at the courthouse in Pocatello. Danny could still see the chalky face of the old man in the witness chair. He could hear the old man begging and could hear his own hard voice insisting that the man take into his hands the notes of his treachery. The man had helped cause the firing of a union activist at Idaho State University. It was fair he should sacrifice his career for the one undone. But his life too? Danny could remember the old man collapsing to the floor, the gurgling far back in his throat, the rolling eyes. The law allows lawyers to destroy lives in other ways, he thought, impelling people into shame, into suicide, into oblivion. For money, lawyers will shield great criminals and torture the innocent. He knew one Washington law firm with a slogan on its pencils: *"A reasonable doubt for a reasonable price."* All of them, however, would be horrified to have a witness twitching at their feet. Yet Danny had felt nothing, no compassion, not even a thin contrition. Why? Because he was in the right and the old man was a Judas? On his high school football team, New York Class D champions in 1962, Danny had been defensive captain, the meanest player on the team. He tackled without quarter and never lent a hand to a fallen ball carrier.

What would Rousseau have said? He turned the pages, but pithiness was not one of Rousseau's virtues. Danny put the book down. There was a quote he knew from memory: *"Law and equity are two things which God hath joined, but which man hath put asunder."* He had studied Holmes and Brandeis to learn the law. Now he was reading the humanists to understand about justice, to find a codicil of the heart. He looked forward to being alone with his books in the monastery.

Stretched out on the couch, Danny closed his eyes. The cushions were covered with a nubby green fabric. All the furniture in the old convent house had been scavenged from junk stores and garage sales. The odd lengths and colors of carpet were warehouse throwaways. Early in the century German nuns had cooked and washed here for the seminary students of Holy Name College, on whose grounds the tall gabled house stood. It had been cobwebbed and vacant when Danny discovered it. In exchange for the refurbishing, the college had let him move in. With him had come Father Bill Davis, his boss at the Ministry for Social Justice, and four more Jesuits involved in other service to the Church. They had named the convent Arrupe House, after Pedro Arrupe, Father General of the Jesuits.

Mr. Silkwood's call woke Danny from his nap. This was their second conversation in as many weeks. The first had been courtesy. Now Danny probed for Mr. Silkwood's grandfatherly feelings about Karen's children. If there was a courtroom award, the kids would be the beneficiaries. "That's fine with me," Mr. Silkwood said, "as long as we can keep it in a trust or something—I don't want their father spending it."

Danny was surprised at the hostility, but he didn't respond. At the moment it was more important that Mr. Silkwood comprehend how a lawsuit could intrude everywhere into Karen's private life. "Kerr-McGee's lawyers will be allowed to ask about anything she ever did," Danny explained.

Mr. Silkwood wavered. Could he have his revenge and still spare his surviving women? "Whatever it takes," he said with deliberation, "I'm willing."

"One thing it won't cost you is money," Danny said. "Sara and Kitty will raise money to take care of expenses." Nor did Danny want a fee, not even a token one. These were conditions no ordinary lawyer would accept, let alone dictate. They aroused suspicion. "What'll you get out of this?" Mr. Silkwood asked cautiously.

"I get to be in charge. When I take a case, I run it. I make all the decisions."

That, at least, Mr. Silkwood could understand. All the other talk of good intentions made him uneasy. He had had almost two years of good intentions. So far he couldn't see that they had resulted in much.

PART THREE

Twelve

Danny ripped another sheet from the yellow pad. He wadded it up and let it drop onto the pile under his desk. Law books with smooth red covers lay open before him. This was Monday, and Mr. Silkwood was arriving from Texas on Tuesday. By week's end, five o'clock Friday, the legal papers had to be in Oklahoma City. Danny had lost track of the days, the weeks. Kitty had had to remind him of tonight's SOS meeting. She had come to his office this morning like a town crier. ("You said you'd be done with the research by now!") She was bringing an Antioch professor along tonight to help get the lawsuit court-ready.

Leaving the paper balls, Danny pulled on a frayed cord for the blinds. The pulley made a dry creaky sound. The glass was flyspecked and filmy, and he had to strain to see the figures below, hurrying home against the final light. A pigeon landed on the window ledge and shook water from its feathers. A drizzle was falling.

It was more than a mile to the EPC, where they were to meet. Out in the street Danny entered a timpanic uproar. Important men without umbrellas, forgetting who they were, shoved and hollered from precarious stances between the white lines of traffic. Taxis hungered from curb to curb like giant pouncing tabbies. Danny walked past and kept walking. He moved into the gloom under the trees of the Hill. The weather twilled his hair into clinging wet curls, but he walked on, rehearsing his explanation.

They were waiting for him—Kitty, Bob, Amber, Sara, and the others. Kitty introduced the law professor, a man severely dressed. Danny glanced down at his own familiar suit. Drat, he thought, I should have gone to Arrupe House and changed to jeans. He coughed; he was catching a cold. He would have liked to dally, perhaps entertain the gang with one of his spellbinders; it was his great charm. But tonight, he knew, he should get right to it. "There's no way we can sue Kerr-McGee for intentionally killing Karen. Not up front," he declared gravely, like a doctor at a postmortem. "We don't have the legal basis for a *wrongful death* tort. No judge will let us through the door."

There was silence. No one moved.

"In *wrongful death*," Danny said to fill the void, "the burden of proof is very similar to homicide. We'd have to show that agents of Kerr-McGee were responsible for ramming Karen into that culvert."

He turned toward Wodka, whose face was the most sympathetic. "What's the alternative?" Wodka asked.

"A civil rights suit. We can file under the Act of 1871, which is an old Reconstruction Period law, and we can get into how Karen was harassed at work, how she might've been wiretapped, et cetera. Plus we can file a negligence tort on her contamination. I've got that much written up already. All I want to do is drop *wrongful death*. Otherwise we risk getting the whole shebang thrown out."

"No, dammit, no!" The words had the curdle of a missionary calling to savages. Kitty was half out of her chair. "What's the matter with you people? We can't let Kerr-McGee get away with killing Karen. She's in her grave because all those men out there were cowards. Are we gonna be the same way?" Kitty's chair toppled over as she moved toward the door. She reached out; her eyes were wet glass. "You've ruined everything!" The disappointment built into hysteria. "I wish *I* could do this suit. There has to be a way. I know there is. You just haven't looked hard enough."

"If you'll sit down, I can explain," Danny said, but Kitty kept right on going. Alone in a corner with her dolls, Amber began to whine. Danny shook his head in a slow pendulum motion. He felt frozen. He felt twelve years old, huddled on the porch in his corduroy pants and flannel shirt, the snow falling.

The meeting was breaking up. Bob went to change Amber's diaper, and Wodka asked Sara if she knew Dingell's latest plans. Danny ducked into the hall, expecting to find Kitty in tears against a wall. The hall was empty.

"She probably left—she had to do guard duty at Antioch tonight," Sara said, putting her arms around Danny. His lips skated lightly over hers.

"Want a ride?" Sara asked. With her eyes she swept his proud, distracted face. At his temples Danny had lines ridged deep in the flesh, perhaps to the bone: from too much thinking.

He tried a smile that did not come out. "Can you drop me off at the office?"

At Antioch there had been a student revolt against heavy-handed guards. In a compromise, the students themselves had assumed the security chores, and once a week Kitty took up a post at a guard desk in the library lobby. Usually she studied until the lights-out stampede at eleven. Tonight, with an hour left on her shift, her books were still in her knapsack. Her head was sunk on the desk. She felt a leaden ache like a tumor.

The ringing phone jolted her upright. "Who is it?" she asked sullenly. "What do you want?" It was probably a paramour of the Tuesday night guard, getting his evenings mixed up again.

"It's Danny. You didn't give me a chance to explain." He began citing the names and numbers of past litigations, some of which Kitty recognized from her classes.

But what good was it to know why something could *not* be done? Why didn't he go to Sara? Kitty steeled herself against the appeal in his voice. She was silent, closed as a fist. She was telling herself: let it go, forget it, think of it as a weight lifted away; you'll have more time for school and the kids, and you'll be healthier. Of late, terrible migraines had been keeping her in bed long into the morning.

Danny created spaces in the conversation for her, but he was forced into a soliloquy. "It's not what you think. I want to find out who killed Karen as much as anyone. We just can't lay it on Kerr-McGee yet. Not to a moral certainty. If we come up with some evidence, we can put her death in the suit later."

"The statute of limitations is about to run out," Kitty said obstinately. "You won't be able to file a *wrongful death* suit later."

"No, but we can amend the civil rights part of the suit. Remember how the feds used the civil rights law to go after the Klan when the local DA's wouldn't prosecute for murder. We can do the equivalent of that." An idea, like a resurrected spirit, was taking shape. "Technically, her death was a civil rights violation. She was deprived of her right to travel freely on an interstate highway."

Kitty's voice softened. *"The right to travel freely on the highway?* That's perfect. Sometimes, Danny, you are a joy to talk to."

"As a matter of fact, we can stick it in the suit right now. It's not gonna leap out at a judge the way *wrongful death* would."

WASHINGTON. NOVEMBER 2, 1976. So far today Bill Silkwood had endured a long plane ride, the misrouting of his luggage, and a taxi ride through bedlam. But his discomfort was nothing compared to his anxiety, the anxiety that at the last minute he might yet be cheated out of his day in court. Only seventy-two hours remained in which to get the legal papers written, typed, notarized and into a U.S. District Court.

"We don't have the time for Meadows," Mr. Silkwood growled. "Why even bring him up?"

Danny patiently repeated his reasoning. "Meadows is the father of the kids, their legal guardian. If his name isn't on the suit, Kerr-McGee could challenge us on procedural grounds."

"But they couldn't get it thrown out because of that?" Mr. Silkwood single-mindedly kept his attention on the suit. "We could get by without Meadows?"

"Yes, we could, but . . ." Danny pulled his chair closer to where the dark-haired grandfather sat. They were in Danny's office at the Ministry for Social Justice. Mr. Silkwood was on the opposite side of the desk, like a truant boy sent to the principal's office. He was sweating in his overcoat. "If we don't take care of this now," Danny said, "it'll bedevil us all the way. We can't have Meadows getting pissed off and pulling some stunt. Everybody's got to be in this together. It's gonna take all of us, legally and *spiritually*."

Through the open door Mr. Silkwood noticed a man in a collar at the drinking fountain. What kind of lawyer, he wondered, is someone who wants to be a priest?

Danny said, "Look, I know you feel Meadows mistreated your daughter. Hard as it is, you've got to forget that."

Mr. Silkwood growled more displeasure, but Danny was hard-nosed. "This is our first disagreement, and I'm settling it. Meadows is in."

Carrying out the decision was not quite as simple. Meadows had his own misgivings about joining again with the Silkwood family, even in this reduced and impersonal way. He wanted no part of press conferences and women in Afros. "But for the sake of the kids, I'd like to cooperate," he told Danny. "If you can talk my brother-in-law into it, I'll go along." The brother-in-law was a lawyer.

So a preliminary draft of the suit was air-expressed to Oklahoma, where the Meadows family still resided. But as the hours counted down toward Friday there was no word from the brother-in-law.

Danny used up Wednesday daytime going through the case once more with Stockton. Wednesday evening was a marathon of writing and research. Kitty and Sara and Mr. Silkwood read Danny's yellow sheets to correct factual inaccuracies. Not until the sun delivered a new day did they go home.

But Danny went without sleep. From his office he took a cab to the OCAW. A sheen of beard made him look sinister.

Mazzocchi and Wodka had briefed him earlier about the atmosphere of fear at Cimarron: the transfers, intimidations, harassments, and, after Karen's death, the polygraphs and firings. "It all adds up to a good-faith presumption they had her under surveillance," Danny said.

"Wouldn't surprise me," Mazzocchi replied. "Nothing does any more." Having put his faith in the AEC, the FBI, and Congress, he was a little short on faith. The chalk questions on his blackboard had become a taunt. Now, when OCAW men in Denver referred to the case, it was with deepening intolerance. Why didn't Mazzocchi leave behind this unproved scandal? Jack Tice and Jean Jung and the ghost of Karen Silkwood were no longer his concern. With the closing of the factory, 5-283 Nuclear had been disbanded.

"Give me your honest opinion," Mazzocchi said in a grizzled tone. "Does this ragtag lawsuit have a snowball's chance in hell of cracking this case?"

Danny was adamant. "If they were spying on her in any way, shape, or form, I'll jump all over them—and you can watch your murderer run for cover."

"Okay, I'm with you," Mazzocchi said, sounding more like his old self. "If you're willing to stick your neck out, I am too. Let's do it."

Wodka was less grand about Danny's capabilities. "Assuming they did have Karen under surveillance, and I'm sure they did, how are you gonna prove it?"

"To start with, Srouji told Stockton she'd seen the actual wiretap transcripts."

Wodka hooted. "Oh Christ, you can't trust Srouji. She works for the other side."

"That's why it's good evidence. Her testimony would be an admission against interest. And if she's got copies of the transcripts, we'll subpoena them."

"She'll light a match to them first. Wait and see, you can't count on her."

"Do *you* have anything better?"

A memory stirred. "In one of the notebooks Karen gave me, she'd written a cryptic phrase: *the company knows something is going on.*"

"Anything else?"

"Let me think a minute." Wodka's mouth went square. "During the time right after Karen was killed, we did a little test. Drew thought his phone was bugged, so he and I concocted a decoy story and talked it up over his phone. Sure enough, it wasn't long before Reading was sniffing around, asking Drew all about it. Course, that's not proof either."

"All we need right now is a good-faith presumption."

"Well, the best of luck to you," Wodka said. "You'll need it." The choral comment chased after Danny as he left. He had heard it many times before.

Now that they were down to the last twenty-four hours, Mr. Silkwood seemed to have the most in reserve. He carted in a good supply of coffee and Cokes; he collated pages; he wrote out longhand supplements; and he was an incisive influence on those matters that had been left undecided till the end.

How much to ask in compensation? Kitty wanted the figures set high. "No price is too high for somebody's life." Danny argued for a deliberately low amount to impress the judge that they were after truth, not money, and Mr. Silkwood leaned that way too. They settled on a request for $85,000 in actual damages and $75,000 in punitive damages.

Which names to put on the title page? The brother-in-law had called at the last hour and said to include Meadows. So the plaintiffs were Karen's father and her former husband as trustees for her three children. The defendants were James Reading, Dean McGee, Jackie Srouji, Lawrence Olson, John Keeney, along with several of their associates and the organizations they represented.

Danny wrote a heading at the top of the page: *Karen Silkwood, by the administrator of her estate, et al. v. the Kerr-McGee Corporation, et al.* But wasn't this needlessly provocative? Why not put the names of

Karen's children first? "No," Danny said, "we're not going to hide behind them. This is not a shakedown suit. We're not going to settle for a few bucks just to send the kids to college. This suit is for their mother. Either she'll be vindicated. Or the company will be. One or the other. Those are the stakes."

Mr. Silkwood grabbed and pumped Danny's hand in agreement.

Where to file? Oklahoma City or D.C.? They had thrashed this through before and decided on Oklahoma City, but now Mr. Silkwood wondered whether D.C. might be safer. What if the papers got lost like his luggage in an airline black hole? "I'm not saying it couldn't happen," Danny said, "but we have a bigger worry. Kerr-McGee could argue that the suit belongs in Oklahoma because it's the principal defendant. If the judge throws us out of D.C., we're dead. The statute of limitations will have run."

"I think a D.C. jury would be better though," Kitty said. "People here are aware of big-time corruption. You wouldn't have to educate them. People in Oklahoma think of Kerr-McGee as a patron saint."

"That cuts both ways," Danny retorted. "Oklahoma jurors might not be as sympathetic, but they wouldn't be as jaded either. When they find out the truth about Kerr-McGee, they might get as outraged as you."

Mr. Silkwood resolved the debate with some straight brainwork. "The trial will last how long? Three, four weeks? No way am I gonna put up with D.C. for three, four weeks."

Danny had divided the lawsuit into three parts—the contaminations, the death, the cover-up—but not in the order they had happened. Count One was his creative effort to define Karen's death legally as the finale to a series of civil rights violations. It accused Kerr-McGee of interfering with her union activities up to and including her uncompleted drive to the Holiday Inn. Count Two accused the FBI and Justice Department, along with Kerr-McGee, of a conspiracy to obstruct justice. Count Three seemed the least consequential. It accused Kerr-McGee of negligence for letting plutonium escape its factory and enter Karen's home and person. The legal logic was blissfully simple. Because the company had a duty to guard the plutonium it bore the blame for whoever poisoned Karen's refrigerator (as long as that someone was not Karen herself).

By two in the morning the papers were ready except for some typing. Danny and the others drifted out for much-needed sleep, leaving alone the typist, a young woman Kitty had enlisted in Tom Sawyer style. She kept awake listening to the wind-chime of the carriage return. When she was finished, she draped the machine with a black cover and pushed open a door. It made an awful screech. Blundering out a wrong exit, she had triggered the burglar alarm. She slammed the door, but the screeching didn't stop. The police had to be called, and they had to get one of the Jesuit administrators out of bed. He was not at all pleased to find an unfamiliar, bleary-eyed girl on the premises without an office staff escort, and Danny heard about it in a gruff reprimand the next day.

But to Danny the incident was a wonderful buffoonery. What the hell? If that was the worst side-effect to this suit, he would walk to Oklahoma on his knees.

OKLAHOMA CITY. NOVEMBER 5, 1976. At fifteen minutes to five the case of *Karen Silkwood v. Kerr-McGee Corporation* was placed on the docket in the U.S. District Court in Oklahoma City.

On a day seen dimly in Downriver Detroit, as through layered ice, the voters showed themselves to be Democrats first and foremost. They elected Congressman Dingell, sex scandal and all, to his eleventh term. Ringed by old pals, Dingell thumped the winner's podium with a young politician's zest. "Of all the election nights I've seen, this is the most satisfying," he exulted.

Earlier, at his Capitol Hill office, an aide had issued a press release. The Silkwood hearings would resume December 2, the day Congress went back into session.

In his suburban home Stockton watched the election results dance across his TV screen. A commentator unveiled a Bicentennial map of the United States. The red states belonged to Jimmy Carter, the blue to Jerry Ford, and the white were still up for grabs. The map was predominantly blue, but Ford's were western states with fewer electoral votes. Carter looked like the winner, which heartened Stockton. New people would soon be sitting at the center of the Justice Department.

Things do change, Stockton thought, mulling about a recent turnover. Nicholas Callahan had been deposed as the FBI's number two cop, forced into a hasty and disgraced resignation. He had been spared the ordeal of a public confession, but the *Times* had speculated with apparent confidence about his involvement in kickbacks from an electronics firm. Half a dozen more of the Old Guard also had been implicated.

Still, if others savored the announcement, Stockton did not. It was the scale of things that bothered him. Kickbacks seemed the least of the Old Guard's turpitude. None of them had been punished for the plot to drive Martin Luther King, the Nobel laureate, to suicide. Stockton wondered at the sense of morality in government. He doubted that morality was the cause of the treadmill mood—Callahan gone, Ford going, maybe Keeney and the other Justice Department men going too. But even if they were all sent packing, would the government be any more moral?

It was during such wonderings that he wished he drank Scotch—and understood much better those who did.

NEDERLAND. NOVEMBER 13, 1976. For the second year in a row the killing frosts were late and the rains were warm. Merle Silkwood was feeding her unfinished breakfast to Frito when she saw that the mums were back in blossom, as if to remind her of the day.

Bill Silkwood needed no reminding. "You be careful now," he said as Linda, his youngest, dressed in a windbreaker for a bicycle ride. He looked and felt uneasy, calling after her, "You sure you don't want me to drive you?"

"No, Daddy, I'll be okay, I promise." Linda tried to remember how her father used to be, up early to paint in the morning coolness, full of energy, building new cages for their backyard zoo, trimming the tall bushes out front: a happy outdoorsman. Not the man who sat in a darkened house, letting the green paint crack and fleck, letting the bushes rise wild and snarled and so thick they blocked sun from the windows. Their home now looked like a place that could be torn down without much loss. Inside there was an air of fear and defense, like a frontier fort waiting for the onslaught after the first skirmishes. She had tried to wheedle her father out of his moods, but when she was in the house her stomach felt jumpy and acidy too.

At school a week ago, with her father in D.C. for the lawsuit, Linda had been called to the principal's office. "Your mother phoned," the secretary told her. "You're excused from class. She'll pick you up out front for your doctor's appointment." Linda was surprised. She had the sniffles, but it didn't seem worth a doctor's bill. She bundled up her books, but a feeling nagged at her. In front of the school a car came racing toward her, a car she didn't recognize. Suddenly scared, she dashed back inside and telephoned her mother at the bank. Then she got really scared: her mother knew nothing of a doctor's appointment.

Linda returned to math class, and the scare was over. All her friends swore they were innocent, and she believed them. They were not such unnatural pranksters. But if one of them had not been the false voice on the school phone, who had it been?

A small rally in D.C. took note of the second anniversary, as did a dozen or so similar rallies across the nation. Sara had lobbied the NOW board of directors into formally anointing the date as Karen Silkwood Memorial Day, adding it to a calendar that celebrated Susan B. Anthony and Alice Paul.

For the occasion Sara and Kitty had wanted to use a picture of Karen for a large commemorative poster. But the perfect portrait was hard to come by. Karen's snapshots had been disposed of in the warehouse barrels, and though her parents had dozens of her in childhood poses, their collection had ended with her marriage. Their lone photograph of Karen as an adult was the one from her Kerr-McGee ID badge, with her curls bunched at the back of her neck. Then Sara remembered that there had been a picture of Karen among her effects in the Pennzoil box. Wodka had kept it, and he gave Sara a duplicate.

The original had been snapped by a friend of Drew in a serious moment at the bungalow. Karen was on the edge of a couch, leaning into the room, engaged in talk, arms uplifted, unaware of the camera. The flash had hidden the right side of her face in shadow. It made her seem a little lost and all the more haunting. Her dark hair was long and sleek, and on her lips was a hint of a girlish smile.

It was not of a quality that could be blown up to the size of a poster, so it had to be put at the center of a smaller handbill, printed on stiff paper. Karen's white features disappeared into a heavy black border, leaving a nose, her forehead, one cheek, the smile. Kitty and Sara argued about which words would best fit the picture—a poem or inspirational quote or political slogan—and agreed on a catch phrase from the *Ms.* article: *Karen Silkwood: Dead Because She Knew Too Much?*

WASHINGTON. DECEMBER 7, 1976. No spitting out his disgust, no dulling the bad news in a burst of work. Not this time. Stockton decided instead to take the rest of the day off. Tomorrow would be soon enough to pack up his Silkwood files.

For once the processes of government had moved quickly. Stockton hadn't expected that, nor had he expected such a complete turn of events. First, Dingell's long-delayed hearings had been delayed again. That had happened last week. The FBI and the Justice Department officials had led him to believe they would honor their invitations, but then, barely within the bounds of professional courtesy, they had begged off. Having been named in Mr. Silkwood's suit, they considered the hearings to be double jeopardy.

Dingell had accepted their logic, while he tried to find a way to subpoena them. To get around Tom Steed, the powerful Oklahoma congressman, he would have had to go to the floor of the House. But since this morning it was all beside the point. In a procedural vote the Democratic Caucus had removed Dingell as subcommittee chairman.

The sex scandal was not to blame. Dingell was the generic casualty of a new order. For more than a century Democrats and Republicans, meeting separately after each election, had divvied up the chairmanships. At one time the old-timers got them all. But then reform had come. It was the reformers who had removed Dingell as chairman, because he also held the chair of another major subcommittee.

That was how Stockton understood it, and how the newspapers reported it. He did not pretend to know more about back-room politicking than the pundits. Still, the vote had let several people off the hook: officials at the FBI, the Justice Department, Kerr-McGee, and Congressman Steed.

Driving home, there were few cars to impede Stockton. It was a different city at this time of day, before the commuters and hookers took over. The calm and his thoughts had a wistful resonance. What a month! From Dingell's halcyon reelection to this! The Caucus vote just about guaranteed that there would be no legislative remedy for the Silkwood family. On Election Day in Oklahoma the political career of Thomas Bamberger had come to an end. He had lost his seat after twelve years in the state legislature. Stockton had half expected to read that Bamberger had been discovered in some sexual peccadillo, but there had been nothing like that. Dean McGee hadn't even worked against him; the lack of an endorsement was enough.

Alaska would be Stockton's next assignment. But still on Dingell's agenda was the long-ago GAO review of the Silkwood case. In the initial review the question of MUF had not even been addressed. Instead it had been left for a larger investigation of security at all nuclear facilities. Like his own, the GAO investigation had never been completed. Perhaps, he thought, they could somehow be combined. Well, he had plenty of time to think about it.

WASHINGTON. JANUARY 11, 1977. "Let's keep this between the four of us," Danny cautioned, closing the door to the Butternut drawing room.

"You've heard from Bill Taylor?" Sara asked.

"Yes. He put out the word through his old CID buddies, and he's starting to get feedback."

"And?"

"More than half the FBI files were never turned over to Stockton. *Top secret* is written all over them."

"Can Taylor get us copies?" Kitty was impatient for results. Against her wishes Danny had insisted that Bill Taylor should get the two thousand dollars donated by NOW, all the money they had. She scarcely knew who Taylor was. An ex-Marine, a Vietnam vet, a tough guy with a knife scar across his belly, a macho man—that's all she knew. Oh, yes, Taylor was now a private eye. Off and on he worked for F. Lee Bailey, which is how Danny had met him.

"The FBI files are under lock and key," Danny explained, "but Taylor talked to somebody who got a peek at them. He's learned two things. There was a big MUF at Cimarrron, and the CIA had something to do with it. Which would explain why the Justice Department won't prosecute. It never does when the CIA is involved."

"I'll be damned," Bob said. "It gets spookier all the time."

"Spooks—that's what we need: A cooperative spook," Sara suggested. "Bob, how about your brother?"

"Who?" Danny asked.

"My brother's a CIA agent, stationed stateside," Bob said. "But he never talks shop. He took an oath not to—he takes the CIA seriously." There was an embarrassed silence at the mention of a family divided.

Kitty said, "What about some of Taylor's friends? Weren't they in the CIA with him?"

"CID. Taylor was in the CID in Vietnam," Danny said. "He's kept up his contacts in the intelligence networks. But he's purposely vague about who they are."

"You're being vague too," she said, a Coke in hand. "What's the CID?"

"CID is the Criminal Intelligence Division," Bob said. "Plain-clothes Marine cops. Mean dudes."

Danny grinned. "You might not want to meet Taylor in a dark alley, true enough, but the war cured him of all that bombast. He quit the Marines cold. Believe me, Taylor's one of us."

Kitty frowned at the possibility. "So what's his next move?"

"He's gonna sail the Caribbean." Danny shrugged helplessly.

"What?"

"We're out of money, and Taylor had to go back to his old job. He's captain of an elephantine yacht down in the Caribbean, sailing some old geezer from port to port."

"We're out of money because Taylor charges a hundred dollars a day," Kitty said bitterly. "I told you we should have tried to hire Stockton."

"But Taylor's a *murder* investigator," Sara said.

"Anybody we get is going to cost us. I can't do this lawsuit on pennies," Danny said. "No one can. We need to scare up a couple thousand more."

"You say *we* but you mean *us*. You mean Sara and me." Kitty glowered at him, daring him to contradict her.

"A lawyer can't go out cup in hand. There are bar association rules. You should know that."

Sara interceded. "There's no sense arguing. We *have* to get more money, that's all there's to it. Meanwhile, I have to load the dish-washer!"

"I'll help," Kitty volunteered. They both left for the kitchen.

Danny turned confidentially to Bob. "What's wrong with Kitty? She was about to take my head off."

Bob knew by rote the causes of Kitty's moods—her excruciating over mid-terms, her pique at the sloppy housekeeping (she would not let Bob pay a weekly maid because how could she justify a tired black woman cleaning up after healthy young white folks?), Amber's teeth-cutting, Shawn's young-boy mischiefs, the growing mutiny within SOS (Wodka was the latest defection), her habitual scheduling of thirty hours into every day (she was now trying to squeeze in a part-time job at EPC). All were good excuses, but Bob felt annoyance at having to make a demeaning apology. "I think Kitty is right. We have to be more economical," he said. "Let's forget about the CIA angle and have someone go to Oklahoma. Let's verify Karen's original list of allegations, sort of pick up where Wodka and Mazzocchi left off."

"I'm for that. We could send Taylor to talk to the workers," Danny said, willing to oblige. "But we still need money, and I don't think we're gonna get any big bucks from the OCAW. This case has pretty well worn out its welcome over there."

"Yeah, I know. I've been talking to Wodka. He and Mazzocchi are getting pressured from above. There's an OCAW vice-president who thinks the suit will give the industry a bad name."

"It'd have been a lot easier to keep the OCAW in the coalition if Kitty hadn't broadcast this as an anti-nuke suit. I know she can't help herself. She wants everybody to help her dig a hole to bury the industry. But the OCAW can't be in favor of lopping off thousands of its own members. She put Wodka into a position no union man could support."

"She's not that much of an extremist. Kitty would be overjoyed if they simply stopped building reactors. And so would I. Anyway, Wodka seems uptight about something else."

"Wodka aside, SOS is pretty shaky. I think we have to emphasize that the suit involves issues other than nuclear. Civil liberties, for instance."

"Fat lot of good it'll do. The ACLU won't come near us because they heard Karen was a loony-tune."

Danny bent to warm his hands over a space heater. "The ACLU will come around, they're good people. Oh, well, let's be thankful for small triumphs. At least the judge rejected Kerr-McGee's motion to have the suit thrown out." He rose and peered at a paper protruding from Kitty's typewriter. "Workman's-comp law? Good subject for a term paper—and a bad law. It doesn't really protect workers; what it really does is prevent them from suing their employers." The paper moved untouched. "Hey, do you feel a draft in here?"

A chill blew up from a small unused fireplace. Bob stripped a blanket off the guest mattress and sausaged it into the chimney. "I keep intending to fix it," he said. Loose mortar and years of soot had made it a fire hazard.

From the mantel Bob took a stapled sheaf of papers. "Have you seen this? It's called the Barton Report. It's supposed to be secret, but it's being passed around the Hill. The NRC commissioned it as a futuristic look at nuclear power. You should read the civil liberties section."

Danny obeyed. "This is right out of Orwell," he said. The Barton Report envisioned a nuclear future where the NRC or FBI would be allowed to conduct surveillance without a court order, detain nuclear critics without filing formal charges and, under certain circumstances, to torture suspected nuclear terrorists.

"This is where I agree with Mazzocchi and Wodka," Bob said. "This is the trap we have to avoid. If we make too much of a fuss about smuggling, public paranoia is going to rise, and the right-wingers in Congress will have an excuse to create a nuclear police state. Can you imagine what it'd be like? The companies would go hog wild. They'd fire anybody who's ever given them any trouble. Probably throw half of them in jail."

"That future is already here. Why do you think Kerr-McGee tried to give everybody a polygraph test?"

"But so far that's an isolated case. I'm worried about it becoming an industry-wide procedure. If that happened, the OCAW would be down the tubes. Precisely as Srouji was advocating at the first Dingell hearing."

"Maybe that's what the FBI and the NRC really want. But as far as the smuggling goes, I have to agree with Stockton. We can't do a cover-up—we'd be no better than them." In his mind Danny had a picture of Mafia-style men at an abandoned airstrip loading lead-lined canisters into a Libyan or Iranian plane. "Whatever the truth is, that's it. We go with it."

OKLAHOMA CITY. FEBRUARY 1, 1977. Danny slouched against the lobby wall, pretending an interest in his newspaper. Near the comics he found a short notice about his clients, subpoenaed into town by Kerr-McGee's lawyers. Today, upstairs in the court reporters' suite, Bill Meadows was to submit to a deposition first, then Bill Silkwood. Danny had a recurring fear: the room would become a boxing ring and he a disjointed referee, helpless as his clients pummeled each other.

Mr. Silkwood was punching a round black button to call the

elevator. It came and went without them. They were waiting for Meadows. Danny didn't want to go up without him.

"There he is," Mr. Silkwood said finally. A man of average height, with a bit of weight to spare, came through a revolving door. Meadows had a nautical walk and brown cowlicked hair slicked back as if facing a perpetual wind. He was dressed in a brown leisure suit. He came over to Danny. "Is there anything I shouldn't say to these lawyers?" Meadows asked apprehensively. He had not bargained for being the first witness called for pretrial testimony.

"Just tell the truth," Danny said. "I'll butt in if they get out of line." Danny shook his hand; Mr. Silkwood stiffly did the same. In the elevator they talked about the weather, and upstairs a receptionist showed them to a room lined on all sides with books that looked too pristine to have seen much use. Depositions are usually lonely affairs, but here there was a crowd like for a cockfight. Reporters and spectators were jammed against the bookcases, and the alert imperious faces of seven lawyers surrounded a single empty spot at a long polished table. One of them grudgingly gave way so Danny could squeeze in with Meadows. Mr. Silkwood stayed with the reporters.

Introductions took a while. Danny kept his eyes on Bill Paul, the chief counsel for Kerr-McGee, a lawyer in his prime. Bill Paul's fading black hair was finically in place. He was a fifth-generation Oklahoman whose family name was heralded by the town of Paul's Valley. In a vested dark suit he seemed rigidly, ponderously circumspect, like a minister about to be televised. In fact, Danny wondered, where were the TV cameras? Kerr-McGee obviously had invited all the newspapers in town.

Bill Paul allowed himself a sumptuous smile and went to work, asking Meadows about his seven years with Karen.

Why was the marriage common-law? "Karen's kinfolks had thrown a fit because we'd run off to get hitched, and we decided it'd be easier just to tell them we had been. We were gonna make it legal when we got older, but we never got around to it." What led to the divorce? "We had a lot of financial difficulties." Was Karen a spendthrift? "No, she did the best job she could with spreading the money out. . . . I didn't really keep up with who we owed how much to or what. I just dumped that in her lap, and if I wanted to spend some money I did, without worrying about the fact it was already committed." Did Karen use illicit drugs? "No, sir, she didn't." Did she smoke marijuana? "No." How about alcohol? "Yes." To an excess? "No." Did she attend church? "Occasionally she did. I didn't."

Did Meadows ever learn of any impropriety on Karen's part? "No, sir." Did he have reason to believe she had been unfaithful? "No, sir . . . I was seeing Kathy, the girl that I am married to now."

A sour signal passed between Bill Paul and his associates. Meadows gulped his fill of water and wished he had something with more of a kick. He wished also that he had never heard of Danny Sheehan—he was being forced to publicize his own deficiencies, and for what? Any sane man could see, by looking around this room, that the company and the government were ganged up seven lawyers to one. What if he lost his job at Mobil Pipe Line over this?

In response to another question, Meadows said, "I asked Karen for a divorce, and she said she wanted to keep the children. She said she could get them if she wanted to. . . . Then one morning I woke up and she wasn't there."

Had she threatened to leave? "Yes, but the way it happened I was surprised."

The reporters raced their pencils. Late in the afternoon, after Bill Paul had done all he could to pick apart the unhappy details, the deposition ended. Mr. Silkwood's turn would come the next day. Danny thought Meadows had been forthright and truthful. So did Mr. Silkwood, who cleared a path for his former son-in-law. They thanked each other. Meadows was relieved but still anguished, and he declined supper.

Entering a restaurant Danny paused at a newspaper vending box for a copy of the afternoon *City Times*. He opened it and yelped as though a bee had stung him.

"What is it?" Mr. Silkwood asked. Taking the paper, he saw. Bold black letters at the top of the page proclaimed: SILKWOOD CALLED CHILD DESERTER.

Twenty-four hours later that headline was replaced by another: SILK-WOOD MARRIAGE "DISGUSTS" FATHER. It was accurate, as far as it went, for Mr. Silkwood had no talent for improvised feelings. Head bowed, face quivering, he had sat miserably all day at the deposition table, wanting to be fair to the absent Meadows, but Bill Paul had brought out all the bad blood.

"Did I do wrong?" Mr. Silkwood asked afterward. In his big coarse hands he held a tall vodka fixed by Jim Ikard, a young local lawyer who was helping Danny.

"Absolutely not," Ikard said. "It's a much bigger mistake to lie."

"That lawyer just kept at me and at me."

Danny waved emphatically. "Karen's marriage is not very important to this suit. On the important stuff you were great." Danny assumed that Bill Paul had wanted something more from the depositions than family gossip. Many of his other questions had been far trickier. Who's behind this suit? Who's paying for it? Whose idea was it? What's SOS? Who's Kitty Tucker? Who's Sara Nelson? Bob Alvarez? Who's behind them? Where do they get their money? Are they in league with Danny Sheehan? What's his motive? Do you personally know anything about the facts in this case, or did Mr. Sheehan tell you everything? Did he talk you into filing the suit? And, finally, "Do you have the feeling you're being used as a tool to wage war on Kerr-McGee and the nuclear industry?" At that Mr. Silkwood had shouted in righteous anger: "All I want is to find out who killed my girl!"

"That was the best answer all day," Danny said in a congratulatory tone. "Bill Paul was hoping I'd suckered you into this. That way he'd get the suit dismissed in a minute. He could even get me disbarred."

Mr. Silkwood accepted a second drink. "To tell the truth, I'm not quite sure why you are in this. But I know why I am."

Thirteen

The lights of Oklahoma City rose up, winking between the clouds. The jetliner slanted down, lowered its flaps, hit an unseen skid of ice and twisted to a stop. Rabbits scampered off the runway. After all this time Kitty was in Oklahoma, as a delegate to the National Lawyers Guild convention. It was her reward for being editor of the Guild newsletter at Antioch. Drew met her at the debarking ramp. He had expected baggy jeans and army boots instead of the monk's-cowl cape and her lavender wool dress. But true to Danny's prediction, Kitty's huge frizz made her aggressively visible.

"Good to meet yuh," he said. He was wearing his cowboy hat. It rode low, front and back, authentic prairie style. In Oklahoma the way a man wears his hat is said to tell how much of the prairie is in him.

"I hope this isn't a big inconvenience. I don't know anyone else here," Kitty said. "I realize I don't know you either, but I feel like I do."

Drew picked up her bags and grunted at the weight of the SOS pamphlets packed among her clothes. "Danny's told me a lot about you," he said.

The Guild convention was at the University of Oklahoma about forty miles away. On the way they stopped for a steak supper. Kitty noticed his broken fingernails and hands with a thousand little cuts, abraded by sandpaper, showing wear beyond their years. "I'm working harder and longer than any time in my life, and enjoying it more —I think," he explained. He was half owner of an auto body shop called the Dolly & Hammer.

"There's so much I want to ask," Kitty said. "What do you know about the fuel rods? If they're really defective there could be a major accident when they're used."

Drew was not so sure. "Don't get me wrong, but I've read a lot of science, and I have to agree with the AEC, with the Rasmussen Report. There are enough safety systems to prevent major accidents."

"How can you say that?"

"I just don't think the problem should be exaggerated."

"Do you think Karen was exaggerating?"

"Of course not. Kerr-McGee was definitely cheating on quality control and they didn't give a damn if we got dosed. You couldn't pay me enough to work there again. But it's the workers who take the risk, not the public. The people who are afraid of nuclear reactors going critical and dosing the countryside aren't being realistic, people like Ilene Younghein."

And like you—Kitty felt the words he didn't say. She coughed hard into a handkerchief but couldn't dislodge the congestion in her chest. It was more adhering than mucus, a heavy unidentified sensation. A female voice on the jukebox wailed about a man who had let his lady down. Chivalry and other male chauvinisms were dying out; properly so, Kitty thought. But here sat Karen's man, cool and enduring, a mature free spirit, and she felt a motherly urge to scold him. No, to *judge* him. She put her palms against the table and pushed up to leave, an extravagant denial of her feeling.

"Want a drink?" Drew asked. He ordered a whiskey straight in memory of Karen. "Yours is a piña colada, right?"

Kitty was startled—Danny must have talked a lot. "Right," she said. She blinked several times to clear the refracted image before her. "Have you met Taylor?" she asked. "He was in Oklahoma last week to interview some of the people Karen worked with."

"Yeah, I really liked the guy. I introduced him to a few people from the old days who I can still call friends."

"From a lawyer's viewpoint, it'd be better to have witnesses who aren't friends. They'd have more credibility."

"There's plenty of them, but they won't testify. Even Jack Tice has reservations about going into court."

"Why? Why's everyone so damn reticent?"

"Zane Grey wrote about it—and it's still true. Out here you've got to prove you're tough enough to win. Nobody's gonna take a risk for a loser."

"But what's the risk? A lot of these people don't work for Kerr-McGee any more."

"Unless you're a cowpuncher, you work for the energy industry:

oil rigs, pipelines, mining, selling cars, fixing cars. Dean McGee's got a handle on more than Kerr-McGee. He's a director of Phillips Petroleum, and he hangs out at the country clubs with everybody who's anybody." Drew drank his whiskey down. "But it's not just economic self-preservation that people are worried about."

"What do you mean?"

"You'd understand if you ever got a visit from Mr. Reading. He's been out to see me two, three times. A real polite guy, icy friendly. You gotta be dense not to get his message. *Get outta town while the getting's good.*"

"But you haven't left."

"I guess I'm dense." Drew raked fingers through his hair, using the move to break the grim rhythm. Reflectively, he said, "I almost did leave the spring after Karen died. There was nobody to stick around for. I was gonna put all my things in a van and head out for the wide blue yonder."

"Why didn't you?"

"Maybe I didn't like being run off. Maybe I like Oklahoma. Who knows?" Drew's voice was distant, diminished.

In his tranquil acceptance of courage, Kitty saw how easy it was to misjudge him. Yet she felt compelled to test him further. "Will you testify if we get to trial?"

"I'm giving a deposition next week. Kerr-McGee subpoenaed me."

"That's not what I mean," she said. "Will you testify for us? *Against* Kerr-McGee?"

"Lady, I can hardly wait. I'll dress up in pinstripes if you want." His sincerity was as bracing as a run in the dew.

The waitress brought the bill and Drew laid out a generous payment.

"What time is it?" Kitty asked.

"Oh, Jesus. I forgot you had to get to the university." He slapped his head to rouse himself and his palm left a small smirch of body-shop grime on his brow like a declaration.

He gunned the Sprite full out, but they were too late to get Kitty a dorm room for the night. Without being asked, Drew drove her back to the city and smoothed sheets and blankets over his couch. At dawn Drew made a skillet breakfast, then drove her to the convention.

"There's a bunch of us going to see Willie Nelson and Emmylou Harris tomorrow night," he said. "Want to come?"

"I'd love to." Kitty kissed him on the cheek and groped her way from the Sprite; it was so low to the ground.

NASHVILLE. FEBRUARY 19, 1977. Water swirled in the two large aquariums. Red-tailed sharks and African frogs choked down the tubifex worms. Engorged, the miniature creatures stared vacantly at a newt caught between the air pipe and a glass wall. The newt was in a frenzy. Jackie Srouji finally noticed his predicament and freed him. She often felt as trapped as the newt, she told a visiting journalist. The analogy was so convenient, he said cynically, that it seemed planned. No, no—she got teary—she was entangled in a skein of events over which she had no control. Everyone had deserted her, even her oldest friends. Rumors about her circulated at parties she no longer attended, and worst of all, she had been lumped in as a defendant in this lawsuit.

A process server had come to her apartment last week with a subpoena from Danny Sheehan. She was to appear in Oklahoma City in a few days with her thousand pages of FBI documents. "Why is he persecuting me?" The final hurt, she said, was that he was of her own faith, a candidate for the priesthood.

Tonight she would meet him at her parish church and explain that she was harmless, a victim, not unlike Karen Silkwood. The meeting had been arranged through the Little Sisters of Jesus whom she had met in D.C.

Perhaps Srouji wants to cleanse her soul, Danny thought, here at St. Henry's of Nashville, among the crimson vestments and sentimentalized icons. Danny had brought Father Bill Davis with him. Father Bill was the director of the Jesuit Office of Social Ministries. He was an ordained priest, a better caretaker of souls and confessions.

Srouji came in. "Where's your lawyer?" Danny asked.

"He's coming."

"Fine, we'll wait for him."

Father Bill did not understand. "Why not talk to her without the lawyer? It'd be less formal."

"I can't." Danny explained. "Bar associations have a kind of Miranda rule against a plaintiff's counsel talking to a defendant. I told her on the phone her lawyer had to be here."

They shifted about awkwardly for fifteen, twenty minutes, until Srouji's tearful voice intruded on the chitchat. "Please, I need your advice. Am I in any danger? Will they try to kill me too? What should I do? Please, I don't want to die!"

Danny turned to her with a cautious sympathy. "You *may* be in some danger. Your testimony and your documents *are* critical to this case. But your best insurance is to be completely forthcoming. Turn the documents over to the court and tell us all you know. Not now. Next week, under oath."

But Srouji kept beseeching him for an alternative, and finally Danny gave her a small gesture of farewell.

"What's the matter?" Father Bill asked, as the heavy carved door clunked shut behind them.

Danny shrugged limply. He felt a foreboding. "I was willing to work out a deal so she could be like an unindicted co-conspirator. But a deal like that has to be worked out with her lawyer, and I don't think she ever invited him. Whatever she's trying to pull, I don't like it."

OKLAHOMA CITY. FEBRUARY 22, 1977. "I don't know what the Washington code of conduct is, but here we have rules of civility," Bill Paul raged. "You're not even counsel for Drew Stephens. You're completely out of order."

Danny bowed a stiff fraction and hid a smile. All morning he had been discourteous and hostile, needling, interrupting, forfeiting forever any chance to play in Bill Paul's golf foursome. Danny's tactic was a reflex, yet a cunning one. He knew how corporations routinely try to settle embarrassing lawsuits out of court, quietly, without admitting liability, to be rid of the nuisance. If Kerr-McGee made a reasonable offer, he might be bound ethically to accept it on behalf of the Silkwood children. But if he could add Bill Paul's ego to the lawsuit, as one of the stakes, then maybe there would be no recommendation for settling, and the case would be that much closer to a trial.

Bill Paul's irritation was at a level with the importance of the deposition. It was going to take three full days. Drew was a frontline witness.

Danny didn't begrudge the time. Bill Paul's questions, charged with taboos, were as revealing as Drew's answers.

Out of unfamiliarity, or perhaps shame, Bill Paul had no success at all on his first foray. "Are you aware of any administration by Karen Silkwood to herself of any illicit drugs through the means of a hypodermic needle?" he asked.

"No, sir. Never," Drew answered.

Again, later: "Wasn't there a syringe, or what I would call a hypodermic needle, found in Karen's apartment at the time of the decontamination?"

"Yes. It was in the kitchen. Karen and Sherri used it for cooking."

"Did Karen smoke marijuana?"

"I'll have to refuse to answer on the basis of the Fifth Amendment." (In Oklahoma marijuana users still went to jail.)

"How about Quaaludes and other sedatives?"

"Yes, she depended on them to calm herself and to sleep during the daylight."

"Did she talk about her children?"

"It was a painful subject. She'd made a logical decision about them, but it was difficult for her to live with it."

"Have you ever heard about Karen engaging in a physical sexual act with any person at the factory—within the confines of the factory?"

Drew shook his head, but Bill Paul rephrased the question several times, seeking any small piece of confirmation. Thwarted, he closed the first day with a number of pleasantries as if to encourage Drew to prepare better responses overnight.

The next day he asked about Karen's bisexuality. "Do you have any knowledge about gay activities in which she engaged?"

"What do you call gay?" Drew parried.

"Let's say any physical sexual act between Karen and another woman."

"That did occur."

"With whom did it occur?"

"I don't know the names."

"Did Karen tell you about it?"

"Uh-huh—there were probably a couple of incidents."

"What was the approximate time frame of these physical acts?"

"Early 1974, while we were separated."

"What was the occasion for Karen telling you?"

"We were usually quite honest with each other." From what Drew knew, Karen had sought love from her girlfriends out of bitterness toward him and Meadows, but the experiment had been short and unfulfilling.

"How close was Karen to Steve Wodka? Was she his lover?"

Drew was candid. "Karen told me she slept with Wodka at the Pick Lee Hotel," he said, "and there was a second time in Oklahoma the night of the cancer seminars."

Danny put down his pencil and relaxed. So that's why Wodka has been uptight: a romp in the hay. Hell's bells, what's more normal than that?

Bill Paul, however, thought he saw the outline of a romantic triangle. "Were you jealous of Wodka?" he asked Drew.

"No. Karen and I didn't have that kind of tie on each other," he answered. "We talked about her being with Wodka, and I accepted it."

"Did Wodka ever say anything about this *nonbusiness* relationship with Karen?"

Drew recalled Wodka's unease at their first meeting, the day at the airport with Karen in semi-shock. "He was surprised I accepted him; he didn't know how to take that." After the AEC grilling and the late-night pizza, Drew said, Karen had been exhausted and had gone to sleep on one of the beds in Wodka's motel room.

Voraciously, Paul asked, "Which one of you slept with her?"

"She slept with me," Drew said.

"Did the two of you engage in any sexual activity?"

"I don't think so."

"Well, did Karen and Wodka have sex that night?"

"No."

Paul talked fast as if he expected to be kept from finishing, but Danny sat scratching his nose. Anyone reading this exchange, he thought, would be sickened. Indeed, Paul looked a little ashen; and Danny wondered if the corporate attorney had reached his limit. But again and again he returned to the voyeurism. Summing up, he asked, "Okay, Drew, I know you're not a medical man, but based on your knowledge do you think Karen was what medical science classifies as a nymphomaniac?"

"No!" The harshness of Drew's voice made the word more a denunciation than a dissent. Throughout he had been gentlemanly, far beyond his obligation, but now his muscles contorted. He cracked his knuckles, rubbed his wrists, flexed them. In these moves was the relishing of a roundhouse swing.

But Bill Paul's next question switched to a new topic—methodically his questions began to move through the events of 1974, up to the present. "Do you know Bill Taylor? Do you happen to know where he lives?"

"Somewhere by the ocean, I think, because he's a sailing nut," Drew said.

Danny was suddenly all ears. How did Bill Paul know about Taylor? And how much did he know? From the tenor of his questions it appeared he knew more than he was letting on. Perhaps Reading already had a background report put together. Danny had to smile a little at the thought. What would Reading have made of an ex-Marine in with the ranks of counterculture radicals?

Bill Paul was almost done. "What can you tell us about this SOS organization?" He seemed to think it was foreign, or subversive like SDS.

"I'm not a member," Drew said.

What did he know about Kitty Tucker? "She likes good country music." What about Sara Nelson? A shrug. Bob Alvarez? Another shrug. Did Drew know the source of their funds? "No." Had Drew given them money? "No." Bill Paul was glad to hear that—last night his wife had been scandalized to see Kitty Tucker on local TV appealing for money to finance the suit.

Afterwards Drew had a question of his own for his interrogator: "Will I get a fee for this?"

"Yes," Paul said. "It isn't much—twenty-five dollars a day—but it'll help offset the time you lost at the Dolly & Hammer."

"Oh, I wasn't thinking about that," Drew said. "I was thinking of endorsing the check over to Kitty Tucker."

With the Guild convention finished, Kitty went exploring. Even here on the prairie, she thought, there must be a thin commonweal for the SOS.

At Jean Jung's trailer a snowman was dripping toward ruin. Kitty was pulled frantically inside. "Dear God, I hope no one saw you," Mrs. Jung said, making anxious noises in her throat. "I don't want Kerr-McGee to get mad. I still work for them, see, in the payroll office downtown. I need the Blue Cross." This compromise appeared not to have saved her health. Her hair was coming out, and recently she had been operated on for a tumor in her neck. She apologized for this as though it were a weakness she pampered.

Mrs. Jung's identity as an eyewitness to the manila folder had never been made public. It was a secret held by Stockton, Mazzocchi, Wodka, and a very few others. Mrs. Jung worried that any parenthetical visit might lead Kerr-McGee to her. Respecting the older woman's fright, Kitty discreetly withdrew.

She found Jack Tice at his secondhand store. He had the pieces of an antique dresser scattered on the floor before him. With wood screws and a dowel or two the furniture of his childhood could be made more valuable than it had ever been. Since leaving Cimarron he had been a day laborer: woodwork, truck driving, construction, whatever—a mean, tired life. The sleeves of his jacket looked as worn as the old dresser. "It's too little, too late," Tice muttered, meaning the lawsuit. "It's not gonna get anywhere. Those company lawyers and the judges are like this." Two entwined fingers made his point. "Look, I'll try to help out. But don't expect much."

Ilene Younghein and another housewife activist, Ann Funnell, revived Kitty with a cup of tea and hopeful words. *They* were the commonweal. Mrs. Younghein had petitioned to become an intervenor, a sort of citizen-lawyer status conferred by the NRC, allowing her to intercede formally against the Black Fox nuclear reactor going up outside Tulsa. In all of Oklahoma, she was the lone intervenor. Being such an obvious and single maker of trouble, however, had not brought any to her. "They don't take me seriously," she said ruefully from her sofa.

Mrs. Younghein and Mrs. Funnell had been unsuccessful in organizing a coffee-klatch fundraiser for Kitty. "Kerr-McGee has people on all the civic committees, the hospitals, the schools, everything," Mrs. Younghein said. "No one wants to alienate them."

"Aren't there people who are a little more, uh, radical?" Kitty asked.

"It isn't that people are conservative, or dumb, or insensitive, but they're used to minding their own business. What we need is a real organizer, someone like you."

Kitty smiled at the compliment. "I've got to get home to my kids, but Sara Nelson might be able to get NOW to pay her way out here."

Nudging open the Dolly & Hammer door, Kitty announced, "I came to say good-bye." Drew clicked off the paint sprayer and pulled a mask from his face. Pinpoint spots of mauve colored his gloves and coveralls. He came out into the dry solid air. It was freezing, so they moved into the office, a shack resting on short platform stilts. "Dammit, lady," Drew said, "I have to tell you I greatly admire what you're trying to do." He had never given such a tribute to Karen, and now he wished he had.

As they talked, Buzz Hirsch pulled in. Hirsch was a Californian hoping to make a film of the Silkwood case. Though the story had enough melodrama, it so far had only one investor. Hirsch had come to Oklahoma with a camera to get material for his sales pitch.

"Hope you two don't mind having your picture taken," he said. "No, not by me, but by this guy who's been tailing me." Hirsch made a face. "He's pretty sharp. It took me a while to pick him out in my rearview mirror. But when I was taking pictures on the highway, he stopped a ways back and started taking pictures of me."

Drew laughed drily. "There's a certain Mr. Reading who likes to be well informed."

"Yes, I know," Hirsch said. "Right after we got going on this movie, Larry Cano—he's my partner—had a weird run-in over a loan. He was lucky: he knew the Pacific Finance branch representative, Mrs. Kirish. She had gotten an official-sounding call asking for Larry's entire financial history. This official claimed to be with the Defense Department and described Larry as some species of revolutionary. Like I said, he was lucky. Mrs. Kirish knows what an all-American kid Larry really is. She signed an affidavit in case this guy ever bothered us again. He had given her his name and number—James Reading of Oklahoma City."

OKLAHOMA CITY. FEBRUARY 25, 1977. Some minutes into Jackie Srouji's deposition at the federal courthouse, Danny understood what the Nashville church encounter had been about. He was seated, but he could feel his knees buckle.

Srouji had a theatrical story to tell. How Danny had played up to her religion, had exploited the Little Sisters of Jesus, had enticed her to a tryst, badgered her, frightened her with assassination talk, how she did not know until later that she was entitled to her lawyer's company.

He was now present, her lawyer, and he talked in high-minded echoes, fawning, catering to her furies. She was providing an opportunity to have Danny kicked off the case. From Bill Paul's look of victorious contempt, that already seemed to have been accomplished.

Danny shouted and slapped papers on the table, his anger hyperbolic, but the outburst cleared his head. He remembered he had taken Father Bill to Nashville. Thank God for the foresight! A priest would be unimpeachable.

Calmer, Danny listened to Srouji's jagged retelling. Fear can paralyze conscience, he knew, and invert the truth. Truth? From what he had seen in different courtrooms—the contradictory swearings of eyewitnesses—truth existed fleetingly in the mind, never static, forever adjusting itself to satisfy illusions and desires. Perhaps in her fear, Srouji had mistaken her enemy.

But when Danny resumed his questions, the worst was confirmed. Srouji had brought only an irrelevant dozen of the thousand pages. The others she had remitted to the FBI. She said this with such glee there could be no mistaking where her allegiance lay.

With quick thrusts, Danny demanded: Did the documents include transcripts of Karen's phone conversations? What did they indicate about plutonium smuggling? Also: Who told her what to say in front of the Dingell subcommittee? Who told her what to write in her book? Was she in cahoots with Lawrence Olson and James Reading? Did the three of them plot to discredit Karen Silkwood?

To all these inquiries Srouji uttered denials or denied Danny the satisfaction of an answer. He probed her eyes: wanton, colorless. Her voice was metallic. Her hair was frozen by lacquer, her smile by insolence. An eight-millimeter lens atop a tripod gaped blandly at her, recording her expressions, and a microphone took in her words. Danny had the judge's permission for the rented television gear, in case Srouji "disappeared" when the case went to trial.

But this celluloid roll would contain nothing of substance for a jury. I've underestimated her, he thought, or *them*. There no longer seemed to be a distinction. He waved dejectedly for the cameraman to pack up. The deposition would be continued at a later date, after Danny importuned the judge. Next time, if Srouji dared not to answer, he would have her jailed for contempt.

"Fine," she bristled. She already had mailed a written complaint to the FBI, and she planned to see the judge too. Next time? If she succeeded, there would be no next time.

OKLAHOMA CITY. MARCH 23, 1977. On the gray humming surface, the pickup raced as if to a rescue. In the valleys the wind had blown drifts of pink sand. On either side of Highway 74 were broad fields of ruminating cattle. "You can't let them eat too much spring grass," Sherri Ellis said. "It's too rich. They get gas and bloat up and die."

"What a terrible thing," Sara said.

Sherri seemed morbidly conscious of their route. "I gotta get liquored up to go out there," she said, and by way of acknowledgment she held out a canteen of rum-and-Coke to Sara, keeping one hand stiff on the wheel. "Go on, have a sip. It's better for you than them cigarettes. No offense, but you smoke almost as much as Karen."

Sara crushed the half-smoked cigarette in the ashtray, in with an accumulation of others, and took a healthy swig from the canteen. The culvert wingwalls had come into view. The pickup stopped in the tall grass off the highway, some yards beyond.

They hiked back, the grass tickling their ankles. At the road's edge, there was a broken rabbit, showing red insides.

This was Sara's first trip to the site, but it was even more of a goose-flesh pilgrimage for Sherri. She hadn't been here in nearly a year, nor to her grandmother's little ranch, which, she indicated with a wave, was off on a dirt road a mile or so away. Sherri had inherited the white two-story ranch house after her grandmother's death, and for a while she had gloried in it as a hermitage. It had no phone, no close neighbors. The winter after Karen's death it was therapy. Sherri fed the animals and typed out a manuscript. A New York publisher had been interested in a book about Karen. In spring Sherri had emerged, driven to town, and shown around the unschooled manuscript, titled *Kill Me . . . You Can't,* in which Kerr-McGee was the villain. Days later, back at the ranch, upstairs at her old Underwood, she had heard the clipped-wing hysteria of her ducks fleeing an attacker. A coyote? She went to get the shotgun, but the gun was gone, stolen. From an upstairs window she saw a man's shadow around a corner of the house. And as she told Sara, "The ducks stopped shrieking and it got quiet. I slid under my bed and held my breath. Stayed there an hour, maybe two, listening for footsteps on the stairs. Couldn't hear a thing. Finally I got bold enough to come out. The man had laid a board across the porch railing and he'd put one of my ducks on the board. It was all stretched out; its neck was snapped. I took it to mean that's what I was gonna be, *dead as a duck.*" So Sherri had run off to a cabin on a wooded Colorado slope and had just recently come back to Oklahoma, lonely, out of money, wanting now to be a beautician.

Sara stood a long time at the culvert. Melted snow, flushed from fields through cylindrical clay tiles, had turned the creek turbulent, reaching high up the banks, drowning the bluestem sprouts. The water rippled under a breeze. Sara looked to the horizon, squinting, tasting dust.

"A norther's starting to blow," Sherri said. "We better git."

Sara massaged her arms through a light sweater. Dusk was closing out the light. Soon there would be nothing to see on the huge prairie; only the sound of occasional cars and the undertone of the creek would be left.

In a whirlwind two weeks Sara formed the Oklahoma chapter of SOS: sympathizers from the Sierra Club, NOW, the Lawyers Guild, plus, of course, Ilene Younghein. At Oklahoma State University, where Dean McGee had been awarded an honorary doctorate during one of Richard Nixon's last presidential appearances, she tried to recruit some students. During her speech a well-tailored older man tried to shout her down. He was not a student; he had come to vouch for Dean McGee. "Never, never could Mr. McGee be involved in anything underhanded."

"If he hasn't done anything wrong," Sara volleyed back, "why won't he come down out of his office and talk to the press?" Afterward several students came to thank her for the speech because so little information about the case was available here.

That gave Sara the idea to call up every news organization in the phone book. Libel lawyers and squinty-eyed editors had to approve her comments before they got to the public, and few made it. But at Channel 9 a young reporter managed to get Sara on the air, as she had done a month earlier with Kitty. Sara felt a stirring of affinity; she asked the reporter if the rumors were true about there being a general blackout of the case in Oklahoma.

Yes, the reporter said, but it hadn't started out that way. In the first weeks after Karen's death, local news stories were alive with the possibility of foul play. But then suddenly the toughness had dropped away like a pose. Why? Well, it became known that the bad publicity was giving Kerr-McGee's board of directors an urge to transfer world headquarters to Houston. Dean McGee himself was against pulling up roots, but he might be outvoted. Pretty soon editors and reporters were having confidential chats with James Reading, and pretty soon their stories were making Pipkin out to be a bit shady and Karen a bit flaky. They had enough integrity not to publicize the worst gossip, but if all you knew was what you read in the local papers, you would have the clear impression that Karen had done herself in.

A few newspeople had rebelled. Joe Pennington, over at radio station KTOK, had gotten a cop to talk off the record and had done a broadcast saying Karen might have known about jimmied books and smuggled plutonium, long before Srouji put forth that idea. But Kerr-McGee sent KTOK a letter, dignified and low-key, pointing out how this was a "national security" issue. Pennington had been reassigned, and pretty soon he left town. Over at the *City Times,* Alan Bromley had kept digging on his own time, and when the lawsuit was filed, he had asked for the assignment. But a week later Bromley had been fired, and he believed Kerr-McGee was behind it.

Several aging basketball players materialized in the downtown YMCA locker room. They kidded Jim Ikard. "Give you odds, Jim: a thousand to one your suit doesn't get anywhere."

Ikard kidded them back. "It isn't *my* suit. Unless we win, of course."

But it was Ikard's lawsuit, as much as Danny's, at least in a technical sense. Under the federal court rules, Danny had been required to find an Oklahoma lawyer to file the legal papers. Not knowing anyone at all, Danny had phoned around, and Ikard was recommended—"quick as a whip, but he's got enough patience to put up with you." In response to a call, just before last November's deadline, Ikard had signed his name and filed the papers.

It had made him the object of much friendly derision here at the YMCA. They were Ikard's friends, lawyers like him and populist legislators from the State Capitol, young professionals a few years and a few dollars shy of country-club exercise. They were young for what they did by day, but evenings they were old men playing a boys' game. One on one, Ikard couldn't be stopped. He had been All-State in 1965, among the best ball handlers, fast and physical, ever to come out of Oklahoma City. Even now, when he felt like it, he could drive the basket, hip-juke, fake-pump, elbow, and lay the ball in, leaving the rest of them grabbing each other. He was something to watch, tall and hard as a steel beam, with a long full beard gone prematurely to salt-and-pepper.

Tonight, after the game he had to go back to his office, four blocks

away in the steepled City National Bank building. Sara was coming
by to pick up a copy of Kerr-McGee's most recent motion. "Hi! Sorry
I'm late." She came bustling in. Ikard was at his desk, a varnished
pine table with chrome underpinnings. The floor was adobe tile.
Artwork for the new age hung on the walls, ferns from the ceiling.
There was a lithograph in bold colors. "Did you get that in California?" Sara asked.

"I got it here at the mall." Ikard smiled. "Not everybody out here
is a hayseed or cowboy."

Sara circled the room, admiring it. "How'd Danny ever talk you
into doing this case?"

"Oh, I figured—what the hell? I never want to work for Kerr-
McGee, and this will insure I never get asked."

"Do you like Danny?"

"He's great. Crazy, but great. I didn't even meet him till after the
suit was filed. Which was a story in itself: filing the suit. Danny air-
expressed the papers with only hours to spare, and I got over to the
courthouse right at closing. I was reading the papers as I signed
them."

"I'd like to ask your honest opinion: do you think we can win?"

Ikard shrugged. "I'm not taking any bets, but, well, a lot depends
on Danny." Ikard showed her to an unoccupied annex with packing
crates and sawdust on the floor. "We're fixing it up for him. He'll
have to be out here practically full time."

NASHVILLE. JUNE 22, 1977. The judge had not believed Srouji's
version of that evening in the church—Father Bill's affidavit was
persuasive—but neither had the judge put her under a contempt
citation. So the deposition was to proceed as before, except that this
time, at Danny's request, Ikard would conduct it. Danny felt too
hostile.

The emotion was unusual, but then he had never been in a litigation where all the participants did not clearly belong to one side or
the other. He hated duplicity. Srouji's presence was like an extra
player on a football field; at any time she might line up with either
team. The dilemmas she caused were remarkably complex. For the
past month FBI officials had tantalized Danny with a quid pro quo:
the Justice Department would prosecute Srouji for perjury if he would
press charges in writing. It was a sure way to restore his lawyerly

integrity, but why should the FBI make the offer? One possibility: If Danny formally accused Srouji of perjury, he could never present her to a jury as reliable. Anything she had said or might say, anything about wiretapping or smuggling, would be forfeit.

Danny watched her face as Ikard took the seat next to her. It was a mask. Ikard's own face was at once amiable and august, with the graying hair and beard that made him look twice his twenty-nine years. For six long hours he did his best, spinning a silky tone and alternately acting stern—but without result. Srouji had a rationale for not cooperating. All her research had been done as a journalist, she claimed, and therefore was confidential and protected.

Ikard's fingers bent stiffly and a pencil snapped. Danny asked again for an adjournment. He was angry at being outmaneuvered, and he could feel bile rising up toward violence. He looked at Srouji; her stare was like a curse.

"Okay, that's it," he said. "I'm going to ask the judge to put a stop to this. I'll have you hauled up on perjury and anything else I can think of."

Outside on the sidewalk Danny kicked at the gum wrappers and winter-dried catalpa pods as though they were obstacles. "All my career I've defended the First Amendment," he said. "So what does this witch hide behind? The fucking First Amendment! She's turning all my old arguments against me. If we get her cited for contempt now, she'll make herself into a journalistic martyr."

WASHINGTON. JUNE 28, 1977. Peter Stockton came out of a hydrocarbon haze and into the smell of Swiss steak and overcooked cabbage rolls. He called out good-naturedly to Bob, "I hear you're poaching on my territory again."

"The Alaska pipeline is all yours," Bob said with the same humor.

Stockton dropped his voice to a mock whisper. "No, I mean the black market."

"That's yours too. I'm working on the gray market."

They filled their trays and cleared off a table and sat down. Stockton had a copy of a GAO report, the one about nuclear security and MUF that had been more than two years in the making. The report was in several parts. But the bottom line was that security at nuclear facilities was "inadequate at best." Thirty-six separate violations had been discovered at one facility alone. Unauthorized visitors had penetrated high-risk areas at two other facilities. Three had man-size holes in their fences; the doors were unlocked and the burglar alarms turned off at another. The GAO had placed part of the blame on the Joint Committee's doting optimism, but that criticism wasn't in the sanitized summary the Joint Committee had released. So Dingell's temper had flared. He had commissioned the report, and by God, he would release the full text. That included information about the cumulative MUF for all U.S. nuclear facilities over the previous twenty-three years. At least eight thousand pounds of plutonium and enriched uranium was unaccounted for.

"No matter what they say, that's a helluva lot," Bob declared.

"I'm willing to believe the report, as far as it goes," Stockton said. "If every facility lost a couple of pounds every year, through spills and whatnot, that would account for most of it. But I'm not willing to believe *all* eight thousand pounds was lost to natural causes."

"You think some was sold on the black market?"

"I think it went somewhere. If there is a black market, and there probably is, then that's probably where it went."

"It'd be a lot easier to tell what's what if we had something more than a composite figure. I'd like to see the MUF broken down company by company, facility by facility."

"I'm working on it," Stockton said.

"In between Alaska?"

"Yeah. I've got my hands on some old records. There's one company that had a gigantic MUF."

"Kerr-McGee?"

"No, a Pennsylvania company. NUMEC."

"How much is missing?"

"A truckload. Cross your fingers that some psycho didn't get hold of it. The NRC guys get cold sweats every time I bring up the possibility."

"The other possibility is the gray market," Bob said.

"Explain that to me, will you? I read the magazine article where you were quoted, but it wasn't very clear."

"This think tank, the Hudson Institute, actually coined the term gray market. I read about it in one of their white papers. That got me interested, so I did some snooping. Used one of your tricks: played dumb. It works. I got somebody to tell me about the World Nuclear Fuel Market, an international consortium of seventy-nine companies from eighteen countries. About half are American. They got a headquarters in Atlanta, which is zippered up pretty tight, but somebody slipped me a consignment list. Some of these companies have been shipping weapons-grade material from the U.S. over to Europe. There were sales of sixty pounds of plutonium last year. Private, commercial sales."

"I thought only the government could make nuclear sales overseas."

"Used to be that way, sure. Five years ago these companies could've been charged with treason like the Rosenbergs. But Nixon changed the rules under his share-the-wealth program. There's been a legal loophole since 1973."

"Jesus, that's the year before Karen was killed." Stockton was looking for a context. "I was on the Hill then. I don't remember any debate."

"Nixon slid it through. As far as I can tell, the vast majority of Congress still doesn't realize what's going on. But the gray market is a reality. American companies sell to European companies who sell to God-knows-where, Pakistan or Iran or Brazil. The NRC has to approve the first leg of the transaction, but after that it's a free-for-all."

"What a hell of a temptation for companies to fudge on their MUF. Jack it up forty pounds, skim off the excess and sell it overseas."

"Precisely! Munitions companies have been stockpiling bazookas and machine guns and selling them secretly for years. Why not nuclear companies? Why not Kerr-McGee?"

"One way or another we've got to find out what the real MUF at Cimarron was. That's definitely unfinished business."

Stockton saw that Bob had disposed of two Swiss steaks while his own unambitious lunch of soup was half to the brim. The oyster crackers had ballooned across the surface.

Bob said, "Did you hear about Seigenthaler's big award, that Sidney Hillman thing for courage in journalism?"

"Yeah, I called to congratulate him. I thought he'd be all pumped up, but he still feels he's under a cloud. The FBI has never apologized. Even with a new Administration."

"I always figured the FBI doesn't give a damn who's President."

"Not that Carter has been much of an improvement—with all due respect to your old boss."

"You mean *presidential adviser* Joe Browder?" Bob grinned. "Well he's having fun. Trying to reform from the inside. So is Wilson Clark, the guy who helped Browder launch EPC. He's out west as Jerry Brown's energy adviser."

"So what're you doing among the peons?" Stockton felt sportive again after the long siege of serious talk. "Holding out for Deputy Secretary of Energy?"

"Not me. Being on the outside is great for your peace of mind."

OKLAHOMA CITY. JULY 14, 1977. A night shadow of gnats stirred from the uncut lawn and trailed Kitty to the front door, swirling around the porch light. "Come in," Jack Tice said. "Fast."

"Thanks," Kitty said. "Like I told you on the phone, I've gotten a small amount of money through the place where my husband works. For a follow-up survey."

"What kind of survey?"

"I'm sending a questionnaire to everyone who worked at the factory, to find out whether they were ever contaminated and whether they've had any health abnormalities since then."

Tice ruffled his mustache. "I thought cancer doesn't show up for years."

"That's right, but radiation causes other things: miscarriages and birth defects."

"That wouldn't apply to too many of our folks. We had mostly men."

"Fathers can also pass on the defects to their kids."

"Damn! I wonder what else there is that Kerr-McGee never told us."

"You probably were told that the doses you got were safe. But as far as I know, nobody's ever done a study of nuclear workers to find out exactly what's safe and what isn't."

"What can I do?" Tice asked.

"Wodka gave me the names of all the workers the OCAW had on file, and I've checked phone books and city directories for addresses. But there are gaps."

Tice stretched out his hand. "Let me see that list."

WASHINGTON. AUGUST 20, 1977. The Butternut attic smelled of avocado shampoo. Sara unwrapped a towel from her smooth cap of hair, drenched as from a storm. Blindly palpating, her fingers produced corkscrew curls. Water sprayed onto Danny where he sat, home for a while from Oklahoma, his head thrown forward over a sheaf of papers.

"I recruited six new members for the NOW Labor Task Force," Sara said. "We're forming subcommittees, we have so many issues to work on. Full employment, J. P. Stevens . . ."

"Sounds great." His eyes did not waver. "This suit is sinking under a flood of paper. All I've done all summer is answer Kerr-McGee's interrogatories. It'll take another year to finish it."

"What about your entrance date at the seminary?"

"I can delay that."

"You could also transfer the case to Ikard," Sara said, forcing the point.

"It wouldn't be fair. I lassoed him into this. He doesn't have the time for a dragged-out fight."

"What you mean is you don't want somebody else to fight *your* fight."

Danny tried to disagree. She wouldn't let him. She touched his cheek, and his hand moved over hers in a happy embrace.

"Let's go dancing tonight," he said.

OKLAHOMA CITY. SEPTEMBER 10, 1977. Jim Smith was built stubby with muscular forearms, indelibly sunburned. Until Cimarron closed he was one of two production supervisors. Before that, for eighteen years he had worked at a nuclear munitions factory for the Pentagon. Now, all of a sudden, these SOS people, people not exactly in sympathy with his lifetime of work, wanted him to turn his back on it. First this private eye Bill Taylor had paid a call. Next a Washington lady, Kitty something-or-other, had sent a questionnaire. Then Jack Tice, the 5–283 man, had phoned. At the moment Karen's father and a lawyer fellow, name of Ikard, were buying Jim Smith a T-bone at the Skirvin Plaza.

"I knew Karen well enough to say hello," Smith said. "She had her own way of doing things, which wasn't my way. But—and I know Old Man McGee would keel over to hear me say this—but I think her heart was in the right place."

Mr. Silkwood said, "Jack Tice tells me they want to stop that health survey, the one that Kitty Tucker is trying to do."

Smith nodded and unfolded a letter from the chief of Kerr-McGee's

nuclear division, which had been sent to all former Cimarron workers. The letter warned them against cooperating with Kitty unless
they wished to get embroiled in the lawsuit. "I got a good temper, I
guess, but this was the first time I ever got mad over a letter," Smith
said. "See, in the morning meetings I was part of management, but
the rest of the time I worked in those two-deck rooms with everybody
else, breathing in that junk. If this lady wants to do a survey, hell,
I'd like to know what she finds out."

"You're no longer with the company?" Ikard asked.

"No, which is another thing that burns my butt," Smith said.
Bitterness sharpened his words. "Kerr-McGee promised us transfers
when they closed shop, but where did they want to put me? Down
one of their damn uranium mines! I've worked in nuclear all my life,
and I've risked my neck before. You might think I'm dumber than a
box of rocks for doing it. But I sure ain't dumb enough to work in no
hot hole." Smith was self-employed at present. He had a stall at the
Old Paris Flea Market, hawking Bowie knives, pistols, swords, insignia patches, beer mugs, crystal goblets, country-rock stereo tapes.

"Can you explain something?" Ikard asked routinely, keeping his
anticipation in check. "The sign in front of the factory says there was
only one lost-time accident the last three years there. How's that
possible?"

Smith sat back. "Easy. We had plenty of accidents but we never
lost production time. We never stopped working. One time, I think
it was spring of '73, a fire broke out and there was radiation everywhere. I went in and told the manager we had to stop and clean up.
He said, 'Let's go out front!'—which meant I was gonna get the axe.
So I put the men in respirators, and they came out hotter than little
red wagons. It was push, push, push—production first and to hell
with everything else."

"Would you testify to this?"

"I'm no snitch," Smith said decisively. "I still believe in nuclear.
The industry's made a lot of mistakes, sure, but nuclear is our best
hope."

Ikard felt the rejection. He spoke quietly. "All you'd have to do is
tell what happened, good, bad, indifferent."

Smith pondered that, as he had several times before. "I guess if I
was subpoenaed I wouldn't have no choice, would I?"

"Thank you," Mr. Silkwood said, his voice splintering between
the words.

They walked into the graying evening, and Smith recalled the last time he had seen Karen. "I stopped by her place. The moon-suits were ripping it apart, and she was standing there, tears running down her cheeks, a scared little girl."

The next morning Danny got a long-distance report from Ikard. "You wanted a John Dean witness? Well, maybe we got one!" Ikard said. "Jim Smith was on the inside at the factory. He went to all the management meetings and he knows a helluva lot. He might even know about the MUF."

Fourteen

The noises had identities. The scratching was Yoko, a coon dog with a long coppery belly. The screen door banging in answer was Shawn. The thumping on the stairs was both of them, Shawn goading the dog to a race. Kitty heard them go romping across Amber's ménage of Play-Doh figurines, and she heard Amber's soulful cries. "Stop it! Stop it this instant!" Kitty sat up in bed. Another of her headaches had put her there. Something inside her head was quivering like a bass viol. She forced herself to the hallway and cradled Amber, warming the wet, deflated toddler face, and she called Shawn back to make his peace.

Then she fell back on the bed. Sara came in and tried to squeeze the knot from the back of Kitty's neck. "It's the tension," Kitty said.

Downstairs in the kitchen a notice from Kerr-McGee was pinned up. It had come in triplicate: deposition orders for Kitty, Sara, and Bob. All week Kitty had been trudging around the house in dread of the depositions. Anything unflattering that came out might someday count against her entrance to the D.C. bar, assuming she graduated from Antioch, which was a separate headache.

At least the house didn't smell of cigarettes. Sara had gone cold turkey. Her throat had itched from the craving at first, making her edgy, too, but today it felt velvety and wonderful. The cigarettes hidden in her dresser didn't even tempt her.

Kitty was relaxing under Sara's fingers. "You said yourself they're not allowed to use our depositions for a fishing expedition," Sara soothed, her hazel eyes quiet like the coon dog's. "Danny says we should tell Bill Paul to go jump if he tries anything."

The depositions lasted three days in mid-September. Bill Paul would have liked much longer. His questions traipsed everywhere through the backgrounds of the Butternut gang. Why was Kitty's last name Tucker instead of Alvarez? How had Kitty and Bob and Sara become political activists? What were their affiliations? Had they ever done anything illegal? (Kitty had to own up to her long-ago arrest at the Orange Bowl cafe.) Who were the other leaders of the SOS? Who was bankrolling them?

Through repetition, Bill Paul made clear his interest in the names and dollars behind the lawsuit. The Butternut gang revealed nothing. They didn't want Kerr-McGee to know they had almost no money, that for months the lawsuit had been sustained only through Danny's goodwill. When Bill Paul got pushy, Kitty erupted in a harangue. "I'm not going to give you any names. Kerr-McGee's harassed enough people."

"My clients have never done anything like that," Bill Paul harrumphed.

"Oh, yeah?" Kitty began rattling off examples, and Bill Paul withdrew the question.

When it was Bob's turn, Bill Paul got a lecture on what was wrong with the nuclear industry. Bob was primed. He had just testified before a committee of the National Academy of Sciences. He had a regular speech about how future generations would have to deal with tons of radioactive waste, how the gray market was making bomb materials available to almost anyone, how Navajos were dying of cancer in uranium mines.

Afterward Bob chided Bill Paul, offering to make himself available at the trial.

"No, no, that's okay," Paul said emphatically. "I'm not going to need you again."

For Sara it took an act of harsh will not to be her habitually open self. But at one point it was she who caught Bill Paul off guard. "Does Kerr-McGee have us under surveillance?" she asked.

Bill Paul's face turned waxen, and he and his partners briefly left the room. When they came back, Bill Paul said, "Off the record, I can tell you that my clients are not spying on you."

Sara asked him serenely to swear to it, but he begged off.

"Why not?"

"Because, well, because it's a preposterous notion. I don't want to dignify it."

WASHINGTON. SEPTEMBER 17, 1977. Last week, Danny's hopes had been pumped up and he had felt dauntless. Jim Smith and another Cimarron supervisor, Jerry Cooper, appeared willing to testify. But Cooper, now manager of a Phillips 66 gas station, had gotten a visit from a Kerr-McGee representative, and he had suddenly remembered that his franchise could be taken away and his mortgage annulled. Smith, on the other hand, had gone ahead and talked forthrightly at his deposition until Ikard brought up the question of smuggling. The company lawyers had stopped him right there. The objection was "national security." Smith's military years had made him respectful of the code phrase, and he had said no more. Danny expected that U.S. District Judge Luther Eubanks would uphold the objection.

"It's easy to tell that he's in Bill Paul's corner," Danny said to Sara.

It was one in the morning, long past time for Sara to go home. Danny had a commandment about eight hours of sleep, but tonight he was the one breaking it. They were at Arrupe House, sitting on the floor in his chairless attic, working on the biggest crisis yet.

Danny leaned back, using his palms on the floor for support. Books of all sizes were in one corner; a bag of cookies was perched on a windowsill.

"Bill Paul isn't what you'd call charismatic," Danny said. "But he's got pull, quiet pull, the best kind. He was president of the Oklahoma bar last year. He hangs around with all the muckity-mucks, and Eubanks thinks he's the cat's meow."

From the beginning Danny had been under a handicap in all the aspects of litigation that are usually decisive: money, legal help, willing witnesses, rapport with the judge. "Eubanks did give us a few breaks, I won't deny it. But as far as interpreting the law goes, he's been beating us flatter than piss on a platter. He can't get it through his head that Srouji should not be entitled to a freedom-of-the-press privilege. She's an FBI operative, not a journalist, which I've explained over and over to Eubanks. But he just sits there like a statue."

By the judge's ruling, Jim Smith wasn't allowed to discuss smuggling, and Srouji didn't have to.

On other rulings Danny had done no better. Judge Eubanks had allowed the FBI, the Justice Department, the NRC, and Kerr-

McGee to hold back most of their records. The rationale: "national security."

Earlier in the year Danny thought he had a way to finesse the judge. A Franciscan order, holding twenty-four hundred shares of Kerr-McGee stock, had agreed to file a minority stockholder's resolution with the Securities and Exchange Commission (SEC). In effect, the resolution asked that the stockholders be allowed to vote on whether to make the internal company records public. But a Kerr-McGee official had gone to a Catholic bishop to get the Franciscans to back off, and when they didn't, Kerr-McGee had hired a Texas law firm which had a former SEC director among its partners. The law firm had waged a successful appeal to the SEC to keep the resolution off the agenda at the stockholders' meeting. Father Robert Taylor, a Franciscan treasurer, had reported the defeat to Danny. ("We've handled dozens of cases for the Interfaith Center for Corporate Responsibility, and we've never run into a company that went to such great lengths to avoid a vote.") The records remained out of reach.

Judge Eubanks had compelled only one witness to talk. He was Buzz Hirsch, the Californian filmmaker. Bill Paul had subpoenaed Hirsch and demanded all the names, notes, and photographs collected for his movie. Hirsch had gone out, hired a lawyer, and filed papers of resistance based on his own First Amendment rights. But Judge Eubanks had cited him for contempt and sentenced him to six months in jail. He was free on appeal, but so much of his time and money was going to appellate lawyers that there was none left for his movie.

Before Hirsch clammed up, though, he had made one mistake. In a room full of hostile lawyers he had coughed out Mrs. Jung's identity. Two afternoons later, while Mrs. Jung was at work at Kerr-McGee headquarters, her trailer had been broken into. It was no ordinary burglary, since her TV set and jewelry boxes had been left behind; only her desk and papers had been ransacked. Shortly thereafter a heavy car with bright headlights had chased her home. The car came within inches of her bumper, braked, wheeled around in a sideswiping move, pulled in front, slowed to a reptilian pace: a terrifying sequence. When she got up the nerve to pass, she was pursued at speeds up to eighty-five miles an hour over gullied rural roads. She made it home; but since then there had been other harassments. Anonymous callers, throaty voices in the night, had been dunning her with cold advice. ("Don't do anything you might re-

gret.") ("Think of your health.") ("Do the smart thing.") The smart
thing, Mrs. Jung had decided, was to go into hiding in Colorado. It
was unlikely that she would return for a trial.

After nearly a year, Danny was accustomed to one adrenaline col-
lapse after another. Even so, everything else had been mere prelude
to the current crisis. Judge Eubanks had placed Danny under a deadline. Six weeks: that was all the time they had left to get their
evidence together to proceed to trial.

Danny's mouth ached; his face was tight with consternation.

"Is that enough time to do anything?" Sara asked.

"Right now it wouldn't matter if we had another year. We don't
have the money to pay Bill Taylor, so there's no way to get the
evidence we need."

All summer Taylor had been at a standstill for want of money.
There had been barely enough for Danny's expenses. Depositions—
the grist of their investigation—had gone untranscribed; a dollar a
page was too expensive. The total budget to date had not exceeded
$20,000, a trickle of ten-dollar and twenty-dollar checks from NOW
members and readers of *Rolling Stone* magazine, which had taken a
flagrante bello interest. There had been just three big checks, from the
Laras Fund of California, the Emergency Civil Liberties Foundation
in New York, and Jann Wenner, the *Rolling Stone* publisher. Had it
not been for free rent and free supplies at Ikard's law firm, the case
probably would have been lost already through attrition.

Danny's desk in Oklahoma City was only a plywood board astride
a pile of cardboard boxes, but it was more than he now had in D.C.
Danny had been forced to choose between the lawsuit and his office at
the Ministry for Social Justice. The Church had other wishes for him.
"It was an accumulation of things, and they were very gracious about
it," Danny explained. "It won't affect my living here at Arrupe
House. But it was also disillusioning. It was *déjà vu*. Like Wall
Street, the Church is willing to do political work, as long as it doesn't
make their big rich contributors unhappy."

"Is it true that Father Bill quit too?" Sara asked.

"It's true, and I feel partly responsible. I got him involved in this
case, and now he's gung-ho to go out to Oklahoma. For which I'm
grateful, of course. He's not a lawyer, but he's good at tracking down
things."

"Maybe Father Bill could do what Taylor was gonna do?" she said
hopefully.

"No, that takes a professional. It takes a guy like Taylor who knows his way around the spy netherworld—the CID, CIA, Interpol —and there aren't five guys like him who'd work for us. At any price."

"I still have a feeling Father Bill would make a good investigator."

"Actually, he might be very good at talking to the Cimarron people, converting people like Jim Smith into witnesses. But we're daydreaming," he said with resignation. "The problem is still money. I'm down to mooching quarters for the candy machine."

"You keep saying that, but it's not getting us anywhere."

"Sara, how can I make you understand? We're at the beg-borrow-or-steal stage. We're out on a limb and the judge is sawing it off."

"What do you want *me* to do? Go ring doorbells?"

"If you have to." There was heat in his voice. "Look, who else is there? Kitty is always busy."

"But it's okay for *me* to drop everything? The J. P. Stevens boy-cott? The ERA? Maternity benefits? Organizing clerical workers?"

"I'm sorry. I hate putting it all on you. But *you* got me into this case."

Sara looked away. She stood and touched her toes, flexing away leg cramps. She opened a window. Free cooling air blew in. She snatched the bag of cookies, chocolate chip, which she had been denying herself. "I'm already committed to a labor rally for the ERA in Virginia, and there's the NOW-Alert for Silkwood Memorial Day. And honestly, Danny, I'm an amateur at fundraising. I don't know the first thing about it."

"Sara, I know you can do it."

"Bullshit."

"Then you tell me what you want me to do."

She set down the cookies. "Okay, how much money will it take?"

Danny scowled in contemplation. "Michael Kennedy figured on twenty-five thousand, and that's about right. In fact, I'm just realiz-ing how right Kennedy was. I've been expecting manna from the skies. We have to get realistic. Let's say twenty-five thousand by the end of October."

"Danny, that is *not* being realistic." Sara did a quick calculation. "Doesn't your evidence have to be in by then anyway?"

"If you get the money, I'll get the extra time. I promise."

"You really are incurably cavalier."

"Optimistic, incurably optimistic."

Sara had the silverware and cups in place on the longboard and a vegetable stew on the stove. Kitty hugged her appreciatively: "You didn't have to fix dinner—it was my turn."

"That's the good news," Sara said. "The bad news is that we need twenty-five thousand dollars." Yoko bounded into the room, whimpering for affection.

"The rest of SOS is completely broke too," Kitty sighed, scratching and stroking the dog. "There's a huge backlog of letters to answer. I've been buying the stamps myself." Paying out of pocket was an old habit to which Kitty had reverted. With money earned as a Hill intern, she had bought helium for ten thousand balloons to be set adrift from the front gates of several nuclear reactors. Landing in backyards after miles of floating, tags on the balloons told their finders that, in case of a major nuclear accident, the winds would be bearing radiation instead of helium.

"Is there anyone left in SOS with fundraising experience?" Sara asked.

Kitty laughed hollowly. "Is there anyone left in SOS, period?"

"I can't raise the money by myself," Sara said. "Can you help?"

"Why doesn't Danny lean on his old Wall Street buddies?"

"That's not funny." Sara was offended. "I'm asking you."

"I can't. I wish I could, but it's too much to do. I'm all used up." Kitty lapsed into gentle weeping. The dog barked and rubbed against her. "Sometimes I think we've created a Frankenstein. We've built up all these expectations, and now we can't deliver."

Sara swayed under the blasphemy.

"I'm sorry," Kitty said. "I didn't mean it." In forgiveness they embraced each other.

Later, alone in her bed, Sara prayed. "If you're going to help, God, now is the time."

COLUMBIA, MARYLAND. SEPTEMBER 19, 1977. "Let me check the agenda," the receptionist said in a lofty tone. Sara's brown arms were lost under sheets of white paper on which she had written fifty reasons why a private foundation should fund the suit. "I wouldn't be this rude, but it's an emergency," Sara said. "I found out about this meeting too late to get invited, but I have to get in. Please!"

The receptionist softened. "Give me your name," she said, "and I'll get you on our list. We have another meeting in three months."

"I can't wait three months!" Sara said firmly, calling up all her determination. But her hands were making broken-wing movements, and her knees were knocking.

The receptionist got up and went behind parquet doors. David Hunter came out. Hunter was executive director of the Stern Fund. "We have a formal procedure," he said. "Other groups got their requests in by our deadline. We can't give you preferential treatment."

A red patch grew on Sara's face, as if from a slap. "I'm sorry," she said sincerely, "I don't want to cause a scene, but I'm not leaving till you at least look at my proposal." Another man appeared in response to the receptionist. He was Herman Warsh, a wealthy environmentalist and husband to Maryanne Mott Manet, an heiress to the General Motors fortune. "You have to leave," he said.

Sara wouldn't. She kept talking about the urgency, the six-week ultimatum. Finally they seemed to understand. Cascading the papers into their hands, she whispered another prayer.

Sara tried to compensate for the lack of time with sheer furious action, filling out forms, calling everywhere, going from one foundation to the next. They told her she was plucky and cute, but no one put pen to check.

Then David Hunter called. After reading her proposal, he was ready to donate $3,000. Maryanne Manet would give $6,000.

That was all well and good, but it was only half, and on Sara's calendar five weeks had been marked off. With a week to go, she went downstairs to the Butternut bedroom off the kitchen. "Come in," said Marion Edey. Marion, a lobbyist and political researcher like Bob, had lived in the house about a year. "Can you help?" Sara asked.

Marion was from a wealthy New York family.

"I'm embarrassed, putting a housemate on the spot like this," Sara said, "but I'm desperate. I'm about to throw myself on the floor and hold my breath." Jokingly she puffed up her cheeks.

Marion chuckled a little. "Don't do it! I'll help." Though she did not like to trade on her past, she said she would this time. "I'll call a few people," she said. "And I have some money. I'll give you five thousand."

The next day Marion sent telephone maydays to the Ottinger Fund and her mother, and Sara did the same once again with her list. When they were done, there were four more miraculous pledges on their toteboard, finely scripted rows of zeros that all together totaled almost $50,000. A happiness filtered through Sara. She felt superb!

Danny was unavailable in an Oklahoma courtroom. But Sara's shouts of "Thank you, Jesus!" from the Butternut porch, and Yoko's yapping hosannas, sounded excited enough to reach the prairie.

OKLAHOMA CITY. OCTOBER 27, 1977. At Kerr-McGee's invitation, local reporters had used the depositions of Drew, Mr. Silkwood, and Bill Meadows to make public much of Karen's private life. But lately the lawsuit had been kept under wraps. No local reporters had been invited to Jim Smith's deposition or to Jack Tice's. Nothing had been in the papers for months, and even attentive followers like Ilene Younghein assumed the suit had dropped abashedly into the past tense.

That was not far from reality. Given the latest orders by Judge Eubanks, Danny predicted a dismissal by Thanksgiving. At their depositions Lawrence Olson and James Reading had refused to answer dozens of questions because of "national security." Olson admitted talking to Jackie Srouji, but he claimed ambiguously that someone else had been responsible for arranging the meeting. Reading could not remember anything he had told Srouji. Asked how he got his dossier of Karen's habits—"Did it fall from the sky?"—Reading grinned sarcastically and said, "Maybe it did."

Danny had emptied his frustrations onto a *City Times* reporter, and to his surprise an article had made it into print. Now other reporters were calling, and the lawsuit was again in the news. Writing about Jim Smith, who substantially contradicted the official version of how Cimarron was run, and writing about Stockton's evidence of a cover-up, the reporters were making Kerr-McGee's innocence seem less certain.

In a fury Bill Paul had cornered Danny. "I've tried to give you every consideration. I've tried to do things in a professional, friendly way, and meanwhile you're manipulating the press. My client is being slandered. You're not a lawyer, you're a, a . . . a hellraiser!"

Today the macho tug-of-war was moving to the federal courthouse. Judge Eubanks had been asked to impose a "gag order" on Danny. It was a slapdash move—neither Bill Paul nor Justice Department attorney Glenn Whitaker had prepared any legal briefs. Rather than defend himself, Danny had asked the Washington-based Reporters Committee for Freedom of the Press to send an attorney to defend the First Amendment. She was Lana Tyree. Danny and Bill Paul glowered at each other while Whitaker and Tyree made the legal arguments. Quoting from an ACLU brief Danny had once written, Tyree said the gag was "constitutionally offensive." Whitaker, an Ivy Leaguer in wing-tips, said it was necessary because Danny had been resorting to headlines to try his case.

Judge Eubanks spread his arms and leaned into the fracas. He had heavy, florid cheeks and a cantankerous style. He said, "You seem to enjoy talking, Mr. Sheehan. What do you have to say for yourself?"

Danny felt no respect and did not feign any. "This proceeding is without merit. I have nothing to say."

"Nothing?" It was an unwilling echo. Danny watched as the judge swallowed. Time stopped, as if Danny had fired a bullet into the wall clock. He had not meant to be so provoking. What was the value? When Judge Eubanks spoke again, though, Danny had a dawning idea. He saw that the judge was at the edge of control: gambler's luck.

Judge Eubanks ordered Danny to stand and face him. Censorship wasn't justified, the judge said, but censure was. As the presiding guardian of good manners, he wished to teach some to Danny. "You are a professional and you should conduct yourself in a professional way." Danny's body registered a sneer, and the judge's red face thrust forward in an acerbic uptake. "I do not want a return to this Roman holiday atmosphere," he said.

"I object to that characterization," Danny retorted with the smallest of smirks. Now he was being surgical, provoking, without furnishing an excuse for a contempt citation. Judge Eubanks aimed a finger and sputtered. "You, sir, are someone who runs off at both ends!" The finger flicked toward Ikard, whose face burned bone-white under the heat of the tirade. "And you, Mr. Ikard, are a magpie!"

The judge seemed lost in combat. Turning, he gave Bill Paul a partisan wink. "Apparently Mr. Sheehan and Mr. Ikard have taken this thing and are running with it and are using the Silkwood parents as a tool," he said, parroting Bill Paul's frequent description of the suit. "This case isn't worth a hill of beans anyway."

Danny whirled, looking beyond the maple palisade to the reporters in gallery seats. (This time *he* had invited them.) Had they caught the judge's unjudicial remarks? They had.

As soon as he could, Danny escaped to a phone and informed those reporters not in attendance.

"I think we did it," he said later, relaxing with Ikard. "I think we just got rid of one crusty old high-hatting hip-shooting judge."

Six days later a reporter notified Judge Eubanks that Danny was drafting a recusal motion to have the magistrate disqualified. Within an hour the judge did what Danny had been waiting for: he voluntarily relinquished his role and transferred the case to another judge.

"All right!" Danny's proclamation carried through the law office. The suit had a reprieve. It would take the new judge three or four months to acquaint himself and log it in.

It was a second victory in as many days here on the twenty-third floor of the City National Bank Building. Yesterday one of Ikard's partners had won freedom for four shaggy-haired members of the Hangmen Motorcycle Club. A topless go-go dancer had accused them of roping her to a clubhouse bed and having their way with her. She might have been believed except that Ikard's partner got her to admit it had all taken place over several weeks while she went willingly to and from the clubhouse. Set free, the Hangmen stumbled up to the law offices and across Ikard's adobe tile, holding aloft jugs of an obscure whiskey. Finding Danny at his plywood desk, they had laced his iced tea to overflowing and wondered why he wouldn't touch it.

Today there was no whiskey, no revelry, only Danny's boasting. He and Ikard thumped each other's shoulders, but temperance fastened onto their mood and sobered it. Leaning against the cardboard boxes, one of Ikard's partners offered some free advice. "Getting rid of Eubanks might not be such a blessing. A judge is one thing, but the juries here are something else. They don't see the world like you do. They got a definite pecking order. At the top are self-made millionaires like Kerr and McGee and at the bottom are the Hangmen. If there's anybody lower than riffraff bikers, it's a topless go-go dancer. The way it is, they'll probably put Karen in with the go-go girls."

"First things first," Danny said cheerfully. "First let's get to trial."

WASHINGTON. NOVEMBER 5, 1977. Amber was nodding asleep to her daddy's medley from *Wonderful Town*. All evening Bob had been entertaining her, but it was no excuse for putting off the phone call. "You better do it," Kitty urged again.

He did not move from the ivory-gray chair. "You know how cranky these research scientists are. They're like hermits. This guy's liable to sic the government on me. He certainly wasn't very nice to you."

"But he isn't too pleased with the government either." An endearing quality got into Kitty's tone. "Mancuso is an important man. He's done the only epidemiological survey of nuclear workers there is." She came over and squeezed onto Bob's lap next to Amber. "Besides, he'll like *you.*"

Dr. Thomas Mancuso, an early riser, had phoned Kitty the other morning while she was sleepily dressing Amber. He was aware of her attempt to survey the Cimarron work force, and brusquely he had set her straight: a survey of two or three hundred workers was too small to be meaningful. You needed to monitor thirty thousand or so nuclear employees to get a true reading about the effects of radiation. For longer than a decade he himself had been at work on such a study. But now—Dr. Mancuso's voice had fallen—the government that had sponsored his research was in the act of suppressing it.

Kitty had tried to ask him more, but, bang, he had rung off.

PITTSBURGH. NOVEMBER 12, 1977. Dr. Mancuso actually had quite a history, and as Bob gained his trust, he confided it. He was from Ohio, like Bob, which made for comfortable small talk. During his 17 years as the industrial-hygiene director for the State of Ohio, Dr. Mancuso had pioneered the "Social Security Method" for tracking down retirees and transients who had handled asbestos, polyvinyl chloride, plutonium, other carcinogens. At that time few studies with human data existed; regarding plutonium there were none at all. Many health standards were little better than guesswork. But by getting access to Social Security records, Dr. Mancuso was able to match payroll lists to obituaries. It was an invaluable breakthrough. An entire history of rubber-tire workers, who were doing a lot of dying in Ohio, could be looked at in one sweep. Industrial causes and effects began to show up. In 1961 the National Cancer Institute had named Dr. Mancuso one of the country's top cancer researchers, and the University of Pittsburgh had recruited him for its public-health facility.

Here Dr. Mancuso was shoehorned into a somber office with as much walking space as a closet. Three brown-tone snapshots of his children were the only relief from drab walls and metal furniture. On meeting him, Bob had the impression of a man shrinking into himself, having to inhale deeply to fill his clothes. Thin, almost withered, his oval face danced above a sweater and tie of some faded fashion.

Over the years Dr. Mancuso had descended into a solitary existence, determined to make Contract E(1101)3428 the capstone of his career. Money for it had come from the AEC, a yearly stipend to follow the lives and deaths of nuclear workers. He had traveled to fourteen states and spent months among the Social Security record rooms. His files glutted two dozen four-drawer cabinets. He made charts and filled them with numbers. The workers who had died, the causes of their deaths, the amounts of radiation inhaled, and other numbers, other variables. The charts multiplied into subcharts. He quit teaching, and he didn't eat much either. Skipping lunch, he would search his files over and over, looking for landmarks, measuring them against a statistical horizon. Because cancer can incubate for so many years, he did not expect to see any real patterns before the late seventies.

So he was bowled over when Dr. Sidney Marks called in June of 1974. Dr. Marks was the AEC health studies manager, and he wanted to use Dr. Mancuso's name in a press release. Another researcher, Dr. Samuel Milham, had come across an abnormally high cancer rate among the Hanford workers in eastern Washington State. Not many Washingtonians live east of the glacial range, except those in Hanford, a huge AEC/Pentagon center known to its residents as "Plutonium City" (also home to the still-unfinished fast-breeder). Until the war Hanford had been an unpeopled patch of desert forty miles from volcanic Mount St. Helens. Dr. Milham planned to publish his finding. The AEC was trying to stop him. It wanted Dr. Mancuso to say Dr. Milham was wrong and the radiation standards were fine and dandy. Dr. Mancuso refused; he wasn't ready to publish any conclusions yet.

In the end there was a gentlemen's agreement. Dr. Milham would let Dr. Mancuso publish first. As it turned out, that didn't make the AEC any happier. Dr. Mancuso enlisted the help of two British researchers: epidemiologist Alice Stewart, tall, white-haired, elegantly efficient; and biostatistician George Kneale, reclusive, skeptical. They put the Hanford numbers through computer acrobatics. They tried different sequences. The readouts were the same. It was an accelerating curve. Hanford workers were dying of cancer, particularly pancreas and bone-marrow cancer, in ever-increasing numbers. They had confirmed Dr. Milham's finding.

The import of Dr. Mancuso's study had not immediately occurred to him, and even now Bob had to prod him. "What does it mean to the industry?"

"I suppose it means they'd have to spend millions and millions to make conditions truly safe for the workers," Dr. Mancuso said. "At present the industry is allowed to expose workers to an average of five rems of radiation a year. But the Hanford workers had an average ten to thirty times lower, well within the safe zone, and they still got cancer."

"Which means the safe zone isn't really safe."

"Exactly. The maximum legal dose should be lowered by a factor of ten at least. To half a rem a year: roughly equal to five full-body X-rays."

"You make it sound like even X-rays aren't very safe."

"No, they're not. Not in quantity. But you must remember that my study is not complete. I only have a pattern for the thirty thousand workers from Hanford. There are nearly two hundred thousand more nuclear workers. I can't be absolutely certain until I finish. But the government won't let me."

Dr. Mancuso had been bowled over a second time when in 1976 he went to Germantown, Maryland, headquarters for the part of the AEC now called ERDA. Without making it an order, ERDA officials told him they didn't want to see his study in print. Already they had cut off his stipend.

"Were you able to check on that?" Mancuso asked Bob.

"According to James Liverman in the environment and safety division, you were cut off because your retirement is imminent."

"Retirement? I have six more years before the mandatory retirement age."

The AEC/ERDA money had stopped five months ago. Dr. Mancuso had been given a year's grace by the University of Pittsburgh to find private funding, and he had mailed out dozens of solicitations. But no luck. Instead: a third shock. Officials of ERDA were circulating a negative critique of Dr. Mancuso's study, reversing the official peer review that had given it high marks. "They're trying to discredit me. The bastards!" He had begun to fear for his health, and he feared the next surprise. It had come two months ago: a call from an official in ERDA's Chicago office. A "priority" teletype had been sent from Germantown ordering Dr. Mancuso to give up all his files and read-outs. He didn't know what to do, so he did nothing; it was a stall, verging on defiance—this neutral, diffident scientist defying the lawyers of government.

Today he was in his office, having walked the eleven wintry blocks from his home. Snow clogged the campus. He was on the phone to Bob when the postman delivered another ERDA letter. In unmistakably stern language it ordered Dr. Mancuso to yield, or have his two dozen cabinets seized. "I thought this sort of thing only happened in Russia," he said.

"They're just trying to intimidate you," Bob said.

"Well, they're doing a good job."

There was a routine now for Karen Silkwood Memorial Day. Rallies, marches, vigils around the country marked the anniversary of Karen's death. Feminist groups had accepted Karen as one of their own. With a lot of work Kitty also had made the day into an anti-nuclear veneration. There was a network of grass-roots anti-nuclear groups, very loosely affiliated, and in a way Silkwood Day helped pull them together. Kitty would help them set up rallies and she would arrange for speakers, though she did not offer herself. On that score she was still too shy.

Sara was the opposite. She was in demand as a speaker, a star attraction, and she would go from rally to rally, from D.C. to Philadelphia to New York. Not just on Karen Silkwood Day either, but whenever there was a chance to talk up the case, and wherever—union halls, campuses, churches. She had an uncommon sincerity in her voice, something that was both hard and soft, and she would leave an audience in tears.

ATLANTA, GEORGIA. NOVEMBER 13, 1977. Bill Taylor, who had never been to a political rally, was not about to start. He was otherwise on duty, working on a new and expedient friendship with a man named William Lovin. They were telling a lot of war stories and Marine jokes.

Taylor still had the look—russet hair cut short, wide shoulders at right angles, massive arms from millions of pushups, muscles that did not stop. And his Marine handshake was often his best calling card, though his pride in it had coldly waned. Like Danny, he could point precisely to the incident that had changed him. Vietnam: 1969. Taylor had seen a man in a jeep throw a firebomb, engulfing civilians at lunch. It took days, but Taylor traced the jeep and the firebomber. Under Taylor's fists, the man told all: how he carried out such assassinations on orders from the CIA. The man went free, and, eight years into a life career, Taylor asked the Marines for a discharge.

Because of Sara's fundraising, Taylor was now back on the case, taking a leave from his cushy skippering job. But instead of Oklahoma City, he was in Atlanta, off on an artful tack that Danny had plotted. ("If Kerr-McGee is using surveillance and smear tactics, other nuclear companies probably are too. Let's look for a pattern we can pull together.") It was a hope based on a deduction, but Taylor had come up with several leads.

In Texas the state police had spied on Robert Pomeroy, ex-Marine, Continental Air Lines pilot, and chief antagonist of a nuclear reactor near his Dallas home. When someone tried to get Pomeroy fired despite an impeccable airline record, he sued and found evidence that the police were in a conspiracy with the owners of the reactor. In northern California a former Marine Pathfinder, Robert Rowen, had been fired from his technician's job after he told the AEC that his employer, Pacific Gas & Electric (PG&E), wanted him to falsify records of radiation levels inside its Humboldt nuclear plant. Afterward Rowen had gone job hunting without success: the local police chief had circulated a dossier saying Rowen was a sharpshooter-revolutionary in the style of the Black Panthers. The dossier had come unsolicited from a PG&E security official. (A state labor referee later ruled that Rowen's firing was due to his "extreme safety consciousness," which finally allowed him to land a job as a football coach and civics teacher.) In another case PG&E had used its friends on the Joint Committee on Atomic Energy to pressure NBC–TV into canceling a documentary critical of nuclear power. The network also dropped the documentarian, Emmy-winner Don Widener. He stayed unemployed and came to feel he was being blacklisted because of "lies" PG&E had spread. He sued for libel and (eventually) won a settlement. In New Jersey anti-nuclear leader Larry Bogart, former assistant to the Allied Chemical board chairman, was now under the binocular watch of private detectives. Three times his VW had been tampered with. Once the accelerator rod was sawed through. As Bogart drove the New Jersey Turnpike one winter evening, heading to a crucial meeting, another car sideswiped him, crunching his car down an overpass incline. Only a guardrail kept him from somersaulting into a pond.

From these and other leads, Danny had separated out one that was less localized. In New Hampshire, agents of Information Digest had been caught infiltrating the anti-nuclear Clamshell Alliance. From his spy-world friends, Taylor got the lowdown on Information Digest. Based in D.C., it was a private snooping firm that for a fee would tell you the names and habits of anti-nuclear leaders, what a New York State report called "raw, unevaluated, editorialized and frequently derogatory information." Information Digest was in the same line of work as Research West, a California firm known for its special way of getting information: burglaries. Of the customers for these services, Georgia Power, owner of two nuclear reactors, was noteworthy, having used both agencies.

Atlanta was home for Georgia Power (and for the World Nuclear Fuel Market of "gray market" notoriety), and Taylor had come here looking for furtive little tracks to follow back to Oklahoma. So far it seemed like a good hunch. Georgia Power even had its own undercover squad with a $750,000 annual budget, nine undercover agents, and lots of fancy-dandy arcana out of a spy catalogue: infrared telescopic cameras, fingerprint kits, two-way radios, a videotape unit, drug-analysis kits, and surveillance cars with a dashboard flip-switch to change headlight configurations and trick a driver being tailed. Georgia Power had justified all this because thieves had been stealing equipment from its Hatch nuclear plant. It appeared, however, that the thieves were corporate executives, not working stiffs, and when William Lovin tried to prove it, he had been fired.

The bar was a gloomy one. Pinpricks of light in the ceiling twinkled like innumerable stars in a wilderness sky.

"I was part of Risk Management: that's the name of Georgia Power's security division," Lovin said. "But it isn't a security division at all, not in the traditional sense. It's a miniature CIA. We kept dossiers on everybody Georgia Power doesn't like. Union organizers, anti-nukers, little old ladies who made a fuss over their utility bills. We knew who they've slept with, who their creditors are, who's got a grudge against them, and why."

Someone put a coin in the jukebox. It kicked in. Taylor ordered another round, and in the fellowship of the drinks, Lovin kept talking. "We even had a dossier on Karen Silkwood. Though it wasn't one of ours. We got it through the network."

"You were hooked into a network?" Taylor raised his voice above the music.

"Yeah," Lovin said. "To be honest, I'm not sure how it worked. But you oughta check out Fort Lauderdale."

"Fort Lauderdale, Florida?"

"Yeah. A lot of the Risk Management guys matriculated from there."

In southeast Florida, some of the Georgia Power men were known. They had been with JM WAVE, the CIA guerrilla army that warred on Castro in the sixties. Over drinks (what else?) a former comrade remembered that one of them later went off to a school in Fort Lauderdale. It had a landing strip out back.

Asking around the airports, Taylor had no trouble locating it. The landing strip had a tall fence and dozens of "Keep Out" signs. The school was in a modern building with smoked windows. The strip and building belonged to Audio Intelligence Devices, Inc. Concealed in bushes, of which there were plenty, Taylor drank coffee and watched unsmiling men come and go.

Back at his motel room, in a steely dusk, he saw that his marker in the doorjamb had been disturbed. He reached in cautiously for the light switch and touched a man's shoulder. Something brushed his scalp, and a blade ripped into his sport coat. He grabbed, feeling for a wrist, and felt metal, then the wet of his blood. But he held on to the blade, found the hilt, and twisted. Now it was his knife. He pushed into flesh, and someone screamed. There was more blood, spurting from the man's side. Voices were yelling. A second man rose up from behind the bed. Taylor's Marine reflexes sent knee to groin, callused flat hand to neck. In seconds the intruders had scurried off, hunched and wincing.

Taylor's room was a disaster area, his clothes flung about, the pockets slashed open, furniture tipped over. His hand was bleeding.

Knotting a handkerchief around it, he called Danny. "It looks good," Taylor said. "We're making somebody nervous."

"Okay, keep charging," Danny said. "But if there's anything more like this, you pack it in. Understand?"

Taylor stayed with it through three weeks of rigor and craft: flirting with secretaries, matching names to license plates and to Cessna fuselage numbers, spying on boats with microwave antennae. One weekend Taylor came home to a burgled apartment and a worried wife. He picked up a tail, doubled back, and ambushed the driver, a thin inky man carrying the credentials of an Iranian secret policeman. Taylor made trips to Oklahoma and to Andros Island in the Caribbean. He talked to soldiers-of-fortune, military friends, spy pantologists.

In early December he brought his report to Danny at Arrupe House in D.C. "Audio Intelligence is the intersection," Taylor said. "It's an international intersection for spies—Iranian SAVAK agents, Chilean DINA agents, South Korean military police. They fly into that landing strip from all over."

"Into Fort Lauderdale?"

"Yep. Audio Intelligence is the place to go to buy the state-of-the-art in spy equipment. There's a scale-model city inside—houses, trees, cars, streets. They call it Surveillance City. You can learn where to place a bug and how to do it in five minutes or less."

"Great," said Danny, "but where does Oklahoma fit in?"

"I'm coming to that. First, let me tell you that Georgia Power has been a real steady customer down here. And so have a lot of local police departments. From a lot of states where it's illegal for cops to have wiretap equipment. Like Oklahoma."

"Has Kerr-McGee been a customer?"

"I don't know. But the OCPD has—the Oklahoma City Police Department."

Tony Mazzocchi's apartment was a jumble of shipping containers. Off the walls came weavings and inexpensive oils. Kitchenware and the boys' favorite games went inside double-strength cardboard. Breakables were padded into a steel-enforced army trunk with labels from Paris and Le Mistral. With the new year Mazzocchi would be a vice-president at OCAW headquarters in Denver, and he would be in good position for a run at the union presidency he coveted. But it was not the happiest of promotions. Always an Easterner, brash and gregarious, he was skeptical about going west. Steve Wodka would have to be left behind in the D.C. office, breaching an eight-year partnership, and Mazzocchi's family was being uprooted just before the holidays.

In the kitchen his wife reached for a large clock with white face and black hands, the kind that hang in classrooms. A dusty foreign object fell off its back.

"Tony, this doesn't seem to be part of the clock."

He squinted at the object, a spool of thin wires and a feathery needle.

"It's a bug, isn't it?"

"What a dirty damn trick!" he said. "Putting it in the kitchen. They didn't even let us have breakfast in private." He rolled it over and over in his hand.

"They must have had a good laugh," his wife said. A tight grimace kept her from joining the unheard mirth. "You've been so careful never to say anything important on the phone, and all this time they had the *apartment* bugged. I wonder if they had one under our bed too."

Danny pulled the metal eavesdropper from a pocket and laid it on Mazzocchi's desk. "I showed it to a friend who's in R&D at the CIA. It's an exclusive model. The needle is the transmitter. It vibrates against the back of the clock, using it like a diaphragm. There's no electrical impulse, so bug detectors can't pick it up."

"It sounds pretty high class," Mazzocchi said. He picked it up.

"It isn't the kind of bug you get in a nickel-and-dime spy store. You'd have to go to the CIA or the National Security Agency or a place like Audio Intelligence."

"Any idea how long it might've been there?"

"This style was perfected about five years ago. Taylor thinks it could've been there that long."

Taylor also had a theory—he was careful to label it as such—about Mazzocchi's blackout accident of three years before. In the CIA's chemical hoard was an LSD potion that produced hallucinations and unconsciousness. Absorbed through the skin, it could not be traced by normal blood analysis. During the Watergate days Howard Hunt had suggested smearing the LSD on the steering wheel of columnist

Jack Anderson's car, an assassination idea that was dropped partly because Anderson often wears gloves.

"I remember you had on that big mackinaw," Danny said to Mazzocchi. "But did you have on gloves?"

"I doubt it. I don't wear them when I'm driving."

"I don't suppose you had any tests run on your steering wheel?"

"No," Mazzocchi said. "It never crossed my mind."

Danny glanced about the room. The blackboard, which for so long had waited for answers to its battery of questions, was scrubbed clean. The desk was blank too. Plaques and photographs were in a van on a highway to Denver.

"Well, if they went and got a poison like that, I'm flattered," Mazzocchi said. "You'd have to be a real pain in the ass for them to go to all that trouble."

OKLAHOMA CITY. DECEMBER 20, 1977. The hearing at the federal courthouse was supposed to be routine. Ikard filled in for Danny, who was in D.C. dickering for further access to FBI and AEC/NRC files.

Judge Luther Bohanon, the new presiding magistrate, growled unsympathetically at the papers from Ikard. They were subpoenas for state and local police officials, a motion to reopen Jim Smith's deposition, and so forth: all together twenty-one requests. The judge did not much like them. He denied twenty.

It was only a month and a half since Judge Bohanon had taken over, barely time to read through the waist-high mound of legal papers and documents. Already he was out of patience. "I'm going to get this case ready for trial whether you like it or not," the judge told Ikard.

"You're not going to allow us to take any more depositions at all? None?"

"That's right. You've had a year. You've had a chance to do everything," Judge Bohanon declared. "You've sued a lot of people that probably should never have been sued. You don't have any reason to sue them. This is a suit up in the clouds in some regards."

"We got our ass kicked," Ikard reported.

Danny hollered into the phone. "We can't go to trial now—Taylor is just warming up."

"We don't have a choice."

"I thought Bohanon was supposed to be the best federal judge in Oklahoma."

"He is, but—"

"But?"

"I've done a little checking. Apparently he owes his judgeship to old Senator Kerr."

Fifteen

Taylor put his .38 Smith & Wesson on the bed under a pillow. He went to the window and looked out, casing the parking lot. He had joined up with Danny and Father Bill in Oklahoma City. They were down to staying in beat-up motels; the money from Sara was going so fast.

Danny took another pillow and bunched it between the wall and his back. His legs stretched out on the floor, away from the water stains. The shower curtain had a rip that was getting wider by the day.

"Karen must've kept her folder in that crawl space above the ceiling," Danny said. "She must've gotten it out the night after they tore up her apartment."

"But that was before she went to Los Alamos," Taylor said, his words coming out in a spray. "And she didn't take the folder with her, or leave it at Drew's house. So it had to be stashed someplace else those last few days."

"She could've left it in her car, I guess, but I doubt she was that dumb."

"I think we can also rule out the houses of her friends. She didn't even tell them she had a folder. She didn't even tell Sherri."

Danny felt jumpy. He got up and paced the room. His brow began to wrinkle. "Have you checked that old place that belonged to Sherri's grandmother? Didn't you say it's near Cimarron?"

"Yeah, it's right off Highway 74. Here, I'll draw you a map." On a piece of paper Taylor made a line for the highway, a dot for the factory, another for the culvert. "I drove that stretch yesterday. I wanted to see if there's any place off the highway where a car could've parked and waited for Karen to go by. There aren't any driveways, but there's a little dirt road." He drew a line intersecting the highway about halfway between the factory and the culvert. "The old ranch is down that road, a mile or so west of 74." He made another dot.

The dot, the next afternoon, became a gray barn, sagging in the middle. Then, over a little rise, there were also a tractor shed, a white house. Taylor was coming at the ranch from behind, through the fields, trying to shake any tail. He blew warm air on his hands. The cut had healed up fine. But his side hurt, just a twinge, along an old scar where a long flat knife had been run through. Of all the times he had been knifed, all the knives he had confiscated, the fancy Oriental daggers, the pearl-handled switchblades, he had kept that long flat knife. It had damn near killed him. But he had pulled it out, and now it was on his office wall, plunged into his Marine coat-of-arms.

Taylor slid open the barn door. Loose boards were knocking in the wind, and Sherri's horse whinnied from a stall. Bales of hay protected that side of the barn. Taylor wasn't sure what he was looking for. Maybe one of Karen's documents accidentally left behind. Some clue. Something. Yesterday he had walked two miles up and down the creek looking at things caught in the underbrush. There had been nothing along the creek. There was nothing in the barn.

He tried the tractor shed. On a shelf there were bottles and other junk and a space where something might have been. Below, on the floor, Taylor saw a white business envelope. He stooped and picked it up. Pigeons had soiled it. There was no postage mark, no address, nothing inside; but in the left upper corner there was the Kerr-McGee logo. And stuck behind a plank: another envelope, brown, also with the logo.

OKLAHOMA CITY. JANUARY 7, 1978. Jim Ikard stroked his beard. White was overtaking the black. The primary cause was genetic, but there was no doubt Danny was contributing. Again they were arguing. Ikard said, "Just because lightning struck once, don't assume it will again."

"We *have* to get Bohanon kicked off this case." Danny waved his hand like a railroad semaphore. "If he stays, our ass is in a sling." Danny handed over a thin folder. "This is what Father Bill's gotten so far."

In his debut as a private eye Father Bill was going hurriedly into

Judge Bohanon's past. From Ikard he got a promising lead: Senator Kerr's personal papers at the University of Oklahoma Library. But the library refused him access. So Father Bill was consulting browned clippings in newspaper "morgues" and talking to John Seigenthaler of the *Tennessean*. It happened that Seigenthaler, while with the Kennedy Administration, had done a background check on Bohanon.

That had been in 1961.

Bohanon was up for a federal judgeship. Senator Kerr was his sponsor. But a review panel of the American Bar Association had hung him up with a "not qualified" rating—Bohanon was an attorney with a few wealthy clients and no experience on the bench. So President Kennedy asked Kerr to nominate someone else. There were three names on the slip of paper Kerr sent back: "Bohanon, Bohanon, Bohanon." At that point Seigenthaler had been dispatched to Oklahoma. It did not take long to understand what it was all about. Kerr, the wildcatter, multimillionaire, undefeated politician, would talk about himself to anyone. One story he told so often it became a prairie legend. At age eighteen, a husky farm boy of meager education, Kerr had set out his goals: "A family, a million dollars, the governor's mansion—in that order." For years he only looked foolish. Money ran out before his college studies did; he sold magazines door to door and apprenticed himself to a judge. Then, at age thirty-five, with a borrowed $25,000, he and his brother-in-law bought up a languishing oil company. It was a time of sacrifice for Kerr, a big, hearty man who liked to eat. ("Sometimes all I had was a plate of beans and cornbread.") After eight fast years, though, he was a millionaire. Dean McGee, the brightest geologist at Phillips Petroleum, became his new partner. McGee ran the business while Kerr ran for governor. Stumping the state in his American Legion commander's hat, Kerr made governor in 1942 on his first try. He was elected in 1948 to the U.S. Senate and was soon enough the "Uncrowned King."

Bohanon had been one of his behind-the-scenes men, helping mastermind Kerr's elections, and he was, besides, a close family friend. Bohanon's appointment to the bench thus became a test of Kerr's clout. As long as Kennedy held up the appointment, Kerr held up presidential legislation. Quickly there came a compromise. The King swung the Senate behind Kennedy's unpopular foreign aid bill, and the President made a federal judge of Kerr's friend.

In sixteen years Judge Bohanon had put to rest his "not qualified" rating. He had ordered desegregation in Oklahoma City schools, ordered prison clean-ups and generally he was well respected. "He's known for being evenhanded," Ikard said.

Danny thought that was being charitable. "He turned us down on twenty of twenty-one motions. I don't call that evenhanded. Face it, an old due-bill is being paid."

Finally Ikard deferred. "Okay, I'll draft the recusal motion."

Contrary to Taylor's better instincts he made himself conspicuous. With Judge Bohanon's abrupt deadline he had to take chances. If the recusal motion failed, the trial would begin in a few weeks.

At an Italian restaurant Taylor ate a leisurely supper. With his gray hunter's eyes he watched the other diners. Three were by themselves: a college kid with a mop of hair, a burly man in a striped shirt, a pretty woman with a rabbity fur hooked across her chair. Taylor drove from the restaurant to a rock concert at the Prairie Lady, a former church with walls and floor done over in tongue-and-groove oak. He got up twice to change seats; he bought apple juice and carrot cake from a concessionnaire. The burly man in stripes was near the door. Stripes! Taylor smiled. With all that nuclear money they should be able to afford someone with less flamboyance. He moved on to Chadwick's. It was like American bars in Saigon, full of greens and browns. Tonight was Chadwick's grand opening; Taylor had gotten an invitation through Ikard. The burly man soon came in. Taylor moved to the rest room and relieved himself, putting his bladder in fighting condition. He banged open the door and walked out a rear exit into an alley. Several steps to his left, away from the yellow sweep of the streetlight, Taylor flattened against a wall, a shadow of lethal calm. Perhaps thirty seconds later the man edged into the yellow. Taylor had the man's features memorized; everything about them was medium. The man walked left through the alley. Taylor's arm chopped. There was an expression of surprise and a sharp, vicious liquid crunch. The man's nose burst into blood, glittering on his shirt. A revolver clattered to the alley brick.

"Okay, buddy, who put you on my tail?" Taylor took on the role of bully. He had the man's arm crooked painfully.

The man gritted and reached with his free arm, muscling fingers into a little belly flab that Taylor needed to work off. Taylor slapped the hand away and expertly skimmed the leisure-suit pockets. There was no wallet, no identification. "C'mon! Who're you working for?" Taylor tightened his grip. "Talk fast, my man."

"Get bent!" The man puckered, hissing gutturally.

A third voice rolled out of the night. "What's going on there?"

Taylor looked up. A security guard stepped out and came into focus. The guard had seen the man following Taylor and thought robbery was his intent. "You okay?" he asked.

"Yeah, sure." Taylor felt his quarry jerk deftly free. The man scooped up the fallen gun and slid away.

Danny tried to eat around the meat in the chili but couldn't manage it.

"Sorry, I forgot to dish out a bowl for you before I put the beef in," Drew said. "How about a grilled Cheddar?"

"I'm allergic to cheese," Danny said. Instead he wolfed contentedly on a lettuce sandwich ladled with mayonnaise.

Mr. Silkwood patted the mound above his belt in salute to the chef. "A good feed!" It was said with sincere warmth. In recent trips to Oklahoma he had avoided Drew—a distance had grown between them. Mr. Silkwood felt the young man had been too candid during his deposition. ("Why did he have to say *anything* about Karen's personal life? Why didn't he tell Bill Paul to sit on a hot poker?") But the meal had helped set the hard feelings aside. Perhaps, as Danny had said, there was no way to keep separate the private Karen and the public Karen. Better to act as if there was no shame in it, hard as that was.

Mr. Silkwood and Drew tossed down after-supper drinks in a jolt; the glasses vibrated with memories.

Danny the storyteller was in form. With winks and gestures, like a one-man game of charades, he was letting them in on some of Taylor's funnier cloak-and-dagger adventures. "So there he was, left flatfooted in this alley with this dumb-fuck guard. The guard was all abeam, thinking he'd saved Taylor from a mugging." There was a chorus of laughter.

It was time to get to a topic far more serious, far more delicate. Danny began describing a scene at the Cimarron warehouse. The description came from a former worker who had been there. "Karen's belongings were in a row of steel barrels—this was a day or so after they gutted her apartment. Company men in 'moon suits' were picking through the barrels like hoboes, holding up frilly panties and laughing, and two plainclothes narcs were watching the show. Kerr-McGee had called them in. It's not hard to guess the plan: find a bag of dope, have Karen busted, and say good-bye to David Burnham and *The New York Times.*" Danny paused while the glasses were refilled. He stood apart, without a glass. "Luckily, the narcs didn't find any dope. So she wasn't busted." Instead, had there been an escalation of tactics? Plutonium in her refrigerator? Hit-and-run on the highway? Perhaps the failed dope bust had not been so lucky after all, Danny thought.

"At the point Kerr-McGee called in the narcs they obviously were aware of Karen's activities," he said. "What we're trying to pinpoint is whether they had been keeping tabs on her all along."

Mr. Silkwood compressed his lips. "You're running this thing, Danny, and I'm not gonna butt in, but I don't rightly see where you're getting us."

You *do* see, Danny said to himself, but you don't want to. You don't want the case to go anywhere near the hated dossier. Aloud, he said, "Let me backtrack a minute to Audio Intelligence. Why are Okie cops getting their training and equipment from this heavy-duty espionage place? Why do you need trained spooks in the middle of Oklahoma? Well, there's only one possible answer. Plutonium. They had to keep their eyes peeled so nobody would steal some plutonium and make a bomb. So, almost without a doubt, the OCPD cops were working with Kerr-McGee. Now, somewhere, somehow Karen got mixed up in this. That's what Taylor's sources have told him. But we need to connect the dots. From Audio Intelligence to OCPD to Kerr-McGee to Karen."

"But what does it matter whether Reading knew all this gossip about Karen?"

"The sixty-four-dollar question is *when* he knew. When did he realize Karen was a troublemaker? Did he have time to put her under surveillance? Did he know she was going to the Holiday Inn that night?"

"You can be damn sure somebody from Kerr-McGee knew that!" Mr. Silkwood put his weight on the metal step of the dentist's chair, defiantly cocking his old shoe.

"You can say that a hundred times, but your saying it won't convince a jury."

"I just don't think all that personal stuff has to be dragged in."

Mr. Silkwood wanted to attend the trial, steadfast on the hard benches, showing mute esteem for his dead daughter. Danny knew the pain it would put on the old house painter's face to listen in public to testimony about Karen's promiscuity and pill popping. But he knew Mr. Silkwood would bear it for her sake. Danny's worry was the effect on the jurors. Karen's way of life, alien for Oklahoma, would somehow have to be made understandable.

OKLAHOMA CITY. JANUARY 19, 1978. Ikard opened the YMCA steam-room door to a blast of heat and lusty laughter. The steamers were enjoying a story about a local straitlaced football coach whose job was at risk because disgruntled alumni thought he should have won a big game he lost. The story behind the story had inspired the laughs. The way the story went, an assistant coach had given the game plans to the other team because the straitlaced coach was messing around with the assistant's wife.

"Why don't the papers ever print what's *really* going on around here?" Ikard said, smiling, folding his towel on the bench for a cushion.

"I see *you* made the headlines this morning," said a scarlet-skinned man. He was shrouded in hot, billowing mist. "Quite a coup, getting Bohanon shot down on top of Eubanks."

"To be technical," Ikard said, "they both stepped aside voluntarily."

"Yes, but I know how they hate to do even that. Federal judges almost never step down—they're feudal lords. Bill Paul must be livid to lose *two* good-ol'-boys."

"I think he's more upset at who's replacing Bohanon," Ikard said. "We asked the Tenth Circuit to give us somebody from out of state, and they did. Judge Theis from Kansas. That's the real coup. Bill Paul won't be able to buttonhole Theis at the state bar meetings."

"Theis? Why does that name sound familiar?"

"He just finished that obscenity case with *Smut* magazine, and he did the Leavenworth riot case a few years back. Remember? He kicked the defendants out for being disorderly. Made them listen from their cells over closed-circuit audio. He's a tough old bird."

"You think *he's* an improvement?"

"Sure! We *want* a law-and-order judge."

The Corpus Christi bell clanged for Saturday-afternoon Mass. Father Bill Davis was out shopping for a motorcycle muffler when he saw the open church doors; he stopped on impulse.

Except for "Jesus Saves" neon, there were no churches in the vicinity of Father Bill's motel. Catholic churches were scarce everywhere; only two percent of Oklahoma's churchgoers are Catholic. This discovery disturbed him less than it did Danny, who was having to rethink his plan to send forth Father Bill in clerical collar to prick the consciences of the Cimarron workers. Out here, men in collars were "mackerel snappers."

The tower bell clanged yet again. Mass at Corpus Christi was unaccountably delayed. Father Bill went in and saw kids squirming about on hard curved-back pews not made for comfort. Their parents did not look very reverent either. Father Bill browsed. In the vestibule the convent sisters were whispering. The parish priest, Father Paul Gallatin, had been called away on an emergency, and his replacement hadn't shown.

"I can say the Mass," Father Bill offered. They looked at him. Collar still in his suitcase, he was an apparition in jeans and work shirt, hair uncombed, cheeks mossy with beard. Uneasily the sisters let him put on vestments and go to the altar.

The next day Father Bill felt a little bad. Suppose some parishioners had been insulted? When Father Gallatin returned from his emergency, Father Bill went back to the rectory again to apologize. "No need to do that," the parish priest said. "But I'm glad you came over. Tell me, how does a priest turn into a legal investigator?"

"Well, I got tired of being a bureaucrat," Father Bill explained. "I was with the Ministry for Social Justice, but you can't wage much of a fight against injustice from behind a desk. I'm forty-one. I felt it was time to get back into the world. I'm not leaving the priesthood, but I want to put my faith to work in other ways."

"I admire you. More priests should act on their faith," Father Gallatin said approvingly. He was middle-aged and plump. He offered coffee. Unexpectedly, he suggested, "Why don't you move into the rectory with me? I'm a good cook, and there's plenty of room. And you could help with Matins."

"It *would* be a godsend to get out of that motel. We're bunking three to a room."

"Your friends are welcome too."

"I should warn you we're a little unconventional. Danny's a vegetarian; Taylor's an authentic two-fisted character; and I've been known to buzz around town on a motorcycle."

"Fine, bring the bike too."

The cycle, a Honda 450, went under a tarp in the rectory garage and remained there. The pavement was icy cruel, and Father Bill had no time anyway. He was keeping company with old newspapers, magazines, books, and political scholars, finding out about the two men whose names and reputations had forged Kerr-McGee. Were Robert Kerr and Dean McGee true giants of rectitude?

Senator Kerr's career had been out in the open, or so it seemed. Once, in response to a *Saturday Evening Post* reporter who inquired about Kerr's sponsoring a tax bill that plainly benefited his own company, the senator had puffed up, jabbing at a diamond Kerr-McGee pin on his lapel. "Why, I founded my company and I wear this badge right out in the open for everyone to see." At the suggestion that he not vote when he had a conflict of interest, Kerr's grin had turned rascally. "Now, wouldn't it be a hell of a thing if the senator from Oklahoma couldn't vote for the things Oklahomans are most interested in?" What was good for Kerr-McGee was good for Oklahoma. He had made junior business partners out of fellow senators, compromising them as well: Senator Clinton Anderson had helped double the price of helium, enabling Kerr-McGee to open a helium plant that could not have competed at the lower price. *"Kerr has been raised in an anything-goes style,"* biographer Martin Haun wrote. *"You did whatever you were big enough to get away with. Which, for him, was considerable."* Kerr was a senator for fourteen years, during which the worth of his company increased seventeenfold. His personal fortune went from one million to thirty-five million dollars. By a magnitude of ten the "King of the Senate" was the richest man on the Hill—King, and Midas too. Not until his death, however, did the fullness of this achievement become public.

Senator Kerr died on New Year's Day 1963 in the stands at the Orange Bowl (Oklahoma's Sooners were in a losing game to Joe Namath's Alabama team). A heart attack silenced him as his critics never could. After a funeral that drew politicians from the President down, Kerr's executors opened an office safe and bank lockboxes. He had stashed away nearly two million dollars in cash, unaccounted for on his books. Bobby Baker, on his way to prison for influence peddling, later testified that $100,000 of the two-mil was from savings-and-loan executives—a bribe paid to Kerr for stopping a bank-tax bill. Baker had been Kerr's protégé; they were like father and son. But Baker said he also had been Kerr's bagman, and the repository of many secrets. Among them: Kerr's keeping of a mistress on the Senate payroll.

Many Oklahomans chose not to believe Baker. But there was no mistaking the real estate bonanza on the Arkansas River. As Rivers and Harbors Subcommittee chairman, Kerr had used billions in public funds to dredge and extend the Arkansas River three hundred miles into his state. Landlocked Oklahoma got a seaport. Kerr got a lake named for him. And a lot of money. He had had the foresight to purchase thousands of acres along the river's new route. His profit, or profiteering, was in the millions. In his lifetime he had bragged about many things, but he had not bragged about his land grab. In fact, he had gone to some trouble to conceal it, using proxies to keep his signature out of the transactions. Reporters found out only in 1965 when his executors posthumously affixed his name.

At about that same time, the Oklahoma attorney general took Kerr-McGee to court for conspiring to inflate the price of asphalt it had sold to the state. The practice dated back twenty years, to when Kerr was governor, but no one had dared do anything while he was alive. Dean McGee, taking over as board chairman, was ordered to pay a $4.6 million fine: the company's first moment of disgrace.

Father Bill read this in puzzlement. How had McGee rehabilitated the company's image?

The Oklahoma newspapers held a dutiful explanation. After paying the price-fixing fine, reduced by half on appeal, McGee had inaugurated a period of goodwill. In 1967 the first annual Governor's Club Cup was awarded to Kerr-McGee for boosting tourism in the state. McGee let local kids swim in the company pool, donated land for a park, endowed science research, and elevated the profile of all this charity. He sponsored Beat Texas pep rallies for the football Sooners and put his research division to work on a camouflaging device so Army jeeps could display *I Ride with Pride in Oklahoma* bumper stickers without attracting Viet Cong bullets. These and other civic doings were reproduced in a twenty-eight-minute movie, which, by the company's count, three out of four Oklahomans saw.

People tended to make a distinction between McGee and his late partner. McGee was an unstraying husband, a man of stern principles, honest, straight as a girder. At the end of Father Bill's research, though, he had one notation to the contrary. He re-located the article from which the note had come. It was a single sentence in a long, boring account of the Arkansas River scandal: McGee's name had been affixed to the same transactions, as a thirty-seven-percent owner, and he had reaped the same tainted profits. Barely mentioned at the time, the impropriety apparently had been forgotten.

WASHINGTON. FEBRUARY 7, 1978. Congressman Dingell sat at his desk. He twirled his gavel, letting his words take effect. It wasn't bad enough that Stockton had gotten in a duel with the FBI, but now Stansfield Turner was sore at him. The CIA director himself!

Stockton's face showed appropriate chagrin. But the depiction of Stansfield Turner waving his arms and acting blustery had a certain obverse appeal, suggesting, as it did, that Stockton was close to something sensitive. It was a hackneyed clue, but usually reliable. Emotion is a good indicator when men take such pride in their detachment from it.

A similar emotion was leaping redly along Dingell's neck, that bulldog temper of his. "I backed you all the way," he said to Stockton. "But what the hell are you into with this NUMEC mess?"

NUMEC was the acronym for Nuclear Materials and Equipment Corporation, the operator of a uranium enrichment factory in Apollo, Pennsylvania. In the mid-sixties NUMEC had had the largest recorded MUF ever, 572 pounds of weapons-grade uranium. Had it been stolen? The AEC figured that 223 pounds had been lost to industrial quirks and another 127 to drainage in the Kiski River, figures later conceded to be highly inflated. Another 16 pounds had been found in a burial pit. Even so, that meant NUMEC was still short 206 pounds of enriched uranium, equal to about seventy pounds of plutonium, or seven small bombs. NUMEC officials tried to explain it away as somehow normal. But Stockton had come up with a Joint Committee memo that said the loss could be considered normal "only if the factory had run seven days a week, twenty-four hours a day since before the Revolutionary War."

Still, not much had been done about it. The AEC's chief investigator had been lured off the case by a high-paying job from NUMEC, and the Justice Department, after a mere nine days of investigating, had closed the case, deciding there was no one to prosecute. A nimbus of lies and small blackmails and "national security" covers had stretched across ten years of cover-up. The CIA had known about the MUF in 1968, and so had President Johnson. And they had known of a nuclear facility on the Negev Desert by the Dead Sea, where the uranium had probably gone, so Israel could become the world's seventh nuclear nation-state. At the AEC, the Joint Committee, the FBI, the Justice Department, certain top people also had known. It had been a cover-up so vast it seemed unmanageable, but it had been managed, and it had gone on and on.

There had been rumors, though, and Stockton had heard the rumors. He had asked around, talking slow, being inquisitive, doing the dull important sleuthing at which he is so expert. He had gotten some officials to talk, and he had found a paper trail, memos stuck in this government cranny and that. The memos had formed enough of a basis to go to the CIA and demand the full story.

Stockton had been given a briefing, learning as much as the CIA wished him to know. But then, that same day, an article had appeared in the *Washington Star.* There had been a leak, and Stockton was suspected. The CIA director had accused Stockton, straight out, with no proof, just a strong dislike, because Stockton had been impertinent throughout, trying to exhume this old skeleton.

"The leak is a trumped-up deal—they just want you to sit on me," Stockton had told his boss. And, indeed, when Dingell confronted the CIA director, the director had backed down.

But now Stockton was impertinently digging further into the cover-up and into the way former CIA Director Richard Helms had handled it. In the rendering Helms gave, he was just following President Johnson's orders. But what had been the real motive? Had the CIA and FBI been inept? (Stockton had evidence that an Israeli Mossad agent had been in place at NUMEC for several years.) Or had there been complicity between the Israelis and the U.S. government? (Veteran journalist Tad Szulc had reported that the CIA was, in fact, a silent partner in the smuggling ring.) At the moment Helms was engaged in a cynical plea-bargain with the Carter Administration. In trying to get out from under an unrelated perjury charge, he had let it be known he could pin the NUMEC cover-up squarely and publicly on Johnson. For his silence, Helms expected to be let off on a misdemeanor. Any interference in the plea-bargain was naturally unwelcome.

Dingell returned the gavel to its desk mount. "Keep at it, Stockton," he said encouragingly. "Let's not have any more blind alleys like that Silkwood case."

News from Oklahoma wended irregularly to the old FBI building. Kitty and Sara dropped in when the lawsuit was doing well. By their long absences, Stockton knew it more often went poorly. He had met Taylor once—working together, he realized, they would have made the perfect Mutt-and-Jeff pair. Mazzocchi also had come by for coffee before heading out to Denver.

Last month, after some delay, Aurora Publishers had released Srouji's book, *Critical Mass,* and someone had mailed Stockton a hardcover copy. The Silkwood case was Chapter Thirteen. There was no mention of smuggling, and in this version Karen was a suicidal fanatic turned into a union patsy. The Atomic Industrial Forum had praised the book and was helping Srouji on her promotional tour.

Last week detective fever had briefly struck Stockton. After much ado about "national security" the NRC had agreed to tell Dingell the final MUF figure at Cimarron. Stockton was sure it would be in the range of forty to sixty pounds, as Barbara Newman and David Burnham had originally reported. But the official MUF was sixteen—handily enough to make a bomb, but below the level Stockton had come to view as statistically sinister. *Sixteen* pounds—he had difficulty believing it. At the first opportunity, he planned to find out more about the arithmetic behind that number.

WASHINGTON. FEBRUARY 8, 1978. Bob remembered the look from Lourdes. After the Army he had hitchhiked across Europe, briefly taking a job as a Lourdes guide, helping cripples to the underground holy water where it seeped from dank rocks. Those who had found healing in the wet touch had left relics: an assembly of blackened crutches hanging like spirits from the grotto ceiling. New seekers clung to the guides and gazed up, mesmerized by the sure knowledge of a cure.

Again Bob was the guide. Dr. Mancuso followed him up the wide terraced steps, past the gun-blue statuary and the red marble pillars. The footing was slippery from a light greasy wax. At Lourdes, Bob knew it was a fraud, but here he was the one giving faith. He had arranged for Mancuso to testify before the Subcommittee on Health and the Environment, chaired by Congressman Paul Rogers.

Dr. Mancuso rested his elbows on the witness table to steady himself. Cloistered in his university cubbyhole, he had lost the easy use of words; they kept bumping into each other. But his plea was burning and sharp. Fourteen years of his life had gone into Contract E(1101)3428. Now they had taken away his funding and they wanted to take away all his data. Two weeks before, the NRC had joined ERDA in demanding his files. On Bob's advice, he had removed them to a private stronghold.

Dr. Mancuso's text rustled in his hands. He looked up, his face maddened and morose.

Later Dr. Irwin Bross would testify about his nine years of study at the Roswell Park Memorial Cancer Institute in Buffalo. By way of different statistics, using the effects of X-rays, he had reached the same conclusion as had Dr. Mancuso: one or two rems of radiation, a dose presumed to be safe, was not. As little as one tenth of a rem increased the risks of leukemia and genetic damage. Last May, two months after Dr. Bross's study became public, his research grant had been terminated.

Up marched Dr. Edward Radford. He seated himself with terse dignity. Dr. Radford was chairman of a committee of the National Academy of Sciences, a citadel of the scientific establishment. Bob had been lobbying the academy, playing up the idea that Dr. Mancuso and Dr. Bross were modern-day Galileos. But did Dr. Radford agree? Standing to one side, tall and anxious in his burnt-orange suit, Bob crossed his fingers.

Dr. Radford did not speak long, but his speech left an echo. All these numbers are real people, he said: people who are dying, people who are deformed. The standard should be made ten times stricter at once.

Bob applauded silently and went to sit with Dr. Mancuso. He looked bedazzled.

A man from the Atomic Industrial Forum came to the Hill afterward, in a small panic, to halloo some of the subcommittee members. They should not get stuck in the sublime, the lobbyist said. "The issue is jobs. Lower the radiation limit from five rems a year to half a rem and see what happens. You think the industry can afford to spend billions on safety revisions? As soon as workers get half a rem, they'll be let go. They'll become as transient as grape pickers. It's already happening. Barflies and summer-vacation students are already being pulled in off the street to do repairs and other hot jobs. They work a few hours, and when they get the maximum dose, out they go. If you tinker with the standard, all you'll have is a revolving-door work force. The OCAW will raise hell."

Soap bars—herbal, deodorant—lay in a happy composition against the linoleum wall. The pink bar was stamped with the name of a Chicago hotel. Attending an anti-nuclear conference there (a weekend of Robert's Rules of Order and purer-than-thou snobbery) Kitty had salvaged the unused soap from her room. She still employed the small economies from her days in Oregon in the lavender school bus. Sometimes she and Sara mused about the turn of the decade when both had lived west. It had been a simpler time. Sara was doing restaurant ballet, balancing hot dishes, gyrating away from lecherous fingers; Kitty was making sand candles for sale to tourists—digging molds in wet ocean sand, pouring in wax, hoping it would jell before the tide rolled in.

Holding the Butternut commune together was probably harder work. But at last the frictions, the egos, the routine of chores and meals, even the Butternut treasury, all were in balance. Weekly the household ate four dinners of fish or vegetables and two of red meat (Kitty and Bob were the cholesterol holdouts). Sunday was leftovers. As the "money fascist," Sara had been too forgetful and Bob too softhearted, so Kitty had taken it over permanently and Butternut no longer ran a deficit.

Money for the lawsuit, however, was still a problem. "We're almost broke again," Sara said glumly. She had saved this announcement until Kitty was snug under a cubic yard of bubbly bathwater.

"I'm not surprised, the way Taylor runs through money," Kitty said. She would perform a masque of delight if Taylor ever did crack the case, but she did not like him or his expense account.

"It costs money to get somebody to risk his neck," Sara said.

"The rest of us are doing it, and we're not getting a cent," Kitty retorted. She turned on the tap to agitate the bubbles. "Honestly, Sara, I don't see how you can defend someone who's macho to the nth degree."

"That's elitist bullshit and you know it. Didn't I just hear you complaining about all the anti-nuke elitists?"

Kitty's face lit red, instantaneous as a struck match. Yes, she had been so disgusted after the Chicago conference that she had talked of organizing the next one herself. But now, her temper rising, lip stuck out furiously, Kitty was reveling in self-righteousness. The campaign to vindicate Karen Silkwood, the campaign she had started, was being taken from her. Sara was moving the lawsuit under the auspices of the Quixote Center, a Catholic social justice organization. The move was advisable for tax reasons, but Kitty, already grieving over the slow death of SOS, felt she was being cut out of any say over how the money was spent. She would rather it went to a scientist who could prove the fuel rods were defective, instead of a private eye who spent it like a sailor and clobbered guys in alleys.

"When we started this, we were gonna carry on Karen's work," Kitty said. "Danny's forgotten all about the fuel rods."

"I thought we started this to find out who killed her."

"I started it to stop what Karen was trying to stop. Stop the fast-breeder. Stop Kerr-McGee. Stop the industry. That's what Karen would be doing if she was alive to do it."

"I know you think that. But you're wrong, Kitty. You can't make her out to be somebody she wasn't. Karen was against the way Kerr-McGee did things, but she wasn't against nuclear power. Ask Wodka or Mazzocchi."

"They're not talking to me: I'm too undiplomatic." Kitty turned her head away, a transition as sharp as splice in a film. Her hair radiated independence. "Karen was an anti-nuker, just like she was a feminist, in the most basic sense of the word."

"You're wrong. The last time Karen was home in Nederland she was telling her sisters how wonderful nuclear cars would be."

"That was months before she was killed. She could've changed. Just because you were *visited by her presence* doesn't mean you know everything about her!"

Sara forgave the apostate. Kitty was not herself: the headaches came so often now that they seemed a great pounding constant. Kitty's evening bath, an hour of submersion, was her major relief. The bubbles were shrinking to silvery pearls. Half of her hair was lank on her neck; it was a halo melting away.

"Taylor's gone back to that yacht in the Caribbean," Sara said. "Danny and Father Bill are all by themselves in Oklahoma."

"Taylor will be back as soon as you raise another ten grand." Kitty steadily buffeted her lower lip. "I'm sorry," she felt obliged to say. It was a phrase she had to use more and more. "Will you rub my neck?"

From a brooding position, Sara moved next to the tub and propped up on her toes. Her voice ran on in a tremolo. "One of Taylor's men got shot in the head—he's lucky to be alive. But all Danny does is smile. He thinks smiling makes him invulnerable."

She pressed on Kitty to the point of hurt. "Taylor may be macho, but he's the only one who can handle this case."

OKLAHOMA CITY. FEBRUARY 14, 1978. A sound above made Danny's heart leap, but it was only ice flying off the telephone lines. The wires snapped and chirruped in the wind. Then the phone rang three times and ceased in mid-jangle: Sara's signal. He timed a minute on his Timex and dialed a phone booth number in D.C.

Danny made himself comfortable in his own booth.

"It's all because of that biker gang, the Hangmen," Danny said. Something in Sara's response made him smile. "No, it has nothing to do with Father Bill. There's a private eye out here, Joe Royer, who helped get the Hangmen off. He found out that the go-go girl was going home in between gangbangs. Anyway, Royer is willing to work for us, and you know how rare that is, with everybody getting scared off." (Recently, there had been the Albuquerque private eye, a war buddy of Taylor's. While checking out a tip that Karen had been tailed to and from Los Alamos, the man was jumped and shot behind the ear. A fluke in the trajectory saved him. There was no telling whether the shooting was related to the Silkwood case, but he wanted nothing more to do with it.) Danny concentrated on sounding positive. "To make a long story not quite so long, Royer was at a bar where the Hangmen go, and he met one of their mamas. She was saying how her best friend has ended up on the opposite side of the law, as a secretary for the OCPD. The secretary's job, believe it or not, was to type up the wiretap transcripts. Well, Royer spent last week going to all the places this secretary goes. When she went shopping, he went shopping. And on, and on. It's an old tactic, I guess—you become a part of the setting, like the mailman or a neighbor. Finally he made his approach. Sure, the secretary says, the OCPD has a Red Squad that does wiretapping, even though wiretaps are as illegal as mother-killing in Oklahoma. Sure, they'd bring her the wiretap cassettes—Audio Intelligence cassettes—and she'd transcribe them. Sure, Kerr-McGee knew all about it. Royer could just see her in the witness box, telling how she'd transcribed Karen's phone calls, blowing Bill Paul away. But Royer's luck ran out. The secretary quit her job about six months before Karen's death."

"So it was a big nothing?" Sara asked, wondering why Danny was so engrossed in yet another dead end.

"We kicked each other awhile too—coming so close and not getting anything. Then we thought: why not run a bluff? So yesterday Royer and I got up with the sun and drove to the cop house. We found this big dude in full artillery—gun, billy club, radio, spats. Big bass voice: 'What can ah do for you fellahs?' So I balls-out told him we knew all about the wiretaps. He got sanctimonious as the devil. 'You fellahs are barking up a tree. We don't even have wiretap equipment.' I told him we knew Karen's calls had been transcribed. He gave me the fish eye. 'No, siree. None of our people did that, not in their *official* capacities.' It was the way he accented the word that gigged me. He knew he'd stepped in it. 'What do you mean, not in their *official* capacities?' I asked. He got hold of himself. 'Nothing, I didn't mean nothing. You fellahs better get yourselves outta here. You're starting to rub me the wrong way.' Royer could see his PI license going into hock, so he pulled me out of there."

Danny could hear a soft ripple of concern on the line. Before Sara could voice it, he said, "We're due for a break, Sara. I can feel it." He was like a little boy unwilling to come down from his tree-house: the potential for seeing something kept him there. "I've been working with a couple of local reporters. To get a line on the Red Squad. You know, that gag order really backfired on Kerr-McGee. The press got the idea they were trying to hide something."

Sara felt pride. "That's a great way to get around not having money: let the press do it."

"It's still a poor substitute for Taylor."

"I'm about to send out a new fundraising letter."

"I just hope I can talk Taylor into coming back." Danny did not tell her the latest. A few days after Taylor returned to the Caribbean, his office had been broken into and his Silkwood file stolen. The burglar had located it despite an elaborate hiding place.

"Say hello to Father Bill for me," Sara said.

"I will. He's out looking for Karen's old girlfriends."

"Tell him to watch out for crazy drivers. You too."

"Sure. Say hi to Bob and Kitty." On a Laundromat window some teenage artists were achieving symmetry—their initials became graceful veins in the frost. They drew a large heart. Danny watched the artistry glaze in the sunlight. It was Valentine's Day, he realized. "Uh, Sara?"

"Yes?"

"Happy Valentine's Day." The words dropped with sudden affection into the mouthpiece.

OKLAHOMA CITY. FEBRUARY 17, 1978. The judge's spectacles, polished with a white handkerchief, gleamed in the light. He settled them onto a brisk, intelligent face and pulled his robes around him. He put on a formal smile.

"Gentlemen, my name is Frank Theis. I'm from Wichita, so you'll have to excuse me if I violate any Oklahoma City customs." Judge Theis cleared his throat with a struggle. He had an aneroid voice box that wanted frequent oiling. "I'm here at the pleasure of the Tenth Circuit Court of Appeals. They always give the good ones to me," he said with a glint of humor.

Judge Theis was not yet prepared to hand out rulings—"but I don't see any good reason why some of these files shouldn't be produced."

Bill Paul's head caught and stopped in a backward tilt.

Judge Theis gathered papers in a country fist. He looked out at the room of lawyers. "There are a lot of ghosts in this case," he said. "And I'm either going to bury them once and for all, or they're going to get up and walk." At the end of that sly prophecy, he stood up and went back to Wichita.

Sixteen

Bob heard the distant cry and rolled over. Groping for the light, he heard it again, much closer. "Stop! Oh, God, don't shoot!" Kitty's fingers were fastened onto her nightgown, her eyes crimped shut.

He shook her gingerly. "Wake up!"

"Oh, God, it was the same nightmare." She sagged against him. Slowly she said, "A man was shooting. He had a monster gun with a hundred barrels, with dials and knobs and spinning needles. I could see the bodies fall. Someone was stacking them in piles. The gun went *whirrrr-r-rr* and hit me right above the heart—right here—in a big purple splotch."

The years dropped away and Kitty was a student again in her second semester at the University of Wisconsin. It was a May morning in 1963. The air was clean and fragrant with warm loam and sweet grass, not the sort of day to learn you are dying. Kitty had touched her throat and felt a swelling. At the student infirmary the nickel-sized lump was diagnosed as a bronchial cyst; routine surgery was scheduled. But a week after the biopsy Kitty was still being wheeled from one hospital room to another. She sneaked a look at her chart and deciphered an ominous word: Hodgkin's. With a two-hour pass she stole over to the library. The books said Hodgkin's disease was a rare lymphatic cancer that usually affects men. That made her feel bitterly privileged. Then she read about survival rates. Only eighteen percent of all Hodgkin's victims survive longer than five years.

Kitty raged at the doctors for their colossal trickery. "What if I wanted to write the Great American Novel? I wouldn't have known I had a deadline!" Her only chance was a series of radiation treatments. The doctors painted a lavender box on the skin over her lymph glands as a target for the X-ray technicians. Lavender was her favorite color, but this box had a harsh birthmark gleam. When the malady spread to her chest, so did the vivid geometry. The treatments made her so tired she would drop asleep over the morning comics. Her hair fell out in honey-colored clumps. Soreness in her throat constricted it. She grew wan and edgy, dwindling to bony ribs, meager thighs. Naked, she did not recognize the creature she beheld in the mirror —perhaps a prisoner just released from the hole. There were only blue eyes against a pallid wasteland. Yet if she whimpered, the doctors might stop the treatments. Finally they did. The lumps were gone.

"That's all over with," Bob said. His arms encircled her and his lips dispensed a patient kiss. He could feel her frailty, her unreleased tightness, the wild floundering of her heart. "It's over with."

"No, it's not!" Sobs welled up. "How many rems do you think they gave me? Twenty? Fifty? A hundred?"

"Don't think about that," he ordered.

The ghastly certainty of disease was on her face. "I wish I'd never heard of Mancuso or Bross or Gofman. I wish I still believed that 'safe' radiation *was* safe."

Bob held her a long time, waiting to see, when sleep came, what it would bring.

Sunday night Sara proofread the SOS newsletter so it could go to a printer the next morning. Monday afternoon she alerted radio stations to a NOW rally. Monday evening she met with Quixote Center directors about the lawsuit. Tuesday she rode the commuter train to New York to discuss a benefit concert with *Rolling Stone* editors. A few of the more socially conscious rock stars, like Bonnie Raitt and Jackson Browne, had been playing at anti-nuclear benefits. "If it's any help," Sara told the editors, "there was a ticket stub for a Bonnie Raitt concert in Karen's purse the night she died."

She took a late train back. Her supper was cooling under tinfoil in the refrigerator.

"How did it go?" Bob asked.

"We might get a cocktail party or we might get a rock concert. Or both. Or neither. It's all up in the air." From the refrigerator Sara scooped out a plateful of eggplant lasagne, but she felt too tired to reheat it. Taking command, Bob put the congealed lasagne into a frying pan. Like a beginning dancer, Sara took off-balance steps to the table. Her eyes were red and puffy, anxious for sleep. "You're trying to live on caffeine again," Bob accused.

She smiled weakly. "I've been sleeping eight hours. Eight hours a week."

It was still early, but breakfast was over and the dishes washed. An unshaded window revealed a forbidding winter day. Wind rattled the front door and blew through cracks. Kitty wrapped her hands around a cup of tea for warmth; she put it to her lips, angling it slightly, and burned her tongue. She prolonged her consultation with the *Post* comics, sitting in her bathrobe, yearning for a Coke.

"Please, listen," Sara was saying. "This woman is on the warpath. She's going around to everyone on the NOW board."

"Isn't she the one whose husband is a scientist for the industry?"

"That's the trouble. She keeps quoting him as the expert, and he says that your article in the newsletter was gross exaggeration. It's hard for me to say this so-called expert is full of shit."

"Great! My best friend won't stand up for me."

"Dammit, don't do that! I told you the article was overwrought. A nuclear accident can't burn a hole through to China."

"That isn't what my article said. It said that if one of these thousand-megawatt reactors went critical, a heat-ball would go straight into the ground. Of course it wouldn't go all the way to China. There'd be a steam explosion when it hit ground water, and you'd get a radiation cloud a hundred miles wide. But the textbook term is 'China Syndrome' because, theoretically, it could blow through the center of the earth."

"But the chance of *any* explosion happening is what? One in a million?"

"If you want to believe the Rasmussen Report, fine," Kitty said hoarsely.

"All I want is to get straight on the facts."

"Facts? The Rasmussen Report isn't based on facts. It's scientific roulette. You can tell the NOW board it's on their heads."

"You're doing it again. People are not baby-butchers just because they don't agree with you."

"I'm getting a headache."

"Oh, so now *I'm* the cause of your headaches?"

"Please, leave me alone."

OKLAHOMA CITY. MARCH 1, 1978. The Corpus Christi bells were silent, and Father Gallatin was asleep. Danny was scalding dishes in the rectory kitchen. "Ouch!" He jerked back his hand. Father Bill adjusted the faucet to get the temperature right.

It was their first chance to confer privately since Father Bill's return from Tulsa. "Taylor's right—this is hard work," Father Bill said. "I had to wait in the car till she got home from work, then I gave her time to eat supper before I knocked, and we must've talked for two hours or so. I was starving by the time I left."

It was a fact, not a complaint, but Danny made a show to fortify Father Bill's morale. "Next week I'll double your salary."

The priest huzzahed. "Two times zero? How much is that?"

"Okay, it's tripled! Now tell me what she had to say."

"About the same as girlfriend number one. They both described Karen in practically the same words—moody, stubborn, romantic, but not suicidal. She was very much a survivor."

"Did she ever go crazy wild on drugs?"

"No. They'd get stoned and go skinny-dipping in Lake Hefner or watch porno movies in somebody's basement. That's as wild as they got. There weren't any orgies. It was sorority stuff, teenage hijinks, all the nonsense Karen missed out on in Nederland."

"What about lesbianism?"

"This girl had gone with Karen to Dallas a few times on weekend escapades. But they always picked up guys. She swears up and down that she was never intimate with Karen."

"You believe her?"

"Yes, I do. She admitted that Karen went through a hate-men stage where she hung out at gay bars. But she didn't think it amounted to anything sexually."

"But Karen told Drew that she'd had lesbian affairs?"

"I asked this girl about that. There's a possible explanation, but you're only gonna like half of it."

"Tell me the best half."

"I'm afraid it's indivisible."

"Typical luck."

"This friend doesn't believe Karen was ever a lesbian. She thinks Karen made it all up to make Drew jealous. To throw in his face when they quarreled."

It was perhaps good news—of a sort—for Mr. and Mrs. Silkwood.

But what else might Karen have made up? A soapy cup slipped from Danny's grip and banged on the floor. Dishwater whooshed down the drain. Where he had held the pans for scouring, there were gray smudges on the porcelain basin.

Bill Taylor fooled with the Hauterus anchor and watched for froth on the glassy swells. The shore of Cape Canaveral was just a few hundred yards away, and a rocket, silver and black and snubnosed, was visible above the palms. Taylor had piloted them into a cove, sneaking past the patrol boats that kept everyone else miles out on the Atlantic, getting them in where they could see the sizzling cinders hit water when the rocket roared to life. It smoked into the ionosphere in absolute glory, leaving a glow on the clouds. Another satellite was launched, and Taylor's gentleman client was happily in awe.

On the way back, with the wind gone limp, the remote ocean seemed to Taylor like the remote prairie, a remoteness that conveyed threat. He began to think of Danny and the unfinished job left behind.

Portside, into a phone, Taylor found himself saying, "Oh, hell, I'll give it another month or so. No charge! But don't let it get out. It'll ruin my image."

Danny reacted with grateful aplomb. "I've got Father Bill and a local guy, Joe Royer, working in the Oklahoma end right now. Why don't you meet me in Nashville?"

They met at the Nashville airport. Then Danny went to call on John Seigenthaler at the *Tennessean,* and Taylor went to look less formally for information about Jackie Srouji.

Seigenthaler now had in his possession, through the Freedom of Information Act, a black-penciled copy of the telex the Memphis bureau had sent to FBI headquarters. On the same page that mentioned his "illicit relations with young females," there was a follow-up note—*the information furnished by the source was unfounded rumor since it could not be corroborated.* Yet it had taken eighteen months to get an apology on Justice Department stationery, and Seigenthaler would not have gotten one at all from Homer Boynton, the man who had bad-rapped him, if he had not run into Boynton at a law-and-the-media conference.

But Seigenthaler had been exonerated. President Carter had appointed him to a committee that nominates judges to the Sixth Circuit Court of Appeals, and the FBI had approved his appointment. The report from the FBI was "all clear." Two years after it began, his nightmare was mercifully, equitably at an end. Or would be, if Danny Sheehan would only let it.

In the city room Danny noticed on the walls the gold still-life of the Sidney Hillman Award for Courage in Journalism. But in his office Seigenthaler had hung a single piece of paper in a frame, a testament of support from the people he worked with.

Through the open door he waved Danny in.

"I read that your recusal motion persuaded Judge Bohanon to step down," Seigenthaler said conversationally.

"Yes. It got us some extra time. But now it's back to the grind."

"Are you planning a third deposition for Srouji?"

Danny nodded. "It may turn out to be a huge waste of time and money, but I've got to know about her. Either Srouji is a fruitcake or she knows one heck of a lot about why Karen Silkwood was killed."

"She's definitely a riddle." Seigenthaler scowled into space. "She's a person who's easy to overlook. She blends in. She sat on our copy-desk rim three nights a week, and no one took any notice of her until this Silkwood case cropped up. That day in my office, when I became her 'confessor,' she showed me a few of her documents. They didn't involve the Silkwood case, but they were supersensitive documents. Someone obviously had a lot of trust in Srouji—her control agent, whoever. I guess my opinion is that she's not a fruitcake."

"What I'd like is an affidavit from you, everything you remember that indicates she's a government operative."

"An affidavit?"

"I have to strip away her journalistic facade. It's the only way I have a chance of getting the judge to compel her to answer."

"I was taught that a newspaperman should never get in the middle of somebody else's lawsuit," Seigenthaler said in hesitation. He scowled some more. Finally he said, "Well, I suppose you have to pursue truth wherever you find it."

Across town Taylor was in pursuit of other truths, such as they were. In Srouji's semi-confession to Seigenthaler she had divided her FBI life into two periods: 1964–68, writing memos for the Bureau about campus and ghetto radicals; and 1975, doing a few trifling favors for old times' sake. In between, she claimed, she had been only mother-wife, free-lance writer, and caretaker of tropical fish. But as Taylor was finding out, Srouji had been considerably more active than she had let on. She was known to a wide society of political groups —the U.S.-China Peoples Friendship Association, the National Solidarity Committee for Cuba, the anti-nuclear Paddlewheel Alliance, the anarchist Catholic Workers Society, the Coalition for the Protection of Political Rights; and under the alias Lelia Hassan she was also known to the Palestinian movement. Frank Russo, founder of a trade-with-China group (predating Nixon's opening of the Great Wall), remembered her. One time, he said, she had insisted he go with her to an Air Force base in Tullahoma, and when they got there she tried to get him to trespass into classified areas. Dolph Honicker, the *Tennessean* news editor who was anti-nuclear, told of an after-hours excursion Srouji took him on to the federal courthouse. They got in through a side door that had been left unlocked. The happenstance of the door got him to wondering, and when Srouji began egging him on to punch a hole in the lobby portrait of President Ford, he beat it out of the building. "I had a feeling the place would've lit up like Christmas if I'd touched that picture." Another time Srouji had whispered around town that she knew where M-16s could be had for the taking.

Agent provocateur? Taylor heard the label over and over—all her political friends called her that, if not worse. But they were hardly objective, as Taylor knew.

Then, by a stroke of fortune, he found someone who had known Srouji from the other side, a government man who was willing to talk: a really good source.

OKLAHOMA CITY. MARCH 9, 1978. The room held odors of unlaundered fabric and vegetable oil. For two days and nights the cleaning lady had been kept out. Danny had been catnapping in his clothes on a bed of rolled-up carpet. A paper sack, discarded under the plywood desk, showed greasy spots from its former cargo of fried okra. Judge Theis was due in from Wichita tomorrow, and Danny had to be ready with a set of new motions and deposition notices.

"You got a summons for Srouji?" Taylor asked.

"Of course." Danny poured coffee into a cup stained from much use.

Taylor sat on the carpet; there were no extra chairs. He began his report, reciting from the notes which he planned to burn later out of respect for burglars. "Srouji was nineteen when she got started with the FBI. You can see how it could happen, a naive kid out for the thrills. What motivated her afterward, I can only surmise—misguided patriotism or maybe just the chance to travel around on government money. The FBI liked her, even though she's unsubtle and a little uneven, a little too coy. Her great asset was her cover: she was a journalist. Even when she dropped out to have her kids, her name stayed in a central data bank. Until one day a low-risk job opened up at the CIA—they wanted an update on the Soviet fast-breeder—and a CIA computer got Srouji's name from an FBI computer. Her credentials fit. Politically she had leftist contacts. Professionally she had a legitimate press pass. And she knew something about the subject; she'd written about nuclear power for a magazine. Best of all, she was from Nashville, not a place the KGB keeps track of. The morning of February 1, 1975, she was shoving Gerber's into her screaming baby—that's her own account—when she got a call from Dominick DeLorenzo. DeLorenzo is a former Army Intelligence agent, fluent in Russian, and top dog at Aurora Publishers. He asked her to write a book. The advance was modest, but her travel budget was first-class. Through the book she got access to Colonel Zaitsev at the Soviet Embassy. Zaitsev accepted her as an author and introduced her around, even got her a pass so she could tour Soviet nuclear reactors. Back at Langley the CIA debriefed her. But meanwhile, Srouji's face had shown up in the FBI's routine surveillance of Zaitsev. That's when things got sticky. Srouji got another phone call, this time from the Bureau. They wanted to put her book to use too."

Danny jumped up. "She was trying to work for both the CIA and the FBI? At the same time? No wonder she came unglued after the Dingell hearing."

"She allowed herself to be pushed beyond her ability. A trained professional would have seen trouble. Apparently all she saw was the glamour."

"Was it the FBI who put her onto the Silkwood case?"

"It's still not clear who sent her to Olson. But it was a natural. Olson was her control agent in Nashville, and she was the obvious one to pack off to see him in Oklahoma City."

"Somebody did send her there?"

"The orders came from one of the intelligence agencies. Olson was told to cooperate too. These were high-up orders."

"And they used him as her control agent again?"

"It looks that way. But she had more than one control. DeLorenzo was her CIA control. And he got real nervous when she started to get into MUF. I saw a note he sent her. *Concerning the nuclear black market —stay away from that because it would really cause a blowup.* I guess the CIA was afraid she'd blab. As she eventually did."

"Except now they've got her back into line."

"I don't know about the CIA. But she's mended fences with the FBI. Olson helped her get her act back together."

"How do you know it was him?"

"Well, the great thing about snoops is that everybody is always recording everybody else's conversations. There's a tape of a phone call from right after the hearing. Olson tells her, 'We've got some real problems here.' She's worried—she says, 'Am I in trouble? Can I get arrested?' And he gives her the old softshoe: 'Everything will be okay if you just sit tight. Don't screw up. Don't screw up . . . everything can be all right with *this* outfit.' "

"You don't happen to have the actual tape, do you?"

"No, just a good source."

"Will your source sign an affidavit? I'd like to get this information to the judge."

"Sorry. He's reliable, but not very noble. Why don't you save this for the trial and spring a Perry Mason act on Srouji?"

"I couldn't chance it in front of a jury. No, I've got to get her and Olson into another deposition."

At the courthouse the next day Judge Theis said no, maybe, and yes with a practiced diligence. He refused subpoenas for the new OCPD names on Danny's list and he deferred the subpoenas for Srouji and Olson, but he did give the go-ahead to bring under oath certain others who previously had been protected by Judges Eubanks and Bohanon.

Of these, the most important was Thomas Bunting, a captain in the Oklahoma State Bureau of Investigation. It was through Bunting that the OCPD Red Squad allegedly had bought wiretap equipment from Audio Intelligence, and if true, it meant OCPD officials had lied to Danny.

Until now, Bunting had managed to keep out of a deposition on the dubious plea of "police security."

This was Friday. "We'll be deposing your client next week," Danny told Bunting's lawyer.

On Monday, at his brother's, Bunting keeled over, never to regain consciousness. The death certificate guessed that a cerebral hemorrhage had killed him at age forty-four.

Danny read about it in the Tuesday-morning papers. Services were set for two o'clock that afternoon. "They're burying this guy without a coroner's inquest," he said to Royer. "Let's get the widow to stop the funeral."

Despite the enormity of the suggestion, Royer was willing to try. He had once been in Mrs. Bunting's employ, on a missing-person case, and she owed him a favor. But this was the wrong time and the wrong request; she shut the door in Royer's face. By nightfall her husband was interred without an autopsy.

The attempt to interfere almost got Danny in trouble. Bill Paul muttered about having Danny disciplined or disbarred, revealing once more the hostility between them. Nothing formal came of it, though, which Danny regretted. It might have been an excuse to have Bunting's body dug up.

Bunting's death was officially in the category of coincidence. The cops he had worked with gave no thought to homicide. What would a pathologist have looked for? A needle mark at the base of the skull? Some foreign substance in the blood? Danny didn't know, but he had grown weary and suspicious of coincidences.

"You're overreacting," Ikard said.

"I'm not overreacting."

"Who would have murdered Bunting? The CIA?"

"All right, sure, that's a pretty alien idea out here under the big sky. But you got to admit this case isn't exactly your straightforward gunfight at forty paces. A young lady is dead from a suspicious car crash; her union boss is almost dead from blacking out at the wheel; the last person to see her alive has been chased down dirt roads at breakneck speeds; and her roommate has been manipulated and intimidated. Not to mention the burglaries, the credit checks, the buggings, the motel visitors, the stray bullets. Or the fact that Bunting is the third person on our witness list to die in the past three months."

The other two had been Leo Goodwin II and Senator Lee Metcalf. Goodwin, heir to the GEICO insurance fortune, had put up the original money for Audio Intelligence. But there had been a falling-out, and Goodwin, dying of cancer, had agreed to an interview with Taylor.

Two days before it was to take place, January 15, Goodwin had died. The death certificate said "congestive heart failure," but the doctor who signed it had not seen the body. Three days earlier Senator Metcalf's body had been found on the floor of his Montana apartment. Metcalf also was buried without an autopsy. With his death only Dean McGee was left to testify about the epiphany in spring 1976 that had ended the Senate investigation.

In his gut Danny did not believe that Bunting or Goodwin or Metcalf had been assassinated. But it was possible; anything was.

WASHINGTON. MARCH 25, 1978. Kitty lay with her back against the synthetic-mink pillows. A month's backlog of magazines spilled off her lap onto the bedspread. With scissors and a yellow hi-liter she attacked them. As usual they yielded clippings for her "Nuclear Waste" file.

The new *Progressive* told of plutonium seeping from a nuclear dump outside Sheffield, Illinois, a region rich in walnut forests and soybean fields. The NRC said there was no health hazard, but cattle and fish were dying of unfamiliar diseases, and local officials were alarmed enough to fence off nearby swimming holes. Kitty's drawer was cluttered with similar reports. At Maxey Flats, Kentucky, plutonium and uranium waste had leaked into underground streams. Radioactive curium from New York's West Valley disposal site had left a trail down the Cattaraugus Creek, across Lake Erie, over Niagara Falls, into Lake Ontario. Cesium and cobalt from the Indian Point reactor on Long Island had settled in the Hudson River. One million gallons of radioactive waste embalmed in metal barrels had been sunk off the coasts of Delaware, Maryland, and California. The barrels, steel with a concrete matrix, were corroding. Men in minisubmarines had begun tests near the Farallon Islands, fifty miles west of San Francisco, after gigantic sponges were found growing on the barrels. About sixty-seven thousand barrels were at the bottom of the Atlantic and another forty-seven thousand in the Pacific. No one knew the exact total; the AEC had destroyed its records of the dumping.

Someday, Kitty hoped, she would have time to edit her clippings into a booklet, a small token in the propaganda war against the Atomic Industrial Forum. There was one government report she wished everyone could read. It described a near-criticality at Hanford, Washington, in a waste trench code-named Z-9. The trench had been closed in 1962. But eleven years later inspectors discovered plutonium waste coalescing at one end. They had to pump cadmium into the trench, a round-the-clock emergency, to prevent what the report called "an explosion like a mud volcano."

For years the AEC, and then the NRC, had said it was impossible for a nuclear-waste pit to go critical. They had pooh-poohed a story from across the Iron Curtain about a dump exploding at the edge of the Siberian plain in the fifties. But in 1976 an exiled Soviet biochemist, Zhores Medvedev, had confirmed it: waste buried near Kyshtym, in the southern Urals, had gone critical in late 1957 or early 1958. Under the Freedom of Information Act, the CIA had been forced to disclose that U.S. officials had known about it from the beginning.

In the past few months some of the Kyshtym survivors had been interviewed by British journalist Andrew Cockburn. Kitty scissored an article of his in the latest *Esquire,* headlined "The Nuclear Disaster They Didn't Want You to Know About." It was vivid reading.

The Soviet dump had been in an area of small villages and nomadic tribes, but the victims filled all the nearby hospitals. The people vomited; their eyes went white. Hundreds, perhaps thousands, died. The ground looked like the surface of the moon, blistered and cracked from the heat. The air had a charcoal taste. Only the chimneys were left standing in one village. The main highway was closed for nine months. When it reopened, there were signs telling motorists to drive through at top speed with their car windows closed. Even after the land repaired itself, radiation lingered. Topsoil had to be scraped off and bulked in a nuclear landfill. Mushrooms and wild berries sprouted and grew huge, to the size of tennis balls, but they couldn't be eaten. Fishing wasn't allowed. Ten years later, pregnant women were still being advised to have abortions. There had been many deformed babies with beveled lips and nubs for arms.

"Lights out!"

Bob's drill-field voice startled Kitty.

"I'm not finished," she pleaded. "Give me another half hour." Every night now they seemed to replay a version of this conversation. Sleep had become an abyss for Kitty, from which she had to be rescued. It was full of dreams formed out of her Wisconsin past and by a current undiagnosed condition—headaches and a fever like malaria—but she had not gone to a doctor, afraid of what she might be told.

"It's no better, is it?" Bob asked. He was unbuttoning his shirt.

"No." She yanked the bedspread, and the sliced-up magazines cascaded under a dresser. Even this single twitchy effort was audible in her lungs. Somehow it seemed a final act. She stayed where she was, moaning softly.

"I brought you a glass of wine," he said.

"Thank you." She drank it in deep swooning sips. Bob watched for signs of languor in her face. "It's no use," she said in defeat.

From the next room came a tiny entreaty, "Mommy, mommy." Kitty got up.

"You don't have to go," Bob said. "She's just talking in her sleep." Kitty listened through the door. Unhappy snufflings and gurglings broke through the silence, then nothing; Amber had located her thumb.

Bob picked up the scissors and the hi-liter. He put them on the dresser next to a gold hairbrush and a college-era picture of Kitty. Taken after her recovery from Hodgkin's, her beauty was captured in soft focus, hair the color of sunlight running in long curls past her shoulders. Her hair had changed, but not her face, at least not till recently. Now it showed gray pockets at her eyes and dozens of tiny furrows Bob had not noticed before.

"Come to bed," he said.

Her dress traveled up her body and over her head. Compulsive fingers roamed across neck and chest. She looked in the mirror and pulled her skin taut, feeling for lumps.

She said, "Can we do something special when I get out of law school?"

Bob smiled indulgently; her graduation was more than a year away. "We could go camping in Canada."

"Canada has those vicious blackflies."

"How about Europe? I could take you to Lourdes."

"Be serious."

He moved over and pulled her onto the bed where his warmth had been. "We'll go anywhere you want."

"I don't want to go anywhere." She looked at him with frightened directness. "I want to have another baby."

WASHINGTON. MARCH 26, 1978. In the Arrupe House living room Father Bill knelt before a cardboard box that could have held a gross of eggs. It contained the long-awaited issue of files from the FBI and the Justice Department. There was another box, about half as big, from the AEC/NRC.

First the duplicates had to be culled out, the pages Stockton had already given them: the memos about the fictitious gale-force wind and the other pathetic details of Olson's investigation. In another stack Father Bill put newspaper articles that an FBI clerk had doggedly reproduced. There were duplicates of duplicates. But none of them was new evidence.

The remainder were the heretofore-unseen pages. They were a scanty, blackened collection, mutilated to the point of being unintelligible. Felt-tip pens had obliterated names and other pertinent words. From gaps in the page numbers, Father Bill could tell that dozens of pages were missing. If any dealt with MUF, they had been deleted.

He separated the most interesting pages into an even lonelier pile, narrowing it eventually to two single sheets. One made it clear—at least as clear as bureaucrats can make anything—that the Kerr-McGee theory of Karen's "self-contamination" had begun as soon as the AEC inspectors arrived at her apartment, even while it was still being torn apart. The other was a copy of an FBI teletype sent by Olson on June 18, 1976, shortly after the Dingell hearings. *"Srouji claimed to have been a (blank) for the (blank) for five years,"* Olson had written. *"It had been suggested that she write a book on the nuclear industry in order to make contacts in that area."*

Father Bill left these on the table for Danny and went to scrub his hands. Outside, in patchwork sunlight, was a spring landscape, a backyard tinted with orchard blossoms. Robins, roosting on branches, fluted high and joyously. It felt good to be back at Arrupe House, even for a few days. He carried two suitcases upstairs. Danny had gone off to talk to Sara about money.

Danny put his arm around Sara's waist as they walked. The street-lamps were springing to life. It was barely dusk; the movie had been a matinee.

A block from the theater it was forgotten. "The NOW board took a vote," she reported in a tone of gloom. "They refused to sponsor the direct-mail campaign."

Danny felt a winter wind come from nowhere. Or was it his imagination? This was not Oklahoma; nearly everyone on the street was in a suit. He humped his shoulders against the wind and the news, not understanding either.

"It was approved on the first vote. But after some of our supporters went home, this one woman jumped up and made a motion for a second vote, the same woman who's been denouncing us for months. To her the case is like a personal threat: her husband's a nuclear technician of some sort. Anyway, it was three in the morning, and the vote got reversed."

For a comfortless moment Danny did not speak. Then he asked, "Could you get the board back together for another vote?"

"They live all over the place. I think the best thing now is to have SOS sponsor it. I'm gonna talk to Kitty tonight."

Except for the banister that Shawn kept shiny, there was dust everywhere at Butternut. The baseboards had turned gray. Spiders had bearded the ceiling corners. The ivory-gray chair stunk of dog. Finally Kitty had had to change her mind about having a maid in once a week ("They have to make a living too"). One was coming next week. Perhaps that should have told Sara something new and different was wrong with Kitty, but it only seemed another concession to her migraines.

Kitty kept to herself the long hours she was lying awake in the demands of her despair—the despair of an obsolete woman with teeth worn to the gums, set adrift on an ice floe. By denying her illness she hoped that somehow it would go away.

Tonight Sara stopped her at the stairs. "Come have coffee with me in the study room."

Kitty's desk was unkempt; an unfinished term paper had been there awhile. She sat on the sofabed with her knees drawn up.

"Here's the direct-mail letter," Sara said. "All I want to do is put it on SOS letterhead. A hundred thousand copies should bring in ten or twenty grand."

Kitty read it quickly. "I don't like it. It's too equivocal. It should say point-blank that we're trying to stop everything nuclear."

"We're sending it to feminists and civil libertarians and unionists." Sara sounded stifled. "It's a cross-section of people. A lot of them aren't anti-nuclear."

"But SOS *is,* and the letter should say so. Or else don't use SOS."

"I don't believe this!" Sara's face recorded the shock. Her eyes closed, her voice blurred, unrecognizable as her own.

"All right, you can send out the letter. But I'm sick and tired of this hypocrisy. Karen wasn't killed because she worked in a widget factory. It was a plutonium factory. People have to understand the difference."

"This is not an anti-nuke case. This is the Karen Silkwood case. For once in your life, Kitty, try to understand we need a coalition to win."

"Great. Wonderful. You go spend your time building a coalition, and meanwhile they go on building nuclear reactors."

"We're all working our ass off. It's gonna take time to stop nuclear power."

"We don't have time!" Kitty's voice shrilled. A police car sped by outside, flashing blue. "Take your stupid letter. I'm tired of talking."

"You're impossible. You really are impossible. You might care about billions of people who aren't born yet, but you don't give a damn about your friends."

"Look who's talking," Kitty stormed. "You don't care if the kids get fed! You call up half an hour before you're supposed to cook and tell us you're hung up in an 'important' meeting."

"Are you saying my meetings aren't important?"

"We all have important meetings, but the rest of us manage to follow the duty chart. You're the only one who's too preoccupied."

"All right, fine." Sara's tone was bold and vehement. "If that's the way you feel, get somebody else to take my place." Her elbow tipped over an empty coffee cup. To remove any doubt of how she felt, she broke the cup into pieces against the wall.

Kitty hiccuped. She started up the stairs, but had to rest against the banister. The tears came in a hot, ungovernable release.

Danny and Sara waited for Bob and Kitty outside the restaurant. A benign sky overlaid the tension. Good food and new surroundings, Danny thought, could lead to a truce. It was a fanciful idea.

Kitty and Sara let their spaghetti dry on their plates. They would not be drawn into a conversation.

Danny tried again. "I think a lot of this is my fault. I've put a lot of pressure on Sara."

Kitty looked up. "Let her do her own apologizing."

"That does it!" Sara threw down her fork, and it bounced off the table. "You're the one who should apologize, Kitty Tucker. You're the one who's been hateful and closeminded."

Bob reached a calm, courteous hand for the fork. "I think everybody here needs a vacation. This is insane. Why are you fighting each other? If Jim Reading could hear you right now, he'd never worry about us again."

"I will not be patronized," Sara said. In the volatile atmosphere the quarrel was expanding and changing shape. It gathered into a storm of latent resentments, promises unkept, a friendship undone.

With brutal clarity Kitty said, "There is no way I'm going to live in the same house with her."

Sara pushed back her chair ostentatiously. "Good, we finally agree on something."

"Wait a minute," Danny shouted, but Sara was up and striding away. In another minute she could not have resisted the temptation of that plate of spaghetti. In her mind's eye she could see horrified waitresses stepping around the strands and fragments of her uneaten dinner, flung in Kitty's face.

Sara's tan Plymouth still had its California plates, by now terribly illegal. She parked by the curb outside Butternut. A retaining wall between the sidewalk and the elevated lawn had never bothered her before. But now it did. It kept her from backing up to the porch.

Arms piled with sorry-looking grocery bags, she began trudging back and forth from her neat attic. The Plymouth took on the look of an overstocked life raft. She crammed in everything worth taking. She was determined not to make a second trip.

In a hurtling stream of traffic Sara drove southeast. At Shepherd Street she made a right. The rows of colonial brick houses gave way to a darkening tunnel of elms saved by some miracle from Dutch elm disease. She turned into a long driveway. Holy Name College, a single, immense building of stone masonry, waited on a short rise. It was a familiar sight, but she felt she was seeing it for the first time. Where the driveway looped around a statue of the Virgin Mother, there was a spur of pavement leading to Arrupe House. The former convent seemed lost in a pink mist. The air was afloat with orchard pollen. Sara blamed it for her sniffling. Behind unruffled curtains she could make out the outline of heads talking and reading, all of them male. Sweet Jesus, she thought.

She gathered her strength; it was not enough to carry the grocery bags.

Danny was in the kitchen mixing colors for an omelette, red and green and yellow. "Great timing," he greeted her. "You can eat half."

Sara's face struggled for control. She lifted it, soft but clear-eyed. "Danny? Are you ready for a roommate who knows how to nail up sheetrock?"

OKLAHOMA CITY. APRIL 6, 1978. Ikard's opinion of Oklahoma journalism improved with each paragraph of the article in the afternoon *City Times*. Reporters Dwayne Cox and Mike Bates had enterprisingly acquired a copy of an OCPD inventory. Included were such items as "wiretaps and disguiseable microphone transmitters," their article said. "Also several beeper devices used in trailing autos, a 'debug' transmitter to check for wiretaps and other equipment to covertly monitor conversations." Eleven of these devices had been purchased from Audio Intelligence in Ft. Lauderdale before Karen's death.

Hallelujah, Ikard thought; score one for our side.

The article was the first independent verification of Taylor's strange reports. Though Danny swore by him, Ikard had no real way of knowing whether Taylor was reliable. Certainly Taylor had the hard look and seedy sophistication of a good private eye, and he got a lot of his information conventionally, from secretaries and the like; but his report on Audio Intelligence had been from faceless sources, the sort who appear in ski masks on TV documentaries. As a lawyer, Ikard had always been lukewarm about such informants: they were of no use in court. But to see in newsprint that the OCPD Red Squad did possess spy tools suddenly made it true.

The discomfiture of the Red Squad commander, Lieutenant Ken Smith, was also apparent. He was quoted: "Most of this stuff was already here when I came in 1975. Honestly, I don't know why it was bought. We can't use wiretaps except in violation of the state law."

NEW YORK. APRIL 7, 1978. All day Sara and Danny had been in and out of offices along Fifth, along Madison, along Park. The people who give away money for a living had given them hope. So did a mild evening rain that rinsed the air and pricked their skin. They inclined their faces toward the pattering drops and walked in no haste to the apartment of a lawyer Danny knew from Wall Street. The spare room had a tall ceiling and a bed with sun-gold sheets. Out a window beaded with rain Sara could see the red flicker of an all-night deli. It had been hours since she ate; she felt weak and empty but not hungry. She felt lighthearted, curiously teenage, awed. She pulled the shade to hide the city. Danny found a wire hanger for her damp dress. It was one of her best, afternoon-sedate and simple, her fund-raising uniform. She hung it in the closet. Inside, on the door, was a picture of Christ on Calvary, edged in gold. She stared: Danny's face looked back at her from beneath the cracked glass. No, it was Kitty's face. The lighting was playing tricks, she thought. It was poor because of the height of the fixtures.

"My head is spinning," she said.

"Why don't you lie down? I'll go get take-out Chinese or something."

"How could I have been so un-Christian? I've never had such a blowup with anyone. Except my husband."

"You and Kitty were trying to be best friends, roommates, comrades-in-arms, all for one, one for all—it was too much togetherness."

"I keep thinking I should feel guilty, but to be honest, I feel great." She was in a silky slip with a hem of lace. Her arms hung by her sides. There was no cigarette held skittishly on her lap, no defensive hand thrown up on shoulder or bosom.

"I think it's good for you to get out of D.C. right now," Danny said.

"What's good is you. You're terrific." Sara kissed both his eyes. "Just terrific."

"Be careful." He laughed self-consciously. "I'll start hanging around like an old hound."

"Danny, I love you," she said softly.

"Do you remember when you told me about your marriage? You said you'd jumped from being part of your father's family to being part of your husband's. You wanted to be free, to be yourself."

"I don't think you can really love someone unless you are yourself."

Danny seemed on the verge of saying something, but he kept rearranging the words. "It'll take two months, maybe three, to wrap up the rest of the pretrial proceedings," he said finally. "After that, we could go somewhere, maybe the Caribbean."

"If we ever take a vacation, we'll have an identity crisis," Sara said.

But her heart swelled at the thought of such an extravagance. She had never known Danny to spend money on anything except the cinema and his litigations.

She had on a touch of perfume; Danny was aware of it as an unusual supplement. He kissed her, a real kiss. For the next several hours they lay in bed, loving, whispering about themselves, wandering through their pasts, taking new routes, retracing old ones, crossing boundaries, finding islands of surprise. Danny told how he had badgered the Idaho regent into a heart attack, and where he had gone afterward to get his bearings: the Indian sweat lodge (wind through thin canvas freezing his naked back, fire burning his face, his soul flying to the sky); Harvard Divinity School (a year of exercising his intelligence); the Ministry for Social Justice (a drastic cleansing, the hope of harmony).

Sara, listening, thought about the Caribbean.

WASHINGTON. APRIL 10, 1978. Into the oven went a slab of beef, overlaid with onion slices like rosettes. Bob shut it in with a sense of achievement and went to sit with Kitty in the living room. "South Carolina is beautiful in the spring," he said. "You'll love it. Honeysuckle, magnolia, persimmon . . ."

". . . mosquitoes, creepy-crawlers."

Kitty's sour appraisal did not faze him. "As guests of honor, we'd get the cabins in the state park."

"I don't have the time. I've missed too much school." Her voice was stuck in a forlorn, sulky register.

"It's on a weekend. The rally will be a mile or so from where they plan to store a couple hundred tons of waste. Your speech can be about the Silkwood case, and I'll talk about Mancuso and his study."

"Who else is speaking?"

"Dr. John Gofman, and—"

"The man who wrote *Poisoned Power?*" The thought of being on the same stage as Dr. Gofman was like a hand on her shoulder, waking her. The book he had written (with Dr. Arthur Tamplin) was her catechism.

"Yeah, the same guy. I meant to tell you he's working with us to get Mancuso's study reinstated. Did you know he and Tamplin went through something very similar when they were with the AEC in California?"

"No, they don't talk much about themselves in the book."

"I heard about it from Ernest Sternglass—he's a professor in the next building over from Mancuso. Sternglass was one of the very first American scientists to raise the alarm about legal levels of radiation not being safe. He wrote an article for the *Bulletin of Atomic Scientists* in 1969, claiming that four hundred thousand people were dying from atmospheric fallout."

"Four hundred thousand?!"

Bob paused awkwardly; he felt he had said too much. "We can talk about this some other time."

Kitty took a broom from the front closet and swept up fallen coleus leaves by the bay window; she wanted the house to look presentable when the maid saw it. But the thought of all those deaths caused her to stop. "If Sternglass wrote about this, how come no one did anything?"

"He was ridiculed by just about everyone: the AEC, the National Academy of Sciences, the *Times,* the *Post.* The National Institutes of Health canceled his research grant, and the AEC even commissioned a team of scientists to refute him. Gofman and Tamplin were still with the AEC; they were still Good Germans. But they were coming up with calculations that refuted the AEC more than they refuted Sternglass."

"Was that the study the AEC wouldn't let them publish?"

"Uh-huh. The AEC jettisoned their project, cut their budget, and tried to demote them. They did the only honorable thing: they resigned. It's taken me a while to figure out there's a small band of dissident scientists scattered around, sort of in exile—Mancuso, Bross, Gofman, Tamplin, Sternglass, and Mazzocchi's two friends, Geesaman and Abrahamson. They were all forced out. Mancuso is only the most recent, though they've been more heavy-handed with him because he has those Social Security numbers. He can point to actual corpses."

"It's great that Gofman will help him. It's so disgusting when these scientists get hung up in petty rivalries. You know, if I had to pick the person I'd most like to meet, it'd be Gofman. Do you think he'll be on a tight schedule in South Carolina?"

"You'll come then?"

"Sure, why not?"

She sniffed the air curiously. Hurrying to the kitchen she opened the oven and got a full blast of the aroma. "A roast? Bob, I love you."

One thought about South Carolina lagged: "What about Amber? Will those cabins be warm enough for her?"

"I thought we could let her stay here," Bob suggested. "Marion and the others can keep her amused."

"A weekend all to ourselves?"

"Us, and three thousand other anti-nukers."

"I hope you fellahs are appreciative." Judge Theis smiled wearily at an official-looking box; its sides were walnut veneer made of cardboard. "I gave up my weekend to read through it."

Bill Paul had tried hard to prevent this moment, but Judge Theis, from the high-backed chair in his borrowed chambers, passed the box of Kerr-McGee files over to Danny and Ikard. Danny lifted the box, heavy as a casket.

Danny was tired and his eyes hurt, but Ikard couldn't wait to hunt through. After some cursing over paper cuts, Ikard located the MUF figures. As he already knew from Stockton, the final MUF at shutdown in 1975 was listed as sixteen pounds. But in 1974, four weeks before Karen's death, the MUF had been forty pounds. According to the inventory sheets, the plutonium had been caught up in the pipes.

"I'm holding back a few pages," the judge said. "They're either not relevant or they border on invasion of privacy. However, I feel you should be made aware of a couple of names from those pages: Steve Campbell and Robert Byler. You might want to talk to those two gentlemen."

Seventeen

All the time Danny was a kid he had put off the ritual. But the time came—Thanksgiving weekend his junior year in college—when he ran out of excuses. So he crunched out to the woods in upstate New York. They gave him a big old cannon of a gun and told him to stand in a windbreak of short pines. Uncle Jim and the others circled around and began the drive. Presently a deer came out ahead of the noise, a big deer, an eight-pointer anyway. Danny could hear it breathe. He aimed and fired, and chips of bark flew. The deer shook as if loosening up for a race and bolted down a hill away from the drivers. That was Danny's plan: simply to scare the deer. He hated the gun and everything else about hunting and he stood there in the snow only because Uncle Jim was getting old. He owed it to his uncle to pretend to try for his first buck. A second deer charged stiffly into the open. More wood chips, and again the dance down the hill to safety. Another one followed, a little spikehorn. As Danny saw it, he saw also that one of the drivers had come up and was watching. The shot had to look real. Danny fired from the hip, as if he were overanxious, and the bullet made a splat, then a bleat. There was a red line in the snow where the spikehorn had fallen. Danny walked over and threw down the gun, and no one in his family ever said a word about how he got his buck.

Now he was back in deer country, although none of it was familiar. This was Wyoming. Out the car window, through sun and dust, the road twisted along the contours of the Wind River Mountains. Crossing the Continental Divide, Ikard slowed down for the turnoff. A bulldozer had scraped this rough path through small boulders that a glacier had left behind. They passed cowboys who were herding Herefords into loading pens. Danny kept his mouth closed against the grit seeping in. At last they came to a valley and land that was flat. The main Thunderhead house stood before them, grand, without being grandiose. Saddle-notched fir logs jutted in crisscross from the corners. Two stone chimneys, exhaling smoke, enclosed the house like bookends.

The Thunderhead ranch was a fantasy come true for Gerry Spence: fifty-five square miles of fantasy. Coyotes and mountain lions controlled the upper, outer reaches. Closer in, closer to the ranch hands and their rifles, were the Simmentals, two thousand head. Spence had the largest Simmental herd anywhere in the country. The cows were a mottled red, and they had a Swiss pedigree. They were worth at least $2 million. It was not a fact Spence bragged about, but others invariably did.

Spence was a weekend rancher. During the week he was a lawyer in Jackson Hole. He had bought the land and the cows with big money earned on behalf of drug-deformed babies and the paraplegics of seat-belt failures. One time he sued a Walt Disney company for spraying the countryside with 2,4-D to kill brush. Thousands of aspens had been destroyed in the process. The case made legal history; it gave trees a status in court. Spence also did murder cases. Currently he was considering the case of the Rock Springs police chief, winner of many quick-draw contests, who had shot an undercover cop dead between the eyes, perhaps in self-defense. In eighteen years as a prosecutor, a personal-injury lawyer, a criminal lawyer, Spence had lost but three cases—they were in the period when he was boozing and his marriage was breaking up. He had sworn off the bottle and was remarried and hadn't lost since. Judges who had seen him perform made comparisons to F. Lee Bailey, Melvin Belli, Percy Foreman. But Spence did not have a reputation anywhere near theirs. Outside Wyoming he was probably better known for his Simmentals.

Danny had heard about him through one of those freaky cosmic revelations that so delighted Sara. She had had a special feeling about a great benefactor who was going to present himself, and one evening before Sara's departure from Butternut, a young man, new to town, had come to dinner. He happened to have worked as a Thunderhead ranch hand the summer before, and he began talking about Spence, what a fantastic lawyer he was and how he hated corporations. Sara got on the phone to Danny: "This is him—Spence is our man." To which Danny had groaned, "We need money, not another lawyer." But Sara had been positive, and so Danny had called out to Wyoming, and after some haggling and hesitation, Spence had wired back a friendly telegram. He would put up the money, ten grand or so, to take more depositions.

Danny brushed off the dust that had settled in disrespect on his suit. The house was on a low hill away from the barns and storage sheds. A large figure hulked in the doorway. "Look at him," Danny marveled.

Spence had a big brown outdoor face webbed with tiny wrinkles. His stance was studied, watchful. A massive twenty-gallon Stetson was down over his forehead. His vest was rawhide and a great dollop of turquoise shone from his belt buckle. "Only the gun on the hip is missing," Danny said.

Spence led them into a room with space in the rafters. "My wife, Emma Jean," he said. "She spells it Imaging." His hat tipped toward a beautiful woman in a dress with elaborate beadwork of her own doing. A ledger book was open on a desk. "Paperwork, paperwork. You can't get away from it," Spence said. "One rancher I know just put a ticker tape in his living room for the market reports. As it is, the market's shot to hell. Five years ago a prime Simmental bull went for twenty-five grand. Now everybody's raising them. The price is going down instead of up." He paused—an expressive pause. Even his most casual comments had stops and starts that were staged. A pickup rumbled up in the quiet outside. It was red, with chrome roll bars and a revolving spotlight on the cab roof. "You can always tell a guy who wants to look like a cowboy. He puts a dog in the back of his pickup, and a couple of fence posts to rattle around, a rifle in the window, and he thinks he's set."

"Don't forget the CB," Imaging said. She indicated her husband, her face alight with mischief. "His handle is Big Thunder."

Spence's mouth opened in a handsome laugh. Then he was serious. "Just so you know, gentlemen. I've turned down a hundred cases that were more sure-fire than yours. Maybe two hundred."

"We're gaining on them," Danny said with genuine faith.

"Getting an out-of-state judge was a master stroke. But you're still a little short on the facts."

"Which is why your help is so providential."

"About that: I've given it a lot of consideration . . ." This pause seemed sincere. "I've talked to Bill Silkwood, and I'm willing to come on as co-counsel."

"Sure, uh, that'd be great."

Ikard had a question. "Mr. Spence, you just—"

"I'm Gerry or Spence or even Big Thunder. Not mister."

"Gerry, you just said yourself the case is a big 'if.' Even if we win, the money will be a pittance. So why—"

"So why am I interested? Let me be up-front. I'm not a Light Brigade lawyer. Never believed in gallant absurdities. Nor do I necessarily see any terrible evil in nuclear power. But I do have a position against abusing the environment, and against abusing people. And I happen to know a little about Kerr-McGee. Their geologists came up to Wyoming a while back. Wanted to rip up our mountains to look for coal, uranium, anything. We chased them the hell out."

"You work with the Sierra Club?"

"No. I'm a rancher, not a conservationist. Getting rid of those geologists was more like self-preservation. And your suit is more in the category of an opportunity. You've complicated it with all this conspiracy crap, but as long as we win that won't matter. The point is to make a nuclear company pay for radiation damage. Let's set that precedent. That's how you're going to bring about corporate responsibility. A swift kick in the pocketbook." Colloquialisms were a natural part of Spence's charm. "Of course, the ante you guys set is ridiculous. A hundred sixty thousand? They're laughing at you."

"How high would you raise it?" Danny maintained an equable look.

"Well, let me get the lay of the land. Let's see what I can get out of Olson and Srouji."

OKLAHOMA CITY. APRIL 13, 1978. Lines of distrust had set Olson's face in a wary limbo. He looked brown, sinewy, tightly coiled: the appearance of a hanging rope.

"Did you ever meet Mrs. Srouji at a motel?" Spence asked.

"In the spring of 1975 I picked her up at her motel here in Oklahoma City."

"That was part of what you call 'keeping her sweet?' "

"Yes, sir."

"Did you do anything else to keep her sweet?"

"Counseling, talking to her."

"How about little-boy—little-girl stuff?" Spence winked. The motel receipt had indicated two people in the room.

Olson became instantly a figure of honor, ready for violence. The mouth went harsh, the voice cold. "The answer to your rather contemptible question is no."

Judge Theis wagged a reproachful finger and announced a break for lunch. Afterward Spence finished making his point. "Did James Reading ever talk to you about Karen Silkwood's sex life?"

"Somewhat," Olson replied. In the box of FBI files there had been a handwritten note. *"She was a pig!"* Olson had written.

"Did you think that was a contemptible inquiry?" Spence asked.

"No. It gave me some handle on the people involved. . . . It was a little hard trying to figure out who were logical suspects. Was this a lovers' quarrel? Was she indeed murdered?"

"You think it gives you a handle if you know something about a person's sex life?"

Olson's lawyer answered jovially for him. "It's interesting, at least."

"I see. It's *interesting* when we're talking about Karen Silkwood's sex life, but contemptible when it's Agent Olson's sex life," Spence said snidely. He was having fun with Olson, but it was fun with little substance. Olson's memory kept failing and, when it didn't, the young FBI lawyer in wingtips inserted himself with irritable alacrity. In a day-long deposition Olson made only one small acknowledgment. Srouji, he said, had belonged to a conspiracy of some sort. "She told me she had been instructed to write her book."

"Did she tell you who had instructed her?" Spence asked.

The FBI lawyer was again vigilant. "Your Honor, that would involve the area to which we object."

Judge Theis appraised the men around the table, his eyes snapping wisely under white spiky eyebrows. There had been more than thirty objections in the name of "national security." But before he could make any sort of ruling, the deposition had to be removed to chambers, away from the reporters. The FBI lawyer, standing but not moving, insisted on an even tighter arrangement. He wished to exclude Spence, Danny, and Ikard as well. That was contrary to ordinary procedure, but acceptable to Judge Theis. He was no doubt curious as to how "national security" was in jeopardy.

An hour later Judge Theis returned with the government men. He sighed, "I don't know about you, but I'm tired." He sat down heavily, shoulders drooping. His face, though, was under the control of the dutiful arbiter. "I've never been so utterly convinced of anything in my time on the bench: these matters just shouldn't have exposure," he said to Danny. "You can assume they're sinister, if you want, but they *are* secret—and will remain secret."

Breakfast the next morning was at the Skirvin. "This judge is no different from the first two," Father Bill said bleakly into the smorgasbord line.

Danny's plate was yellow to the edge with scrambled eggs, and white in the center with mayonnaise. He said, "There're still a few openings to charge into. We'll get through somewhere." The football metaphor was odd since he pretended not to know sports any more.

"I'm inclined to go full-bore at Srouji today," Spence said.

Danny agreed. "It's a good guess that they told Theis about Srouji working for both the FBI and CIA. Ergo: there goes her First Amendment privilege."

As they entered the courthouse Srouji grabbed Danny's wrist, exhibiting unusual strength. "God will stop you," she crooned strangely, in a voice somewhere between a laugh and a sob. Inside she gave everyone else a cozy smile and looked right through Danny.

Before her deposition could get under way, this third time around, there was still the question of who she was legally: newswoman or undercover agent? Judge Theis was not like some judges who try to find a middle course merely to create an impression of fairness. He was too careful of the law to be so capricious. In nine years on the federal bench very few of his decisions had been reversed. Yet he was good at splitting differences, granting both sides about half of what they wanted, or about what they had a right to expect. Today he ruled in Danny's favor. Based on yesterday's closed-door revelations and on the affidavit from Seigenthaler, Judge Theis formally identified Srouji as a government agent. But there was a loophole in the ruling. As an agent, she now was entitled to the same security cloak Olson had used. She could stay mum on the same questions.

Spence held out a mangled sheet of paper. There was a pile of papers at his elbow; they were Danny's trophies from all the accumulated months of struggle. This was the FBI teletype: "Srouji claimed to have been an (blank) for the (blank) for five years. . . . It had been suggested she write a book on the nuclear industry in order to make contacts in that area."

"Mrs. Srouji, do you deny that you wrote your book at the behest of the FBI or CIA?" Spence asked.

"Object to that, your Honor," the FBI lawyer said alertly.

"Sustained."

Other areas were off limits for other reasons. Spence tried to ask Srouji about a statement she had made in a defiant moment to a *Tennessean* reporter. "I know who killed Karen Silkwood," she had said then. "I can name the murderer, but I won't."

Judge Theis did not like how Danny had originally slipped murder into the lawsuit ("the right to travel freely on the highway"), and he did not like Spence's line of questioning. "This is not a coroner's inquest," he said in denial. "I don't intend to allow you to get into murder unless you can really prove it."

"How can we prove it if we can't ask about it?" Danny griped, but he shut up under the judge's chastening gaze.

Spence switched topics. "Do you have any evidence of pressure brought on the FBI to curtail the Silkwood investigation?"

"I did hear that the Oklahoma City bureau wanted to do more, but the Justice Department ordered them to cease," Srouji said. She would not elaborate.

Spence dug out another paper from the pile before him. None of the papers had come harder than this one, an affidavit from Stockton.

Stockton had been in a difficult spot, caught between Danny and Dingell, between the needs of the courts and the privacy of Congress. Danny wanted an affidavit telling how Srouji had bragged about seeing wiretap transcripts of Karen's conversations. "As much as I'd like to, there's no way I can," Stockton had said on each of the several times Danny had asked. An affidavit was one step from taking the witness stand, and if Dingell let Stockton do it, other pestering lawyers would expect the same treatment—and there was no end to the lawyers trying to drag congressional staffers into court. But then came the release of the FBI file box. One of the censor-lined sheets, which at first looked like all the others, proved on second look to be a classic FBI smear. It was a memo from an unidentified FBI agent in Oklahoma City, apparently based on information from Reading, referring to Stockton's time in Oklahoma City. "(Blank) did learn from certain of his sources that Stockton didn't accomplish too much because Stockton spent most of his time visiting local prostitutes and not working." Anyone reading this—the judge, say, or a reporter— was bound to think it held a smidgen of truth, though it was as fictitious as the smear against Seigenthaler. The people at the FBI, it seemed, could not resist the force of habit. But their little maneuver, so unoriginal, had blown up on them. Dingell had changed his mind; he had let Stockton sign the affidavit.

> Srouji indicated she was surprised at the incredible detail of conversations and events in Kerr-McGee documents supplied by Jim Reading. She said she discussed this with Reading, who indicated his group had conducted surveillance of Silkwood. Srouji claimed she had copies of transcripts of what appeared to be the product of phone taps and bugs.

As Spence quoted from it, Srouji kept her eyes on her lap, like an unprepared student hoping the teacher will pass her by. "Now what exactly did Mr. Reading tell you?" Spence inquired.

"Oh, gee, I don't remember. . . . I think Karen had singularized herself and she had, naturally, come to the attention of Kerr-McGee. In that respect I think they were very much aware of her existence. . . . But I can't remember specifically what Mr. Reading told me."

A dozen repetitions of the question did not cure her amnesia, but she was plainly flustered. Danny draped his arm across the back of Spence's chair and whispered, "Ask her about her publisher."

Spence selected another paper. He eyed it as if it were Delphic, but this one was a prop: the words on it were gibberish. "How long have you known Mr. DeLorenzo of Aurora Publishers?" he asked.

"I met Mr. DeLorenzo when he asked me to do the book."

"Does he have some relationship with the government?"

"Uh, yes sir."

"What is it?"

"You know, I can't—" Srouji looked wildly toward the FBI lawyer. He sat, an impassive form. Why didn't he object? Danny had a grim thought: he doesn't need to object; he knows she'll cover for the CIA.

"Just tell me what Mr. DeLorenzo told you," Spence said benignly. He rustled the paper, a card dealer's motion.

"Uh, I don't want to get somebody else in a lot of trouble." Again her hands and eyes appealed to the FBI lawyer, and again he did nothing. Danny's thoughts leaped: the prop *is* working—or maybe the lawyer only cares about the FBI, let the CIA watch out for itself.

"I know, but you can just tell me," Spence said.

"You have to understand. I didn't know all this when I signed the contract, okay? He told me this after I turned in the manuscript."

"All right, but what did he tell you?"

"He said he was with the CIA. I swear to God I didn't know that. I did a straight book. He paid me, and he published it. And that is all I know." Weeping and incoherent, she covered her face with Kleenex. "I'm sorry. I'm just a woman. I can't help it."

Sitting down to supper, Father Bill had a realization—it came to him that Spence and Danny were very much alike. Both worked in the same way, reveling in the naughty freedoms of the courtroom. They enjoyed the combat like other men enjoy a disreputable night on the town. And, in the manly talk after a good day, both tried to be lord of the supper table.

Danny had the upper hand at the moment. He was telling his Idaho State University story. "We were in the exact same courtroom where Clarence Darrow defended Big Bill Haywood on that trumped-up charge of killing the governor, and we had a similar cast of characters. My client was a local union president who'd been fired from the university in a trumped-deal, and Jess Hallie, the grandson of the original prosecutor, was the attorney against me. Naturally, I had Darrow's seat." Danny paused. The others shared a laugh while he speared a *sopapilla* from the dessert plate. "I found out the Idaho regents had conspired to get rid of this guy during one of their regular meetings. Normally all their meetings are recorded, but the secretary had been ordered to destroy this particular tape. *However,* she'd saved her notes, which I got hold of. Then I subpoenaed one of the regents. He got up on the stand. I was out to ruin him—I wasn't taking any prisoners. I shoved the secretary's notes under his nose. His mouth went up and down. He started breathing funny, gasping, grabbing at his chest. All of a sudden he was down on one knee, pulling himself across the floor like a swimmer. I was hollering, 'Get back here.' I wouldn't let him go till they brought the doctors in. Well, he had to have open-heart surgery and almost croaked. So I subpoenaed two more regents. They wouldn't show up. They sent word they'd had heart attacks. I thought they were hiding out, but they produced the hospital records. One of them had open-heart surgery too. They all had coronaries out of absolute stark terror."

From the other end of the table Spence boomed a reply that echoed above them. "Every great lawyer has to have a dark spot of anger in his heart. It's what he draws on when he gets a witness in his sights." Danny fell silent. He loved his story for its drama and almost had forgotten how he had shocked himself with his lack of feeling for the wounded men.

"You should all come up to Wyoming for deer season," Spence was saying.

"Are you a trophy hunter?" Ikard asked.

"No, I go for the venison. My dad taught me to eat everything I shot. Otherwise it's a waste."

"Hunting is always a waste," Danny said, a bit defensively. "What does it give you? Besides a moment of power."

"You think it's wrong because it makes some people feel good?"

"Pull the trigger and you're giving in to instincts that go back to the caves."

"Danny, I like you. I admire you. I wouldn't say this if I didn't. But I've listened to you talk about how we got to disarm the military, defrock the generals, spread peace and love. But, sitting here, I think the most violent guy at this table is you. There's violence in you, Danny. There's anger and there's violence in you." Spence paused. "How does that make you feel? Everything I just said, how does it make you feel?"

"Well, first of all, I don't think I agree with your analysis."

"I didn't ask what you think," Spence said. "I asked how you *feel.*"

Danny's mouth clamped around an unspoken retort. He was rarely bested, but this was one of those rare times.

Taylor had dropped several pounds and grown a beard. "Danny's gonna turn you into a monk too," Drew kidded him. He opened the Pizza Hut door, firing the sun briefly into its dark interior. A waitress gestured them to a table.

"This is the place you and Karen met up with those two cops?" Taylor asked.

"Yeah, but we had no idea that's what they were. All we knew was that Bob Byler was a security guard here on the weekends, and Steve Campbell was his sidekick. They were both into photography—that's why we asked them back to the house. Karen had some vague notion to build a darkroom. Thinking on it now, she might have asked them about darkroom techniques. So she could figure out how Kerr-McGee was doctoring the photomicrographs."

"Could she have mentioned the photomicrographs to Byler or Campbell?"

"Oh, now, I don't think so. Is that what the judge told Danny?"

"The judge just gave us their names. I tracked Byler to the OCPD. He does camera work for the Red Squad. Campbell isn't actually a cop. He's a freelancer, a groupie."

"But you, uh, think they were spying on us?" Drew was having trouble enunciating.

"It's in their line of work."

Drew put his head down. "That blows me away, it really does. I thought they were friends." A throbbing started at the back of his head, the old pain, the old undefined fear. He thought about the .38 Special Chief, which he no longer had, and how defenseless he felt without it. "What a sucker I was, what a four-star rube."

"Take it easy. We don't know for sure that they did anything."

"They did, they did. And I let them. Dammit to hell. I, uh, I never said anything before because it didn't seem important, but I let Byler take pictures at a party we had, and I let Campbell photograph my diary, plus my list of 'strange happenings.' I wanted him to have photographs of everything in case my place got ripped off." Drew looked at the pizza the waitress brought; it might have been a rubber bone thrown as a joke to a stray dog.

Taylor took a slice from the half with mushrooms. Drew had become suddenly young to him in the strain and self-disgust of the betrayed friendships. Taylor felt compassion. The lawsuit was an odd torture for both Karen's friends and her enemies; the wounds of memory were not allowed to heal.

But he also felt a new excitement. He asked, "After you met Byler and Campbell did they attach themselves to you? Did they show up unannounced, run into you on the street, that sort of thing?"

"Not Byler, he was more reserved. But Campbell did that. Exactly that. He came to my place right after Karen was killed. Popped in uninvited."

"Okay, think a minute. When did you first meet them? Give me as precise a date as you can."

"Oh, boy, that'd be hard to reconstruct." Drew snatched at drifting bits of history. "It was a few weeks before Karen was killed. It must have been a weekend because I'd borrowed a friend's Volvo, and I had to get it back so he could do his National Guard duty. Yeah, I remember now, he'd left an M–16 in the trunk. In fact, I got the damn gun out to show Campbell."

"Your friend had an M–16 from the Guard?"

"Yeah, he'd signed it out to go target practicing."

"Okay, if he signed it out, there's got to be a record. You can count on the military to have it in triplicate."

OKLAHOMA CITY. APRIL 28, 1978. Steve Campbell had scrubbed choirboy looks; his soft blond head tilted impishly in the air. The more specific Danny's questions, the less specific Campbell's answers. Campbell was good at not being specific. How many times had he been to Drew's house? "More than once and less than a thousand," he said. His voice trilled in phony sweetness.

Campbell had been with Byler at the Pizza Hut late on a Saturday night sometime in the fall of 1974. Byler worked at the Hut, moonlighting on weekends from the OCPD. There was a guy in the parking lot that night who Drew thought was a tape-deck thief, or maybe Karen did, but somehow Byler got into a conversation with them. Campbell, hanging around, got into the conversation too. When the Hut closed, they all went back to Drew's bungalow. The visit might have gone unremarked had it not been for the M–16. Drew made a show of it. And the next day, or a day later, Byler mentioned the rifle to his superior at the OCPD, Commander Robert Hicks of the Red Squad. What were Drew and Karen doing with an M–16? Planning to attack the factory?

Commander Hicks thought it was a matter for Kerr-McGee, and so Byler, Campbell and Hicks got together with Reading a few evenings later at Byler's house. Out of that meeting Campbell had gone to work informally for Reading: by becoming a deliberate friend of Drew. The photographs Campbell had taken, he had delivered to Reading.

"You took these photographs with the knowledge you were going to show them to Reading?" Danny asked.

Campbell's shoulders heaved. "Yes," he said, somewhat off balance. "Reading said he was interested in the information."

"Did you go to Reading's house?"

"Yes."

"How many times?"

"More than once and less than a thousand." He had recovered his poise.

"Did you show the photographs to Hicks?"

"Once. I don't think I did it more than once."

"But you could have?"

"I could walk on water, but I don't."

Danny hit his hands together sharply. "Now don't be silly. You can't walk on water, but you could have shown him the photographs more than once."

"Well, I might have in the sense I might have done a lot of things." Campbell wouldn't leave his sanctuary of vagueness. Danny asked about Byler's involvement, whether Byler had given any pictures to Reading. Campbell said he couldn't remember.

Danny moved closer, the fury of his words inches away. "Don't tell me you don't remember, Steve, because you will get your ass thrown in jail for perjury if you keep this up! And no one's going to rescue you!"

The FBI lawyer, who had been half listening, came to attention. "I'm going to object. If you're going to act this way, Mr. Sheehan, I'm not sure we should be here."

"I don't care whether you're here or not," Danny said, not moving a fraction from Campbell. He looked hard at eyes that were obviously trying not to blink.

"If I can pause here, I will try to remember," Campbell said. A small spasm was worrying the blond face. The eyes were bright with fear.

"Good, good," Danny said. He smiled in satisfaction. He wanted Campbell to leave the deposition a little shaken. The fear was more important than this answer. The really important answer of the day had already come out: Reading definitely had been getting information and pictures about Karen surreptitiously through the OCPD.

"In the old days, I suppose, the cops would have done it out in the open and been proud of it," Danny said. "They'd have busted up the union and that would have been that."

Drew, nodding sagely, went to a window. An almost invisible figure was on the lawn fighting through a windy rain. Lightning branched in the sky. "Jesus, what a night," Mr. Silkwood said, coming in. His jacket was soaked. Hair streaked down his forehead. The wind lashed the door out of Drew's hand, spinning it on its hinges. "Tornado season," he said, handing Mr. Silkwood a towel.

Danny was oblivious to the storm. "I was just saying how clever these cops are. Everything they did was *unofficial*," Danny said. "Commander Hicks didn't do anything *officially*, Byler and Campbell didn't do anything *officially*. All they did were a few favors for good-ole Mr. Reading."

Drew's last visit from the big security chief had come a few months ago. An unexpected shadow had fallen during lunch one day at the Dolly & Hammer. Reading's face was even more puffed out and spongy, his round eyes incongruously small, marooned in a red capillary sea. The toe of his shoe had dug a hole in the dirt as he made small talk about how tough it must be for young guys starting in their own business. Then Reading had spit and walked away. Drew had not had a drink for weeks, but that night he had drunk himself sick.

Danny began talking louder to drown out the sound of rain on the roof. "It turns out Reading was an OCPD big shot for years, before Kerr-McGee hired him away. He goes way back with Hicks, Byler, all of them except Campbell."

"And Campbell did it for what? The money?" Anger showed on Drew's cheeks like a rash.

"Who knows? He did get paid. Reading has admitted paying Campbell for the pictures."

"The little prick. I'd like to hear him sing soprano." Drew reached for a hunting knife that hung in its sheath on a hook. He began slicing a lime for gin and tonics.

"Don't do anything crazy," Danny said quickly. "I mean it. Let me take care of these turkeys."

"I don't get it. What kind of pictures was this Campbell fellow taking?" It was Mr. Silkwood, tousled and uncomfortable in his wet clothes.

"There were at least four sets of pictures. A set Campbell took of Drew's diary, a set Byler did at a party here, a roll from Drew's camera—"

"I gave it to Campbell to be developed," Drew said miserably.

"—plus a roll from Karen's camera."

Drew cut the air with his knife. "That had to be from the camera Karen bought in Los Alamos, the one that was ripped off."

"Unfortunately, there's no way to prove that because the pictures didn't come out. Or, if they did, no one's saying. Byler says Karen must have forgotten to open the thingamajig in front of the shutter. The film was still virgin."

"Could this have been out of her old camera, the one she had before Los Alamos?" Mr. Silkwood interrupted in a slow, deep wondering.

"I guess it could. Sure."

"In other words, they might have stolen that one too? Before she was killed?"

Danny had not thought of that particular possibility, and said so. But the larger possibility—that Reading had employed Campbell to spy on Karen while she was still alive—was very much on Danny's mind. He was obsessed with it. Father Bill had gone all over town to find Drew's friend, Bob Ivins, the M–16 marksman. Danny wanted something as exact and incontrovertible as a National Guard log. "It's real interesting, real interesting," Danny said. "Reading says he never heard of Karen till the apartment contamination. He swears up and down he didn't even know her name till then. You should've seen him at his deposition. Smug as a bug. He's gonna get one big shock when we hustle Ivins into that courtroom."

Mr. Silkwood looked blank.

Danny went on. "Father Bill tracked Ivins down, and he was real cooperative. The National Guard claims to have misplaced those particular records, but Ivins has a friend who kept a logbook. It shows he had the M–16 checked out on October 12, which was a Saturday. It also shows he never had it out on loan after that. That was the last time. That has to be the date Byler and Campbell saw it. We can be almost positive. And we know from his own testimony that Byler went in to the OCPD and told Hicks about the M–16 a couple of days after seeing it. And bingo, Reading got into the act. All within a week."

Drew began writing on the back of an old Dolly & Hammer work order. October 10—Karen organizes OCAW seminars. October 12 —we run into Campbell and Byler. October 16—OCAW wins election. October 17 (or thereabouts)—Campbell and Byler meet with Reading. November 5, 6, and 7—the contaminations. November 13—the accident.

He gave the paper to Danny. "Is this right?"

Danny nodded. A look came over Mr. Silkwood, a sad tenderness.

It had been a while since Danny had held one of these briefings. Mrs. Silkwood, in her kindly way, had let him know to keep them infrequent. Each small advance toward a solution wrung from her husband new hope, new anger. Each setback left him disgusted. Like Stockton, Danny had peculiar, indirect methods that seemed to prolong everything. So much of the case now involved the doings of spies-for-hire, government agents, maybe smugglers, people so foreign Mr. Silkwood could not associate them with his daughter. Yes, he knew she had been a spy too; but a make-believe one, not the real-life kind.

He craned forward toward Drew's scribbling. Impatience took over again. "I don't see where this gets us. Are you saying Campbell or Byler knew about the Holiday Inn? Are you saying they were the ones who told Reading?"

"Not necessarily. I still think Kerr-McGee found out about that from a wiretap."

"Then what the hell good is the stuff?"

"I'll tell you. On the evidence we have I can make a good-faith presumption that *someone* knew Karen was going to be on Highway 74 that night. Then I have to ask myself: who had an interest in knowing? I can make another good-faith presumption that certain individuals at Kerr-McGee did. But who had a way of finding out? That's where a presumption is more difficult. We have Stockton's affidavit that there was a tap on Karen's phone, which is information he got from Srouji, who allegedly got it from Reading. It's second-hand and thirdhand evidence, but it's evidence. Also, we know that the Red Squad, with Hicks as the commander, invested in wiretap equipment from Audio Intelligence and sent undercover men to Fort Lauderdale for training. Good evidence, but no direct tie-in. Until now. Now we've got the tie-in. Hicks is the one who put Campbell and Byler in touch with Reading. The OCPD was working hand in glove with Kerr-McGee all along." Danny stuck the sheet of dates under Mr. Silkwood's shrouded gaze. "Take another look," he said. "On October 17, give or take a few days, Reading meets with Campbell and Byler. That's right after the decertification election. No jury is gonna think that's an insignificant coincidence. Forget what Campbell and Byler did or didn't do. What's important is that Reading was using snitches. And these snitches were pretending to be friends with Karen and Drew."

Mr. Silkwood frowned at the paper. He looked out the window at the storm. He fiddled with a drink that tonight did not taste right. "But when it's all said and done," he persisted, "we don't know any more about what happened on the road that night, do we?"

For a moment Danny's composure left him. There's no pleasing this old man, he thought sourly. Only fatigue and a censor in Danny's brain kept him silent. Suddenly the racket outside reached him, hail pebbling on the pavement. He reminded himself that for nearly four years Mr. Silkwood had endured on a string of good-faith presumptions. "We've turned a corner, I think," Danny said quietly. "We're getting the evidence, piece by piece."

Father Bill found Harold Sebring in Stillwater, Oklahoma. Sebring's car dealership here was larger than the one in Crescent, but that was not the reason he had left. No, with the factory closed and jobs hard to come by, his customers weren't making their payments. Along with the owners of the Hub Cafe and several more of Crescent's prominent citizens, Sebring had given up and moved away.

"Make me a trade on a Honda 450?" Father Bill asked.

"What do you have in mind?" Sebring looked prosperous, his hair neatly coiffed, his clothes new: a pale blue sport coat and a dressy tie knotted over a good shirt.

"Just kidding," the priest said quickly. "I'm here because of the Silkwood case." Father Bill sometimes wore his collar, but he always made clear his real role before questioning anyone. Affecting any sort of pretense made him uncomfortable. Once Taylor had wanted him to sneak a tiny microphone under the collar, but Father Bill thought that was going too far. ("I'll do one or the other, but not both. It's a clash of symbols. With one I'm telling people I can be trusted, but with the other I'm deceiving them.") Today he was without either. Being so much on the run, he hadn't the time for any sort of costume. He might well have been an auto-accessories man trying to make one more sale. His hair was trying to escape down his neck and his clothes hung in folds.

Harold Sebring's new showroom was actually the first stop for Father Bill in a three-state travelogue, but it was not his first travelogue. For some weeks he had been off chasing after a number of characters who might have been of help, but weren't. There had been Robert Bathe, a 5-283 member, whose car was sideswiped and almost forced off Highway 74 shortly after Karen's death. But Bathe wouldn't talk, and the OCPD had written it off as a prank of drunken teenagers. There also had been John Thomas Cook, an oil rigger in Woodward, Oklahoma. Someone thought he was leaving a clue when he scrawled the letters "AEC" on a wall in blood from a shot in the head. But his message had nothing to do with the government AEC: it was about a sex triangle and jealousy and suicide.

Sooner or later, though, Father Bill's luck was bound to turn. Harold Sebring, for instance, was someone who could say, yes or no, whether the dents in Karen's car were the result of it being winched out of the culvert. A. O. Pipkin and two other experts (Dr. Ernest Martin, an Albuquerque chemist, and Gerald Greene, an Albuquerque metallurgist) had run the dents through chemical tests and put them under high-power magnification. According to the tests, metal had struck metal; the concrete wingwall was not the culprit. This was close to a scientific verity but not quite one. Sebring could contradict the experts, and if he did it would be bad. The jurors might never be able to sort it out.

More than once, in his sleep, Sebring had seen the little white car rising on his winch line from the muddy water. Always he was standing on the grass, watching. One assistant worked levers in the tow truck; the other guided the line to conjunction. The car came out backward, tugged bumpily up the bank, perpendicular to the creek, up onto the shoulder.

"Where was the car in relation to the wingwall?" Father Bill asked.

Sebring's hand opened and shut with mechanical rapidity. Back in Crescent he had not wanted to say anything against Kerr-McGee that would throw the town's economy out of whack. He had always been truthful, but no one had asked all the right questions. "We pulled it out over the grass," he said, "so we wouldn't scrape it up any worse than it was. It was a little foreign job, you know, squashed like a tin can in front." He remembered it exactly. "It didn't come close to the wingwall."

Father Bill scribbled like mad in his notebook. "How far away would you say it was?"

"It was a good five, six feet away."

"So there was no way that it could've hit the wall on its way out?"

Sebring looked quickly toward the door as if hoping for a customer. Then he shrugged. "The car did not hit the wingwall. However the dents got there, it wasn't our fault."

"You'll swear to that?"

"It's the truth."

From Sebring's showroom it was on to the flatlands of eastern Colorado. Jean Jung had found a bookkeeper's job there. It was in a small town that had a name of no importance unless you happened not to know it, and almost no one in Oklahoma City had cause to. Mrs. Jung had quit her job at Kerr-McGee and moved away, pledging her few friends to secrecy, and Father Bill had to prove himself a detective to get her new address. He arrived at a building that had been flung onto the ground. The roof and walls ran together in a triangle of corrugated tin. It had no windows and no sign of life. But behind a blank front door Father Bill found a saloon, and at a desk in a side room Mrs. Jung was counting receipts. She gave a half-smile and raised a hand to straighten her wig.

Out of habit she touched the spot on her neck where the tumor had been cut out. Packaged in preservatives, the tumor had been put aboard a plane—for Los Alamos she had believed—but it had been somehow detoured to the Dominican Republic, then lost. Whether it was infected with plutonium she could only guess, and so her days had become a nervous, despondent succession.

Father Bill explained himself.

"Is Kerr-McGee gonna come looking for me too?" she asked instantly. "I ain't got no place else to run."

"If there's a way to keep you out of the trial, we will. But right now we need your testimony. You're the only one we know who saw Karen with the documents."

"I could lie and say I didn't see nothing."

Father Bill shut the door behind him, conveying with a gesture a gentle reproof. He said, "Is it that hard to stick up for Karen? Was she that awful a person?"

"You think you can make me feel bad, is that it?" Mrs. Jung's hand went to her face. Her heavy rouge was scarlet against unhealthy skin. "You can't make me feel worse than I do. I feel terrible about Karen. A kid sister, that's what she was like. Sometimes she'd get depressed and I'd give her my shoulder. But the truth is, Karen was the one that kept me going. Me and a lot of others. She was so smart, so full of grit. The way I wished I could be."

From atop a cabinet Mrs. Jung took down a latticed gold frame from which her daughter smiled out, mugging for a camera. She held the picture and felt its solid assurance. "I remember everything. Do you want to hear it all?" She began to repeat for Father Bill the whispered words Karen had said as she left the Hub Cafe.

Father Bill looked up from his notes. "Did Karen indicate whether she knew anything about MUF?"

"It seems like she may have. But, oh gee, if I had to swear it, I . . ." Mrs. Jung tried to recall the exact scene, Karen against the flimsy paneling, the others hurrying out, Alma Hall poised to follow . . . "Alma Hall! She was right there. She must've heard every word! Ask her—please, why don't you ask her?"

Alma Hall had since married—"a nice-looking fellow, but didn't catch his last name"—and moved to a small Kansas town. Edmond perhaps? Or Thayer?

Father Bill went to Thayer and found an eatery that looked similar to the place where everyone used to gather in his Montana hometown. The lady at the cash register said, "Why sure! You mean Alma South. Moved up here two years ago. Real sweet. Has a job over at—oh, but she won't be there today. She'll be tending one of her kids. He's down sick with the flu."

Exactly as described, the former Alma Hall was home being a nursemaid. Yes, she remembered Karen and Mrs. Jung talking at the Hub Cafe. But over the commotion their words had been muted, too soft to hear. If there was any talk about MUF, she didn't hear it. "All I can tell you was Karen had a folder. A brown one. Chuck full of papers. I did see them, as God's my witness."

BARNWELL, SOUTH CAROLINA. MAY 10, 1978. The blue-jeaned regiment, about three thousand strong, went marching across the madly vining morning glory and last year's corn stubble. For fifty dollars a day they had rented a soil-bank farm field near the Barnwell nuclear facility. T-shirts declared "Better Active Today than Radio-active Tomorrow." A watery ointment, a secretion of garlic, was passed around and rubbed over forearms. ("Mosquitoes hate it.") Long-haired carpenters, hammering arches over a double-deck stage, were an hour or so from finishing.

Kitty sat under a billowing green tent, fussing with her speech. It required all of her strength not to lie down on one of the cots. Just yesterday she had been ready to let Bob come by himself. She had felt so miserable. In her mind she kept returning to the Wisconsin hospital, to the X-ray guns, the delusory IV bottles draining away months and years like an hourglass, the stink of antiseptic foretelling the tomb. ("Oh, please God, don't let me die!") Was she praying to the God of St. Anthony's, the God of her parents, the God of her brother the priest—the God she had rejected? No, it wasn't God who had kept her alive. Nor the X-ray guns. The pact she had made fifteen years ago was with herself. Her own will had saved her. She had willed herself healthy. Even the doctors had said so. They had been amazed. Remembering, she felt better. She would will herself healthy again; the borrowed months and years were not to be squandered.

Bob came into the tent. With him was an older man in brown

tweeds. A passel of reporters trailed in and encircled them. One reporter said: "Dr. Gofman, you live three thousand miles away in California. Why should you be upset with nuclear waste being deposited here at Barnwell?"

"There was a time I wasn't. As you say, why should I? It's not going to affect me if it leaks into your drinking water." Dr. Gofman pressed his eyes shut a moment. He was a gentle, scientific man, and as glad as he was for the educational value of the TV cameras he wished to be rid of their shoving, besieging handlers.

Kitty dug a can of Coke out of an ice chest for Dr. Gofman. Something in her gesture was transferred to the reporters. They seemed to become more polite. A large man from the ABC affiliate in Augusta spoke. "I'll grant you that the industry hasn't yet solved the problem of waste disposal. But suppose it does. Will you drop your opposition to nuclear power?" It was a hostile question, put forward civilly.

Dr. Gofman answered. "All right, let's suppose there was a hundred-percent solution. I doubt it'll happen, but let's say we could bury it all in the salt mines of New Mexico without worrying about any sudden geological shifts a couple thousand years down the line. That's just the final phase of waste disposal. There'd still be all the other phases: sealing it in drums, transporting it, loading and unloading it, and so forth. In the last four years there have been more than three hundred traffic accidents involving nuclear shipments. Outside Denver a truckload of uranium yellow cake lay on the ground for twelve hours, blowing about loose because everyone else was confused about who was responsible for cleaning it up. Nuclear waste is escaping into the environment all the time. By early next century, not so far in the future, radiation from waste and other nuclear sources will be killing two hundred thousand Americans a year with cancer."

The reporter's lower lip fell. He might have had a reply, but outside the carpenters were finished and it was time for the rally to begin.

A girl dressed as Reddy Kilowatt moved to stage center. She acted out a satirical skit, making Reddy out to be a greedy little monster. (After her last public performance she had been arrested under an old anti-Klan law against wearing political costumes.) Next came Bob: he told about Dr. Mancuso's fight and how fifteen grand had been raised through EPC to stave off his eviction. A farmer walked on and hollered out surprising statistics about how nuclear facilities drive down the value of adjoining land.

Then it was Kitty's turn. Her walk up the stage steps was tentative and Bob wondered if her spirit might fail after all. She began, "If Karen Silkwood was alive today . . ." but stopped, fumbling, uncertain. An unwelcome blush crossed her face and slowly she raised a fist. "If Karen Silkwood was alive today, she would be *here* today." Whether or not it was true, Kitty believed it. Her voice became a warm flow, and when Dr. Gofman stepped up to give his speech, he bowed in tribute and squeezed her hand.

After make-do suppers, the rally leaders gathered in the tent and gave hearty support to Kitty's idea of a national anti-nuke convention. She volunteered to organize it by August. Bob warned against the rush and aggravation, but Kitty insisted she could handle it. Only through hard work, not prayer or piety, would her heaven be gained.

The next morning, with the dawn still buried, the anti-nukers rolled out of their sleeping bags for a hike to the nuclear dump. They would have to walk double file two miles along a road, and when they got there riot squads and police buses would be waiting to haul them away. Kitty had an impulse to go with them, even though an arrest at this point might sabotage forever her chance of becoming a lawyer. But first there was an obligation she had delayed all weekend. Kitty had promised Sara (they were talking to each other through intermediaries) that she would ask Jackson Browne to donate a concert like Bonnie Raitt was doing. Jackson had played to great ovations at the rally and his trailer-van was still in the cornfield. He was on the back stoop, strumming a ballad for a wide-eyed youngster, his son. He laid the guitar aside at Kitty's advance. She gave him an SOS newsletter and said her spiel, fighting shyness all the way. Jackson smiled. "That was you who gave the speech, wasn't it? Hey, I'm convinced. I'll ask my manager if I have an open date, and it's yours."

Kitty stammered a thank-you. This was a genuine celebrity!

Then she joined the others, walking hand in hand with Bob. She was in her robin's-egg-blue dress. Hymns rose in chanted syllables from the procession, and from bushes next to the road the cicadas sang. At the nuclear dump the police were gentlemen. They gave everyone a choice between being a bystander or getting arrested for trespassing. Kitty chose not to go to jail.

That afternoon the U.S. Geological Survey made public the results of a two-year study. According to the government's own experts, there was no such thing as a "fail-safe method of storing nuclear waste" and never would be.

WASHINGTON. MAY 15, 1978. Stockton had heard nothing but compliments lately. He had been doing fine productive work, finding scandal and calumny in the trans-Alaska pipeline, the capping of still-gushing Texas oil wells, the supertanker mess. Even the NUMEC case had been more or less a success. It was all but certain that bomb-grade uranium had been removed from the NUMEC factory and smuggled to Israel. Stockton had been proved correct. But for all his good cause to gloat, he looked downcast. The government men who had lied for years about NUMEC would not be sent to prison, nor suffer public disgrace of any sort. The plea bargain of Richard Helms and a general apathy at the Justice Department had seen to that. It was maddening.

Stockton was walking fast with Danny through a thin morning mist. "What's happening?" Stockton asked. "What've you come up with?"

"I told you about Steve Campbell. He made friends with Karen and then went to work for Reading. A nice arrangement." Danny found them seats in a coffee shop. Other customers were arguing about the Carter Administration. "And we finally got Srouji to admit that her book publisher is with the CIA."

A waitress took their order.

"Still looking for the great CIA conspiracy, huh?" Stockton asked in a joshing accent.

"Yep. Just like you."

They laughed. It wasn't often that they bantered with each other. Stockton was a regular guy, offhanded, quiet with his wit. He had never gotten used to Danny the storyteller, Danny and his facial cues, his reach for drama. How different than Win Turner, good old Win Turner, gone from the Hill into semi-retirement, working as a political consultant.

Stockton sat with his hands folded to avoid the temptation of the hot rolls in the basket. "Is this judge going to let you get into the cover-up?" he asked.

"I don't know. Both Olson and Srouji pleaded 'national security,' and he went along with it."

"Any new theories?"

"Just the same ones as before. Kitty thinks the nuclear fathers all got together and put on the Big Clamp to save the fast-breeder. Et cetera." Danny made a sound with his teeth. "The only theory that makes sense is the smuggling theory. Your theory."

"It's just too damn bad the final MUF figure was only sixteen pounds."

"But you still think it *was* smuggling?" Danny asked, uncertain.

"I think it's a possibility. NUMEC is proof that smuggling goes on. But . . ." Stockton finished off his glass of water; beer was just a Sunday drink now. "But maybe we've made it out to be more complicated than it was. Maybe they were just doctoring the photomicrographs. That's Wodka's theory."

"Kerr-McGee would've had the same motive either way," Danny said. "Smuggling or photomicrographs."

"But it might've been different people. Smuggling would've had to involve some top people. But the photomicrographs were being handled at the production level. One of the supervisors could've been operating on his own. Cheating on the welds to speed up production."

"How could a supervisor have found out about Karen's documents? He wouldn't have had access to wiretap transcripts."

Their breakfasts had arrived. "He could've seen Karen snooping around the files and put two and two together," Stockton said. "Then he could've followed her to the Hub Cafe. Or he could've waited in the Cimarron parking lot till she drove by on her way back. It would've taken him about a mile or so to catch up to her, which is right where she went off the road."

"And he didn't grab her documents because he freaked out when he saw he'd killed her," Danny said, completing the theory.

"It's even possible he didn't know she had the documents with her. It could've been coincidence, after all," Stockton said. "Kerr-McGee could've found out about the documents after her car went to Sebring's garage. The Highway Patrol could've informed Kerr-McGee. They're all buddy-buddy. Just like Reading is buddy-buddy with Olson and Olson is buddy-buddy with Srouji and on and on."

"One way or the other, though, somebody stole the documents out of the garage. And that's when the cover-up started," Danny said. "There had to be something in those documents. Something more than photomicrographs."

"Yeah, I have to agree with that."

The waitress suddenly had her hand out for their plates. They had to shoo her away. "Taylor has a theory about the CIA. It's the ultimate conspiracy theory." Danny shifted deeper into the booth and lowered his voice. "Well, no, I shouldn't say it's Taylor's theory. It's the theory of one of his informants."

"And?"

"The theory is that the CIA, or some other intelligence agency, was involved in this all along. Right from the beginning. That they knew about plutonium being smuggled out of Cimarron, and they killed Karen because she found out."

"Does this informant have any evidence?"

"Well, he's the one who told Taylor about Srouji's publisher being CIA, and that panned out. I don't think he has any paper evidence, but the CIA does keep popping up. Taylor found out that the CIA had men stationed in Oklahoma because of Cimarron, and there are all kinds of CIA overtones to Audio Intelligence."

"Did you ever take that deposition from the head of Audio Intelligence? What's his name?"

"Jack Holcomb. No, Holcomb got tipped off, and he took off like a bat. He's out of the country. We can't get to him. Same thing happened when Taylor tried to serve a notice on Bill Lovin, the guy at Georgia Power. Somebody really must've spooked Lovin. He took his whole family to Germany. Never even bothered to sell his furniture. Every stick is still in the house."

"And it's all supposed to be part of the same conspiracy?"

"If you believe Taylor's informant, yes, it is."

Stockton was aware of the intensity of Danny's declaration. "Well, you know what they say about conspiracies," Stockton said mildly. Unfortunately, he thought, that doesn't make them any less real.

Eighteen

At first Arrupe House was the strangest place Sara had ever lived: the guarded, brittle looks; the confusion in the dormitory-style bathroom. And the smell: the smother of old pipe smoke, dust, mildew, the sour staleness from men keeping house. But now the rugs were beaten, the floors swept, the plastic insulation taken down from the windows, the place aired out. Some of the men had even pitched in and helped. Arrupe House seemed like a home, especially now that Danny was back.

He had timed his return for the Bonnie Raitt concert (with James Taylor, Carly Simon, John Hall) and a cheese-and-wine fundraiser at which his panache was a great asset. Afterward Danny realized he had never paid Sara a compliment for what she had accomplished. Not with the house—he hardly noticed a difference—but with the fundraising.

It was remarkable what she had done in the past few months. Things had gotten bad, very bad. Danny and Sara and Father Bill had hit bottom. None of them had an income; they did not know how they would eat. Only through the grace of the Quixote Center, which put them on staff, had they kept going—and kept the lawsuit going. But now the foundations were giving money again. Stern, Levinson, Veatch. More cocktail parties were in the works, and the Jackson Browne concert was all but arranged. The total already had topped $100,000.

The breakthrough had come with the creation of the Karen Silkwood Fund. It had finally become clear why Sara was getting such a mixed bag of responses to her requests for money: the requests were a mixed bag—some on NOW stationery, some on Quixote Center stationery, some directly from SOS. The Karen Silkwood Fund had solved that. It was a new organization, or rather a coalition of old organizations. Yes, after all the talk about coalitions, there actually was one. Sara had made up her mind and had gone from meeting to meeting, getting each organization to set aside rivalries and petty conflicts for the sake of Karen Silkwood. It was something of a first: a coalition of feminists, environmentalists, unionists, civil libertarians, the Church.

NOW and the Quixote Center were in the coalition, and the EPC. They were more or less expected. But the National Emergency Civil Liberties Foundation (NECLF) and the ACLU, which had once been one organization years ago and had split up in a nasty fight—they were both in. (The NECLF deserved a lot of credit. It had bailed out the lawsuit in the very early days and had even paid the original filing fee.) The SOS was in the coalition too, and the OCAW had joined in an ad hoc way. The differences between Kitty and Wodka, and between Kitty and Sara, were by no means patched up. But maybe now they could be.

It would also be easier now to raise money. The Youth Project, highly respected in funding circles, would be the fiscal sponsor. The Karen Silkwood Fund would have its own set of accounting books. The IRS would be happy. So would the donors. Sara would be the coordinator; Anne Zill, a veteran of fund-raising campaigns, would be the liaison to the foundations. And Alison Freeman, an organizer from such events as "Sun Day" and "Earth Day," was coming aboard to do half the work.

"It's truly remarkable," Danny said. It was an observation and compliment both.

In the morning Sara had trouble pulling on her jeans. Leaning to touch her toes, she put unusual pressure on her abdomen. It didn't strike Danny as anything significant, though. After a movie, they went to an ice cream parlor and ordered double-dips. Probably Sara was overeating a little, he thought.

"Ikard called," Danny said. "The judge wants us to wrap up the depositions. I have to go back."

"When?"

"Tomorrow. I have to take a deposition in Florida and then get to Texas by Sunday. We've identified the Audio Intelligence salesman who handled the OCPD deal, and we have to serve him notice."

"Isn't that Taylor's job?"

"Have you seen Taylor lately? He's a regular hundred-pound weakling." The joke was meant to take the hurt out of his leaving. "Anyway, Royer will serve the notice. But I want to be there, so I know it's legal and so we can get this guy into court right away."

"Be careful," Sara said.

"Oh, sure." Thinking of the time ahead, Danny suddenly felt a spasm of loneliness. Nothing had been said of the Caribbean vacation, not since that one time. But sometimes Sara would get a faraway look, and it seemed as if she were quietly reminding him. "There'll be a break once the depositions are over," he said. "It'll take the judge a month or so to rule on the rest of the motions. I thought maybe we could go to St. John then. You can get a beach hut there for next to nothing."

Sara smiled, perhaps at the notion that paradise could still be had at a bargain, but she said nothing.

"Tourists don't generally go near St. John," Danny said. "There's no air conditioning, no casinos, no golf courses."

"Water and sun is all I want," Sara said. A vague half-asleep smile glided into her eyes, that faraway look again.

"Great. It's a date, then," Danny said. He hugged her.

They had been walking without direction. At dusk they found themselves with a merry dance step by the Reflecting Pool in front of the Lincoln Memorial. Slowly Sara squeezed Danny's hand. "I have something to tell you," she said. "I've been having trouble coming to grips with this . . . but you and I are going to have a baby." He understood then about the fit of her jeans. "By the doctor's timetable, it would have been that weekend in New York," she said.

Danny did not immediately try to take stock of what a baby would mean. If his times with Sara had given him anything, it was the ability to care about the single moment, even an ordinary moment. Of course, this one was most extraordinary and soon became more so. Words usually spoken much earlier in courtships now tumbled into the open, strained and severe at first, then tender, ecstatic, like water over a cliff, a splurge of joy, spoken freely, eloquent in its foreignness.

FLOWER MOUND, TEXAS. JUNE 11, 1978. Danny met Joe Royer in Dallas; then they drove the hour north. J. W. Hand, the Audio

Intelligence salesman, had a landscaped lawn and a house set back from the street. It was early Sunday afternoon. At the front door Royer tried to talk his way past Hand's wife with a tale about papers to be signed. The woman left the chain latched and went to talk to someone deeper inside. "I'm not accepting any papers," she said on her return. Quickly Royer identified himself and plunged the subpoena through a crack by the chain. She jumped back. "I didn't touch it! You can't say I did!"

"Tell your husband he's been legally served!" Royer shouted tersely, retreating to Danny in the car.

"Let's get out of here," Danny said.

Five minutes or less from the house, Danny heard behind them the swerve of a car in fast pursuit. The rearview mirror revealed an unmarked white car with a red flasher on the dashboard. A headline sprang vividly to Danny's mind of three Northern civil rights workers shot down in 1964 and buried in a shallow Mississippi grave. "Take out your license and the registration," he instructed Royer. "We don't want to be reaching for anything when he stops us." Royer braked onto a lonesome dirt shoulder. They got out slowly, locked the doors, and stood facing their pursuer. The man wore a baseball cap, a soiled T-shirt, jeans, tennis shoes. He looked as if he had been called away from a Little League game, except for the snub-nosed revolver strapped in a hip holster. He declared himself a policeman and asked for Royer's ID.

"Now yours," he said to Danny. Danny kept his hands flat and stubborn at his trouser legs. "I was a passenger in the vehicle. My ID is none of your business," he said—to show he knew the law, and to show he expected conflict and was not intimidated. The cop lowered the bill of his cap against the sun and hooked thumb and index finger in place on his gun. "I'm ordering you."

"And I'm ordering you to tell me why you came chasing after us," Danny said with adamancy—a piece of theatrics he should have forgone.

"Okay, buddy, you're under arrest."

"For what?"

"For refusing to identify yourself and for resisting arrest." Danny raised his arms, a quaint gesture turned serious, and the cop swung him around against the car. His chin hit a chrome edging and his legs opened under a sharp kick. He felt handcuffs close around his wrists.

Royer was yelling. "You can't do this. He's got to be in Oklahoma tomorrow. He's got depositions to take."

"The way I hear it, ain't nobody gonna miss him up there. They don't much appreciate what you're doing, and we don't either."

Two other cops sirened to a stop. "These the two litterbugs?" the fat one asked, indicating Danny and Royer in a jest that filled his cheeks. He had with him a paper folded lengthwise. Danny recognized the subpoena last seen vanishing into the foyer of the Audio Intelligence salesman. The cop placed it on Royer's palm with a small cunning look. "I believe you fellas dropped this."

At the local jail Danny was fingerprinted, his mug shot taken. He had to give up his wooden cross and his belt. "No Sunday arraignments," the desk sergeant said. "You get your turn after the drunks in the morning."

Danny's cell was old, stained with rust and vomit. A green crust of bread was on the floor, and cockroaches. An iron bed rack flopped down on loose hinges from a cement wall. There was no mattress. Danny wiped the fingerprinting smudges off and lay down to read. In the morning, after sleeping fully dressed, he arranged himself on the floor in his usual meditative pose. He put his palms together, fingers linked, as if still manacled. "Rise and shine." A turnkey banged a truncheon on the bars, and somewhere a drunk began a woeful prayer. A plate of watery oatmeal slid into Danny's cell. "Eat up. It's jail rules." But the breakfast stayed on the damp floor; Danny too. After two hours, when the unfocused look had not left his face, his keepers grew angry and slightly alarmed. They let him make a second phone call.

It went to the office of Judge Theis in Wichita. The idea had come to him on the floor. Whether or not his arrest had been a set-up to disrupt his schedule, that had been the effect, for which he deserved compensation. Maybe overcompensation, if Judge Theis could be persuaded. With a little more time, a few months, Taylor might be able to identify more of Reading's boys. Sara would understand, Danny thought—we could postpone St. John to late summer.

The judge's clerk accepted the call and listened to the events that had befallen Danny—arrested without just cause, interfered with in the service of a federal subpoena, thrown in jail, denied arraignment. "I'll tell Judge Theis," the clerk said.

On Monday afternoon Danny was ushered before the local magistrate. Onlookers took notice from the gallery; a few had pencils ready. Taylor and Father Bill had called Texas newspapers, the Dallas archdiocese, everyone they knew in high authority. They wanted it known that Danny was in jail, to put the jailkeepers on notice, to lessen the chance of Danny's getting laid out by random violence. It took three days before the phony arrest was gaveled out of court, and Danny went back to Oklahoma City with a big hole in his schedule.

The attempt to wheedle more time out of Judge Theis, however, was a failure, and so the pretrial discovery phase was essentially at an end. It was bad luck that Danny had missed out on a few final depositions.

But one very enlightening deposition had already been taken, that of Roy King, the former personnel director, now retired. King had been a changed man since Karen's death. One night, shortly after it happened, King woke up feeling cold and a little dizzy. It was winter, the windows were closed, and he could smell gas. A gas-company repairman came and checked, even taking the meter apart. Apparently someone had crept in, turned off the gas in the heater, waited till the pilot light went dead, then turned the gas back on. Apparently someone had tried to kill King. It might not have had anything to do with Karen's death, King thought; and then again, it might.

King had gone to the Guthrie Hospital to identify Karen's body the night of the accident. "Then I called her family long distance," he said, "and then I went by the police station."

"What happened at the police station?" Danny asked.

"A highway patrolman made a comment," King said. "He said, 'There's a lot of things in her car that have Kerr-McGee insignia on them.' "

"Anything else?"

"The patrolman told me, 'I would like for you to join with me tomorrow and we will go down there and get those things.' Well, the next morning, about the time he was supposed to be coming and getting me, the patrolman showed up. And he said, 'Well, somebody has already got those things. So there's no need in us going down there to pick them up.' "

It was not exactly a confession. But fitted in with something Ted Sebring had told Father Bill, it was the most revealing word yet on the fate of the documents.

"Do you know if any Kerr-McGee people went to Sebring's garage after the car had been taken there?" Danny asked.

"I don't know anything about that."

"Do you know if any Kerr-McGee people went to the garage and took Karen's documents?"

"I don't know if it was *our* people who took them out of there. I don't know."

Danny had a chart that tracked the day-by-day movements of Karen, Drew, Reading, everyone through the fall of 1974. From November 5 to November 14 it was an hour-by-hour progress—to which he had added these new furtive facts.

MINNEAPOLIS. JUNE 25, 1978. As Bob immediately divined, the Health Physics Society had constructed an ambush for Dr. Mancuso. The panel was stacked with industry scientists, their fear of his findings concealed beneath sarcasm. When Dr. Mancuso tried to defend himself, the moderator told him to wait his turn. When it came, the moderator cut him off because his remarks were "too political." Dr. Mancuso was in shock, discomposed, realizing he had been lured here to be brought into line. He shouted, hands shaking, then was quiet. Bob could feel the other guests and members settling down, like bullfight fans after the banderillas are in place. Suddenly Bob grabbed a microphone and began reading a letter from Congressman Rogers that told how the AEC and its successors had been all for Dr. Mancuso until his study put a lie to the radiation standards. Bob was six sentences into the letter when a man in a Navy uniform wrestled the mike away and shut it off. The scientific discussion ended in near-bedlam.

On the plane ride back east the next morning, Dr. Mancuso was in curiously high spirits. He was a scientist transformed, no longer the timid hermit alone with his numbers and graphs. In his archives it had been easy to believe in the pure neutrality of science. With the destruction of that myth, he had become a fighter. Yesterday had been a catharsis. He had gone through the fire and had not recanted. He had shouted at them, stood his ground. Oblivious to the airline's free eye-openers, Dr. Mancuso was musing aloud. "Only a half-century ago the book-burners were still burning science texts—Scopes lost, remember. But the way scientists are today, they're no better than the book-burners. Science, it's the new religion. All these scientists, they're trying to be high priests. They're the men of purity. Not the purity of what the numbers show, but the purity of blind faith."

"At least we left them arguing among themselves." Bob gave up on a catnap. "I can almost feel sorry for some of them, having to face up to the fact that thousands of workers may die because of their standards. It's a heavy burden."

"Yes, but they knew all along radiation could cause cancer. They were even hypocritical in the way they set the standards—one for workers, another one for the public. A worker can be legally dosed with five times as much as a regular citizen. Why? A worker isn't five times more immune."

"The difference is the profit margin," Bob said.

"That's right. They set standards at a point where the industry could make a profit." Dr. Mancuso was trying to adjust his seatback. "I used to think it was unprofessional to speak out against fellow scientists. Not any more."

It was an opening for Bob to fulfill a promise to Danny. "Would you be willing to go to Oklahoma?" Bob asked. "To testify at the Silkwood trial?"

"I don't see why not." The jetliner had found a bay of blue in the white froth; a brilliant sun sprayed onto their laps. "Before I met you, I would have said a courtroom is not the right forum for a scientist. But I thought that about Congress and look what happened." Congressman Rogers had taken it on himself to help get money for Dr. Mancuso's study. He was in league with Bob, EPC, the United Auto Workers, the United Mine Workers, the OCAW, the steel workers' union, the machinists' union, and the AFL-CIO's health-and-safety-committee. For the hard-hats it was an act unheard of; in the past they had exempted the nuclear industry from construction strikes. Winning over the union men had been a real coup. Bob had gotten their attention with tough talk: "Are there quotas in your contracts? Are twenty-five or fifty workers allowed to die for each reactor?"

Even Wodka had been impressed. Bob had run into him one day on the Hill, where Wodka was testifying about nuclear safety. Wodka had become the most respected and radical of the environmental-unionists in D.C., as even Kitty had to acknowledge.

"See you at the trial," Bob had said.

Wodka had stopped in mid-stride. "Yeah, see you . . ." His hand was awkward at his side. "Strange to think of going back. I haven't been there in three years, but it's like it was yesterday."

ST. JOHN, VIRGIN ISLANDS. JULY 31, 1978. The first three days were just to slow down. Danny and Sara couldn't believe they were really here. Basking in the sand. Floating on the waves. Snorkeling. They lived with their bodies and let their minds go free. It seemed the natural state of the climate. They couldn't remember ever being happier. Sara turned a golden ruddy color. Danny turned red.

"You're getting fat." He was rubbing her belly.

"I'm catching up to you." She laughed.

"Have you thought of any names yet?"

"That's your job. Fair is fair."

LOUISVILLE, KENTUCKY. AUGUST 15, 1978. Into the terrible heat they came, in old vans with fat smooth tires, in microbuses and cars, on the luck of their thumbs. As they signed in at the University of Kentucky campus, Kitty was surprised and gratified; all three hundred delegates had made it to the first national convention of the anti-nuclear movement.

From the nostalgic headbands and knapsacks, many looked as if they had been part of the loyal opposition since anti-war days. But others mingling with them were definitely new to the Movement. Kitty, a victim of her own past narrowness, had reached for diversity in inviting the delegates: the former Alabama assistant attorney general; the dying Army sergeant who had seen the bones in his fingers at a Nevada atomic test; the Navajo miner who had won medals in Vietnam. Ilene Younghein had to stay at home in obedience to her doctor—her health had suffered in a long as-yet-unsuccessful effort against the Black Fox reactor outside Tulsa—but her colleague Ann Funnell was here. From Minnesota a farmer had driven down in a running-board pickup. Up north the utility companies had crisscrossed the land with megawatt power lines. You could hear the electricity crackle and feel it like a heavy tingle. It was electromagnetic radiation, and it was scaring cows to death, killing them with heart attacks. Some farmers had become midnight raiders, toppling the towers with bolt-cutters. An undercover agent had infiltrated their group, posing as a reporter, but the farmers had found him out and left him to walk barefoot out of a frozen swamp.

Jeanine Honicker arrived from Nashville. She was the wife of Dolph Honicker, the *Tennessean* editor the FBI had spied on. She had just filed a federal lawsuit to have nuclear power, all forms of it, declared a menace to the public safety. It made no difference that the suit stood zero chance of success.

Bob and Kitty had come through Appalachian coal country in their decrepit station wagon, its rear door plastered with bumper stickers. Amber came with them. But Shawn, at an age for wanting to know his real father, was in Oregon this summer. When in his last letter he had asked to stay on with his dad, Kitty had heard a sound in her heart like the quiet at the end of dance music. Shawn had been all she had in those years before Bob and Amber. How could she give him up? Not that his father, her ex-husband, was in any way unfit. Once he had even seemed perfect—outgoing, handsome, an Air Force MP—in every way acceptable to her parents except that he was black. When they excluded him from the family Christmas her junior year in college, Kitty had flounced from the house, driven back to campus in a snowstorm, cashed her scholarship check, and eloped. The marriage had ended in Oregon. But he had married again, and for Shawn there were half-brothers and half-sisters. It might be best for Shawn to stay, she thought, realizing with horror what Karen must have gone through. You gave up a part of yourself more alive than your hands or legs when you gave up your kids. You needed an awful courage. The Movement could never fill the void if she lost her son.

But Kitty had no time to dwell on it in the whirligig of the convention.

WASHINGTON. SEPTEMBER 10, 1978. The voice from the grave said, "Steve, we have eighteen- and nineteen-year-old boys who didn't get any schooling, so they don't understand what radiation is." The voice grew simultaneously softer and higher. "They don't understand, Steve! They don't understand!"

Wodka turned off the Sony. "I wish now I'd recorded all of our conversations," he said. "At this point," Danny said, "we don't know if the judge will let it in as a trial exhibit. But we have to get everything ready. Ikard and Father Bill are wading through the files for the umpteenth time."

"Well, it's all yours." Wodka lifted the tape out of the machine.

It contained forty-five minutes of conversation: the phone call from Karen of October 7, 1974. Made at evening rates, it had cost her $14.10.

Sara played the tape several times in the Arrupe attic to decipher all the words. She got so she had every lilt of Karen's voice memorized, the screech, the profanity, the anger, the melancholy—she got to know the pace of syllables like a guitar beat: where Karen's throat was taut, where she swallowed, where asthma choked her breath. The posthumous Karen, the mystical soul of the lawsuit, became more human with each spin of the magnetic coil. A lot of the tape was technical slang, and after all this time, not much was a surprise. There were expressions of faith in the future and even a show of swashbuckling. "Kerr-McGee's scared of a strike!" This was from the first week of Karen's plunge into subterfuge, when she still felt enchanted and unassailable. She talked about the photomicrographs in her folder, talking with a cheer that would have echoed in any eavesdropper's ears.

Just before she hung up, Karen had mentioned a public hearing scheduled for the next day at the State Capitol. It involved the Black Fox nuclear reactor near Tulsa. Representative Thomas Bamberger was inviting people to come and give their opinions. "I think one of us ought to go over there," Karen had said. "Somebody's got to tell them they better hold off on that shit!"

Sara heard the severity in Karen's voice, and she could imagine fingers jabbing the air. So Kitty had been right. In the last month of Karen's life she had been ready to join the Movement. *They better hold off on that shit!*

Sara thought she should play the tape for Kitty.

"I didn't know you two were on speaking terms again," Danny said.

"That old stuff is over with," Sara said. But it wasn't. Out of affection for their damaged friendship Sara had tried to mend it. Kitty had acted warm, and happy for Sara's six-month belly, but it was surface warmth. Holding a grudge was Kitty's nature, part of the obsessiveness that was also her best virtue. It might lead her to accomplish great things, if it did not first destroy her.

But now the voice on the tape had stirred in Sara a vague yearning to visit Butternut, to sit again with Kitty on the ivory-gray couch so they could buck each other up about how this would all turn out.

"Just make sure she doesn't give the tape to some anti-nuke radio station," Danny grumped. "That tape is evidence." He did not miss Kitty. True, her verve and advice had been useful, her code and sacrifice were to be admired, and probably there never would have been a Silkwood crusade without her. But this was not a one-person crusade. So many people had given of themselves, no one was indispensable. Not even Sara, who more than anyone had held things together. The crusade had a momentum and life of its own, it seemed. It would go on and on.

Though the lawsuit might not.

Judge Theis was pondering Bill Paul's latest motion to have the suit thrown out. The legal argument involved the Civil Rights Act of 1871, on which two of the three counts were based. Congress had enacted the law after the Civil War in honor of the freed slaves. Over the years it had been a legal resort for many other "classes," even the Democrats whose Watergate offices were bugged. That was the hitch. To use the law, you had to fit into the legal definition of "class." According to Bill Paul's motion, Karen didn't fit. She wasn't a person of color or of an ethnic minority. She was too regular, too average. In Danny's voluminous answer to the motion he had argued the opposite. If being a union organizer in Oklahoma didn't make you part of a minority, then the law was cockeyed.

Still, Danny was having a bad time of it, waiting for the judge's ruling on this final hurdle before trial. He was with his books in the attic when Sara yelled up a week later. Ikard was on the line—his tone was heavy; the worry had been justified. Judge Theis had dismissed Counts One and Two. He had decided, in effect, to kick the legal dispute up to the appellate courts before spending time on a trial that might be disallowed. That made a certain sense. But meanwhile, Olson and Srouji and the others would not be hauled into the dock.

There remained yet Count Three, which had to do with the plutonium in Karen's refrigerator, the negligence tort that Danny had tacked on. It was a tort narrowly defined; it did not begin to address the question of who killed Karen.

"Is there a way to expand it to get in some of the other evidence?" Sara asked, bear-hugging him, trying to nuzzle him into a smile.

"We can try," Danny said without his usual gleam. She saw in his slack hands that it was possible for him to fall into pessimism. He explained, "Count Three could get dismissed too. The judge left the door open for Bill Paul to file against it. Which he's sure to do. It'll be another month or two before we know whether there'll be any trial at all." After the judge's earlier vow to get at the truth, this seemed like a betrayal. Danny's face was white. He felt hot. He went outside with Sara and stood under a tree. "The CIA has been reformed, isn't that what we've been told?" he said into a luminous sky. "The Rockefeller Commission, the Church Committee, the Pike Committee, they reformed it. What a crock! Anytime the CIA doesn't want a case prosecuted the case doesn't get prosecuted. Justice be damned! Same as always—nothing's changed." They walked in an oblong path. The crush of tall grass under their feet was oddly comforting.

They came again to the tree. The day was dying on the horizon like the death of an old year. Sara could feel their work dying too; she felt it as a dream. All this time, she thought with a pang, we've been creatures in a labyrinth: induced past endless corners, sent dashing toward false openings, led on, doubled back, fooled again, turned around till every direction was the same, perhaps brought at last to this final dead end.

NEDERLAND. NOVEMBER 2, 1978. Although the great oil smell still hung in the air, change had come to the town where Karen grew up —those scuffed, dirty streets had been paved with boiling tar, the bogs mostly drained, mosquitoes placed under control, fast-food vanes erected, the population doubled—changes had happened gradually.

But the changes at Bill Silkwood's little green house were as recent as last month. And about time, some neighbors said. They were tired of the disheveled foliage and peeling paint, and a little tired of the man himself, a man who once had been so polite and reserved, never aggressive or tiresome about his war record or his children's school grades, a man who now talked ceaselessly about his poor dead girl and that damn-fool lawsuit. Why, the way the neighbors heard it, those lawyers had even brought in a psychic. (In fact, there had been more than one. None of them had turned up new leads, though they gave intriguing accounts of the car crash. A Houston psychic had an impression of two men, one of a swarthy complexion, ramming a long ponderous vehicle into Karen's car, forcing it into the culvert. But the impact of the wingwall hadn't killed her. A hammer blow on the head had, as she threw up a defenseless arm.) This sort of voodoo did not sit well in Nederland. Folks here had absorbed heartbreaks in their own lives, as a river absorbs a rainstorm, and gone on with their lives, like the river. At the football stadium and other gathering spots, a suspicion ran that Mr. Silkwood's head had been turned by the hope of a big-money settlement. They did not know that he was of no mind to settle for a cashier's check and that, in any event, all money would go to three grandchildren he barely knew.

It was when the lawsuit appeared completely lost, however, that the neighbors saw and heard the change. One day part of the green roof was ripped away, then the gray one over the garage. The wall between was knocked down, doubling the size of the living room. A row of pine angle-rafters rose up, and over them a spiffy one-color roof. In the vast new space he had created, Mr. Silkwood put in paneling, maplewood shelves, a brick fireplace, kitchen counters, a built-in oven, brand-new furniture. As the fourth anniversary of Karen's death approached, as the backyard mums shriveled under the cold and Frito huddled in her cage, Mr. Silkwood was working again, doing something that was in no way connected with the lawsuit.

He kept at it even after Danny informed him Count Three might yet be salvaged. Danny and Father Bill were in town with an update. In a curious twist it seemed that the price for getting Count Three to trial would be removing Bill Meadows as the co-plaintiff. Counts One and Two, as civil rights actions, had belonged in federal court, but it could be argued that the proper jurisdiction for Count Three was an Oklahoma state court. That was the gist of Bill Paul's latest motion on behalf of Kerr-McGee. The judge had given Danny thirty days to respond, and his response was to ask Meadows to drop off so the litigants would be Bill Silkwood of Texas and Kerr-McGee of Oklahoma. By splitting the jurisdiction between two states, Danny hoped to keep the case in federal court. How Judge Theis would react to this sleight-of-hand was anybody's guess.

"It's up to him," Danny said. "It could go either way."

Danny's other reason for coming was to tell the family of a big rally planned for Karen Silkwood Memorial Day at Robert Kerr Park. What better place to have it than right across the street from Kerr-McGee world headquarters? While talking, it occurred to Danny that if Dean McGee had moved the headquarters to Houston, as the board of directors had once wanted, Mr. Silkwood would be having to quit the suit so it could be Bill Meadows of Oklahoma versus Kerr-McGee of Texas.

"You can tell Sara—I assume she's organizing this rally—that I'll be there," Mr. Silkwood said. "But only for the day. I got work to do here."

And, he thought, work to do at his cabin. The last improvement had been the outdoor shower stall years ago. Karen had used it once, that Thanksgiving weekend in 1973, her last time at home. After the turkey dinner and the shopping, Karen had asked impulsively to go with him to his private world. He understood it, or chose to understand it, as her way of reaching out after the years of that marriage which had separated them. He remembered every hour of the visit: their walk in the woods; the wild grapes going brown, drooping like forgotten holiday ornaments; the heady, wine smell; the corn they put out for the deer and coons. He had never seen her alive again.

Now the cabin needed fixing—new screens, windowpanes, locks, paint. Vandals had gotten in; and insects, rain, rot, doomed memories.

SAN FRANCISCO. NOVEMBER 18, 1978. The plane dropped low over the city, revealing nothing but fog, and Danny instantly regretted giving up his chance for a weekend in the tropics. Right now he could have been landing in South America. Congressman Leo Ryan's party had invited him along to look after the First Amendment rights of the cult members who had followed the Reverend Jim Jones to Guyana. He had been tempted to go for the diversion. Instead, Sara had insisted he come with her to a series of West Coast fundraisers and political rallies.

Danny's speech four days ago in Robert Kerr Park had gone well. The sizable crowd, young and curious, had clapped and saluted. He had spotted Bill Paul, trying to stay inconspicuous among the lifted fists, and had interrupted himself, like a Vegas performer, to introduce and chide his opponent, much to everyone else's delight. Certain members of the SOS chapter, having located Dean McGee's address, had driven out after the rally to see the Old Man. They had left a selection of newsletters on his doorstep. He lived in a pale modern house, unfenced, exposed to public view. Not really palatial, it was, however, the alluring sort that factory workers might wish they could afford, not realizing how much they had paid toward this one.

In San Francisco the rally had been organized locally by NOW and the anti-nuclear Abalone Alliance. The stage was a flatbed truck. In a cold, weeping fog Danny and Sara spoke to the black tops of umbrellas. They needed no text for the words, gone over many times before, but they were thrown off a little by listeners who had radios rudely to their ears. A football game? Rock music?

No, most were tuned to all-news KCBS. Late on the previous day, five of Congressman Ryan's party, including Ryan himself, had been gunned down in Guyana, and there were rumors of more deaths, mass deaths. Danny and Sara received the news numbly.

From San Francisco they traveled south to try to talk to Norman Lear, Ed Asner, Burt Lancaster, other celebrities not yet tapped. If Count Three did reach trial, there would be bills galore for witness fees, restaurants, motels, phones. But Sara had underestimated how long it would take to get themselves placed on Hollywood schedules; three days quickly grew into a week. Suddenly her baby was due in fifteen days.

"The airlines aren't gonna let you back on the plane," Danny worried.

"We have to see Jane Fonda's people tomorrow, and I have to thank Bonnie Raitt and Jackson Browne again for their concerts; then we can go. I'm feeling fine, really. The baby only kicks when I'm lying down."

Sara was sincerely unconcerned, which made Danny be more protective. "Your doctor's on the other side of the country, and no matter how good you feel, you're thirty-six years old. I'm taking you home."

They stayed another eleven days, through the first week of December. Promises of money had begun to spring forth, perhaps because of the season. At Los Angeles International Airport, it took Sara's best smile and a bulky, shapeless overcoat to get herself past the check-in clerks.

In D.C. four days later, December 12, with a tape of Baghavad Gita playing on a portable recorder, the baby was born: a boy. Decidedly awestruck, Danny stayed through the whole thing. At Arrupe, friends welcomed them home with a bassinette, diapers, and a birthday cake for the baby. Sara's mother flew in from Phoenix and went immediately to a department store, where she filled Sara's old Plymouth with baby things and a color TV for the household. She returned to find Danny holding the baby. Sara, one day out of the delivery room, was already back on the phone, trying to pin down the promises of Hollywood to exact figures.

Two phone calls in the morning had renewed her, buoyed her.

One, from Kitty, contained congratulations and an invitation to come by Butternut next week for Amber's birthday. The other, from Ikard, was full of even louder exclamations. "Get your bags packed again! That little kid's gonna be an Okie for the next few months," Ikard had trumpeted over the line. "The judge just made his decision. Merry Christmas! We're going to trial!"

PART FOUR

PART FOUR

Nineteen

This was a determined Danny, determined to have it his way, but not for himself. He said, "It'll be hard enough to get the jury to accept Karen. Believe me, a loudmouth like me will only make it worse."

"But this is your case. You put it together. I know you want to do it."

"Of course I want to do it. I'd like nothing better than to go head to head with Bill Paul."

"And I'm supposed to help deprive you of the chance?"

"Sara, I can't let you change my mind." He knew her disappointment was for him, but his tone was accusatory. "I told you before: I take cases to win them. And Spence can win this for us. He's the old pro. The jury will have confidence in him."

Sara was stacking plates and saucers and bowls in a moldering cupboard, china borrowed from the Corpus Christi rectory. The apartment was new—well, it wasn't really new; it had cracked windowpanes and a rag of a carpet—but they had rented it just yesterday. Sara and Danny had moved to Oklahoma City for the duration of the trial. "I just can't believe that you, of all people, think we should pay Spence fifty thousand to do it," she said. "Fifty thousand!"

"Okay, sure, it's outrageous. From where we sit. But for him it's bargain-basement. Usually he takes half of whatever the jury awards. *Half,* which in this case could be five million or more, since we upped the damages to eleven-point-five. Fifty grand is one percent of his regular cut—if you want to look at it that way."

Sara picked up more plates. "I don't know. The strategy may be right, but the money seems wrong. Why should one person get paid when everyone else is working pro bono?"

"This is real life now."

"All right. In real life fifty thousand is a lot more money than I can get out of Hollywood."

"What about the Youth Project? Can't we get another advance through them?"

Sara sighed and put her arms around Danny. "I'll ask. I'll try my best."

Asleep in the bedroom was little Danny-Paul, not yet a month old. He had been christened at a Mass back in D.C. For all practical purposes, if not legally, Sara and Danny were married. But Sara was still Sara Nelson and Danny was Danny Sheehan, which had made the baby's last name a matter of some discussion. Finally they had hit upon a plan. A baby boy would get Sara's last name, a baby girl would get Danny's. So it was Danny-Paul Nelson in the crib.

OKLAHOMA CITY. FEBRUARY 1, 1979. Ikard lobbed a paper ball across the tile and into a corner wastebasket—a shot that he seemed never to miss. He continued down his checklist. "Father Bill has performed one heckuva miracle," he said. "I count fifteen ex-workers who're willing to testify."

It had been up to Ikard to pull together a list of witnesses for Count Three, but he owed a large debt to Father Bill. The priest was so willing to look at snapshot albums or listen to saloon talk or knock a long time on a front door, anything, to get the trust of the men who had once worked with Karen. More names were being added to the list all the time.

"And the expert witnesses are squared away too?" Danny asked.

"Yes. Bob and Kitty were real helpful. Gofman, Mancuso, and the rest are pretty well set. I'll do the formal interviews in the next few weeks and have everything ready for Spence."

Spence was still in Wyoming, busy with another lawsuit. But a different savior in different lawyer's clothes had shown up unexpectedly in Oklahoma a few months back. He was a friend of Stockton's. "My name's Angel," he had said. He was Arthur Angel, and he was traveling cross-country on his way to private practice in California after three brilliant years at Harvard and three more at the Federal Trade Commission. "Stockton said to be sure not to miss Oklahoma," Angel had grinned. "So here I am." He had proved a fast study. Working with Ikard, he had taken the depositions of several Cimarron supervisors, drawing out a picture of a company hell-bent on producing fuel rods over Karen's objections. ("She was weird," said one company man. "She went to all these liberal parties.")

Sandy curls and a boyish intellectual face were Angel's most prominent features. He didn't wear glasses, but it seemed as if he might have in school. He was quietly aggressive; it was no surprise to find out he had been a smart jock like Danny and Ikard—in his case, at Berkeley and Harvard.

Angel had delayed for some months his return to California. What kept him here, as a temporary partner in Ikard's law firm, was not any cause or seduction of the heart. But a legal doctrine. It was called "strict liability." He had helped Ikard research it, and they believed it could be applied with success to the negligence tort. "Strict liability" went back to English common law. Say a lion gets away from a traveling carnival and mauls a farmer. The carnival owner is held strictly liable for the injuries even if he didn't purposely let the beast out of the cage. The owner avoids liability only when the farmer himself is the one who unlocked the cage. The way the law sees it, a lion is different from a dog or a raccoon; a lion is an ultrahazardous possession, imposing a greater responsibility on whoever has it. Plutonium was Kerr-McGee's lion, Karen the farmer.

Other nuclear workers, like the Navajo miners, had never been able to use "strict liability" in their court cases. They were prevented from doing so by the worker's compensation law. But Karen's case was different. She had not been contaminated at her place of work. "The fact that it happened in her apartment: that's the key," Angel said. "And if we win, it'll be a precedent." The chance of setting a precedent was genuine. It so intrigued Angel that he kept testing and retesting the doctrine in his head. "I think it's perfect. I think it really is."

"Almost perfect," Danny said. He did not have to be sold on using the doctrine, but today the three young lawyers were adversaries. They were playacting. They were trying to pick apart one another's logic to prepare for court: a dress rehearsal. "It's perfect, except for two things," Danny went on. "Number one, Bill Paul will say there was no injury to Karen."

"That's exactly what he'll do," Ikard agreed. "He'll try to hide behind the standards. He'll bring in experts to swear the plutonium in Karen's lungs and liver was within the margin of safety."

"It'll be *our* experts against *theirs*," Angel said. "But we have

Gofman and the others—they did the primary studies. They'll testify that Karen had cancer from the moment the plutonium got inside her. What did you figure her dose at? Fifteen or twenty rems?"

"About that," Ikard said. He was the mathematician in the group.

Danny had moved to a position by the wastebasket where he could intercept Ikard's next lob shot. But—whish—the paper ball went in. "Whatever way you guys want to handle the experts is fine by me. What we really have to watch for is Bill Paul's number two line of defense. Which is really big number one. *She did it to herself!* I can just hear him saying it. *Karen the kook—she did it to herself!* Kerr-McGee hasn't deviated from that line. Not once."

"They've dropped the vagina theory, though," Ikard said. Bill Paul, however, had a new theory. He assumed Karen had lied about having a folder of documents. So, to satisfy Wodka and Mazzocchi, she needed something else, and a wild idea had come to her. She would add extra plutonium to her fecal and urine samples; she would spike the bioassay kits that had been part of her routine since her accidents in July. When the samples showed up hot, it would appear another accident was at fault. It would be a trick. Then, at an emotional point in the contract negotiations, she would whip out the fake bioassay report. She would bitch and holler and blame it on the mess at the factory; she would bitch till Kerr-McGee gave in and set up a health-and-safety committee. The way Bill Paul imagined it, Karen had somehow outfoxed the factory sensors and brought some plutonium home. But before she could pull off the trick, it went awry. In her bathroom one of the urine kits was juggled; the concoction spilled and splashed. Later some got on the baloney package when she set it on the toilet back. Some also got on her, and without knowing, she spread it about the apartment. Accidentally, but by her own hand, she had contaminated herself. That was how it had happened, according to Bill Paul.

Danny held his chart, the chronology of November 5, 6, and 7. "That theory fits some of the facts, but not all of them," he said. "The bathroom spill wasn't until the seventh, so it doesn't account for the contaminations on the fifth and sixth."

"Bill Paul may try to say that the fifth and sixth took place at Cimarron like everyone originally thought," Ikard said. "That would mean Cimarron was as messy as Karen said it was. But if he talks fast enough, it may fly."

"Let's give him his due: let's say it does fly. There must be half a dozen other ways we can knock the theory down."

"The baloney. Karen put the baloney back in the fridge. If any urine from her kit had gotten on it, wouldn't she have thrown the baloney away?"

Angel joined in. "Why would she spike her samples at home anyway? Wouldn't she have done it at work? Much safer—why take the risk of smuggling plutonium out of the factory?"

"Good, good." Danny was waving his chart about. "And don't forget the other contaminations. There had already been seventy-odd contaminations at Cimarron. Somebody made this point once before —I guess it was Kitty. Even if Karen had gotten away with her alleged trick, what would it've accomplished? Diddly—that's what. One more contamination! After seventy-odd, who's gonna care? Not the company negotiators. They weren't gonna roll over because of one measly contamination."

Ikard lobbed another paper ball, and Danny almost toppled over trying to block it. Angel had to laugh. He began crumpling up old newspapers too and firing away. A bank shot; a rim shot; then he got the range; whish, whish, ten in a row, he was on a streak. He quit before his luck ran out. "Whew," he said. "Where were we?"

"The bioassay kits," Danny said. He never lost track of a conversation.

"Well," Angel said, "if Bill Paul has an ace, it's the fact that some of Karen's kits were actually spiked. I mean there's no disputing that fact."

"But we can turn that around and use it against him," Ikard said.

"Exactly. Because whoever spiked the kits did it in a way that was bound to be caught. *Insoluble* plutonium was added to the urine kits, and every lab tech out there knew that if you legitimately had plutonium in your urine it'd have to be *soluble* plutonium. So as soon as the kits went to a lab, the spiking was bound to show up. It was gonna get caught."

"The classic setup! Frame her, discredit her, shoot her down!" Danny was yelling. "Better than a gun."

"Here's what I think is the clincher," Danny said. "It's right here in their files." He had spent weeks combing through the Kerr-McGee boxes—anything in them would be evidence of the best sort. "The baloney package was the hottest thing in the apartment. They can't deny it. Their HPs did the counts, using their alpha counters. Four hundred thousand dpms. That's the count. Now, have you ever heard of the mother-lode doctrine? It's the same as when you go prospecting for gold. You've got to find the mother lode, the highest concentration. That's your source. Four hundred thousand dpms, that's the source. Somebody must've put plutonium on the baloney. When Karen set the baloney down in the bathroom, that's how the back of the toilet got contaminated. From the baloney. Not vice versa."

"But why couldn't everything have come from a spill?"

"Because the baloney had four hundred thousand dpms and the toilet only had one hundred thousand. If it was from a spill, the counts should've been identical."

"Karen could have wiped it up off the toilet."

"No. The toilet was covered with one of those fuzzy things. Like a rug. The spill would've soaked in. She couldn't have wiped it up. At least not three hundred thousand dpms." Danny sat back with satisfaction. He cocked his arm. Whish.

"Next question: who put the plutonium on the baloney?" Danny said, answering it himself. "It had to be one of Kerr-McGee's dirty tricksters."

"It could've been some guy Karen wouldn't go to bed with."

"That seems very unlikely. This wasn't done in a fit of passion. Somebody had to get the plutonium out of the factory, sneak it into her apartment, sprinkle it on the baloney. And add the insoluble stuff to her kits. The whole thing was diabolical. A spurned lover wouldn't act like that. He'd shoot first and think later."

"All we have to prove, though, is that Karen didn't do it to herself," Angel said. "That's the main advantage to 'strict liability.' We don't have to give the jury an exact scenario of how it happened."

"But the jury will want something," Danny said, "and we should have something to give them." With his chart Danny had worked out a theory he thought matched up pretty well to the facts. As he had reconstructed it, the three days of contamination were part and parcel of a campaign to get Karen to quit. The baloney was poisoned with an amount of plutonium that was not lethal, just menacing and malicious. On the first morning, the fifth, Karen made a brown-bag supper out of the baloney. She ate it at work shortly before the alpha counter went crazy. Presumably her supper was the source; presumably she got plutonium on her face and hands and inside her when she ate it. She went home clean that night, and the next morning, the sixth, she did not pack a sandwich—it was the first day of negotiations and 5–283 was buying lunch. However, the night before, *after* being cleaned up, she had eaten a midnight snack. The snack was another baloney sandwich. Presumably that accounted for the plutonium on her face and hands when she arrived at work on the sixth. Again, on the morning of the seventh, she did not bring a lunch. But she had carried the baloney package around in contemplation of a sandwich. So when she got to Cimarron she was already contaminated.

Like the other theories, this one was not without its own riddles. Still, Danny was sure this was it, this was a theory that would make sense to a jury.

"But we should concede we can't prove it one hundred percent," Ikard said.

"It's circumstantial, sure. But that doesn't make it less valid. Half the murderers in prison got sent there on circumstantial evidence."

"I'm just saying we shouldn't theorize too much. Mud Springs: isn't that what Spence calls it? 'Don't get bogged down in Mud Springs.'"

Angel cleared his throat. "Everything—in the end—everything is going to boil down to who the jurors believe. Okay, I know it's a truism. But we've got a client, a client who's dead, and we've got to get the jurors to believe her. The defective welds, the safety abuses, all of her allegations—the jurors have to believe she was telling the truth. And that Kerr-McGee has been lying."

"The MUF is critical," Danny said. "It establishes a motive."

"Agreed. Motive is the bottom line."

Danny was on his feet, bouncing on his heels. "If they start to believe Kerr-McGee was involved in smuggling, with or without the CIA, that's it. We've got 'em."

They were almost finished. There was just one more topic to discuss. Ikard broached it. "Did Sara get the fifty grand?"

"Half of it," Danny replied. "We'll have to ask Spence to take twenty-five down and twenty-five at the end of the month." He tried to laugh. "If not, it's you and you and me against the empire."

Not until five days before the start of the trial did they know one way or the other about Spence. It began to seem that Danny had been too optimistic again, this time stupidly. He began to prepare himself. Could he and Ikard and Angel pull it off? Well, why not? Sure they could.

The announcement that Spence would come, however, was absolutely cause for a celebration. Not that there was time for one; briefings of every variety had to be crammed in. Ikard, Angel, and Father Bill made a quick trek to Wyoming with their briefcases full. Danny did not go. It had become apparent that ego, as much as money, was behind Spence's hesitation. Danny had the title of chief counsel and Spence was to be trial counsel. The titles were meant to make them separate but generally equal. During a trial, though, there could not be two leaders with two separate plans on how to proceed.

Spence took a room at the Skirvin Plaza, kitty-corner from the upreaching granite of Kerr-McGee headquarters. There was an edge of winter still in the wind and leftover snow on the ground. Danny and Bill Silkwood were his first visitors. The three of them had a talk. It was important that Spence feel comfortable. The trial might last a long time, two months or more, longer than he had ever spent away from his wife and home. Everyone was cutting corners, but Danny did not even presume to ask Spence to eat in cafeterias or forgo regular calls to Thunderhead. The suggestion would have been ludicrous. The reality was this: there would be no orders given to Spence —not from Danny, not from the collected team. Not only did Danny promise this to Spence, but the next day he told everyone they had to go along.

OKLAHOMA CITY. MARCH 6, 1979. The federal courthouse is a four-story structure. Sculpted by chisels and fine-tooth rasps, the figures of five women—three in prairie bonnets, two in Indian dress—hold hands in the sandstone over a side entrance. The blindfolded woman is elsewhere, holding her scale.

Spence came into the courtroom with his High Noon hat on his head. He had a look right off a horse, a booming down-home manner veiling a keen mind. He stepped to the table closest to the jury, the one normally reserved for the defense lawyers, who were Bill Paul and his six associates. Spence was a master at minor courtroom maneuvers that often count for a lot; he liked to sit next to the jurors and look them in the eye. He wanted that table, and before the Kerr-McGee men realized it, Spence had slapped his Stetson down like a claiming stake. "You've got twice as many guys, so you can have the big table over there, and we'll take this here small table" was how he commandeered it. Bill Paul started to argue, thought better of it, and led his men to the big table farther away.

Ikard and Angel sat in front with Spence. Danny sat in the gallery with Sara and little Danny-Paul. It was Danny's decision to take this back seat; he wouldn't let anyone tell him different. Spence would be in charge in the courtroom.

Suddenly all whispering and squirming ceased. Judge Theis entered and peered down from behind a tall maple barricade. His old eyes were sharp and strong. Tufts of gray-white hair made a crown for a face of lines and ridges. He had once run Democratic politics in Kansas, as chairman of the party, and it was clear he would run this trial. The scrutinizing and haggling over jurors was completed without ceremony in one day. He let the lawyers take part in the *voir dire*, but he made them stick to basic questions. Do you have a prejudice for or against Kerr-McGee? Do you think $11.5 million, the amount being demanded, is outlandish? Have you read newspaper stories about the case? Have you already formed an opinion about Karen Silkwood? Do you think you could render an impartial verdict? Narrowing the panel from thirty-one to twenty, Judge Theis dismissed those who were too frank with their answers and a few others for whom a long trial would have been a hardship. Spence and Bill Paul were allowed five peremptory challenges apiece. Spence removed a legal secretary and four family men. Bill Paul had five women step down, all of them middle-aged; he seemed to be wary of Spence's sex appeal. That left ten jurors, four of them alternates. As a group, they were reasonably well educated. They all had finished high school and some had gone to college. They were from the middle span of society, white and employable. If they had ever been discriminated against, it was not obvious what the cause would have been. One man had a beard, but nicely trimmed, and they all might have worshiped unnoticed at any church in Oklahoma.

The next day, the second day of the trial, was entirely for the lawyers. It was the day for opening statements. Spence spoke first. He made little use of notes, but he did rely on favorite phrases from previous trials. "The law sometimes seems powerful, but really it is a frail institution. The law cannot return those November days to Karen Silkwood; the law cannot remove her terror or her cancer—it cannot change any of that. It has only the little insignificant power of allowing you to give out a money verdict." Spence looked over at the jurors. They looked back with dispassionate regard. "This lawsuit is principally about a young woman who, you will be relieved to discover, wasn't perfect. She had a different life-style. Her views may have shocked you. But at the bottom, Karen Silkwood was a very ordinary woman. By 'ordinary' I don't mean common. I mean she was a plain regular person like you and me. . . . She was trying to make it alone in a lonely world. She was trying to make her life count for something." He inserted longer pauses and several miscellaneous words, then picked up the thread. "This lawsuit is also about Karen's suffering . . . and about some plutonium that escaped from the Kerr-McGee factory. Not just the minuscule amount that got into Karen's apartment and into her food, but somehow there was another forty pounds that got out too. Forty pounds! We will be asking Kerr-McGee, the men in gray, to tell us during the course of the trial how that got away. It may be that we won't get any answers. It may be that all we'll get are accusations against a woman whose lips are sealed by death, who's helpless to defend herself."

It was almost time for lunch when Spence went back to his seat, yielding to Bill Paul. Bowing, Bill Paul approached the judge. There was something in the background he didn't like—something about the gallery, packed with the curious, the media, local SOS members. And Father Gallatin of Corpus Christi. And Mrs. Younghein.

Up at the front, Bill Paul whispered, "Your honor, can you ask Mr. Spence to take Miss Silkwood's children outside? I'm not sure they should hear what I'm going to say."

The kids—Kristi, Michael, and Dawn—were in their Sunday best in the front row. They were with their father, their stepmother, and their grandfather. Danny, the peacemaker, had arranged this tableau to let the jurors see Karen's two families and to make Bill Paul think the distance between them had been bridged. For today it had been.

Judge Theis stroked his chin, weighing Bill Paul's request. He looked a little perturbed, as if he had not expected such trouble so early in the trial. Stroking, sighing, he recessed for lunch and invited all the lawyers into his chambers. It was the practice of Judge Theis to oversee and settle most disagreements out of the presence of jurors or spectators.

While this was going on, Father Bill took Mr. Silkwood and the Meadows family down the street to the informality of Ikard's office. The kids wandered about, eyeing the wall posters of their mother. Michael and Dawn, the two youngest, remembered her only through vague supper talk and Christmas presents from Nederland. But Kristi, now twelve, uttered a cry of recognition. She pointed at Karen's portrait above the slogan *Dead Because She Knew Too Much?* There was a shy bit of boasting—"it doesn't really look like her, the hair's too long"—which revealed only Kristi's better memory. None of the kids exhibited any homesickness for the home that Karen had left. It had been seven years, and anyway, that was a home they could never return to. They seemed to have taken to their warmhearted and enduring stepmother as their real mother. She stood off to one side, awkwardly, over by the photocopier, talking in question marks to Grandpa Silkwood. "How've you been? What's the weather been like in Nederland?"

Bill Meadows had Michael by the hand. "What's gonna happen?" the boy inquired. "Is the judge gonna put somebody in jail?"

Back in chambers, meanwhile, Spence was needling Bill Paul. "If you're ashamed to say your piece in front of the kids, maybe you better not say it at all."

"I'm not ashamed. I'm just trying to extend a courtesy."

Finally, after quite a while of this, the lawyers and jurors and spectators were reassembled, but, by Meadows' choice, without the children or their parents.

Spence's opening statement had been by turns folksy, softly emphatic, sad, angry, deadpan: emotions and tactics called up at will from his repertoire. He had pointed to the other table—Bill Paul and associates had become "the men in gray." By design or coincidence all seven of them were dressed in the same dark color. Spence wore brown, as he would every day, for all the weeks to come.

Now Bill Paul advanced to the lectern. There was a defiant squeak of new shoes. He pushed his glasses to the bridge of his nose and patted the wood. He brushed his sleeves. He smiled. "If my gray suit offends you, I do apologize." He could be folksy too. He laid out his theory of Karen, how she had been desperate because she had no documents. Much of the statement was civil, even genial, and not at all voyeuristic, except for a few euphemisms about Karen's time with Wodka. There was so much geniality you could have gotten the impression Karen had not been evil, just gung-ho. "Karen was go, go, go for the union. It was kind of an obsession with her. It got so it caused trouble in her relationship with Drew Stephens." Suddenly, with clarity and economy, Bill Paul came to the whole of his argument. It wasn't Karen who had been the bad guy; it was Wodka. "That little union local, 5–283, which really mattered to her, which had become her life, was in a life-and-death struggle. Wodka had put her under pressure to produce, and she told him she would. . . . There is the motive."

Bill Paul's manners were a resource, like an inheritance, and he had put them to good use. But before he sat down, he let loose with a soft threat, reminding everyone he could play dirty if he had to. "You heard Mr. Spence talk about the hell Karen must have lived through from November fifth to November thirteenth. Well, it's our duty, distasteful though it may be, to let you know about her hell before then, what her life was like before then. . . . If the facts discredit Karen Silkwood, then it just has to be. If they do, that is your decision, not mine."

In her seat Mrs. Younghein set aside her rug-hooking implements, the latch hook and coarse yarn. She watched as Dr. John Gofman, the first witness, was sworn in. It was his article in *Intellectual Digest* that had started her on the way to this spot, as his book had influenced Kitty.

Dr. Gofman had a *curriculum vitae* that filled three pages: degrees in medicine and nuclear physics, honors, awards, the best credentials. While still in college he had discovered the existence of a certain uranium isotope and had come as close as anyone to a Nobel Prize. He had been an AEC researcher with few peers. But when in 1969 he tried to publish, in the form of an attack, the study he had done on the radiation standards, the AEC had cut off his funds. Now he was the most prominent of all the critics of nuclear power. His was a mission of dissent. Or was it, as Bill Paul tried to picture it, a mission of destruction against those who had rejected him? Was he now a scientist in decline, bitter, prejudiced? A crackpot?

Nothing in the man who took the stand marked him as anything but normal. Dr. Gofman was short, robust, balding, bearded, dressed in gray. He seemed steady and commanding. Stepping from the witness stand to a blackboard, he began a lecture. He became a professor (which was how, at the University of California, he now made his living). From him the jurors learned all they could wish to know about plutonium. It was a lesson in physics and biology, a lesson in a strange new language, a lesson in what it all meant. "To say that a small amount of radiation won't hurt you is an absurd notion. It's the same as saying that if you take the back cover off a Swiss watch and stab it with an ice pick, you'd still expect it to work. Or that you could take a color TV set, surround it with machine guns, shoot away for an hour, and still expect it to work." Dr.

Gofman had a clear, vivid way of teaching. The judge even came down from his place at the bench and sat next to the jury box with its better view of the blackboard.

Spence had referred a few times to Dr. Gofman as the "Father of Plutonium." Now he asked for an explanation. Dr. Gofman reflected a moment, as if he had forgotten why. He leaned back. "I was at the University of California in 1943," he said, "when I got a visit." It was from Dr. Oppenheimer himself, the bomb doctor. He was in a great tizzy. They needed a quantity of plutonium at Los Alamos—not much, but enough to be seen and handled in the bomb labs. At that time plutonium's existence was known, but no one had seen it, except as an invisible glow of alpha particles. Gofman had figured out two ways to separate the minute particles of plutonium from uranium, and had patented both, but he had never put them to a real test. For country and flag, he was asked to try. Revving up a primitive cyclotron, and his nerve—this was in the realm of unknown danger—Dr. Gofman had sizzled a ton of uranium salt for three weeks and obtained for the War Department a spot of pure liquid plutonium, the size of a teardrop. It was a part of his past he did not advertise.

"Are you ashamed of it?" Spence asked.

"No, I have no apologies whatever for my work. We were at war. We were dealing with an enemy without morals." The risk was worthwhile then, he said, and to a certain extent, it still is. But it's a risk that should be taken by soldiers, and scientists, who are told in advance their lives are at risk.

"Be more specific," Spence said.

Dr. Gofman fell silent and considered his reply. "The license to give out doses of plutonium," he said, "is a legalized permit to murder."

Spence raised his eyebrows. "At what level does radiation kill?" he asked. "Was Karen in danger of dying from the plutonium inside her?"

"Yes, she was. The amount that was found inside her was more than enough to cause lung cancer in a person of her size and her sex and with her smoking habit. It was one-point-three times more than enough. Once the alpha particles hit her cells, she was unequivocally married to lung cancer from that day forward."

There was a recess, and then the cross-examination began. Bill Paul gave the task to one of his associates, Elliott Fenton. Fenton had to try to make the "Father of Plutonium" seem human again. Or, at least, make him seem like an outsider. Wasn't that what he was? A scientist on the fringe?

Not nearly as much as he had been, Dr. Gofman said. The data and analyses of Drs. Mancuso, Bross, Stewart, and others affirmed what he had predicted. The standards were falling into disrepute. "They were never more than thin air and guessing to start with."

The stronger the declaration, the calmer Dr. Gofman's manner, and the more upset Bill Paul looked. In the margin notes of watching reporters Dr. Gofman emerged as an "American patriot" and the "last of the great individualists." But whether the jury, in its expressionless vigil, was of the same mind, no one knew.

Bob had taken a leave from the EPC. Kitty, only her senior thesis away from graduation, had done the same from Antioch. They flew to Oklahoma City with Amber (Shawn having moved in more or less permanently with his father), and set up housekeeping in a duplex three minutes by foot from Sara and Danny's apartment. There was a reunion, a merry scene. Bob and Danny cooked. Kitty and Sara caught up on the news. Away from D.C., it began to seem as if the break between them had never happened.

The original SOS leaders were all now in Oklahoma, or almost all. Only Wodka was missing.

But the big news was Dr. Karl Morgan's arrival. As much as Dr. Gofman, he was a nuclear father, the "Father of Health Physics." For thirty years Dr. Morgan had been the AEC's foremost HP. The Health Physics Society was, in large part, his creation. Although he had been on the panel in Minneapolis that treated Dr. Mancuso so badly, he had stood out from the others by his courtesy and his support, and he had been active in the effort to get Dr. Mancuso's grant restored.

Dr. Morgan was by no means naive about censorship. One time, twenty-four hours before he was to address a symposium in Nuremberg, Germany, his superiors at the AEC had destroyed all two hundred copies of his speech. They had ordered him to read a speech that did not make any criticisms of the fast-breeder, however mild. And he did have criticisms. The fast-breeder was now five years overdue, and it had exceeded its budget by $800 million. Even so, Dr. Morgan believed that nuclear power might still be made safe someday. In the overall debate he was nonpartisan. Kitty explained this to Spence. "That's fine," Spence said, "as long as he's on our side tomorrow."

Dr. Morgan was a towering, furrowed, authoritative figure. He had agreed to testify because of Bob and Stockton, whom he knew and respected, and because of the files. He had read them. The history they described, the spills, leaks, dirty respirators, had made him sick. "The operation at Cimarron was callous, almost cruel," he testified. "It was like sending someone into a lion's cage and not telling them there were animals inside." Strong stuff, for a nonpartisan.

Spence asked about the radiation standards. They were the work of a prudent scientific establishment, Dr. Morgan said. He had been a member of that establishment, and not just a member, but one of the very men who decided the standards. It was a time of ignorance, he said. So much more is known now. There is a radical need to update the standards. All radiation standards should be cut in half, at a minimum. Plutonium-239, however, is so hazardous that the dose standards for it should be reduced 480 times.

Bill Paul rose for cross-examination. He was circumspect; he asked permission to repeat the question. Had Dr. Morgan misspoken? Had he meant to say *four-hundred-eighty* times too lax?

In this way he was made to repeat the answer five or six times, and no one on the jury was able to miss it. Spence, Ikard, Angel, Danny, Bob, Kitty—all beamed. After Dr. Morgan's testimony, Spence decided, there was no need to bring in Dr. Mancuso or any of the other scientists.

Jim Smith was having second thoughts, and third and fourth ones. While most Cimarron workers were happy to be out of the nuclear business, Smith was looking to get back in. And while most had been hourly men, Smith had been a supervisor with a top salary. He had supervised the "wet end." By coming to the witness stand, he would make himself into the only member of management to testify against Kerr-McGee. But he came anyway, in from his stall at the Old Paris Flea Market. He threw wisecracks at worried friends who figured this would blacklist him for all time. Pride was important to Smith. In Korea he had been given the Bronze Star for hiking miles through swamps, hurt and starving, to save a buddy and himself. And he was proud of his seventeen years with the Pentagon at Rocky Flats. But coming here was a matter of pride too. Lounging about the hallway, waiting to take the stand, he talked to reporters. "I'm not here to win any medals. But a man has a duty to tell what he saw. A right, too. I ain't gonna keep quiet. There's been too much of that already."

From his appearance Smith was every inch a prairiebilly—strong, not easily exhausted by work, neck red-burnt.

Yes, he had known Karen, he testified, and he knew *of* her even more. She might have been a conventional person someplace else, but not at Cimarron. She was an emblem of disloyalty and revolution. Her idea of reform was to scrap all of the gloveboxes and most of the fuel rods and start over. It was difficult as well as infuriating to talk with her. *But*—but she had been right, Smith testified. Shoddiness and shortcuts and profiteering were everywhere in the factory. Karen's list for the AEC had been true in spades. One time, Smith said, he had to buy a hundred gallons of white paint to brush over the walls. The walls were cinderblock, full of crevices, in which plutonium had gotten lodged. The paint was to seal it in. But paint is not very permanent, and before long, thousands of tiny flakes, embedded with plutonium, were in the air. Also, behind the factory, on nine hundred acres, there were waste ponds for low-level debris. Ducks and migrating geese would swim and cavort in the ponds, enchanted in their ignorance. And runoff from the ponds once got into the Cimarron River. Whitening and distended, sand bass were washed ashore. A company crew had to take shovels and dig cemetery craters for hundreds of dead fish.

Smith was on the stand three days, all told. He had a lot to tell.

The "surprise" inspections of the AEC were a sham, he said. He and the other supervisors knew of them in advance. Morgan Moore, the Cimarron manager, passed the word to them and they passed it to the workers. In that way a considerable number of violations were kept from the AEC. In addition, there was the incident of April 1972. Two maintenance men had been repairing a pump when a gasket seal ruptured above them. A plutonium mist had rained down. But the two men left for lunch, a meal they ate that day at the Hub Cafe, and all through the beef stew and corn bread, they had no idea their hands, hair, and clothes were hot, no idea at all until they got back to Cimarron. But no HPs were sent to the Hub Cafe, even though, by law, there should have been an all-out cleanup: the stools, napkin holders, salad bar, toothpick jar, everything. No one was notified, not even the AEC. "Management didn't want to risk a public panic," Smith said. The AEC inspectors did find out, but not for more than a year and not from Kerr-McGee. It was told by Mister Anonymous to Mrs. Younghein and reported by her to the AEC.

Surprise and anger were heard in the gallery. But for all the headlines Smith gave out, the journalists were so far a little disappointed. There had been a big buildup—Danny had hinted that Smith would testify to something dynamite—and finally MUF was introduced, the call letters of excitement.

"Did Kerr-McGee tell you what the final MUF figure was when the factory closed in 1975?" Spence asked.

"No," Smith replied, "which was unusual in itself, because I was the one doing the cleanup. I made sure the pipes were flushed out. I don't know how many times we ran boiling nitric through. We tried to get every last gram of plutonium."

"How much was left in the pipes when you finished?" Spence asked.

"On our last flush-through we got three grams, which is way less than an ounce."

"So if a Kerr-McGee witness gets up here and tells the jury that forty pounds is still in the pipes, why, he wouldn't be telling the truth, would he?"

"Let me put it this way," Smith said, "if there's forty pounds still at Cimarron, I don't know where it is."

During a recess the hallways in the courthouse were noisy and crowded: people hanging out by the drinking fountains, reporters lined up for the pay phones, Spence pulled into strategy huddles. The Kerr-McGee men liked to scout around for an empty room to get away from the mill. But today the extra rooms were full of jurors from other trials. Bill Paul and associates had to stand in the halls. They were trying to be closemouthed, but by leaning, reporters could pick up bits of the conversation. Put with the additional wisdom of the usual anonymous sources, the result was a reasonably good insight into how Bill Paul thought the trial was going.

It appeared inside the courtroom that Dr. Gofman and Dr. Morgan and Jim Smith were shaming Kerr-McGee. The newspaper headlines had been rude as well. NUCLEAR EXPERT TESTIFIES SILK-WOOD CANCER CERTAIN. STANDARDS CALLED "MEAN-

INGLESS." WITNESS SPOOFS NUCLEAR SECURITY. HEALTH EXPERT BLASTS KERR-McGEE. But Bill Paul was not overly dismayed. The jurors were pledged on their honor not to read the papers or watch the TV news, and regardless, Bill Paul put a lot of stock in the fact that his witnesses would have the last say, weeks from now. By then the jurors might well have trouble recalling how Spence's witnesses had looked or what they had said. No, Bill Paul was not dismayed.

Dr. Gofman had testified that Karen was infected with lung cancer. But Dr. George Voelz, the health director at Los Alamos, an up-to-date government HP, would be here later to say it was hooey. As for Dr. Morgan, who had labeled Cimarron unfit to work in, there would be Gerald Phillip, the kindly AEC inspector, to testify that the factory was no worse than any other nuclear facility. And Jim Smith's testimony about the pipes' being flushed out? Well, that was testimony in a vacuum. There was no confirmation of a forty-pound MUF—Smith admitted he hadn't been privileged with the figure. Whatever Spence said about the MUF wasn't evidence; he had to get a witness to testify to it. And he had to prove that Karen had known about it. That was the ultimate proof. But failing that, where was the motive for killing her and covering up?

The burden of proof was still heavily on the Silkwood team. At a minimum, there had to be witnesses to swear, as Karen had sworn over and over to Wodka, that the welds were defective and the photomicrographs were perjured. No fraud meant no manila folder, no documents. That was what Bill Paul's theory was all about. If Karen had no folder, she must have spiked her kits to give Burnham something to write about and to keep Wodka from losing face.

The gray stone YMCA where Ikard played his basketball had a plaque at the front door that said the building was a gift from Robert Kerr and some friends. But it was not a place Kerr or McGee or any of their executives would ever frequent. That was just as well. The YMCA had become the domain of the Silkwood team.

Every afternoon, after court was adjourned, they would walk over and take in the steam bath and whirlpool. Along with the four lawyers, this group included Bob, Father Bill, and one more volunteer, recently come from Arrupe House to Oklahoma, the faithful Father Wally Kasuboski, a Franciscan-Capuchin priest who had numbered and categorized a room full of files and now was keeper of the trial exhibits. Sometimes Buzz Hirsch, the would-be movie producer, came with his partner Larry Cano; also the fifth and newest attorney, Rob Hager. All the women were excluded, a point of irritation. The lawyers had picked a place for their strategy sessions that was men-only.

Vapors from the whirlpool had formed a huge winter breath. Shoulders deep in the water, Spence felt a sudden concern about his next witness. "Can we get this cop to wear his uniform?"

"Hammock doesn't need to," Father Bill said. "He has the most honest face you'll ever see. It's better than a uniform."

Ron Hammock took the oath the next day and then surveyed the room—a prosaic, straightforward gaze. It tarried briefly on the auburn curls of a young woman. She nodded in recognition. She was Robyn Petty, one of two legal secretaries who had been holding together Danny's makeshift office, in times of money and in times of none. The other secretary was Pat Austin, who had worked with Danny at the ACLU office in Denver. Robyn and Pat had been on their way to Texas, just driving through Oklahoma City, when they ran out of gas and money. Through a Christmas card Danny found out they were in town and talked them into staying. They had been on the team for eighteen months.

Robyn knew Hammock from a day last October. Robyn had chained herself to a bulldozer on the construction site of the Black Fox reactor outside Tulsa as part of an anti-nuclear protest. Cops had come in riot helmets, carrying bolt-cutters, and sliced through the chains. Hammock had been at the police station where Robyn was booked. That was his job. He was a Highway Patrol officer assigned to Tulsa.

He had short, black hair; his eyes were clear, knowing. Even in civvies, he would have been taken for a cop.

"What did you do before you joined the Highway Patrol?" Spence asked.

"I worked at Cimarron."

"Did you have any experience in quality control?"

"Yes, I did. We had to make sure the fuel rods met specifications before they were shipped out to Hanford." Hammock's hands tightened on the sides of his chair, as if for an ordeal.

"Did you ever see fuel rods that did not meet specifications but which were nevertheless shipped?"

"Yes, I did." Hammock's lips, like a ventriloquist's, scarcely moved. He had promised Father Bill he would testify—and he had shown up, a man of his word. But from the way he sat, straight, then straighter still, Spence began to fear for his memory. At moments like this, memories had a way of going weak.

"Can you tell the ladies and gentlemen of the jury what you saw?" Spence asked. His voice was flat.

"I saw the rods that were shipped—the ones we had rejected—the people that—it was actually the inspectors." Hammock shook his head to clear it. He held on to the chair. Slowly, he said, "We would take rods that had been rejected—they might have a bad weld or too large a weld—well, we would take them and use sandpaper to grind down the welds. Even though they'd been rejected, we'd go ahead and ship them because production was so far behind."

"Who told you to ship them?"

"My supervisor."

Spence let the words hang in the air. Then he said, "Thank you very much, Officer." Bill Paul seemed to be forcing his face into a sneer. It was not half as convincing as Hammock's pained honesty. A pencil bounced and rattled onto the floor. Spence turned. He folded his eyeglasses and took a while sticking them in his coat pocket. He bowed from his waist—a restrained, almost imperceptible gesture. "I think you may cross-examine."

Bill Paul did not rise. Instead Elliott Fenton, his associate, staggered up. "Your Honor, would it be appropriate to take a recess?" he asked.

After the recess, however, and after a full-tilt cross-examination, Hammock's testimony stayed on the record, unshaken.

For a week the Oklahoma City papers had headlined testimony from four former workers. From what the workers said, the files from Kerr-McGee had not told the half of it. The true number of contaminations might have been twice the number in the files. Red-alert machines had sat for hours without graph paper when they should have been recording air purity. Randy Snodgrass said he had been contaminated once by radioactive waste that fountained from a barrel "like water from a garden hose." Sometimes workers had to wear rubber gloves home; even with their hands rubbed raw, the plutonium wouldn't come off. "The contamination was everywhere," testified Ken Plowman, a former HP. "No real effort was made to control it. The supervisors didn't control it. The men didn't control it. It was just a battle that was lost."

Some workers took part in a morbid race "to see who could get hottest the fastest." Didn't they know they were fooling with cancer? No, not in so many words. William Apperson said he first learned about cancer at an OCAW seminar. Snodgrass didn't know until he read newspaper coverage of the trial. Not Plowman, not Apperson, not Snodgrass, not Hammock—none of them had heard the word cancer during their Cimarron orientations, nor did the word appear in the company safety manuals. Kerr-McGee had played down the danger from the get-go, and when the workers got contaminated, Kerr-McGee played down the contaminations, leading to carelessness and more contaminations. In a general way the workers knew the contaminations held a secret jeopardy. But it had been Karen—and Geesaman and Abrahamson—who had tried with their seminar to end the half-truths.

Fogging and sweat and poor fits often made the much-used respirators near useless, the ex-workers testified. When chemical fumes fogged his respirator, Snodgrass said, he took it off. For Karen, with her narrow face, Kerr-McGee had promised a special respirator, but in two years it never arrived.

Spence held up one of the respirators. He played with it, turned it over and over in his hand. This trial did not have the great visual props of a murder trial—the photographs of a victim lying in death. But the respirator was a good prop. Spence got Wayne Norwood to put it on—Norwood had been the chief HP at Cimarron. With its hard edges and odd angles, its construction of black rubber and blue plastic, the respirator might have inspired one of the alien faces in *Star Wars*. In seconds there was sweat on Norwood's neck. "How does it feel?" Spence asked. Norwood shook his head helplessly. His answer couldn't be heard through the mouthpiece. Spence gently rapped the lectern. "That's my point."

The Cimarron oxygen tanks had been as reliable. On at least two occasions while workers were lying on their backs, deep inside storage vessels, the tanks had run out of air. The workers had ripped off the top of their suits to breathe. What they had breathed, of course, was radioactive.

In the "wet end" of production, nitric acid had been a villain. It rotted the rubber gloves and ate away at the gaskets. The acid had to be neutralized when radioactive dregs were placed in waste barrels, and the whole of it had to be solidified before the barrels were trucked to a nuclear dump near Morehead, Kentucky. But sometimes the process wasn't permanent. The acid reverted to a liquid, and the radioactive dregs looked like "ice cubes swimming in acid." In this condition the metal barrels would not long hold out against the acid. Underground in Kentucky, the barrels might disintegrate, their contents might seep out. Radioactive dregs, in fact, were floating in underground streams outside Morehead, though it was not certain the Kerr-McGee barrels were the cause. One afternoon at Cimarron, however, a barrel that was still in port had been ruptured by the acid. Waste had run out, onto the truck floorboards, then through the floorboards, onto the open ground. Parts of the truck, and cubic yards of dirt, had to be buried. For all this terrible mess, Kerr-McGee did not switch to a better process at Cimarron until much later, and then not until after Mister Anonymous called Mrs. Younghein and set off her chain reaction of complaints.

In her seat Mrs. Younghein smiled and nodded at the belated kudos. Except for the reporters, she was the only spectator sitting every day in the gallery. She had finished one hooked rug, a handsome mosaic of sunny orange in a blue-green field, and she was starting another.

But at the mention of tornadoes, her hands fell quiet. She remembered the AEC inspectors telling her how the plutonium was to be moved into a vault during tornado alerts. So many of the AEC reassurances had turned to ashes, and now the ex-workers were saying that that hadn't been the truth either. The vault had gone dusty with disuse; it had been too much of a hassle; the fail-safe procedure had been a farce. But the inspectors never caught on. Perhaps they had been naive and even lazy, but also they had been fooled. There had been nothing to their "surprise" inspections, nothing but a joke. Before the inspectors arrived, hasty cleanups were ordered, spills painted over, broken equipment hidden away. And when the inspectors were around, the workers had orders to keep a tight lip. Hearing this, Mrs. Younghein did not feel appalled so much as rueful. The lies and deceptions were reaching a point of numbness.

The ex-workers who testified were not from Karen's 5–283 circle; they were more like the young hip cowboys who had razzed her. As such, they were a frustration to Bill Paul. They seemed candid and apolitical, and they had nothing but expiation to gain by coming forward now. They were extremely effective witnesses, Spence thought. And they probably had their most profound effect on him. He had come to the trial with his own smidgen of doubt about Karen. Had *everything* she said truly been on the up-and-up?

Braced against the sides of the YMCA whirlpool, the water frothing, Spence spoke of his new awareness. Steamy faces turned to listen. "If this keeps up, I'm gonna go home a radical."

"You better hope not—you're too rich to get radicalized." Danny slapped at the water with his legs, a smart-alecky gesture that drew retaliation. The whirlpool became a playground for men who were suddenly boys. Pleased with themselves, chuckling at jokes that were not all that funny, they splashed up and out: hairy legs and pink chunky middles in several wet sizes.

Dark clouds raced across the sky, raced like wolves. As quickly as they appeared, they were gone, leaving a blue-gray monotone. The morning was March 19, and the witness was James Noel.

As Noel settled in, the elevated witness chair looked unusually roomy. He was a slight young man, just into his thirties. He had thin wispy hair, a slender face, and the meager, unformed features of an ascetic. Currently he was a science teacher at an Oklahoma City high school. Teaching had been his ambition from youth. Even while working at Cimarron, he had studied part time at Central State University. Forced into a choice between his job and his studies, he had left the factory in 1973, some months before Karen's death. If you wanted the exact day and exact circumstances of his leaving, Noel could accommodate you. He was a meticulous and voluminous diarist, a prairie Robinson Crusoe. As a rule his evenings ended with a pen and a logbook.

Noel had been a friend of Karen's and, at times, her confidant. Because of that, because of his partiality, Noel had been low on the list of potential witnesses. His first interview with Father Bill had been short and routine. "You probably won't have to testify," Father Bill had said. "We have plenty of others who know everything you know." But then, only days before the trial began, Noel had been interviewed again. There were things about Karen that Father Bill wished to understand better. She had had so few friends, and Noel was one of the few.

Chatting loosely, but in fits and snatches, Noel had talked about

Karen's metamorphosis from nuclear cheerleader to muckraker. "She'd liked science in school," he remembered, "but she didn't know beans about plutonium when she started out. None of us did. We were just grateful to be there. It was a good job. Though for Karen, I think it was more than a job. Cimarron was supposedly at the cutting edge of modern science. When she realized what a hoax it was, how they didn't give a hoot about quality or safety, it was very disillusioning. I got out of there—thank God for that—and I sort of lost touch with Karen. Oh, I'd see her at a party now and again, or when she was blue sometimes she'd phone me. The last time was two weeks or so before her accident. She told me she'd been snooping around Cimarron. I didn't quite understand what she meant. She was rambling a lot. She told me how shocked she was. Shocked and scared. She was afraid they'd find out what she was up to. Maybe someone would grab her from behind in the file room, or catch her with documents in her purse. She was having nightmares. I advised her to get another job. Or go back to school. She had wanted to be a teacher once. Around kids, you know, she really lit up. But she was stubborn as a goat. She wasn't going to quit till the union got a new contract. She was bound and determined that the place could be reformed. 'It has to be cleaned up, it's a disgrace.' She must've said it ten, twelve times. I knew it had gotten worse since I left, but I'll be honest, some of the things she said were a little wild. I remember when I wrote them down—"

"You wrote them down?!" Father Bill had been immediately alert.

Noel, shrugging, had gone to his desk. "Yeah, I'm pretty sure I was writing in my logbook."

Noel's logbook for 1974 was the size and shape of a small hard-bound novel. As a piece of evidence, it was more trustworthy than any piece of memory or, for that matter, any typewritten memo in a file. A memo can be manufactured by the use of a typewriter ribbon as old as the memo is supposed to be. But it is almost impossible to fake a logbook. The entries in Noel's logbook, stitched in place, written in ink, enclosed on either side by a chronology, had to be taken as genuine.

"Yeah, this is it."

As soon as Father Bill read the logbook he knew there would have to be a change in the list of witnesses. Noel would have to be moved up, right to the top.

Now, under Spence's prompting, Noel took the diary from his lap

and respectfully exhibited it for the jurors. The entry that had so
stirred Father Bill was from October 22, 1974, about a month into
Karen's undercover assignment. She had phoned that evening in a
voice "shocked and scared."

"Did she tell you anything about MUF?" Spence asked.

"Yes. She referred to material unaccounted for. MUF. Specifically
I remember she mentioned seventeen kilograms." Noel ran his hand
down the spine of the logbook.

"Seventeen kilograms—how much is that in pounds?"

"About forty."

A buzz started in the gallery. Noel's revelation, though stated in
a calm, matter-of-fact manner, was the most exclamatory of any in
the trial to date. Danny telegraphed a look of admiration to Father
Bill. The priest, the greenhorn investigator, had succeeded where no
one else had been able to. With Noel's logbook, it was now established that Karen had known about a forty-pound MUF in the fall of
1974, a time when such knowledge was very rare and perhaps quite
dangerous.

"A great day! It couldn't have gone better." Spence distributed congratulatory whacks on everyone's shoulders as they walked two blocks
in twilight to the YMCA. Everyone was in high spirits. How could
Bill Paul's witnesses, well dressed and articulate though they might
be, explain away the logbook? Undressing in the YMCA locker room,
the Silkwood team rehashed the day, savoring it. Their smiles grew
huge: winners' smiles. The yakking was flip, confident.

"There's still one big loose end," Ikard said, edging in a sensible
caution. "I've gone through the inventory sheets in the file boxes.
Forty pounds was missing, all right. But that was in 1974. By 1975,
when they closed down, they had done a reinventory and accounted
for it. That's what Kerr-McGee will say. And that's what the AEC/
NRC will say."

Spence looked suddenly blank. He had mastered a great many
details, and much of the nuclear vernacular, but this statement did
not compute. "Is forty pounds missing or isn't it?"

"It *was* missing. Karen must have come across the MUF figure
when she was collecting documents. At that point, October 1974,
forty pounds was missing. But later it was accounted for, according
to the inventory sheets."

"So it's no longer missing?"

"Sixteen pounds still is. At shutdown the official MUF was sixteen."

Spence had lost his smile. "Up in Wyoming you told me forty pounds. And I told the jury forty pounds in my opening statement. Now you're telling me it's sixteen."

"Let me back up. Sixteen is the number they gave to Dingell's office."

"Whoa. Back up even further," Spence said sharply. "If the jury starts to think we've been shining them on, they'll nail us."

Ikard stopped undressing; he was down to a shirt and shorts. He looked squarely at Spence. "Maybe I better start at the beginning."

"Maybe you better."

"Okay, for two different months in 1974, March and September, the MUF was way high. Forty pounds. The AEC had to come in and do reinventories. But the way Stockton explains it, and the way I read the inventory sheets, all the AEC did was numbers-crunching. They decided the MUF was in the pipes. They call it 'holdup': the amount held up in the pipes. And it wasn't until shutdown that an honest-to-goodness reinventory was done."

"That's where sixteen comes from? The final MUF was sixteen?"

"Officially, yes, sixteen," Ikard repeated himself. "However, I think I've got the *real* MUF figured out." A smile, a flash of teeth in his old man's beard, broke across Ikard's face. "The inventory sheets are a jungle of numbers, numbers scattered all over—three-point-two kilograms in this category, four-point-four in another. So it took me a while to catch on. First you add up all the numbers under 'statistical variation' or 'inventory difference.' You get seven-point-eight kilograms. Or sixteen pounds. That is the amount officially gone, vanished, disappeared. But to get the total MUF you have to add in 'holdup,' the amount that is still supposedly in the pipes. That's ten-point-eight kilograms. Or twenty-four pounds."

"And sixteen plus twenty-four is forty." Spence was glowing again. With a shoe in hand, he thumped the benchrest. "You're a real education."

Ikard tossed his shorts into the bottom of the locker.

Spence kept thumping. "All we have to do now is get it on the record. Because we've already proved it ain't in the pipes. Ol' Jim Smith swore up and down he'd flushed them out down to the last ounce."

As acknowledgment of Ikard's better head for numbers, Spence left it to him to present the rest of the MUF story to the jury. The chance came a few weeks later. Ikard walked tentatively to the front; he introduced himself to the jurors, the first time his voice had been heard in the trial. The witness was a Kerr-McGee man, William Shelley, the director of regulation and control. Shelley did not seem happy to have been invited. He took a rather intense interest in the floor and ignored the tall bearded lawyer who stood before him with the inventory sheets.

Slowly Ikard took everyone through the clogged-up arithmetic. His unrelenting questions colored Shelley's face, colored it and warmed it.

"A couple more numbers, and we'll be finished," Ikard said finally. "I think you've said there were eighteen-point-six kilograms all together. Ten-point-eight in 'holdup' and seven-point-eight in 'inventory difference'?"

"Yes, sir," Shelley replied.

"How many pounds are there in eighteen-point-six kilograms?"

"Thirty-nine-point-six. About forty, I guess."

"Forty-point-nine is what I come up with." Ikard wrote the number on the blackboard, a large, striking chalk number. "So today, as we sit here, there are forty pounds, almost forty-one pounds, of plutonium that are either in 'holdup' or 'inventory difference'?"

"That is right."

There was a final addition to the MUF story, a trial exhibit from one of the boxes: a memo that a former Cimarron security man had written. "With such a large holdup in the pipes, it is difficult to feel safe that we are not losing plutonium."

Twenty

Wodka was in his room at the Skirvin Plaza, emptying a single suitcase. A loud rapping on the door gave him momentary pause. It was Drew, with a Budweiser six-pack in tow.

"How's it going?" Wodka asked. He grabbed the six-pack and Drew's hand.

Drew shrugged. "They won't let me watch," he said, meaning the trial. "Prospective witnesses aren't allowed in."

"Hey, you're gonna miss Bill Paul's performance. I hear he plans to carve me up and serve me to the jury."

Drew did not know whether to laugh; so he didn't. "Don't let Bill Paul get to you. He's blowing smoke."

"I just hope this trial turns out to be worth it," Wodka said. "All the work, all the time. Do you realize it's been four and a half years?" He opened two of the beers. "Jesus, the last time I saw you was . . ."

"Yeah." Drew tugged on his beard. Wodka had grown a beard of his own during those years and shaved it off again. But he had kept the mustache, and, in his navy blue suit, he looked much the same. Maybe his eyes were darker, their sockets gouged deeper.

The Budweisers relaxed the two men. Stiffness began to drop away. The question of Burnham came up. "I don't think he's gonna get out here," Wodka said. "His editors have him running all over D.C. They don't want him near the trial. They get uptight whenever Danny says anything. They think he's a crazy monk."

Now Drew laughed. "I never could see Danny in a monastery. A guy with his brains." He had a sudden observation. "I guess Sara finally saved him from all that." Just the other evening, at an artisans' festival over by City Hall, Drew had run into Danny and Sara and

Danny-Paul. They had stood around together and watched tiny figurines take shape in the hands of a glass blower. They had tapped
their feet to a country band. From a distance, Drew had spotted a
blond head in the festival crowd: Steve Campbell. Running to catch
up, he began to imagine Campbell's face after a good beating. Drew's
handsome cowboy hat, with a spangled feather for decoration, went
flying. And Campbell, suddenly aware of his pursuer, did too, his
blond head disappearing among scores of others.

"Another beer?" Wodka asked, popping two more cans.

Below on the street, there was the screech of tires. Drew swigged
the beer, head back, bouncing on the edge of the bed. He got up and
examined the motel room as if looking for something awry. He felt
jumpy. It was the room. It was being in a room with Wodka,
listening to traffic outside, waiting for nothing to happen, and thinking. Thinking, of course, of that fateful night.

And of guns. At home Drew had a closetful. The arsenal did not
include the .38 Special Chief from those weeks in 1974—the weeks
of the dead-bolt lock, the weird phone-booth vigil with Rosemary,
the forlorn absence of Karen's voice, no more "Drew, honey" or "See
you later, alligator." A panel truck had parked outside his bungalow
the day after Karen's death. A police undercover vehicle with one-
way windows? Posted there in broad daylight to spook him? Well, it
had. As had the noises at night, when he would wake suddenly,
knees like jelly, his mouth wondering where to go for a breath. But
Drew wasn't the sort to carry a pistol with an eye over his shoulder.
After the panel truck left and the noises stopped, he had given the
.38 away. The guns now in his closet were not there from paranoia.
Guns were his hobby, since cars had become his livelihood. And yet
it was true that the guns felt good and made him feel safer: the
Lugers, the Police Specials, a Colt six-shooter, a derringer: objects of
loving. Twice a week Drew went to a firing range and clamped on
ear mufflers; the shots would come so fast you couldn't hear the bam-
bam, just the full roar of a fusillade. In his living room Drew would
plug lead and smokeless powder into empty shells to save on ammo.
He had become a marksman. Over in Norman he had placed sixth in
a big run-and-shoot meet; the only shooters to beat him were cops.
Someday he wanted to test himself on a live target—perhaps a charging Arkansas boar, snout lowered, tusks aimed.

Sara did not like the sign over the pancake house—the neon letters THEY'RE STACKED BETTER and the bosomy waitress made of aluminum and paint. Sara was reminded of her time in California when she had organized a union of waitresses, and once this trial is over, she thought, that damn sign is coming down. She even made a plan—picketers on the sidewalk to embarrass the management—and began to recruit. But the response was unsettling: "I don't have hospital insurance," one woman said. It had never occurred to Sara that a peacefully conducted picket line could be dangerous. Then she remembered where she was.

It may well have been, as the crime statistics indicated, that the streets here were not as bad as in D.C. But there was a different feeling in Oklahoma City, a feeling of violence merely in the way men opened a door—grab, shove, slam. The Wild West was here. So was Urban America. They met here. Not far from town, northeast, there were low hills, the Cooksons, hells of rock and brush good only for rattlesnakes and men on the run. An outlaw accused of raping and murdering three girls had hidden in the Cooksons for an entire year: the year was 1978, last year. A few months ago a man had walked into a steakhouse, announced a holdup, smoked the place with a pair of .45s, left six dead, and driven away with a few hundred dollars. And this very week the remains of a murdered woman had been found scattered through a twelve-block circle, a circle that took in Danny and Sara's apartment, Bob and Kitty's duplex, Art Angel's house, the Corpus Christi rectory, the State Capitol. Dogs had been fighting over the dead woman's arms, legs, torso. Violence was part of the landscape.

Someone—he would not give his name—had called the law office with a tip last year. "I got a friend who's a trucker," the man said. "He was on a run up north a few weeks ago. Pulled in for coffee at a little joint, and seen this guy, who's hauling empty. They got to talking, one thing led to another, and this guy asks my friend to throw in with his gang. A gang of whatchamacallits, hit guys. They work for the Mob. The hang of it is, they don't use guns. They use semis. Run people off the road. They've done jobs in Seattle and down in Albuquerque and one right here. That Silkwood girl." Trying to confirm the man's story, Taylor and Father Bill had spent several wasted days in which they had heard more rumors about more gangs of hit-and-run assassins. Also, they had heard a rumor that an attempt might be made on Danny's life. For Danny to have believed the rumor would have meant living in unreality, or in a reality so bad and desperate and scary it would have been like unreality. So Danny hadn't believed it. At least, not till after the coin flip.

The coin flip was with Father Bill. Danny lost, so he had been the one to go pick up Wodka at the airport. Tossing Wodka's suitcase into a borrowed Toyota, Danny accelerated out the drive, back toward town. In the I-35 flow, Danny eased up at fifty miles per hour; being a driver brought out his conservative side. He zagged around a bump in the road and suddenly he had in his hands a disconnected steering wheel. He felt it, felt the empty sensation, but he did not comprehend what he felt. He tried to keep the car straight, but it was sliding to the right. That was when he hit the brake. The car slowed in a hurry, and the suitcase crashed forward across the back seat. Horns squawked all around. Danny was praying. The car nosed onto the shoulder and bumped against a guardrail and faltered; the engine stalled. Wodka's face, bloodless, was flat to the windshield. Danny rubbed his belly. The steering wheel was wedged between him and the dashboard. They examined themselves for broken bones, then scrambled out to examine the car. A bolt that locks the steering wheel into place had worked itself loose. Or had someone loosened it?

The car belonged to Art Angel, who was in D.C. to testify to a congressional committee about price-listing at funeral homes, a project left over from his FTC days. For twelve hours—until Angel got back and explained that the bolt was a chronic problem—Danny and the others had discussed arming themselves, taking on the sensibilities of the natives. "We could borrow some guns from Drew—he's got a whole nest." "I remember Mr. Silkwood used to pack one when he first came up here." "Probably still does; he's a commonsense man." "It's your show, Danny. You want everybody running around with a gun?" "Shit, I don't know." Danny didn't know. For a moment, the guns almost made sense. Was it because he was the one who had almost been killed? Or because of Sara and Danny-Paul? Well, those were three good reasons.

Even after Angel's explanation about the bolt, the jitters hung on. "Let's be careful," Father Bill said. "Nobody should go wandering off alone." To which Spence replied, winking, "I'd rather go it alone. If we move around like a mob, they could get us all with one pop." Everyone laughed, warily. The mood, half-farce, half-fear, went with them into the courtroom.

In a gallery seat, handy to the door, Danny held the baby and a diaper bag. Sara and Kitty sat near the front, listening together. It was for the two women a rare appearance. Neither could spare the time to watch the trial. Kitty was frantic about finishing her graduation thesis, an analysis of radiation and the law, which was to be printed as a handbook for uranium miners. Sara's time was going toward a big publicity effort and the endless phone calls and letters —pleas for more money: the additional twenty-five grand for Spence, plus thousands more for expense overruns. Mrs. Younghein had tried to arrange a fundraising party at the mansion-home of a wealthy, charitable widow, but at the last minute the widow had lost her nerve. ("They got ways to get even. They could raise my taxes sky-high.")

Sara and Kitty were in court today to hear Wodka, but not only him.

"You had a telephone conversation with Karen on October 7, 1974?" Spence asked.

"Yes, I did," Wodka said.

"And you made a tape recording of that conversation?"

"Yes."

The court clerk attached an exhibit number to the tape, and Wodka was replaced for forty-five minutes by a large stereo-tape machine. The tape spun through. An intense, preachy Texan voice came out. "I've got a weld I'd love for you to see," the voice said, "just how far they ground it down to get rid of the voids, the occlusions and cracks." Jurors strained forward to hear. Karen's voice might have fitted any number of anonymous faces. Sara wondered what the jurors were imagining. An arrogant mouth? A soft, pretty one? The eyes of an actress? Or a face full of outrage and pity? She wished they could see the haunting half-smile on the black-and-white poster of Karen. Even more, she wished they all might have known the woman to whom the voice and face belonged, been able to judge her for herself.

Outside, a rainstorm flattened Sara's coat against her. She drove back to their temporary home, the car shuddering down chuckholed streets from one gray pond to the next. Distractedly, she watched the wipers in their losing contest with the rain.

Her sleep that night was full of speeding cars, headlights flooding the rearview mirror, tires spinning in the air, a lifeless hand flickering shyly through a broken window.

The next day there were more trial exhibits: the two notebooks Karen had given Wodka before she left for Los Alamos. The clerk marked each, and they were passed among the jurors for inspection. In a cramped, scared script Karen had written, *The company knows something is going on.* Asked by Spence if he could explain the note, Wodka said he had learned, long after the fact, that the AEC had broken its promise about the confidentiality of the September 27 meeting in Bethesda: an AEC official had alerted Kerr-McGee. Knowing Karen's bosses as he now did, Wodka said, he presumed they had put her under careful watch. But he had no firsthand evidence of surveillance, and even if he had, the jurors would not have heard it. Judge Theis had ruled inadmissible any mention of wiretaps and the like because of its "highly inflammatory" nature. That is, because it might inflame the jury against Kerr-McGee. By the same reasoning, although for the opposite effect, Judge Theis also had put limits on any references to sex or drugs.

Instead, Bill Paul had to fence with Wodka over euphemisms for sex. "That evening in Washington, did you have a *private* conversation with Karen?" "No, we went out to dinner with Tice and Brewer." "How about after dinner?" "It was a grueling day; we might have relaxed a little." "In Oklahoma, how much were you and Karen together?" "Pretty much." "Did Karen stay in your motel room?" "We all did—Drew and Karen and me." At that answer, Bill Paul smiled with mischief. "I better not get into that." Several jurors smiled too and nodded.

Bill Paul seemed to be picturing a casual, fun-loving Karen. But there was little in Wodka's testimony to suggest she had been. Maybe once upon a time, but not when Wodka knew her. After the contaminations, he said, he could see something was wrong. She was shaking with nausea, her color was terrible. Brown skin had faded to blue-white, showing the depth of her fright.

Bill Paul presently returned to a more favored subject, the trial's central, recurring theme. "When Karen gave you these notebooks," he asked Wodka, "why didn't she also give you the photomicrographs and the other documents she supposedly had?" Bill Paul inclined his head, canting it to one side as if listening for an answer from across a ravine.

Wodka stared, without alarm, but without much hope in the jury.

He said, "She told me she had them in a safe place. At the time she was more worried about her health, and so was I. We had planned to get together as soon as she got back from Los Alamos. Burnham was going to fly in. The manila folder was for him."

"So she never showed you her documents?" "No." "You can't swear she had any photomicrographs?" "No." "You don't know, one way or the other, whether there was any faulty welding?" "Karen told me there was, and I believed her."

Whether or not the welds would in fact survive in the fast-breeder was as yet unknown. Fire-up of the fast-breeder, scheduled to begin the same week as the trial, had been postponed again, and only four welds out of some hundred thousand had been tested. One of the four had appeared defective, but with such a small sample it had no meaning.

Mazzocchi, as combative as ever, followed Wodka to the stand. Spence wanted the jurors to see that a man of age and experience had been behind the OCAW strategy. Indeed, Spence wanted them to understand that there had been a strategy. "Phase One was to win the decertification election," Mazzocchi testified. "As a matter of general history, unions almost always lose such elections. We won at Cimarron largely because Abrahamson and Geesaman had raised the level of concern about health and safety. Then we went to Phase Two, which was to get a good contract. The press wasn't interested in health and safety, but they were interested in fraud. If Burnham did a front-page story about the welds, we figured it'd put Kerr-McGee on the defensive in the negotiations."

"Did Karen realize there'd be no front-page story without proof?" Spence asked.

"Absolutely. We told her it was just a wild assertion otherwise. Nobody would print it."

"What makes you think she actually got the proof?"

"She told us she had gotten it. If she hadn't been able to, the kind of person she was, she'd have called and said, 'I'm sorry, I couldn't get it.'"

Then Bill Paul gathered himself, his walk aggressive. He leveled his glasses at Mazzocchi. "You've been very frank here about your strategy," he said.

"Well, it's because of our strategy that the charge against Karen has to be untrue. She had no reason to contaminate herself. It wouldn't have helped our strategy. On the contrary, it was very disruptive. Karen was supposed to keep a low profile. She wasn't even handling any grievances during this period. It was her nature to react to grievances any time of day, but we told her, no, let Tice handle them, you get your proof together. So her getting contaminated disrupted our strategy."

"Can you tell me *how* it was disruptive?" Bill Paul acted contemptuously curious.

"It came at an inopportune time. It made Karen highly visible, and it was of no news value. It was just one in a series of contaminations that'd happened over the years. Kerr-McGee was the only one to benefit from it."

"What do you mean by that? Of what possible benefit could it be to Kerr-McGee?" The question was archly asked.

"By blaming it on her, doubt was cast on her credibility. And it gave Kerr-McGee an excuse to go into her apartment and search for her documents."

Bill Paul's face jerked. He had asked one, maybe two questions too many. If Spence had asked the same questions, and had an objection been raised, Judge Theis undoubtedly would not have let Mazzocchi answer. The answers were in the realm of opinion.

Moving smoothly on, as smoothly as he could, Bill Paul tried to argue that Karen's credibility should have been in doubt.

The *Times*, in its treatment of the case, seemed to have acknowledged as much. Burnham's articles had never made the front page. Even the one about Karen's death had been printed guardedly and inconspicuously inside, and for the trial the *Times* was using wire-service copy.

During the morning recess of March 28, Associated Press reporter Michael Bates had phoned in his first report of the day. Emerging from the courthouse press room, he held up an annunciating hand. "Something's gone wrong with a nuclear reactor in Pennsylvania. All hell's breaking loose." Within minutes Kitty and Bob were on separate phones to Movement friends who last year had tried, and failed, to prevent the NRC from licensing Three Mile Island Unit Two.

Kitty went back to the courtroom, but her ears were tuned for more running feet from the press room. Her daydreams verged on nightmares. Was Three Mile Island actually going to melt down? The Butternut commune was only an hour and a half downwind of the reactor. Finally she went back to the phone and dialed home. "Get on a plane and get out of there. Please!" Three days later, nearly one million people around Three Mile Island were notified to stand by for possible evacuation. Loudspeakers blaring from civil-defense vans advised pregnant women and small children to leave right away.

A succession of human errors and machinery breakdowns—by themselves not at all uncommon—had brought the reactor to crisis. A large hydrogen bubble, never dreamed of in NRC computer simulations, had been formed and trapped in the reactor dome. If it continued to grow, it could push into and paralyze the cooling pumps, causing a meltdown. It was a real crisis. There might be real victims.

The Rasmussen Report probably would have been the first victim, falling to the raw scorn of real life. But the Rasmussen Report had already been scuttled two months before. In a spasm of public doubt, after years of saying a meltdown was a million-to-one shot, the NRC commission had declared the report "unreliable." Talking to a reporter, Kitty said, "The NRC admitted it: they have no idea what the odds really are. A meltdown could happen once every twenty years, or every ten, every five. Nobody knows."

Kitty and Bob, and their counterparts in every part of the country, were all of a sudden in demand. Reporters from straight newspapers were calling. In the past, anti-nuclear lore had usually been given short shrift—Kitty and Bob and the rest were too passionate. But now they were being sought out because they could expound, off the top, on a history that might otherwise take days to research.

Three Mile Island was neither the first major nuclear accident nor (as it turned out) the most severe. In 1957 and again in 1969, fires inside the Rocky Flats weapons factory, between Denver and Boulder, had burned through smokestack filters, shooting plutonium dust into the air. In both cities the cancer rate was now sharply on the rise. Carl Johnson, the county health director, had made a map of where the wind blew the plutonium. The more plutonium around, the higher the number of cancer deaths. All together he attributed five hundred to radiation. The deaths from the waste explosion in Siberia, as far as is known, were never tabulated. But twenty years later, villages in the southern Urals continued to molder away, uninhabited. Both the Fermi fast-breeder outside Detroit and the Windscale reactor in England had been junked after partial meltdowns. When the Fermi crisis happened, in 1966, local mayors and civil-defense teams went on alert, but the citizens hadn't been informed until months after. In 1975, at the Browns Ferry reactor in Alabama, a lighted candle, clumsily used to check for air leaks, had set fire to a forest of control wiring. One safety system after another had cut off. Only a jerry-rigged backup had prevented a meltdown. The fire, raging for six hours, had cost $150 million. In Minnesota in 1971, fifty thousand gallons of radioactive liquid had gone from the Monticello reactor into the drinking faucets of St. Paul. In Japan that same year, a crippled jetliner making an emergency landing nearly strayed nose-first into a nuclear reactor.

The Three Mile Island bubble had shrunk to gumball size and the panic was over before Spence got really excited about it. What excited him was an AP report that defects in the fuel rods, conventional uranium-filled rods, might have set the bubble afloat. "I wonder," Spence mused, "I wonder if those rods could have come from Kerr-McGee's uranium factory?"

"I've already checked," Bob said. "Kerr-McGee sold its uranium rods to Babcock & Wilcox, which, it happens, is the supplier for Three Mile Island. I don't know if the ones that broke down were Kerr-McGee rods, but the NRC would know. You can ask their guys when you get them on the stand."

Getting wind of this, Bill Paul asked for a mistrial. This was not his first attempt. He had made the same request when *The China Syndrome* opened in Oklahoma City. In the movie a nuclear company uses a hit-and-run goon squad to frighten whistle-blowers. Bill Paul argued that the current furor over nuclear power—on the screen and in real life—made a fair trial impossible. He wanted to scratch this one and begin another when the furor slackened. To Danny, entering the argument in chambers, this was a last-ditch maneuver to deprive Karen of due process. A mistrial, he said, would be tantamount to a Kerr-McGee victory by default. It would be nigh unto impossible for her side to finance a second go-around.

At the head of a long polished table Judge Theis sat as the fulcrum, physically and legally. On one side were the four lawyers for Mr. Silkwood; on the other were the six for Mr. McGee. The judge glanced at his robe, hanging on a coat peg, and at the clock. For fully an hour a day, on the average, the trial was being conducted out of earshot of the jury. He was trying to keep out the invective. Any mention of vehicular homicide was verboten, as was any mention of marijuana and lesbianism. By the same token the jurors, though not sequestered, were to shy away from newspapers, magazines, libraries, TV newscasts, the *Encyclopaedia Britannica,* and any neighbors or relatives who liked to discuss the news of the day. If they read anything, they were to read books from before World War II or ventilated newspapers, which their spouses had excised with scissors. When they talked among themselves, they were to talk about their court-bought lunches at Anna Maude's cafeteria, and little else. Even the weather was touchy; springtime was tornado season, and tornadoes had been injected as an issue in the trial.

Explosively, Judge Theis now injected himself. He said no to Bill Paul's mistrial request and no to Spence's question about the Three Mile Island rods.

The Three Mile Island scare might have been mirrored on Gerald Phillip's face. He looked distraught and totally fatigued. He slumped deep in the witness chair. As the AEC/NRC man most knowledgeable about Karen, and as a touted Kerr-McGee witness, Phillip seemed miscast. He knew of no facts, he said, that singled out Karen conclusively as a malefactor. It was his opinion she had spiked the kits, but, on Spence's objection, that opinion wasn't allowed in.

Nor, in counterpoint, was the research Bob had done. Much of it dealt with the AEC/NRC's high regard for Kerr-McGee, dating to former AEC chairman Lewis Strauss's friendship with Senator Kerr in the fifties. The company's monopoly on uranium mining and milling was due largely to $400 million in AEC contracts—ten times what any other single uranium producer ever received in public money. Once Kerr-McGee got a contract even though its uranium had to be ferried four hundred miles to an AEC facility, bypassing five other mills along the route. In 1962 the Uranium Institute, a band of small companies, formally complained to the Justice Department that antitrust laws had been broken. They said Kerr-McGee's "political influence" was bankrupting them. Nothing came of it, though their prediction of their demise proved correct.

The limits placed on Phillip's testimony probably made him out to be more neutral than he really was. He came across under Spence's cross-examination as a man defensively distressed, but honest.

"Was the baloney package ever submitted to you for fingerprints?" "No, sir." "But you could have taken fingerprints if you'd wanted to, couldn't you?" "I assume we could have." "And that is true with the rest of the apartment?" "Yes, sir." "But you didn't?" "No, sir."

"Now the extra plutonium in Karen's kits came from Lot 29, as the ladies and gentlemen of the jury already know from Exhibit 78–1, but let me ask you: did you discover Lot 29 had been shipped from the factory in August, two months before the kits were spiked?" "No, sir, I didn't discover that." "Well, if you take those two facts —that the plutonium came from Lot 29, and Lot 29 had been gone since August—and you combine them with the fact forty pounds were unaccounted for, wouldn't these be facts you'd want to investigate further?" "I didn't try to make anything out of them." "You didn't even know about them until I gave them to you just now, did you?" "No, I guess I did not."

"Did you know forty pounds were missing or unaccounted for?" "I knew in a very general way there was some MUF, but I didn't get involved with it." "You didn't pay any attention to it, is that right?" "It was not considered part of my investigation." "Well, in an area where valuables are unaccounted for, whether it's gold or plutonium, one of the first things an investigator does is check the financial records of the people involved. Did you check the finances of the people at the factory, including the people in management, to see if anyone had gotten a sudden windfall?"

Phillip's answer was halted by a gritty, scraping noise. Bill Paul was pushing his chair backward over the floor. For six weeks, going on seven, he had called out so many objections that he seldom bothered any more to raise his hand. Now his hand went up. He jumped to his feet. "The question is argumentative, improper, outside the scope of direct, and irrelevant," he said. Judge Theis agreed.

Spence's eyes widened at the judge. Then he studied the jurors, a slow hypnotizing look, as if he was counting to be sure they had all made it back from lunch at Anna Maude's. Taking his cue from the set of their mouths, the tension in their hands, sensing a certain "vibe," he decided that his point about MUF had been clear.

"Now, Mr. Phillip," he said, "did it mean anything to you that Kerr-McGee took every single thing out of that apartment down to the Durkee's dressing and salt and pepper shakers. . . . Did it mean anything that they had the opportunity to review every scrap of paper, every item, right down to the last hair?"

Again Bill Paul was on his feet, and again Judge Theis sustained his objection.

Spence scowled. He towered over the witness. He said, "Did you learn that Karen's apartment was usually left unlocked?"

"I believe either she or Sherri told us that."

"Did you report that fact in your report?"

"I don't believe that specific fact appeared in the report."

"I see. I think you mentioned that when you saw Karen on November 8th she was very sincerely upset?" "Yes, sir." "And she was crying?" "Yes, sir." "And she broke down?" "Yes, sir." "And she thought she was going to die?" "Yes, sir." "It'd be fair to say the contamination had very seriously upset her?" "Yes, sir."

"You told us you brought along a public relations man?" "Yes, Jan Strasma—to provide information to the press." "The press hadn't been advised of this by Miss Silkwood, had they?" "Not to my knowledge." "She didn't try to cause anybody any trouble over her contamination, as a matter of fact, or try to embarrass Kerr-McGee . . . She just didn't want anybody else to get contaminated. . . . She wouldn't kiss her boyfriend Drew Stephens on the mouth because she was afraid she'd contaminate him. You discovered that, didn't you?" "Yes, sir."

"Karen gave you a detailed account of where she had been and what she had done that week, didn't she?" "Yes, sir." "She didn't attempt to conceal any facts that you know of?" "No, sir." "As far as you were concerned, she was honest?" "Yes, sir." "And you had no reason to disbelieve her account of the situation?" "No, sir."

Half the sky was still light, but blackness in the other half announced the tornado. Sara, at her desk, saw the clouds, coiling fatly, whirling into view. And she heard the wind. It flayed the countryside in its rampant advance. A gigantic gust out of the north broke through the balcony door, blowing turmoil into her stack of fundraising letters, overturning a card table bought from the Salvation Army. In his crib Danny-Paul was awake and clamoring. Sara calmed him, holding him with one hand, and with the other battening down the apartment.

By nightfall all was quiet again. On the eleven o'clock news Sara and Danny heard that the tornado's fury had left limbless a few scrub trees and made carrion of a cow. Although slight, the damage had been done within five miles of Cimarron. "No doubt about it—God's on our side," Danny said gleefully. "Next time they lie, they'll be afraid of lightning striking."

Just yesterday a Kerr-McGee official, a member of the Cimarron design committee, had sworn the factory was not located in the middle of a Tornado Alley. "I don't believe Oklahoma has a Tornado Alley," he had testified. "'I've never heard of one."

Sara, snacking on yogurt, made an arc with her spoon. She smiled. In the cosmic order of things even tornadoes had a good side. Eerie or not, everything these days seemed to serve the anti-nuclear cause: the popularity of *The China Syndrome,* the discrediting of the Rasmussen Report, the national trauma over Three Mile Island. Both Sara and Danny had long since become full-fledged members of the Movement. At the last NOW convention Sara had helped push through an alliance with anti-nuclear groups, and she and Kitty were among fifteen anti-nuclear leaders invited onto the political board of Musicians United for Safe Energy (MUSE). Danny had gone equally public. Reporters from Los Angeles, Dallas, and San Francisco, who flew in for a lengthy look at the trial, had quoted his one-liner: "Kerr-McGee is not alone in this—the whole concept of nuclear power is on trial." The rest of the industry had in fact exhibited concern for the jury's verdict. A "mystery man," seen coaching Bill Paul in the hallway, had been identified as a veteran D.C. lawyer, fire-eating and fire-breathing, and affiliated with the Atomic Industrial Forum.

Danny was in much the same role for the Silkwood team. When an idea struck him, he would scribble furiously, then reach the note up to Spence. On the weekends, though, Danny was again in charge. He had taken on the title of morale-booster. He had organized birthday parties for Angel and for Sara, picnics at Red Rock Canyon, ice cream extravaganzas at Kaiser's, and "pig-outs" at inexpensive good-food restaurants. Here in beef country, an all-devouring Spence and a healthy Kitty were king and queen of the banquet, the two loudest exceptions in a plant-preferring crowd. (Bob had renounced red meat on learning he was prone to gout.) Weekend nights were movie nights. Danny had led three separate expeditions to showings of *The Deer Hunter.* After each showing, and after *Norma Rae, Hair!, The China Syndrome,* there had been lively, eclectic debate over ice cream.

Spence, at forty-six, was the team's oldest member, also the newest. In court, he was now the most important. Out of court, he was the most unlikely, the least in step. He showed his age and chauvinism in his heedless fetch-it orders and chuck-under-the-chin rewards. He was not liberated, and though he could be kidded about his etiquette, he was not about to change. On Kentucky Derby weekend he and his wife had jaunted to Louisville. As much as anything, it was to escape more moralizing about *The Deer Hunter,* more disrespect for the holy order of hunting. Still, Spence felt as disrespectful toward institutions just as hallowed. Last week, in the grip of a manly, radical, pompous anger, he had held a press conference in an annex off the courtroom. His arms swooped; his voice berated. "Have you been watching? Have you seen these Kerr-McGee witnesses? We must be up to six or seven now. Half the time, it looks like the same guy over and over. They look the same; they talk the same. They tell us everything was shipshape out at that factory. They didn't know anything was wrong. Or if it was wrong, it wasn't their responsibility. Somebody else was responsible. The AEC was responsible. Or the workers were. Or Jim Smith was. Or somebody else down the line. If you want to know what this trial is all about, that's it. That kind of corporate mentality is the biggest menace to freedom today. It's destroying the individual. It's already destroyed all semblance of individual responsibility."

Ikard and Angel had tried, diplomatically, to rein in Spence. No good and much bad could come of public intemperance. Judge Theis might do more than frown on it; he might begin to lose his sense of humor and fair play. More seriously, if scuttlebutt about Spence should reach the jurors, they might later rebuke him with their verdict. Most immediately, the reporters were miffed; they resented being lectured to.

But Danny wasn't bothered. He might have given this sort of tirade brashly in the courtroom. Once, with the ACLU, he had. The Idaho Falls city council had banned *Last Tango in Paris,* and Danny was in court to remove the ban, on First Amendment grounds. The jurors were all Mormons. If they went along with censorship, Danny told them, their sin would be as wholesale as any in the movie. The statement got Danny kicked out of court, but it had its effect. In Mormon theology the Bill of Rights, including the First Amendment, is considered divinely inspired. While the judge had banished Danny, the jury had let *Last Tango* into the local theater.

Between Danny and Spence there had developed a kinship. They each had style, an exuberant bravado, an unflagging demeanor, a striving to be the perfect advocate, and the closer they came, the more they showed off. On the team they were the sagamore figures. At the breakfast round tables Ikard was perhaps the best at analysis, Angel the quickest with case law, Father Bill the most perceptive at reading witnesses, but for ideas that evoked or infuriated or amused they relied on Spence and Danny. At Red Rock Canyon, an outcropping shelter of soft rock around a meadow of virginal green, there had been a rambunctious game of touch football one Saturday, everyone grunting and running, except for the two fiercest competitors, who sat on the sidelines talking.

Opening night at *The China Syndrome,* with everyone from Mrs. Younghein to Robyn Petty along, the group occupied thirty seats. On their way out, moving as a pack, they encountered one of Bill Paul's junior partners. He was a portly young man, easygoing, rather engaging. "What did you think of the movie?" he was asked.

"I liked it—I always like fairy tales," he drawled. "It was almost as good as watching you folks."

When Bob was an Army medic he would sometimes use his hypodermic to pull rank on swaggering captains and colonels. "Your medical chart says you're due for a cholera booster," he would lie, making them roll up their sleeves. Now as the Kerr-McGee vice-presidents and division managers took their turn in the witness chair, he was reminded of that giddy power. The company men would talk at length about their qualifications, their efficiency, their nobility, swelling up under their clothes with a thickness that was not muscle; then Spence would poke the needle in.

Today's witness was Morgan Moore. He sat erect. He was fifty-two, an engineer, a fast-serve tennis player, a company man for nineteen years. In 1974 he had been manager of Cimarron. After Karen's death Dean McGee had made Moore president for all nuclear operations, from yellow cake mines to the finished product. Robust, clever, distinctly corporate, Moore had an ungenerous chin and a spitfire attitude. He was the highest-ranking company man to have dealt first-person with Karen. He had been the man sitting across from her at the negotiating table.

For his cross-examination Spence moved back and forth as he always did, interrupting the line of vision between the Kerr-McGee table and the witness chair. He had been waiting for Moore to get up there; Spence was gunning for him.

"Mr. Moore, you were at Karen's apartment on November seventh, weren't you?" "That's true." "It's also true she wasn't allowed back in her apartment. She had to stand out in the street—some say she was crying. Did you see that?" "I saw she was upset." "Would you say she was shocked?" "Very upset, shocked, whatever." "Did she appear to be genuinely hysterical?" "I would say she was." "Okay, here's a woman who is shocked, genuinely hysterical, and what was your approach to her? You provided an attorney to interrogate her, didn't you?" "He visited with her. I don't know if he interrogated her." "Did you provide her any medical treatment?" "No sir, not that night."

"Your crew tore the apartment asunder, didn't they?" "I don't remember us tearing it down." "Are you denying it, or you just don't remember?" "I don't know whether we did or not." "But it did provide you with an opportunity to search even behind the walls, isn't that true?" "I would have to agree with the way you phrased it; yes, sir."

"On November thirteenth, the very day of her death, you put special restrictions on Karen, didn't you?" "Yes, sir." "I'm holding Exhibit 291. Can you tell us if it bears your signature?" "Yes, sir; it's dated 11–13–74." "This went to your security staff?" "Yes, sir." "Let me read part of it. This is what you underlined: *All movement past the guard station must be with an escort.* The last affirmative gesture you made to Karen before she died was to put her under escort. I want to ask you: Did the AEC require that?" "We would have done it without an order from the AEC." "I didn't ask that. Did the AEC require you to put her under escort?" "I'm not just sure how they would have phrased it." "Just a minute. This is a very simple question. Did the AEC require you, or did you do it on your own?" "I would have done it on my own anyway." "I didn't ask you that. For the fourth time, I want to know if the AEC required you to do it." "The AEC required us not to have her in a radiation area." "I didn't ask that. Now, for the fifth time, did the AEC require you to put her under escort. Yes or no?" "No, sir. *I* put her under escort."

Moore had begun to hunch forward, knees pressed together, his eyes shaded with thought. Exhaling, he touched his nose and rubbed the back of his shoulder.

"Now, Mr. Moore, you were still the Cimarron manager on December seventeenth, a month after Karen's death?" Spence asked.

"That is correct." Moore's lips quirked in an incipient smile.

"Do you recall that five workers were contaminated that day? Four when a gallon of plutonium liquid leaked on the floor, the other while handling a scrap package?"

"I don't recall the details, but I'm familiar with the situation."

"Didn't Kerr-McGee claim it was a put-up job, and report it to the AEC as such, and use this as an excuse to shut down the factory and give everyone lie-detector tests?"

"We did shut down; yes, sir."

"Didn't you take the position publicly that it was the result of sabotage?"

"That was the headline, yes."

"Didn't you yourself claim it was a put-up job? That it was sabotage? Didn't you tell that to the FBI?" Spence reached for a piece of paper. "Now, before you answer, let me say I have the FBI report."

"I'm sure I would've said it."

"Thank you. Now, those contaminations weren't contrived at all, were they?"

"There was a thermocouple connection leak."

"Yes, I see that's what it says in Exhibit 192–28. Mr. Phillip of the AEC came in and made this report, didn't he?"

"Yes, sir."

"After you claimed it was sabotage, Mr. Phillip found it wasn't sabotage at all. It was a thermocouple leak in Room B–01 resulting in high airborne concentrations of plutonium, isn't that right?"

"That's how it is defined here." Nothing in Moore's face changed, nothing.

"So, even after Karen's death, it continued to be easy for you to make false accusations against other people, didn't it?"

"Just a moment." Bill Paul disturbed the furniture again, vigorously, showing his exasperation and hoping the jurors would share it. "That's argumentative and improper," he said. "It describes motivations the testimony doesn't back up."

"Sustained," Judge Theis said.

A twinkle appeared brightly in Spence's eyes. "Okay, strike the word *easy*."

It was the ninth week. Spence had used five weeks for the plaintiff's presentation, and Bill Paul was matching him week for week, witness for witness. To rebut Mazzocchi, a man near the top of the OCAW, he had brought in Moore, a man in the same position at Kerr-McGee. But there was one big question mark in Bill Paul's strategy. Would he be able to bring in the Old Man himself and upstage everyone? Reporters tossed the question about, making a game of it, but even Bill Paul didn't seem to know. Mr. McGee had a mind of his own.

At the afternoon recess on May 3 the Kerr-McGee legal team exited quickly. A pair of watchful reporters circled around and followed, down three flights of back stairs, through plate-glass double-doors, out a side entrance. By the curb, under the sandstone relief of the five women whose time had passed, stood a new-model Cadillac. It glinted dully in the spring heat, like part of the pale pavement. A man in a black suit stepped militarily from the back seat. He was swallowed by his entourage, men with walkie-talkies to their lips. They rushed the Old Man up the stairs, a route curiously furtive, as if maniacal anti-nukers might be waiting out front to hurl themselves, clawing, at his face.

Mr. McGee's face was seventy-four years old, but barely eroded. His presence in the courtroom had the effect of a magnet. From nowhere, it seemed, women in bouffants and high heels—secretaries from down the hall and from down the street—came filing in behind him. Mr. McGee approached the bailiff, raised his right hand, and was sworn in. He was a portrait of unsparing discipline, strong and knotty, a man of obvious pride despite the humility in his folded hands.

A smile tucked in place, Bill Paul led his witness through the familiar accomplishments of Kerr-McGee, the contributions in taxes and jobs (hadn't Karen Silkwood been given one?), the years of being well managed, scrupulous, humane. Before the OCAW poisoned some minds, Mr. McGee said, it had been a happy company, top to bottom. His testimony was predictable. But that was not the point; it was that the Old Man was here saying it. None of the jurors had ever seen him up close. They listened, eyes locked in concentration, chairs angled forward in symmetry. As a civic leader, Mr. McGee was first among equals.

For Spence the challenge was unsurpassed. How, in a few hours, could he bring low a reputation that had been so long in the making?

From the file boxes Ikard selected memos and press releases that Mr. McGee had signed. One was about a private meeting he had two months after Karen's death with James Keppler, the AEC/NRC regional director. "Now, Mr. McGee," Spence said, "did you express a concern to Mr. Keppler that Karen and the other union officials should have brought their list of complaints to you instead of the AEC?"

"Yes, I did. There was a provision in the union contract that required them to do that, and they didn't follow it."

"As a matter of fact, you blamed the union for trying to get the AEC on your back . . . wasn't that your position?"

"I raised that with Mr. Keppler, yes."

"Were you aware the AEC/NRC was planning to conduct a series of in-depth inspections at Cimarron?"

"I think he told me; yes, sir."

"And did they make the inspections?"

"I assume they did. But I never heard from them after that, so I assume it did not turn out very badly."

"Do you feel the AEC/NRC was fair with you?"

"I felt it was a tough regulatory agency. At times it was dictatorial. But overall we had no complaint."

"Are you aware there were over seventy-five violations of the AEC/NRC code at your factory?"

"Well, I wouldn't know the exact number. As I understand it, most of them were class-three violations that didn't present any harm to the employees or the public."

"Is that what the people below you in the corporation told you? That nobody's health had been endangered?"

"Well, we have a policy that if anybody's injured, I get a report immediately. And I got no reports from Cimarron."

Spence walked back to the table and took from Ikard another paper. "Now, Mr. McGee, I want to talk to you about credibility. I guess you know that when any witness takes the stand his credibility is a subject of inquiry. And so is a corporation's."

This induced a hard cough in the Old Man. He put a coarse, blue-veined fist over his mouth to control it, but another cough shook him. A signal perhaps? Striding forcefully, almost at a lope, Bill Paul headed toward the witness chair. "I object, your Honor. It's argumentative. It's not a question."

"Well, come and talk to me about it," Judge Theis said. With a billow of robe he extended an arm, indicating both tables. Mr. McGee was excused for the day, and the lawyers adjourned to chambers. In an instant the discussion was at full pitch. "It's unfair," Angel said. "You can't let them whitewash the company's credibility without giving us equal time." Normally self-contained, Angel was in a rage at the prospect of preferential treatment for Mr. McGee, and Spence was going up and down in his seat like a piston. "I can show specific examples where Mr. McGee told falsehoods," he shouted. "This press release that he put out is a blatant lie, saying the workers weren't subjected to any danger. . . . And another thing, we should have the right to ask Mr. McGee about going to Senator Metcalf to get that congressional hearing stopped."

"You can't show he did that," Bill Paul protested shakily. "He didn't go there to stop it. He simply told Senator Metcalf what the facts were."

"Just a nice little talk about the facts." Spence made the words writhe.

"And the next morning the hearings were called off," Angel said. "So some epiphany occurred."

Judge Theis let them go on like this for a while and then said, "Well, I don't think the Metcalf affair is proper cross-examination. It wasn't brought up on direct. Mr. McGee came here for a limited purpose."

"What purpose?" Spence burst out, too loud.

"Well, I don't know, I assume it was for some aura of respectability. Nevertheless, he has no real knowledge of the details. You've gone through everything with other witnesses, and I've let you go to work on them. You did a good job, I thought. You made monkeys out of some of them. But this is the top man: he has to rely on his subordinates. Your theory is that the top man should know everything, but corporations don't work that way."

"Then who *is* responsible?" Spence was speaking not just about this corporation and this man, but of the phenomenon. As he spoke, though, he grew solemn. Slowly his jaw stopped moving. He said, "All right, your Honor. I can see your feet are set in concrete on this."

Next morning, at the side entrance and at the front, there were TV cameras focused for a reappearance of the long car and the Old Man in the black suit. They might better have waited a hundred paces south at world headquarters. Mr. McGee was back in his penthouse. Judge Theis had canceled the remainder of his cross-examination.

The possibility that suicide had been in Karen's mind was a lurking part of the case. It had first surfaced as a city-room rumor, apparently springing from Reading's dossier, then Srouji had gushed about it at the Dingell hearing, and Drew had been asked about it at his deposition. Now, for ten weeks, Bill Paul had been trying to put it on the trial record. Whatever basis it had came from a girlfriend of Karen's. Late one evening in 1973, according to the girlfriend, Karen had called, sobbing, talking low but not in a whisper, casting about for commiseration. Drew had stormed out earlier, and Karen was emptying her medicine chest, slipping pills one by one past her tongue. The girlfriend drove pell-mell to the bungalow. By then Karen was vomiting. She sat on the couch, held her friend's hand, and vomited some more. Going to bed, Karen was already recovered.

Judge Theis was willing to have the jurors hear of that evening, but only if there was more to it, only if there had been a pattern of suicidal thoughts and attempts. Otherwise it was an isolated incident, a one-night spree of desperation, a night removed by a year from the fall of 1974.

Giving Bill Paul the chance to produce more evidence, Judge Theis had postponed a ruling. But then Bill Paul himself elicited a fact, until now unknown, that seemed to make suicide much less of a likelihood.

Dr. George Voelz, the health director at Los Alamos, was testifying about the events of November 10, 11, and 12, how, because Karen had been drinking, she had gotten lost among the rocks and ponderosa on the way to Los Alamos, how, on her arrival, she had undergone an *in vivo* test, and how anxious she had been about the result. Afterward Karen and Dr. Voelz had had a private patient—doctor talk. "Will my reproductive organs be okay?" she had asked. "What I mean is: will I be able to have any more children? I have to know."

"I reassured her that there would be no effect on her ability to have children," Dr. Voelz now testified. "I told her it wouldn't be a problem. She looked relieved."

Obviously Karen had hoped for another marriage, another family, a future.

With that testimony, and when Bill Paul could not show any pattern of suicide attempts, Judge Theis ruled that the evening of the pill overdose should not be told to the jurors.

Dr. Voelz had been brought in as the counterpoint to Dr. Gofman. Alert, composed, often volunteering more than asked, Dr. Voelz was a government man and a man of science. He was presented as a premier expert on the hazards of radiation. On cross-examination Spence tried to belittle that expertise, scorning him as an expert "bred, fed, and led by the feds." The young Voelz had sprinted through college in three years, medical school in two, all on a government scholarship, and had spent his career at Los Alamos. He was now the director of health research.

Dr. Voelz, a solid figure in suit and tie and shiny black shoes, defended the radiation standards. He said the standards had been arrived at scientifically, without regard for industry profits. He said that Drs. Gofman, Mancuso, Morgan, and Bross—and Carl Johnson, who had counted the deaths around Rocky Flats—were deliberately misreading the numbers. He said they were prejudiced. He said they were the messengers of scare stories. He said that working in a nuclear facility, or living in a house next to one, was no less safe than riding at thirty thousand feet in a jetliner.

As Dr. Gofman had done, Dr. Voelz ran the *in vivo* numbers and autopsy numbers through his slide rule and pocket calculator. But where Dr. Gofman had said the magnitude of plutonium was a "guarantee" of cancer, Dr. Voelz calculated the odds at only five in ten thousand. Starting with the same numbers, he had traveled to an opposite conclusion.

When Dr. Voelz stepped down, Bill Paul rose, revivified. The presentation of Kerr-McGee's case was complete. The trial had come full circle.

Throughout, Danny had carried in his banged-up briefcase a summary of the evidence accumulated for Counts One and Two—a summary of the interplay between the FBI, Kerr-McGee, and the OCPD —all of it excluded from the trial as either irrelevant to Count Three or too prejudicial. Long ago Danny had given up on seeing Reading in the witness chair. Reading would not be summoned, nor would Srouji, Olson, Campbell, Byler, Hicks; not for this trial, anyway. But Danny held out hope for Roy King, Ted Sebring, and William Clay. Their testimony, he felt, legitimately belonged here, in this courtroom, in this trial. It was the best proof that the documents existed.

William Clay, a Guthrie police officer in 1974, had been called auxiliarily to the culvert that night. But no one had interviewed him until last year when Father Bill did. Clay's recollections of the culvert were still clear: the mangled car, a dried trickle of blood, the papers blowing in the night. Yes, absolutely, there had been papers, he told Father Bill. Forty, maybe fifty. Strewn in the red mud, floating sluggishly on the creek. They were put back in the car and committed to Ted Sebring's garage. Minutes later a Highway Patrol officer had phoned news of the accident to Roy King, the Kerr-McGee personnel director. The officer asked if King could formally identify the body. He also told King about the papers: *There's a lot of things in her car that have Kerr-McGee identification insignia on them. I'd like for you to join me tomorrow and we'll go get them.* That was what King had testified to, under oath, when Danny took his deposition. King and the officer had made plans to visit the garage first thing in the morning. But shortly after midnight, in Crescent, a Kerr-McGee official awakened Ted Sebring, asking him to unlock the garage so Karen's car could be examined for radioactivity. Sebring didn't know the car had been gone through with an alpha counter only three days before or he might have thought the request stranger still. As it was, he called the Highway Patrol for approval. Approval was granted, and Patrolman Rick Fagan was dispatched to make it official. About two o'clock in the middle of a harsh night, Sebring opened the garage for Fagan and four Kerr-McGee men. (King was not among them.) They searched every inch of the car, under the seats, under the hood. Four years later, Sebring did not think they had stolen any of the papers. He had watched them "like a hawk," he said. But his attention had been diverted, he admitted, while Fagan was rummaging through Karen's purse and yuk-yuking about two marijuana cigarettes. In the morning, when Sebring opened for regular business, he sealed Karen's belongings in a Pennzoil box. At King's home, meanwhile, a Highway Patrol car pulled up. A patrolman got out. He told King: *"Somebody's already gathered up all of Kerr-McGee's possessions. They're not there now. So there's no need in us going down there to pick them up."* About noon, Drew arrived with Wodka and Burnham at the garage, and Sebring gave the box to Drew. In it were a few papers, no more than a dozen, plus a windbreaker, a hat, a first-aid kit, a snapshot, miscellany. The papers did not have Kerr-McGee insignia—they were OCAW papers from the contract negotiations. Nor did they have spots of dirt or water; indeed, they showed no sign whatever of having blown about a creek bed.

Now, with the trial in its final phase, all the lawyers were again in chambers. Judge Theis was setting guidelines for the closing arguments, and Bill Paul was saying, "If Karen actually had documents, why didn't she give them to Wodka when he was in town on November 8th and 9th? I think we should be allowed to argue that point from heck to breakfast."

"Well, I can let you argue that her documents were worthless as a deuce, but I don't think you can say she didn't have any at all," Judge Theis said. "She was like a guy playing poker with three aces —she wasn't going to turn the aces over till the time came."

"So you're going to let them argue that she *did* have the documents?" Bill Paul asked, his voice rising.

"That's what the evidence is," Judge Theis said, referring, in particular, to Mrs. Jung's talk with Karen at the Hub Cafe. Mrs. Jung had not testified at the trial; she was still in her hiding place in Colorado, but her account of seeing an "inch-thick" manila folder had been allowed on the record, in deposition form.

"I can let you argue that the documents were nebulous, Mr. Paul," the judge said, "but you can't flat-out say they didn't exist."

"That's unduly restrictive, it seems to me," Bill Paul said. "Aside from Mrs. Jung, no one else said anything about documents."

Danny thought immediately of King, Sebring, and Clay. Judge Theis had the same thought. Everyone in the room had it. The jurors knew nothing of the three forbidden witnesses, but here in privacy their testimony had been discussed often enough.

"If Mr. Paul is going to get cute in his closing argument, then we should have the right to reopen testimony and confront him head on," Danny said. It was said as a challenge. It was said to bait, to agitate, to badger, to provoke: a tactic both sides had used to advantage in the long course of the litigation.

Judge Theis had seen dozens of such scenes in dozens of courtrooms. No matter how talented, a lawyer was only as good as his ego. When it failed, so usually did his client. Egged into a bad decision, a lawyer could blow everything. In a matter of minutes a ten-week trial could be lost. With a spark of levity, the judge tried to steer Bill Paul away from confrontation. "I don't want to have to open the gate and let you die of your own poison, so to speak."

The tendons in Bill Paul's neck began to work against the skin. "Judge, I'll have to confer with my client first, but I'm giving serious consideration to turning Sebring and the others loose. Let Danny waffle around in it if he wants. I'm not sure it'll hang together."

"Well, it doesn't matter to *me*," Judge Theis said, pulling into a stronger pose, like a stern father. "But I didn't allow it in before because it's so prejudicial to your side. If it creates the inference that your side stole the papers, Bill, you've had it."

"Well, I'd just like to give it some thought."

"Yeah, you give it some thought," Danny mimicked. The tone of the room suddenly mounted in drama. Bill Paul's hand shot out as though to yank on Danny's tie. "You think all night about it," Danny said savagely. "Because we'll bury you with it."

"Well, I don't know who will bury whom." A rumble in the judge's throat silenced Danny; it silenced everyone. Bill Paul withdrew his hand and patted his hair into place. "I want this settled by Friday, so we can have closing arguments on Monday," Judge Theis said. "Give it some thought, Bill, as you say. Don't let someone badger you into doing something because you think they're bluffing. I think we're all aware of the shell games you guys play on each other: your wars of nerves."

By retreating, Bill Paul won. He agreed the next day to soften his closing argument in order to keep King, Sebring, and Clay from the stand. As a result, it seemed possible, even likely, that his client might also win.

Danny walked back to the office. The sun was dropping low, and the shadows were long. He looked up. It was really a small downtown, he thought, not like Houston or Dallas, not like the really big boom cities. Tall buildings were on every side, but there were only a few, in a clump. You could almost reach out and touch them all. He saw how the shadows fell. The biggest shadow came from the Kerr-McGee building, three hundred feet tall, and it seemed to fall across the whole city, down the street, past one corner and the next, across the courthouse, the YMCA, and beyond.

Twenty-One

Monday, May 14, windswept and white and hot, blew up across the sky. In the courtroom Spence placed his brown Stetson on the plaintiff's table. Every day it had sat there, in the same spot, while its owner roamed the room, boot heels sounding on the floor. Sometimes Spence would stop and eye the huge hat, as if it had wondrously caught his notice. Careful not to be too theatrical, he might pick off a speck of imaginary lint. The hat was his trademark, good luck charm.

The court clerk called Spence over. "Would you mind putting the Stetson on a chair, out of sight? Mr. Paul objects to it."

Spence put on a show of good will. "Sure, anything to make Mr. Paul happy. I had no idea he doesn't like Stetsons."

"I think it's only yours he doesn't like," the clerk said drily.

Spence gave the hat into his father's hands. Both his father and mother had come from Wyoming to watch him in action. After nearly two hundred trials in which their son had been a star act, this was a first for them. Spence had paid their way here today, to hear the "best damn closing argument I've ever written." Three days of red-eyed absorption had gone into the scrawled pages held in his hand. He had struggled hardest over the question of cancer. If there was no cancer—if there was no injury to Karen—there would be no damages for Kerr-McGee to pay. The autopsy had not revealed cancer because it could not have been detected so soon, not by the most powerful microscope or the most expensive of medical tests. How then could he convince the jurors that damage had truly been done? That there were cancerous cells already in her lungs, just sitting, waiting to rampage through her system some future day, like a time-delay poison.

How to explain it? Now, after a prologue, he gave it a try. "Flying over Wyoming, you can see the ant hills, huge round spots on the landscape, like polka dots. For years they tried to get rid of the harvester ants, so there'd be more land for the sheep, and," he smiled, "more sheep for the coyotes. But, let me tell you, the harvester ant is a most intelligent insect. They put out poison for the ants to eat, but as soon as some died, the others stopped eating it. They put out poison that's absorbed into the ants through their legs, but when the ants saw what was happening they built little bridges over the poison. It was the same with every poison they tried. But then, a few years ago, a scientist came up with a poison that would work. A time-delay poison. It was one that did not work till four or five weeks after the ants ate it. They stayed fat and sassy for those four or five weeks and forgot about the poison. But all the time it was waiting inside them. And one day, just like that, they were all dead."

A nod or two escaped from the jurors. Through fifty-four days and forty-two witnesses, the jurors had been attentive, but stoically so, with almost no hint of inner thoughts.

Spence boomed on, giving other analogies, he explained to them the legal, medical, and factual issues at stake. Soberly, giving each word a heavy accent, he recalled for the jurors the testimony about a forty-pound MUF and Karen's awareness of it, the testimony from an "honest cop" about sandpapered welds, and so forth, hastening along to the heart of his argument.

"Ladies and gentlemen, we brought in worker after worker to tell you what it was like out there—the leaks, the fires, the contaminations, the overtime in respirators, all those horror stories. But who did Kerr-McGee bring in? All we got was a parade of company men who told you the company line. Kerr-McGee didn't bring a single worker to this stand. . . . Nor did they bring in Mr. Reading. Remember, Mr. Reading's the one who knows more about this case than anyone. He's been investigating this case for five years, reporting directly to Mr. McGee. Now, if they'd brought Mr. Reading in, and put him under oath, and let me cross-examine him, maybe we'd have found out what all the facts are. But he was never called. He's the man that Bill Paul bypassed.

"I don't want you to think Mr. Paul is an evil man. I don't think he is. But all lawyers have a free choice to represent who they want, and he chose to represent Kerr-McGee. He's done the best he could for his client. . . . If there was an ugly way to interpret something about Karen, he did it. You know what Will Rogers said about slander? 'Slander is the cheapest defense going.' He was right. It doesn't cost anything to slander someone.

"Now who was Karen Silkwood really? Was she the woman the company men described? Was she uncouth, unreliable, moody, vindictive, sloppy, a miserable hatemonger, an unmitigated bitch? Or was she someone like you and me? Someone who came from where we come from? Her mother and father told you she was a happy child, a good child, reared correctly in the church; she was a scholarship student, a chemistry major; she was very bright. But more than anything else she cared. And she had courage. Do you remember her telling her supervisor: 'A woman fainted in the Met Lab, and your damn oxygen tank didn't work, and I'm going to report it'? No wonder Morgan Moore despised her. And what did Mr. Moore do when Karen was contaminated? He accused her of doing it to herself. Right from the get-go, before any evidence was in, he pointed his long, white, bony finger at her. The blame syndrome. Blame the workers; blame a weak, defenseless woman; blame the dead; always blame somebody else.

"It's unfortunate, but the rule in this trial is that we can't take you past the time Karen left the Hub Cafe. But do you remember what she said to Mrs. Jung? She said: 'I've got the materials—I've got them right here in this folder.' Fifteen minutes after she said that she was dead. Karen knew about the horrible conditions out there; she knew about the bad welds, the falsified records; she knew about the forty pounds. She knew too much.

"Well, she's dead and the factory is closed. . . . There's only one thing that can come out of this trial now, and that is the truth. Your verdict will tell everyone the truth, as it's been revealed to you. . . . That's what your verdict will do. . . . And, if you speak to this company in the language it understands, the universal language of money, you can make it so expensive to lie that the next time they may think it's a bargain to tell the truth. . . . If you will do that, then I'll go home and sleep for two weeks—because I'll have done my life's work all in this one case."

Spence sat down. It was Bill Paul's turn. He nudged his glasses up his nose. He did not roam the room. He stood behind the lectern, stiff at the knees. "You've heard Mr. Spence tell you a lot of stories. Let me tell you what I think is the saddest story I've ever heard. It's how Karen Silkwood has been used, terribly, brutally used, both before and after her death. It started with Mazzocchi and Wodka. They had a strategy. They made no bones about it. They turned Karen into a spy; they had her spying around, sneaking around. Ladies and gentlemen, have you heard anything about Kerr-McGee using anybody to spy or sneak around? No, you haven't."

In the gallery Danny stared in disbelief. You sonuvabitch, he said silently to Bill Paul. You sonuvabitch: if Counts One and Two ever go to trial I'll make you eat those words, word for word, lie for lie.

Bill Paul went on talking. "Poor, poor Karen. Mazzocchi and Wodka were relentless. They told her, 'You've made the charges against Kerr-McGee. You've got to come through! You've got to come through!' They put awful pressure on that girl. And Karen was flunking out. She was flunking out because she couldn't get the evidence about defective fuel rods. How could she? There wasn't any. So the pressure was on. Mr. Burnham was coming to town on November 13th, and she was flunking out. . . . But I don't blame Karen for what she did. She spiked her sample kits, but I don't blame her at all. No, I blame Mazzocchi and Wodka.

"Now, ladies and gentlemen, let me shift gears. Dr. Gofman came in here and told you that factory was 'a license to kill.' That was a monstrous lie from an unbelievably angry man. Most of the plaintiff's witnesses were angry men. They were mad at Kerr-McGee, mad at the AEC, mad at the NRC. Nobody suits them. They're mad at the whole industry. They're mad at the whole world.

"Kerr-McGee operated that factory well within the standards. You might say it's something to be proud of. And I do say it. I ask you to believe it. It is the truth. . . . Mr. McGee and Mr. Moore are not evil men, and their company is not an evil company. . . . They have done nothing wrong. They're asking you to put an end to this nightmare. They're entitled to a full exoneration."

As the plaintiff's lawyer, Spence would get to say the last word before the jurors left for the jury room. But first there was a recess and a short palaver in chambers. The day was almost gone when Spence stood again and began his arm motions, coaxing, commanding, uplifting. "Mr. Paul says Karen Silkwood was a silly woman who contaminated herself. She isn't here to defend herself, of course, but you listened to her voice on a tape talking to Wodka. Did she sound like a kook to you? Did she sound nuts? Did she sound like a stupid broad who would put insoluble plutonium in her urine kit, which immediately tipped off everybody that it was spiked?

"Mr. Paul says it was despicable for Mazzocchi and Wodka to use her. Do you think it's despicable to try to clean up a factory as filthy as this one? Do you think it's despicable to try to uncover a cover-up? No, I think Karen Silkwood's name will go down in history as a prophet, not anything biblical, but as an ordinary woman who became a heroine. I think she may end up saving thousands of lives. What Mr. Paul calls despicable, I think, was the greatest service, the greatest sacrifice."

Spence glanced at the table, reflexively looking for his Stetson. He felt its absence. "Can I have five minutes, Your Honor?"

Judge Theis nodded. The jurors stretched their legs, as did everyone in the jammed gallery. Spence walked by himself to the drinking fountain, swallowed deeply, then walked back. He had one more story to tell. It had been told before, but, in this setting, the telling had a churchly air.

"This is the story of a smart-alecky boy. One day he caught a tiny bird. Holding it in his hands, he decided to trick a wise old man, 'Old Man, what do I have in my hands?' he asked. The old man saw the bird's head peek out and said, 'A bird, my son.' 'Ah, but is it dead or alive?' Whatever the answer, the boy thought, he'd fool the old man. If the old man guessed dead, he'd let the bird fly free. If he guessed alive, he'd crush the bird with his fingers. But the old man only smiled. 'My son,' he said, 'it's in *your* hands.' "

Spence paused; the heavy draw of his breath could be heard in the silence. "Ladies and gentlemen, it's in your hands."

The Saturday before, at the Dolly & Hammer, Drew had bent over an electric emery, honing a steel rod to a fine point. An ancient anger had moved him. He went outside. Behind the shop were the hulks of old cars, huge metal insects in the spring weeds. He propped up a rusting hood and carved a crude bull's-eye in the rust. Stepping off fifty paces, he lifted his arm and leg, in a facsimile of a baseball pitcher, and hurled the rod. It bit into the hood, inches off target. He retrieved it, fired it, retrieved it, fired it, again and again, until the hood was like a sieve.

Most weekends Drew worked. He no longer went to the racetrack or the bars. Only his closetful of guns, and a catamaran that he sailed on Lake Hefner, broke up his routine. But one Sunday he had been talked into an Emmylou Harris concert at the Zoo Amphitheatre, an outdoor cathedral of grass and crumbling stone. Afterward, walking back to his car, tugging down his hat against the sun, he saw a stranded car. Smoke was pouring from it. A security cop was gaping dumbly. No one was in the car, but thousands of Emmylou fans had to pass by. Drew went over and rolled down a window to relieve the pressure building up inside. He heard a shout. "Hey, that ain't yours —leave it alone!" The security cop was waving with his nightstick. Drew began pushing the car, shouting over his shoulder, "Give me a hand, smart-ass, before this buggy blows up." In the spray of insults that followed, Drew was handcuffed and put under arrest for "interfering with an officer." He had to cool his heels in jail for a few hours before they let him go.

Emotions had been building in him. At the artisans festival he had run into Bill Paul. "See you in court," Drew had yelled. But he had not been called to testify. Talking it over, Danny and Spence had decided that Drew's emotions made him an undesirable witness; love and hate and anger made him undesirable.

For much the same reason, Jack Tice and Sherri Ellis also had not been called. With their lives still in upheaval, their emotions ran high too. Mr. and Mrs. Silkwood, however, and Rosemary and Linda, had testified, the final witnesses in the plaintiff's presentation.

Except for one day, when he flew to Connecticut to accept an award from the American Ethical Society, Mr. Silkwood had been every day faithfully, devoutly in the front row. All that time he had stared through Bill Paul, refusing to acknowledge him. Since the day of Mr. Silkwood's deposition, when Bill Paul had suggested that this man from Nederland was not his own man, not a word had passed between them, not even when Mr. Silkwood took the witness stand at the trial. Indeed, he had had the shortest stay of any witness, about ten minutes. Spence had asked just enough to establish Mr. Silkwood's basic patriotism—fifty missions as a bombardier—and to force out, from that deep dry space within, a few painful sentences about Karen. And Bill Paul had opted not to cross-examine at all.

But it had been left to Karen's mother and sisters to give form and personality to the tape-recorded voice the jurors had heard. Mrs. Silkwood described the happy child, the girl who wrote poetry and loved science, the daughter who loved the summer reunions in Kilgore, the woman who in her last few months had been intense, scared, purposeful, who had "one last thing to do" before coming home for the winter. Rosemary described the big sister who "was like a mother to me—who was always there when I needed advice." Linda said: "Karen had a great love for animals and for children. I was just four or five when she was a Candy Striper at the hospital, but I remember once she took me there, to the nursery, to see a little blue baby. And she explained the procedures they were using to make the baby live. Karen was the most caring and loving person I ever knew. I guess the best way to put it is that I idolized her."

Linda had preserved her idolatry in a photo album—Karen in first grade, Karen with her pet rabbits, Karen marching in the band, Karen in her prom dress. In one snapshot the three sisters were lined up in front of the green house, obediently on display in their Easter dresses, all new, lacy, and white. Karen was seventeen. She had a tiny waist, bird-like legs, an upturned mouth. She looked young and vulnerable. There was no suggestion of future belligerence. On the final page of the scrapbook Karen's name was in block letters on a gray headstone, out in the sun, a few feet from the shade of a leafy sumac. Linda had inscribed a quotation, the one Karen had chosen for herself in her high-school yearbook: *It is not only the most difficult thing to know oneself, but the most inconvenient thing too.*

The scrapbook, submitted as Exhibit 279, had gone with the jurors into the jury room.

Thursday, May 17, was the third day of deliberations. This month was Kerr-McGee's golden anniversary. Fifty years ago Robert Kerr had given his name to a company now worth in excess of two billion dollars. Hoopla on a grand scale had originally been planned for Kerr Park. But, apparently because of the trial, the plans were canceled. That had been a low point for Bill Paul and his men. They had begun talking openly, spitefully, in the hallway. "This trial is a farce— Congress should be deciding these issues, not a jury. What do six people from Oklahoma know about nuclear science? Why should they have any say-so? They're just six ordinary people. Nobody elected them." Specifically, the company lawyers objected to the jurors having a choice between the testimony of Dr. Gofman and Dr. Voelz. The MUF, and all the rest of it, would have been beside the point if Judge Theis had ruled that the radiation standards were an automatic alibi. There wouldn't now be this white-knuckle doubt about the verdict.

For all of that, Bill Paul's optimism had been steadily on the increase the last few days. The longer the jurors stayed out, the better he felt. As Thursday elapsed, the guess in the pressroom was "hung jury." A stalemate.

In Danny's group, feelings and guesses were on a teeter-totter, although general paranoia was up. A man had been phoning acquaintances of Ilene Younghein, cross-checking her references on a job application. She had found out when people began asking her about the job—she hadn't applied for one. To be the object of intelligence-gathering gave her new stature in the Movement, and she took rueful pride in it. She wasn't intimidated, she said. But talk of self-defense had begun again. The previous month two Movement leaders in Houston, Texas, had been gunned down, assassination-style. Michael Eakin, twenty-eight, a writer-activist, had died on the operating table; Dila Davis, forty-six, the mother of two, survived with a bullet next to her spine. The shootings had been preceded by vandalism, burglaries, and beatings of other Movement members in Texas and Oklahoma.

Taylor's sudden arrival over the weekend, then, had caused a stir. Had Danny sent for him? Had some new violence occurred? "No," Taylor said, "I'm here for the verdict."

So everyone was waiting. The jurors, now sequestered, caucused through the day and late into the evenings, till ten or eleven. The bailiff guarded their privacy, shooing away anyone near the jury room. The centers of activity were the pressroom and the front entrance of the courthouse where TV trucks were stationed. The courtroom was empty except for a few Movement people stretched on the benches. Most everyone else moved about, unable to sit still. On the radio a Kenny Rogers song played over and over—it was tops on the Country Hit Parade—"The Gambler." Spence hummed along. The husky timbre of the singer's voice and the song's philosophy were much like his own. The words became part of the mood.

Karen's sisters had returned to Nederland. Rosemary, remarried, was a part-time teacher's aide. Linda worked for an auto-parts distributor. But Mrs. Silkwood had stayed here in town with her husband. At the bank they had insisted she take the time off, and there was no need to hurry back for Frito's sake. All winter the old coon had crouched feebly in her cage, without energy to beg for scraps. Just before the trial, Mr. Silkwood had buried Frito in the backyard.

Bob and Kitty were going around saying good-byes they might not have time for later. They had plane tickets in their pockets. For weeks there had been demands for them on the East Coast. On Saturday, if the verdict was in, they were supposed to be in Connect-icut to meet with shipyard workers at a nuclear submarine base; many of the workers had cancer.

Sara was the only one not at the courthouse; the fundraising had to go on. She couldn't leave town until the hotels and restaurants, at least, were paid.

Outside the courthouse, parking tickets were accumulating on the windshields of the TV trucks. Each time Spence or Danny or Bill Paul came out the front doors, the klieg lights would blaze on, then off again in disappointment. Big-time reporters were here, from the *Times,* the *Post, Time* magazine, CBS, ABC, NBC. Over the years the Silkwood case had been an inspiration to the networks—A *Lou Grant* episode had been based on it and two TV movies were in the works —but now Walter Cronkite was also interested. However the verdict went, it would get top billing on the evening news.

Mrs. Silkwood was at the courthouse early on Friday. She saw Judge Theis arrive with suitcase in hand, packed for Wichita. The court clerk followed him into chambers, then came out with an explana-tion. A unanimous vote had been achieved the night before. The jurors had slept on it and were now ready. Mrs. Silkwood's heart began to act funny; it was as if the morning, barely begun, had been a thousand hours long. There was no one in the courtroom she knew. Now that the moment was here, there were only friends of Kerr-McGee, smartly dressed, members of the city's top drawer. But in the hallway she found a familiar face. "Hurry, hurry! Go find every-one."

With Danny-Paul in his carseat, Sara sped through yellow lights and parked the Plymouth in an illegal zone. Danny and the other lawyers came on the run from Ikard's office. In the YMCA dinette Bob and Kitty and Father Bill threw money on the table and aban-doned still-steaming breakfasts. As they ran, the first sprinkles of a thunderstorm caught them. In minutes the whole team was assem-bled in the courtroom.

They needn't have hurried. Judge Theis waited a full hour, allow-ing everyone to get into position. The TV cameramen set up down-stairs; the reporters took courtroom seats close to the door; and the other spectators divided into groups like rival tribes at a wedding. A strange set of forces, utterly unique, had brought into this room the ghost of a girl from Texas and the ghost of a pioneer-king, two people who in life had never met. Concentrated here, from the simple and the mighty, were all their invocations, all their work. But now it was all background. Now the only reality was the verdict. The thunderstorm created a drumbeat. Ka-boom, ka-boom!

"Ladies and gentlemen, have you reached a verdict?"

"We have, Your Honor."

They were three men and three women, faces steely but familiar, everyday faces. They were the people next door: a retired schoolteacher, a structural engineer, a secretary, a foreman for the electric company, a supervisor at the phone company, a housewife. The housewife was their forewoman. She handed the verdict form to the bailiff, who passed it to Judge Theis. He read it to himself. It was hard to tell anything from the many lines in his round face. Mr. Silkwood looked away, looked down; his wife was worrying a handkerchief; he put his arm around her. Father Bill crossed himself—a small sign easily missed. Sara squeezed Danny's hand. So much of Karen's life had been a progress from dream to mirage, she thought; would this be too? The court clerk took the verdict; it was his duty to announce it.

He read the first question: "Do you find by a preponderance of the evidence that Karen Silkwood intentionally carried from work to her apartment the plutonium that caused her contamination?"

He read the answer: "No."

Then the second question, "Do you find by a preponderance of the evidence that Kerr-McGee Corporation was negligent in its operation of the facility so as to allow the escape of the plutonium from the facility and proximately cause the contamination of Karen Silkwood?"

And the answer: "Yes."

The thunder had quit. In an exceedingly quiet room, no one moved. Karen's name had been cleared. She had not spiked her urine kit or spilled it on her baloney. That was the verdict! The plutonium in her refrigerator had been put there by someone else, and because it was Kerr-McGee's plutonium, the company was at fault.

Now it was a matter of money. Spence had asked for $1.5 million as payment for Karen's injuries. But did the jurors believe that the plutonium had done her any injury?

"Yes," the clerk read, "the jury awards actual damages in the sum of five hundred and five thousand dollars."

The crowd made a noise, an oddly soft babble. But the clerk was not finished. There was a last question. Should Kerr-McGee be assessed a penalty for how the factory was operated, the penalty that the AEC/NRC had never imposed? Before the trial began Spence had raised the request to $10 million, a stiff penalty.

The clerk read, "The jury awards punitive damages in the sum of ten million dollars."

Bill Paul was a man stunned. Blundering up, he asked to have the jurors polled. Judge Theis ordered each to stand, and each affirmed the verdict in ringing tones. Then the jurors left; and as they did, all the pent-up feelings in the gallery roared in their ears. Spence pounded the shoulders and backs around him, and everyone pounded his. Eyes brimming, Mrs. Silkwood fell against Mr. Silkwood, and Danny supported them both. "Thank you, thank you, thank you," Mrs. Silkwood said.

Minutes later, on the sidewalk, Danny and Sara and Kitty and Bob stood before the TV cameras, arms around each other. Rain was falling, a tattered sheet of silver in the klieg lights.

Back at the office, Danny's first call was to Stockton. "Did you hear?"

"I heard, I heard." Between the two men there was a feeling of victory. A partial victory, but a victory nonetheless. Stockton said, "Did I tell you I saw Keeney at the Justice Department? I had to go over on some other business, but naturally the Silkwood case came up. You know what? He says he's always personally believed Karen was killed. He just couldn't get the evidence."

Shortly after dawn the next morning, Saturday, a pickup truck pulled off Highway 74 next to the culvert. Two men got out. In a flat space by the creek they marked off five and a half feet and set to work with a hole-digger, the old-fashioned, two-handled kind used on the range for fence posts. Soon they had two mounds of red dirt and two deep holes. By then they were not alone. Cars, vans, a motorcycle, and more pickups were in a line on the road shoulder, half buried in bluestem and goldenrod. They heard a hollow clop-clop. Sherri Ellis rode up on her horse, coming from her grandmother's old ranch, where she was now living quietly, rewriting her book. The horse snorted, pawing the ground. All eyes were on the men and the holes, and an awkward wooden marker—shiny pine boards, squared off and bolted to two cedar logs. A local artist, with wood chisel and paint, had created on it a modestly fair likeness of Karen, her hair long, a smile on her lips. Swaying a bit under the weight, the men planted the marker. It tilted, then righted itself, settling in. Earth was packed around. News photographers took pictures against a purple and maize sky, a poet's sky.

Drew parked and ran up. He saw Danny, Spence, Father Bill, Taylor, several others.

"I talked to Stockton. He sends his best," Danny said, shaking hands. He was holding Danny-Paul.

"Is Stockton still in D.C.?" Drew asked.

"Sure is. Still raising hell six ways to Sunday. He was the one who got the NRC to admit off the record to the forty pounds. That's why we knew it was true."

"I kept planning to go see him. Take a tour of Capitol Hill. Never made it, though."

"You might still get a chance. This case might really crack open now. The AP guy told me we're on the front page of every paper in the country this morning."

The mood immediately after the verdict had been exuberance. Leaving the courthouse, they had whooped and shouted, like happy drunks. Danny had danced a jig down the sidewalk, linking arms with one partner, then another. Passing by Kerr-McGee headquarters, Kitty had fixed it with a look of contempt, as if her fervor could make it come tumbling down. The walk, begun in the rain, had ended under a rainbow. The gray sky had released a streak of rich light. At the Skirvin Plaza, upstairs in a ballroom, there had been a press conference, Danny and Mr. Silkwood sitting at the center of a long table with Spence and Ikard, Angel on one side and Sara, Kitty, Bob on the other. Danny had proclaimed the victory and predicted another. "Let the message go forth that we will be back. Let the people who killed Karen Silkwood beware." Afterward Sara and Kitty had hugged, their first hug in quite a while, then Kitty had gone off with Bob and Amber to Connecticut.

Now Sara was moving down the bank toward the creek. She stopped under the wooden marker. The others stayed up near the culvert, by the north wingwall: a small congregation. Drew pulled off his hat and held it over his heart.

"We're gathered here this morning to honor Karen Silkwood," Sara said. "But before I say anything about Karen, I'd like to mention another woman, a very close friend, Kitty Tucker. If it weren't for her, none of us would be here now. She couldn't make it this morning because she had a commitment to talk to some nuclear workers in Connecticut. I'm sure Karen would have understood."

Applause stopped Sara for a moment. "It's important to realize that Karen was a regular person," she said. "She had a personality like all of us, with good points and bad points. What she did was something we all could do, something we all should do. She chose to stand for truth instead of deception."

The creek shone in the sun, and the grass glittered. On the marker, Karen was holding the scale of justice and underneath was this caption:

BORN	2-19-1946
DIED	11-13-1974
VINDICATED	5-18-1979

EPILOGUE

WASHINGTON. APRIL 15, 1981. "Come on up," Sara said. "You know who you are—come on up!" She gestured and conjured with her hands.

They came up. Stockton and Danny and Kitty and Bob and Father Bill and Mazzocchi and Wodka and a few more from the SOS cast came out of the audience, up to the rented auditorium stage. Sara introduced them and praised them for their sacrifices, their gumption and faith. Her voice strained against the applause.

Mazzocchi took the microphone and jumped into a speech. It was an evening for speeches; four hundred people had paid five bucks apiece to listen. In the two years since the verdict in Oklahoma City, there never had been a real victory party. As much as anything, this was it.

"Maybe you thought the Silkwood case was over," Mazzocchi said. "You were wrong. It isn't." More cheers. Hats and plastic buckets and sawed-off milk cartons were circulated hand to hand. "Pitch in. Help us take the case to the Supreme Court."

To be precise, there were two cases, both of them on their way to the Big Court in D.C. One was being brought by Kerr-McGee, which had filed to overturn the $10.5 million judgment. Jim Ikard and Art Angel, now a two-man law team in Oklahoma, were handling the Silkwood side. The other had been filed by Danny: a last-ditch plea to get Counts One and Two reinstated. Both appeals had lingered for some time at the Tenth Circuit Court in Denver, and no one knew whether the Supreme Court would accept the cases or how long it would take to obtain a final decision.

A woman guitar player struck up a tune. Mazzocchi's speech was over, and he went back to talk to the others. He was a visitor in this city. His future was in Denver, or so he hoped. The following night he would be speaking at another fundraiser, one for himself, for his campaign to win the OCAW presidency. On his first attempt, in 1979, he had been fifteen hundred votes short, about one percent of the total. Now there would be a second attempt. "It's all or nothing," he said. The current OCAW president did not suffer rivals well. "If I lose, I'll be out on my ass. Thirty years of trade unionism down the tubes." He shook his head in a solemn way, but then wrinkled his nose like a street kid. He stuck out a hand to well-wishers who shouldered up.

Wodka stood with him. They would win or lose together.

"How's it going?" The hand belonged to David Burnham, who, with his tie askew, still looked every bit the newspaperman. But he wasn't, not any more. He had left the *Times* to write a book about new technologies—how they were superseding everything, and how they would, in turn, be superseded.

The room was full of writers. Danny was writing a Judeo-Christian blueprint for the eighties, and Bob was at work on a book about the victims of radiation. Although Karen had been the first victim officially recognized in court, the toll of the dead and dying long preceded her. Out west in the fifties the army had ordered GIs into foxholes near the epicenter of atomic tests; scores of men, maybe more, had come away with leukemia or other forms of cancer. A cancer had killed John Wayne, a cancer caused perhaps by nuclear fallout. One of the big bombs had been blown up when the Duke was in Utah for the movie *The Conqueror.* Half a dozen others from the movie set had died of cancer too, as had the many Navajo miners, and all those nuclear workers on Mancuso's charts, and some others, more unlucky yet, killed in freak accidents by radioactive substances that ate them alive. If there was any redemption to this, it was the men of science, the Gofmans and Mancusos, still fighting for tougher radiation standards.

Someone asked about Dr. Mancuso. "His grant got cut off again," Bob said. "Reaganomics—that's the new excuse." He shrugged. "We'll have to get cranked up all over again." Again: just last year the grant had been restored, after Bob had lobbied and talked his throat raw and pulled in improbable allies like the AFL–CIO. As political miracles go, it was a small one, but it was a miracle nonetheless, and having worked it once, Bob could think of repeating it. "Nobody's giving up. We'll go all the way to Reagan if we have to."

Kitty linked her arm with Bob's and posed for a photographer. Nick Thimmesch, the syndicated columnist, was in the crowd, taking notes. *Karen Silkwood, even in death, is a surefire draw for True Believers, even in a Washington consolidating itself in the Reagan era,* Thimmesch would write. *It was a rally reminiscent of activist times. . . . There was guitar strumming, folk singing, a salute to the luminaries of the Karen Silkwood movement.*

Being written about: it went with their funny kind of celebrity. Danny's name had been all over the papers since the victory over Kerr-McGee. His latest lawsuit was against the NRC on behalf of the neighbors of Three Mile Island. Kitty had made headlines with her work on a national anti-nuke rally, the first of its kind, held in D.C. in 1980. And there had been bigger headlines after an anti-nuke rally in New York where Sara was a featured speaker. That rally, in 1979, had been the best attended political happening of the decade, some three hundred thousand strong. Everyone connected to the Silkwood case now had an instant credential. In the "Style" section of the *Washington Post* there even had been a picture of Bob and Kitty dancing at an SOS party.

"Kitty Tucker, Esquire, I presume?" Stockton asked, being jolly. "Is it Esquire or Esquiress?"

"Women lawyers don't care about titles." Kitty grinned, catching the spirit. "We only care about making money."

Kitty had graduated from Antioch and, despite considerable grousing but little study, she had scored a top grade on the D.C. bar exam. There had been much celebrating, flowers and cards competing with a huge cake for space on the longboard. Amber, old enough to understand, had climbed into her mother's lap to get closer to all the happiness. Shawn had punched the air, "You did it, Mom! You did it!" He had returned; he was back to stay, back at Butternut, back with Kitty.

Now, off to the side of the auditorium, a long-haired bartender began serving from a table covered with white linen. Stockton offered to buy a round. Kitty wished for a piña colada. But the table was not well stocked—the mixes were for gin and whiskey. She settled on a Coke. The atmosphere was like a school reunion, with half-remembered stories and half-serious jests. Kitty's grin twinkled. "When are you bigshots gonna find me some clients?"

"I'll be your client," Stockton said. "You can sue everybody who's out to get me. What more could you want?"

"I told you: money." More laughter, more mock pomposity.

But this was serious. About a year ago Stockton had gotten mad, thinking how Karen had been smeared, and Dingell, and Seigenthaler, and himself. He had talked to Danny, who suggested the obvious. "Why don't you sue?" Indeed, why not? So Stockton had, alleging libel and violations of his civil rights and a conspiracy to keep him from carrying out his duties as an officer of public trust. The defendants were familiar: James Reading, Jackie Srouji, Larry Olson, as well as the institutions they represented—Kerr-McGee and the FBI. Stockton's suit had revived the chance that these alleged conspirators would yet wind up in the dock. And, once there, what might the upshot be? Would someone explain about the missing forty pounds? Or reveal secrets still left from the night of November 13, 1974? Would someone confess? Stockton and Danny were letting their dreams run wild, but who could say?

Behind the table bar, Danny-Paul was running about, running hard on tiny legs. Danny crouched low to pick him up. "Me too, me too"—another little boy's voice. Jacob, the son of Pat Austin, tagging along. Danny crouched again, hefting both up to see the activity on stage. Sara was introducing another speaker. The two boys began playing a game just made up, using Danny's head as a sort of tether ball. He found Father Bill and dumped one off. They were all family, all living at Arrupe House—Danny, Sara, Danny-Paul, Father Bill, Father Wally Kasuboski, Pat Austin, and Jacob. Pat had been one of the legal secretaries in Oklahoma, and she was still typing up Danny's legal briefs at hours of the night no other secretary would. Danny had put together his own version of a law firm. The office was in another old house twelve blocks from Capitol Hill. Called the Christic Institute, it was not so much a place for lawyers as for people of conscience. Everyone from Arrupe worked there. In the group too were Rob Hager, an attorney who had assisted at the trial, and actress Jehane Dyllan, whose one-woman play about Karen was getting critical acclaim.

Father Bill had moved to the stage. He relieved Sara of the microphone. "I wanted to tell you something that Sara forgot," he said. "She's told you about everyone else, but she hasn't said a word about herself. So let me say it: this case couldn't have happened without Sara Nelson. If there was one person who held things together, who held all of us together, it was Sara." The auditorium had emptied out a little—parents with sleepy kids had departed—but a thunder from the remaining hands filled the place.

Danny, beaming, was the final speaker.

Then, on a five-by-seven-foot video screen, faces and prairie scenes came into color: a BBC documentary: the story of Karen's death and Stockton's detective work and Danny's litigation. Watching, shifting from foot to foot, Danny and Stockton acted a little embarrassed. "Who they gonna get to play you in the movie?" "How about Redford?" "Nah, not enough charisma!" They laughed.

But movies, in fact, were under way: a documentary, *Dark Circle,* and a Hollywood film. After years of bouncing in and out of studios, Buzz Hirsch had finally made a deal with ABC Films. The gossip was that Meryl Streep would play the part of Karen. Like so much else, though, that was not resolved. Three different scripts had been written with three slightly different endings. That was the paradox of the Silkwood case: there had been so many endings—the car accident, the FBI foreclosure, Metcalf's dropout, Dingell's loss of jurisdiction, the dismissal of Counts One and Two, the trial—endings, each of them, but each had led to another beginning.

Bill Taylor was home. For him the end had been the trial verdict. But then again it hadn't. One evening some weeks afterward Taylor's phone had rung: a call from one of his informants. Sneaking about the file rooms at FBI headquarters, the man had opened a top-secret drawer and found a lengthy report. "The FBI knows," the man said, "the FBI knows exactly what happened. It's all right there on page three." There was a narrative of that night, he said: from the Hub Cafe to the highway culvert. Karen had been followed as she left the cafe. She had driven south on Highway 74, toward Oklahoma City, but then she had swung west, making a detour down a dirt road, to the old barn on the ranch of Sherri's grandmother. Coming back to the highway, Karen encountered her pursuer. There was a brief chase; the other car banged into the Honda. Karen jockeyed about and ended up on the shoulder. The other car raced alongside. And seconds later there was the sound of a crash, then quiet, except for the fleeing wheels and the howl of the wind, a howling like a ghost gone mad.

In broad terms this was pretty much as A. O. Pipkin had first outlined it. That hardly surprised Taylor. But how could the FBI be so specific, so definite? Details like these could not be known. Unless . . . unless the entire story was somehow known. Known, but hidden away in those top-secret files.

In the summer of 1979 the editors of *Newsweek* asked a question on their front cover: WHERE HAVE ALL THE HEROES GONE? Inside the magazine was an essay, touching on an empty spot in America. Teddy Roosevelt was long in his grave and Joe DiMaggio was doing coffee-maker commercials. The Duke was gone too. Things had been simpler once, perhaps heroism had been easier then. Perhaps our heroes today can't survive the overexposure of television. Or perhaps everyone is looking too hard for heroes. Or not hard enough. Well, the *Newsweek* editors had made their own search and had found ten modern heroes. High on their list was Muhammad Ali, for sacrificing his title belt rather than taking the easy way. Ali could have staged boxing exhibitions in Vietnam, but he had stuck to his principles. Right behind him on the *Newsweek* list was a woman who had died because of principles—and for a cause she had barely envisioned. *She was obscure in life, and the auto crash that killed her remains a mystery,* the editors had written. *But after her death, Karen Silkwood's name became a rallying cry for anti-nuclear forces around the globe.*

Karen would not have believed it: being called a hero of her time. At one time, no one would have believed it—except those few ordinary people who had stuck with her, people not unlike Karen herself.

The acclaim for Karen was not quite the same as that for Spence and Judge Theis. Spence had been profiled in *Time*, and touted as a legal gunslinger, "the best in the West—perhaps even the nation." Judge Theis had been named "Trial Judge of the Year" in 1980 by the American Trial Lawyers Association for his handling of the Silkwood case. All of them, the lawyers, the crusaders, they could feel proud. But Karen would never read about herself, never know she had mattered after all. Somehow that made her press clippings all the more mythic. And all the more sad.

Acclaim of a sort had come also to Ilene Younghein. She was being talked about as a nominee for the Oklahoma Hall of Fame. It was the idea of Thomas Bamberger, the former state legislator. "Mrs. Younghein has more fortitude than half the men we got in there," Bamberger said. But there would have to be a lot of politicking before she was let in, if ever. Oklahoma was still home for Kerr-McGee. Things had changed, and things had not. In 1980 the people of Oklahoma had elected a U.S. Senator. Robert Kerr Jr. had run for his daddy's old job, but Junior had lost, lost badly. The Kerr-McGee political machine had lost. But, in doing what it does best, the company was doing well. In 1980 Kerr-McGee had earned $182 million. Things had changed, and things had not.

Drew was working fifty, sixty hours a week at the Dolly & Hammer. On weekends, when he took them off, he might be at an auto show as a spectator or judge. More likely, he would be at an abandoned sand pit or a dry creek bed, shooting practice holes in pop cans, scrap lumber, somebody's old cowboy hat. He had gone hunting for the first time since he was a kid. In brown terrain, elevated, but not high enough to be mountains, he had shot a goat. He butchered the meat, and took the head, with its curved horns, to a taxidermist. In his closet Drew had more guns than ever.

Karen's parents were still in Nederland, still in the little green house. Life was back to normal, as normal as it would ever be. In one corner of their remodeled living room there was a simple geometry of hardwood bookcases. No books were on the shelves, though. Photographs sat there, lined up in a shrine effect, photographs of the three girls—showing off prom dresses, excited, their smiles toothy, features vivid and highboned, Karen in her drill uniform, Rosemary in a beauty-contest pose, Linda twirling a baton—photographs from a time that was gone, photographs such as might be found in a million other little houses. In the evenings, golden lamplight shone on them.

There were two other photographs, both of Karen, in soft black and white, hanging in heavy wooden frames on the walls. Enlarged to a size bigger than life, they dominated the room. One was from Karen's work badge, the other from the poster—Karen as she had looked on her first day at Cimarron, and as she had looked two years later. She might have been two separate people, the expressions were so different; one staring respectfully, the other plainly of an outlaw. Yet they were Karen. You had only to look at the way she held her head, chin up. It couldn't be mistaken even at a distance.

On a spring weekend in 1980, Merle Silkwood packed a suitcase for Kilgore. Karen's grave had to be tended. But neither Rosemary nor Linda could get away, and Bill Silkwood was going as usual to his cabin. Mrs. Silkwood would have to go alone.

"You going or not?" Mr. Silkwood saw her suitcase still on the bed.

"Yes. Yes, of course."

"Oh." He paused. "I thought, if you wanted to wait a week or so, well, I thought you might like to come up to the cabin."

"With you?"

Who Killed Karen Silkwood?

"You don't have to. I just thought I'd ask."

"I'd love to. I really would love to."

So Merle Silkwood had walked with her husband that weekend and deposited corn on the trails for the deer, her heart girlishly light. And later she had made the drive to Kilgore, to the cemetery full of new green. The gray stone lay in the open, in the sun. But each year, as the sumac branched ever wider, the shade was coming closer, a restful, leafy circle. Someday it would cover the grave. With the weeding done, Mrs. Silkwood knelt a moment. Beyond a fence, there were fields and low worn hills hurrying to a red horizon. A cattleman's herd was grazing, a herd of Angus cows, some white, some black. Once, Karen had strolled in the fields here and danced her silly little dances and dreamed her big dreams. Kids were playing somewhere, down in an old swimming hole. They could not be seen, but their teasing carried in the dry air. Karen's mother fussed a little more with the flowers, alive for another season, and then pushed herself up. It was time to be getting home.